NEVER AGAIN

NEVER AGAIN

Germans and Genocide after the Holocaust

ANDREW I. PORT

The Belknap Press of Harvard University Press

CAMBRIDGE, MASSACHUSETTS | LONDON, ENGLAND | 2023

First printing

Library of Congress Cataloging-in-Publication Data

Names: Port, Andrew I., author.
Title: Never again : Germans and genocide after the
Holocaust / Andrew I. Port.
Description: Cambridge, Massachusetts : The Belknap Press of Harvard
University Press, 2023. | Includes bibliographical references and index.
Identifiers: LCCN 2022037046 | ISBN 9780674275225 (cloth)
Subjects: LCSH: Germans—Attitudes. | Genocide—Germany—Public
opinion. | Genocide—Cambodia. | Genocide—Bosnia and Herzegovina. |
Yugoslav War, 1991–1995—Atrocities—Bosnia and Herzegovina. |
Rwandan Genocide, Rwanda, 1994. | Cambodia—History—1975–1979.
Classification: LCC HV6322.7 .P65 2023 |
DDC 364.15/1—dc23/eng/20221123
LC record available at https://lccn.loc.gov/2022037046

CONTENTS

NEVER AGAIN

Prologue

When Europe's worst massacre since the end of World War II took place in July 1995, most German politicians were on vacation. Parliament had begun its summer break two weeks earlier, just as frantic reports began warning that the besieged Muslim town of Srebrenica was about to fall to Serb forces. This was the Serbs' latest offensive in the bloody war that had been raging in Bosnia since the spring of 1992, and they hoped to consolidate their hold on the eastern part of the multiethnic state by "ethnically cleansing"—that is, expelling—all Muslims from the region.

Reports of atrocities began to appear shortly after the fall of Srebrenica on July 11, accompanied by claims that the Serbs had arrested and sent all Muslim men between the ages of sixteen and sixty to internment camps. This took place right under the noses of UN peacekeeping forces stationed there as part of an agreement made two years earlier, when the international organization had declared the town to be one of six demilitarized "safe zones" and vowed to protect its disarmed inhabitants. The fate of the arrested men remained unclear for weeks, but unconfirmed reports of massacres and random killings soon began to surface.

The reports produced a great outcry in the German media, which, citing UN sources, claimed that this "unimaginable barbarism," these "veritable scenes from hell," belonged on the "darkest pages of human history." Chancellor Helmut Kohl spoke about "crimes against humanity," and some public figures even began to contemplate sending

German forces to help stop the bloodshed. On July 14, four prominent politicians from across the political spectrum issued a spectacular public statement in response to the fall of Srebrenica: "We grew up in a country that burdened itself with infinite guilt [and] is responsible for the most inhumane genocide in history. We grew up with the conviction that that should never again be allowed to happen." That was why, they concluded, "only military protection" could save the people in Bosnia and why "we, as Germans," must be "prepared to accept such a risk."[1]

It was in this context that Joschka Fischer of the oppositional Green Party published an open letter of his own decrying the recent events in Bosnia. Fischer, a gifted and media-savvy public speaker, was arguably the best known and most popular member of his party—formally known as Alliance 90/The Greens, which had its roots in the environmental, peace, and dissident movements of the 1970s. His letter of July 30 skillfully argued that Srebrenica had confirmed once and for all that diplomatic solutions and sanctions were not working in Bosnia, and that this demanded a rethinking of official policy toward the region—even on the part of the traditionally pacifist Greens. The proper response now, Fischer concluded, was to offer the remaining Muslim safe zones a "military guarantee."

This placed his party in a difficult position, he acknowledged, because it brought into conflict two of its fundamental principles: a commitment to nonviolence, and a commitment to protecting life and liberty. But it had to make a choice. The German Left was in "danger of losing its soul," Fischer continued, if it "shied away" from confronting this new form of "fascism." In fact, the former student radical continued, if the members of his generation did not "use all means at their disposal to counter this horror and do all that was humanly possible to prevent further sacrifices," they ran the risk of a "political and moral failure" like the one their parents and grandparents had experienced under National Socialism.[2]

The letter caused a storm within his party, which was no doubt Fischer's intention. Following its publication in leading leftist newspapers, his supporters and detractors engaged in a strident public exchange involving nasty recriminations and personal attacks. At the same time, both sides offered solid arguments reinforced by solemn references to the weight of Germany's past.[3] For Fischer, the primary lesson of

National Socialism was "Never again Auschwitz." His opponents placed greater emphasis on a different dictate: "Never again war."

We now know that Bosnian Serb forces systematically murdered more than 8,000 Muslim men and teenage boys after Srebrenica fell. International courts subsequently ruled that genocide did indeed take place there in mid-July 1995.[4] But the term *genocide* began to surface widely only after Fischer's letter had been published and after grisly details about mass shootings and mass graves had appeared in the media. The new revelations had an even greater impact on the Green politician, who gave a remarkable speech at a gathering of party leaders in late September. The war in Bosnia, he said—and "even more so" the massacre in Rwanda a year earlier, when Hutus had killed approximately 800,000 Tutsis over a three-month period—ineluctably called for an "active international policy" against genocide. In fact, he argued, the UN had an "obligation to intervene" when the "threat" of genocide arose.[5]

Fischer had now upped the ante, and his most prominent critics in the party responded publicly with a series of pointed questions. How could one determine early enough whether genocide was taking place, given that it usually became known only after the fact? What "magnitude" was necessary to trigger intervention, and what should that look like in practical terms? There were approximately forty wars taking place around the globe at the time, and one could, they argued, apply the term *genocide* to most of them. Did that mean that the UN—and, by extension, Germany—should intervene in places like Kashmir and Kurdistan, East Timor and Tibet? Fischer's suggestion would be a "gateway," an "intermediate step" on the path to unbridled military action by the Federal Republic, grist for the mill of German conservatives who hoped to make their country a "great power" once again.[6]

Fischer shot back with an equally scathing response. How could a "leftist, much less a German leftist," disagree with his recent statements, especially in light of international law? The UN Genocide Convention of 1948 clearly stated in its first article that the signatories would "undertake to prevent and to punish" the crime of genocide. Germany had acceded to the Convention four decades earlier, and if his critics disagreed with that commitment, they should demand that the country withdraw from it. "My view may no longer be in fashion," he continued, "but German history still counts as a weighty political argument for me in the present. The UN Convention was a direct response . . . to the genocidal barbarity of the German Nazis"—"a response to Auschwitz." The implication was that this imposed a special obligation on their country. Responding to concerns that this would lead to all sorts of foreign entanglements, Fischer pointed out that the Convention was clear about what constituted genocide: a series of specific "acts, committed with intent to destroy, in whole or in part, a national, ethnical, racial, or religious group, as such." How, he demanded, could that possibly justify arbitrary global deployments of the German military?[7]

The two sides had an opportunity to hash out their differences at a major party conference that December in Bremen, where delegates voted on competing foreign policy motions. Fischer's allies called for a "clause" that would oblige the international community to intervene in instances of genocide. Germany, precisely because of its own genocidal history, had a special duty and "moral obligation" to support this, they contended. If such a commitment had existed in the 1930s, "thousands of Holocaust victims might have been saved."[8]

There was a great deal of commentary about the "genocide clause" in *Die Tageszeitung (taz)*, the leftist daily newspaper closely associated with the Green Party. In early December, its editors asked several public figures whether military operations were justified in response to genocide. Opinions varied. Ignatz Bubis, the chair of the Central Council of Jews in Germany, believed that they "absolutely" were. Jens Reich, a leading dissident from former East Germany, concurred, adding that it would have been the right thing to do in Rwanda. But there were also more skeptical voices. The well-known Catholic theologian Uta Ranke-Heinemann was dismissive of this supposed attempt to justify war by "cloaking" it in moralism. A series of letters to the editor objected to characterizing what had happened in Bosnia as genocide, a term that could only be "associated with Auschwitz." Critics further accused Fischer and his allies of "relativizing" the Holocaust and "instrumentalizing" it to promote imperialist wars ostensibly fought in defense of human rights. Besides, a military intervention in former Yugoslavia could not "compensate for Auschwitz" or "atone" for the crimes committed decades ago against the Jews. Sending young men into harm's way now was not the way for Germans to "rise morally" above their parents' generation, argued sociologist Sibylle Tönnies: "We are and remain the country that has a sign of Cain on its forehead and we will not become normal again by covering it with a steel helmet."[9]

Emotions ran high also at the party conference in Bremen, where Fischer recounted his own evolution on the issue of force in an impassioned, highly personal speech. After years of trying to come to terms with Auschwitz, he explained, a "boundary had been crossed" for him in Srebrenica. The resolution calling for a "genocide clause" received only 38 percent of the vote and thus failed to carry the day, but Fischer and his allies did not consider this a defeat. For one, they had not expected even that much support, given previous votes on the possible use of force. It was "almost a breakthrough" and their "radiant faces" showed it, one journalist commented at the time, venturing that the party "as a whole" was moving in Fischer's direction—a prescient prediction.[10] Following federal elections in 1998, the Greens formed a coalition government with the other major opposition party, the Social Democrats, with Fischer serving as the Federal Republic's first Green foreign minister. A half year later, in March 1999, German soldiers participated in their first combat mission since World War II—a decision Fischer would justify by pointing once again to the scourge of genocide in former Yugoslavia, this time in Kosovo. The future foreign minister may have lost the battle in Bremen, but he and his supporters would eventually win the war.[11]

Introduction

The Consummate Country of Contrition

The atrocities in Bosnia in the 1990s sparked the first prolonged debate in postwar Germany about what to do in response to genocide—which was remarkable, given that the Federal Republic was an early signatory to the UN Convention on the Prevention and Punishment of the Crime of Genocide. But it was not altogether surprising. The Convention may have given pride of place to the term *prevention* in its very title, but its articles paid scant attention to the issue of deterrence, addressing it in only the vaguest of terms.[1] German officials had acceded to the Convention four decades earlier, in fact, without seriously discussing that aspect of the international covenant. Their focus was instead on its potential political benefits for the Federal Republic, which was understandable so soon after the defeat of Nazi Germany. Hardly anyone, least of all the Germans, would have wished or expected the unarmed, semisovereign country to involve itself in the internal affairs of far-off foreign states, much less take military action abroad.

When the UN General Assembly adopted the Genocide Convention on December 9, 1948, it stipulated that the agreement would become international law after twenty member states had ratified it—a goal achieved in January 1951. The document, the brainchild of the Polish-Jewish legal scholar Raphael Lemkin, fixed the legal norms for defining and punishing genocide, a term he had coined, as well as for determining which actions constituted this "crime of crimes." There was a great deal of debate about these issues in the lead-up to the vote at the UN, but as nonmembers, the two postwar German states did not have an opportunity to participate. One of the Convention's articles did allow non-member states to join, however, and on December 20, 1950, just weeks before the Convention formally went into effect, UN secretary-general Trygve Lie sent Chancellor Konrad Adenauer of West Germany a letter inviting his country to "accede" to the Convention. Over the next two years, officials at various agencies of the Federal Republic weighed in on the pros and cons of doing so. Far from having any "fundamental objections," Erich Kaufmann, the chancellery's legal adviser, encouraged the government to sign on—and "not just because the behavior of the National Socialist government was one of the reasons" for its adoption. "Corresponding crimes were and are being committed in Soviet-ruled countries," he wrote, and accession would give the Federal Republic the opportunity to "intercede there" on behalf of its own interests.[2]

Kaufmann's explicit acknowledgment of a connection between the Convention and Nazi crimes was a rarity among West German officials, yet his emphasis was clearly on the international agreement's political advantages *for* the Federal Republic. That was politically expedient, from his perspective, hardly an attempt to downplay Nazi crimes. Kaufmann, a professor of law and prominent legal scholar during the Weimar period, had suffered persecution during the Third Reich because of his Jewish background, and had eventually fled the country following Kristallnacht in November 1938. Other officials similarly focused on the Convention's potential benefits. First and foremost, it would allow the government to apply pressure and take legal action against the Soviet bloc for crimes committed against ethnic Germans: the millions expelled from Eastern Europe after World War II, and the thousands of soldiers still in custody in the USSR.[3]

Not everyone was enthusiastic about acceding to the Convention. It might subject the Federal Republic to decisions by an international court of justice, some feared, or it might lead to foreign demands for the ex-tradition of Germans for earlier crimes. That would have been inopportune at a time when the government was busy granting amnesty to former Nazis.[4] In the end, the Ministry of Justice and the Foreign Office dismissed such concerns and came out in favor of accession. But that was not the end of the matter. A stipulation in the West German constitution required the adoption of a new federal law in such cases. The challenging work of translating the Convention and making sure it conformed to domestic law now got under way, leading to a great deal of back-and-forth among officials about the difficulty of finding appropriate translations for legal terms that were foreign to or had a different meaning in the German legal tradition.

An initial draft law was completed by the spring of 1953, and it came to the attention of none other than Raphael Lemkin himself, who sent Adenauer and other high-level West German officials a lengthy memorandum outlining his grave concerns about the translation. Certain language choices failed to capture the spirit of the Convention, he argued; even worse, they undercut the original intent by limiting its scope. To make his objections more palatable, he explained why that should be of special concern to German officials: a more literal translation of the original document would support West German efforts to secure the release of Germans still captive in the Soviet Union.[5]

Lemkin apparently feared that his objections might be ignored, so the tenacious legal scholar resorted to one of his preferred pressure tactics: a public appeal through the press. In a series of leaks, interviews, and letters to the editor that appeared in West German newspapers and German-language periodicals in the United States, he outlined the Convention's political advantages for the Federal Republic, as well as his concerns about the current draft. He then made sure copies reached officials in Bonn.[6] The father of the Genocide Convention, who had lost dozens of relatives during the Holocaust, strategically couched his arguments in terms of West German interests, but his underlying motivation was different. Lemkin was fighting a rearguard action against efforts to pass an international resolution that, he feared, would undermine the Convention by enshrining in customary law the principles established at the Nuremberg trials. This would have made genocide a crime only if committed during a war of aggression—and that would have meant that the postwar expulsion of ethnic Germans from Eastern Europe could not be considered genocide and therefore would not come under the purview of international law. His arguments prompted a good deal of debate among West German officials, who were also being pressured by the Sudetendeutsche Landsmannschaft, an organization representing the interests of ethnic Germans expelled from Czechoslovakia after World War II. The group's leadership vigorously supported Lemkin's efforts, calling for the modifications he had suggested so that action could be taken at the UN.[7]

On January 21, 1954, just as Lemkin was carrying out his media campaign and furiously writing letters to West German officials, the German parliament held its first discussion of the invitation to accede to the Convention. Minister of Justice Fritz Neumayer began by briefly explaining the goals of the new law and the challenges involved in its drafting. Two things were curious about this speech. For one, Chancellor Adenauer had apparently rejected the Foreign Office's suggestion that he deliver it himself. Equally noteworthy was the exclusion of a solemn passage in the original draft stating that the government supported the law "not only conscious of its great responsibility for Germany's future fate, but also in recognition of a *special responsibility* toward the past."[8]

The statement's absence was not altogether surprising. At the time, most public figures remained silent about Nazi atrocities, especially those committed against the Jews. That was *not* true, however, of those who responded that day to Neumayer's address. Carlo Schmid of the Social Democratic Party (Sozialdemokratische Partei Deutschlands, or SPD) one of the drafters of the West German constitution, specifically mentioned the "millions of Jews and hundreds of thousands of foreigners" whose "massacre" had "stained Germany's name with shame" and placed a "heavy responsibility and liability on our people." In his next breath, Schmid also mentioned the "violent" expulsion of millions of Germans after the war, which had led to the "almost complete destruction" of the ethnic German minorities in those regions. The coupling of Jewish and German suffering was not uncommon, even among West Germans with impeccable antifascist credentials. Heinrich Höfler of the Christian Democratic Union (CDU), a former prisoner of the Gestapo, spoke in equally poignant terms about the "deep regret" Germans felt about the death of millions of Jews and foreigners. This was something that filled them with "burning shame," he said, quickly adding that "we also think with great pain" about the millions of Germans expelled from the East—just "because they were German."[9]

Each speaker expressed enthusiastic support for the Convention and the new law, which the Bundestag sent to its judiciary subcommittee for consideration. A lively discussion in the committee turned once again to the question of language, the main sticking point all along. This exchange was just as noteworthy as the one in the Bundestag for what it revealed about how Germans reflected on their country's recent past. Franz Seidel, a member of the conservative Christian Social Union (CSU), opened the session by laying out the changes made in response to Lemkin's recent criticisms. He highlighted the decision not to use the ethnonationalist term *völkisch* because it had been "so heavily misused" in the recent past. Adolf Arndt of the SPD suggested that *rassisch* also be stricken from the law—even though the word *racial* appeared in the Convention—because it was "similarly fraught." Karl Weber of the CDU, a future minister of justice in the mid-1960s, disagreed. The term *rassisch* may have left a "certain bad aftertaste" because of the Nazis, he said, but using it again would help restore its "good old meaning"— whatever that might have been.[10]

The significance of language was also attracting attention among prominent German academics and intellectuals like Victor Klemperer, who voiced concern about the persistent use of words tainted by the Third Reich. It is doubtful the officials were familiar with the academics' work, or that they shared their belief that Nazi terminology had helped paved the way for the regime's worst atrocities by shaping attitudes and mentalities. But they were clearly attuned to the delicate issue of language.[11]

In the end, almost all of Lemkin's suggestions carried the day, and the proposed law was brought before the Bundestag for final approval on July 8, 1954. Seidel thanked Lemkin for his "selfless efforts" in drafting the Convention and his "suggestions" for improving the language of the new law. The only response to the Bavarian politician's remarks came from Jakob Altmaier of the SPD, a German-Jewish journalist and World War I veteran who had fled the country in 1933. One of the few Jews who had returned to Germany after the war, he was also the first professing Jew elected to the Bundestag, in 1949. Accession to the Convention was not, Altmaier hoped, "just a legal measure for us Germans" but also "a matter of the heart"—especially at a time when one could once again hear "voices" spouting "hate" for certain "fellow human beings" solely because of their background. "We have still not overcome the spirit that led to genocides carried out by Germans misusing Germany's name." Altmaier placed the events of the 1940s in historical context, referring to the "trail of blood" that had begun with the "slaughter" of the Armenians during World War I. He praised ethnic Germans such as novelist Franz Werfel, who had directed the "civilized world's" attention to those "sinister events," but expressed regret that this had not prevented the mass murder *by Germans* of a "still unimaginable number" of people because of their nationality and religion. Altmaier, who had helped initiate the payment of restitution to Israel a few years earlier, then added this familiar sentiment: "Injustice begot additional injustice," namely, the expulsion of ethnic Germans from their ancestral homelands in the East. This, too, he declared, was a form of "genocide" (*Völkermord*).[12]

The Bundestag approved the new law unanimously by acclamation. The Bundesrat, the upper chamber, gave its approval a week later, and Chancellor Adenauer officially declared on October 9 that West Germany had acceded to the Convention. Six weeks later, on November 24, Hans Riesser, the country's permanent observer at the UN, formally deposited a declaration of accession with that body—a task that must have been especially gratifying for him. A German Jew, Riesser had gone into exile after the Nazis had fired him from his position in the Foreign Office.[13]

And what about East Germany? On December 6, officials at the Ministry of Foreign Affairs met to discuss preparations for joining the Genocide Convention—even though the UN had not extended an invitation to the German Democratic Republic (GDR). There was a simple reason for that. A precondition to joining was membership in one of the UN's "special organizations" or involvement in the statute of the International Court of Justice at The Hague, and the GDR satisfied neither of these conditions. The officials advised the foreign minister to submit a formal request to the UN for an invitation. Accession would be "useful," they reasoned, because it would improve the country's "international standing" at a time when East Germany was wrestling with the Federal Republic for international recognition and diplomatic ties. The foreign minister's entreaty was unsuccessful, however; the GDR did not accede to the Convention until two decades later, in 1973, when it and West Germany both became members of the UN in the wake of détente. Within a decade, the East Germans would join other Soviet-bloc states in condemning supposed acts of genocide—by none other than the Jews of Israel.[14]

Forty years separated West Germany's accession to the UN Genocide Convention from the acrimonious debate triggered by Joschka Fischer's call for outside military intervention in Bosnia and an international "genocide clause." These two episodes introduce us to important themes at the heart of this exploration of German reactions to post-Holocaust genocide. Most important by far is the question of how Germany's tarnished past has weighed on its postwar present: how memories and perceptions of the Third Reich and the Final Solution shaped attitudes and influenced behavior in response to reports of genocide in *other* countries, and how they were modified in return.

This question has larger significance beyond Germany. The international response to state-sponsored mass murder and questions about the legitimate use of force are vitally important foreign policy issues. German reactions help us better understand how powerful Western states choose whether to intervene in humanitarian trouble spots across the globe. Still, as the country most intimately associated with the "crime of crimes," Germany's case is a peculiar if particularly instructive one. It keenly demonstrates how political interests and domestic debates about the past—how it is interpreted, its "meaning"—influence such decisions. To what extent did the mass murder of the Jews shape postwar foreign policy and public discussion about Germany's "proper" role in the international arena? How frequently did Germans make comparisons, direct or oblique, between Nazi atrocities and ones that took place later in foreign lands—and to what end? Did that change over time, especially following the unification of the two Germanies in 1990, when, now fully sovereign, the Federal Republic began to consider—starting with the Gulf War of 1990–1991—a more interventionist political, humanitarian, and even military role on the world stage?[15] This leads to other important questions. Were reports of atrocities elsewhere used to "relativize" or somehow diminish Germany's own past crimes—and, if so, did this contribute to a backlash against what some critics came to regard as a national obsession with *Vergangenheitsbewältigung,* that is, with "coming to terms" with the twelve most fraught years of their country's history?

But why a focus on reactions to genocide?[16] What Germans wrote, said, and ultimately did (or failed to do) about crimes against humanity elsewhere offers novel insights into how they came to terms with the National Socialist past. Tackling the question in an indirect, roundabout way—beyond the usual focus on solemn statements and massive monuments—provides a more unvarnished look at how Germans dealt with the heavy mortgage of their past by uncovering meaningful hints and traces that are more revealing and more reliable than carefully crafted speeches at orchestrated unveilings.

The baggage of the Nazi past was always somehow present in both German states after 1945. Each considered itself to be the "renunciation" of the Third Reich, their "most important negative historical point of reference."[17] Debates about how the two Germanies confronted that history usually focus on two issues: their different approaches to the past, and the question of silence and the extent to which East and West Germans ignored or suppressed discussion of Nazi crimes against the Jews. There is a popular misperception that most Germans repressed all memories of the Nazi past right after the war and that the Third Reich remained a taboo topic until the late 1960s, when progressive youths suddenly rediscovered the horrors of the 1930s and 1940s and condemned the criminal and moral failings of their elders.

That is misleading. There was indeed a tendency during the first postwar decades to forgo an honest, more open reckoning with the recent past, especially when it came to German crimes. The emphasis instead was on *German* suffering. Public officials rejected the notion of collective guilt, the press downplayed Nazi atrocities, and textbooks took an "uncritical" approach to the Third Reich. Efforts to bring criminals to justice remained lax, with the focus instead on granting amnesty to those who had been sanctioned during the short-lived process of denazification. Physical reminders were removed or destroyed, all part of a "compulsion to forget."[18]

But that was only one side of the coin. There were also efforts to deal with and eliminate aspects of the Nazi past in a different, more constructive way, which under the tutelage of the Allied occupiers involved doing away with the very institutions and structures that had supposedly paved the way to dictatorship, war, and genocide. In that respect, almost every feature of public and private life during the early postwar period was, in *both* German states, a direct or indirect reckoning with the tumultuous Nazi years. No subsequent period witnessed as much *Vergangenheitsbewältigung* as those early years, in fact—depending on how one defines that elusive term. A public preoccupation with the genocide of the Jews would not come until the late 1970s in West Germany, and it never really took shape in the GDR.[19] But "mastering" the past did not mean just confronting the Holocaust, a term that only came into wide use starting in that decade. This is an important distinction, because a failure to differentiate between postwar responses to the Nazi period in general and a more specific discussion of the Final Solution has generated a good deal of confusion about Germans' efforts to reckon with the past and how they changed over time. Recognizing the nature and evolution of those responses is crucial for contextualizing and understanding later reactions to genocide elsewhere.

It is nevertheless true that a "pragmatic," self-exculpatory approach to the past did indeed characterize the first postwar decades. There were a variety of reasons for this, ranging from pressures at home to integrate former Nazis in the interest of domestic stability to external pressures during the Cold War. That gradually gave way to a more "moralistic" tone, a more self-critical approach in the West, where Nazi atrocities eventually took "center stage." Another important shift accompanied this: a growing concern with formally acknowledging and remembering Nazi crimes.[20]

Whatever their shortcomings, those earlier developments lay the groundwork for the later transformation. The first signs of change appeared in the late 1950s and gathered steam in the early to mid-1960s. There were several reasons for this, including a disturbing wave of openly antisemitic activity in the Federal Republic in the winter of 1959. The shift was most evident in popular media, high culture, and the national press, where a more critical discussion of the causes, consequences, and crimes of National Socialism gradually took shape. It culminated in 1968, when West German youths—the so-called sixty-eight generation—vociferously confronted the older generation for having failed to resist Adolf Hitler and for supposedly having swept the Nazi past under the rug.[21]

But the crucial point here is that even in the late 1960s, the focus was not on the persecution of the Jews but on the Third Reich and the wartime experience as a whole. Public discussion of the horrific crimes committed against the Jews remained rare. If mentioned at all, it was usually in tandem with German suffering, an implicit equation of "victimhood" and the sort of collapsing of distinctions on display during the Bundestag discussion of the Genocide Convention in 1954.[22] But was the intent of those who spoke in the same breath of Jewish victims and German expellees from Eastern Europe, or of the Final Solution and earlier genocides, to relativize German wrongdoing? Not necessarily, given that irreproachable figures like Jakob Altmaier also drew such parallels—comparisons that would later draw fire when non-Jews made them.

The discussions in the Bundestag showed that at least some public figures did indeed speak openly about the genocide of the Jews. Public discussion of the Final Solution resurfaced in much more spectacular fashion in the first half of the 1960s. Parliamentary debates about whether to extend the statute of limitations for crimes committed during the Third Reich played a role, but the trial of Adolf Eichmann in Jerusalem and the Frankfurt Auschwitz trials were especially crucial. For the first time, the genocide of the Jews took center stage, with survivors telling their harrowing stories in a large public setting. This period witnessed other important changes: the first public acknowledgment of the "specificity" and exceptionalism of German racial crimes; the opening of exhibitions about the Final Solution and the unveiling of the first memorial sites at Dachau and Bergen-Belsen; the start of school visits to concentration camps and to Israel; the publication of biting theatrical pieces, critical essays, and searching studies by artists, scholars, and intellectuals who called for a more open and critical discussion of the Third Reich.

This produced a backlash by some public intellectuals, who demanded that West Germans move on and "draw a line" under the past. But the new tenor of discussion set the stage for an even more definitive shift away from the defensive discourse of the first postwar decade. How had such crimes been possible, members of the sixty-eight generation wanted to know, and what had the older generation done to stop or, worse, abet them? This "critical turn" did not appear out of nowhere, but it was nevertheless an important turning point.[23] For one thing, it marked the first instrumental use of the Nazi past for domestic political gain. But that was not all. The word *Auschwitz* was now on many lips as well, part of a post-Eichmann spike in the use of this and other code words, in West Germany and elsewhere, for the mass murder of European Jewry. This became even more common during the second half of the decade, when leading figures of the West German student movement detected contemporary parallels to Nazi atrocities everywhere, giving rise to the use of inflated rhetoric and analogies intended to impugn political elites and West German society as a whole. But was this a reckoning with the genocide of the Jews?

The sixty-eight generation was heavily influenced by the social theory and critical philosophy of the renowned Frankfurt School, which saw fascism, Nazism, and even the Final Solution as by-products of advanced capitalism. Many believed that the Federal Republic was a deeply authoritarian, "pre-fascist" state that shared a number of "structural continuities" with the Third Reich—a car wreck waiting to happen. The United States, West Germany's most trusted ally, supposedly displayed fascist tendencies as well. It was, some argued, committing genocide in Vietnam, where American soldiers were setting up "concentration camps" and acting like members of the mobile killing units that had carried out the Final Solution in Eastern Europe. At home, some in the sixty-eight generation began to refer to themselves as the "new Jews," that is to say, as self-styled victims of "crypto-Nazism" and an "oppressive power structure." After landing in jail, the leaders of the Red Army Faction, a radical minority that turned to domestic terrorism in the 1970s, spoke of their "special treatment"—*Sonderbehandlung,* a Nazi euphemism for state-organized murder—and of their imprisonment in an "imaginary gas chamber."[24]

The genocide of the Jews was clearly now a topic, but such inflated rhetoric and careless invocations of Auschwitz were deeply problematic. Intended or not, the sixty-eight generation relativized and arguably trivialized what had happened in Germany by stressing the "universality of genocide." By taking the Final Solution out of historical context, critics charged, they robbed it of its historic "specificity." At the least, such hyperbolic language deflected from the horrors of the Holocaust and obscured its particularities. That very question—the extent to which the genocide of the Jews was "unique"—has indeed been the source of much acrimonious debate.[25] But another important issue was at stake. Did claims about uniqueness unwittingly desensitize Germans (and others) to atrocities being committed elsewhere? This is significant, because if it did—if the portrayal of the Holocaust as unique hindered efforts to prevent other genocides—then it was clearly a macabre victim of its own success.

The discourse became less shrill at the close of the 1960s, with the election of Willy Brandt and Gustav Heinemann as chancellor and president of the Federal Republic in 1969. Like younger Germans of the sixty-eight generation, the two Social Democrats introduced a more moralistic tone into the public discussion of German history, acknowledging and accepting much more openly German responsibility for earlier misdeeds. But they did so in an understated manner. One thinks of Brandt's solemn genuflection at the Warsaw Ghetto Memorial in December 1970.

The upshot was a major shift in public awareness and acknowledgment of Nazi criminality. Memorials and monuments proliferated, novel cultural and scholarly approaches emerged, and the Third Reich became an integral part of German history. Yet, the genocide of the Jews was still not a major focus of public attention, and there was even a backlash in the mid-1970s against the moralistic self-flagellation of the Brandt-Heinemann years. Their successors, Helmut Schmidt of the SPD and Walter Scheel of the Free Democratic Party (FDP), pushed back against "reducing" German history to the twelve years of Nazi rule and called for a more "balanced" portrayal of the past—something Helmut Kohl of the conservative CDU would demand even more energetically after becoming chancellor in 1982. It was therefore not surprising that Helmut Schmidt did not explicitly mention the Jews in his brief speech marking the first visit to Auschwitz by a German chancellor, in November 1977—but did remark that the Germans themselves were Hitler's "first victims."[26] The absences in Schmidt's speech would have been inconceivable two years later, following the airing on West German television of the American miniseries *Holocaust* in January 1979, a major media event that dramatically changed how officials and ordinary West Germans "reckoned" with the Final Solution.

What about "memory work" in the GDR? There is a common misperception that it lagged far behind the Federal Republic.[27] That was certainly true after the sea change of the late 1960s, but before that there were striking similarities on both sides of the Iron Curtain. For East and West, the Third Reich served as a "negative utopia," a reminder and a justification—sometimes more overt, sometimes less—for the policies and behavior of both states. There were, of course, important differences. GDR officials claimed they had eliminated fascism root and branch through a series of far-reaching socioeconomic reforms in the late 1940s; after the arrest, expropriation, and elimination of capitalists and aristocrat landowners (*Junker*), all remaining fascists had supposedly fled to the West. This made a continued reckoning with the past unnecessary, they believed—or at least less urgent than in the "fascist" Federal Republic, where tainted individuals still held prominent positions of power.[28]

That is not to say that the Third Reich was ignored in the GDR. There were certainly concerted efforts to explain Nazism, supposedly a product of advanced capitalism and imperialism. The same held true for the genocide of the Jews. Official ideology reduced antisemitism to a mere by-product of "finance capital" and "class warfare," a side issue intended to distract the masses from focusing on the "real" culprits—capitalists and large landowners. But the essential point is that the Final Solution was not a central focus in either German state early on. In fact, Jews *as Jews* remained behind workers and communists in the East German "hierarchy" of victim groups, their grief overshadowed by the suffering of others tyrannized under the Nazis.[29]

But the Final Solution was by no means completely ignored or "marginalized."[30] In fact, one of the first German films about the persecution of the Jews was made in the East in 1947. There was an official commemoration of Kristallnacht in 1953; a Western play based on Anne Frank's diary was shown in Dresden in 1956; and a variety of films and novels dealt with the Third Reich and even touched on the Final Solution in the second half of the 1950s, just as interest was growing in the Federal Republic. Still, Jewish victims continued to play a subordinate role on both sides of the Elbe. A major memorial consecrated in the spring of 1960 at the Buchenwald concentration camp made no mention of Jewish prisoners, for example. But as in the West, Nazi crimes started to receive greater attention and more critical reflection in the 1960s, a decade that witnessed an uptick in radio documentaries, grassroots commemorative activities by local Jewish communities and Protestant churches, and scholarly research on antisemitism and the persecution of the Jews. Peter Weiss's controversial play about the Frankfurt Auschwitz Trial, *Die Ermittlung* (*The Investigation*), premiered in 1965 in more than a dozen theaters in both German states.[31]

Public discussion of Germany's genocidal past was nevertheless much less pronounced in the GDR, especially after the late 1960s. It is difficult to know what ordinary East Germans thought about the persecution of the Jews; most were no doubt preoccupied with everyday economic and political challenges. In fact, life under yet another autocratic regime fueled a widespread sense of "victimhood" that likely offset any feelings of shame or responsibility for what had happened in the 1930s and 1940s.[32]

Yet for all their differences, each state influenced memory work in the other in unexpected ways. An East German campaign that began in the late 1950s to expose former Nazis still in positions of power in the West spurred greater sensitivity for the Nazi past in the Federal Republic. In turn, the airing of the *Holocaust* miniseries had reverberations in the GDR, where many people watched West German television. But there was something more at stake here than the mutual influence each state had on memories of the Third Reich in the other. East German efforts to expose former Nazis in the West unwittingly stimulated a more open confrontation with the past that, in the long run, may have made the Federal Republic a more liberal and democratic society.[33]

That is an intriguing paradox. If true, it provides one answer to a question seldom explicitly posed or explored because the answer seems so obvious: Why *should* we care about how Germans—or any societies, for that matter—deal with and talk about their past, especially its darker aspects? That may strike some as "impious," but as Charles Maier once remarked, "some questions are useful just by virtue of their being posed."[34]

Most work on the "collective memory" of a given country, society, or group deals with its more theoretical aspects: the nature of memory—how it is formed and evolves, the relationship between societal and individual memory—and how it "functions." The reasons for our preoccupation with memory and for the "memory boom" that began in the 1960s have also received a good deal of attention. But *why* we should care about or privilege the study of memory receives far less attention, likely because of a usually unarticulated conviction that the reasons are "obvious." After all, how we conceive or talk about the past influences the actual behavior of individuals and society in the present.[35] That may be a truism, though a difficult one to prove.

The same holds true for speculative ideas about the purpose memory serves and what is at stake. Memory, some suggest, creates, molds, and reinforces national or group identity, unity, pride, and a sense of belonging. It is mobilized in support of certain political goals in the service of a particular "political culture," and it shores up political institutions through the creation of a "legitimating" or "master" narrative. Memory helps us understand the present and how the world works. It gives voice and succor to oppressed or disenfranchised groups, not least by recognizing and paying respect to their victimhood; it heals the "traumatized" by the telling of sacral redemptive stories. This all seems reasonable and important, especially if it is true that how we "represent" the world in the stories we tell about ourselves and the past constitutes our primary or even sole social reality. But such claims are speculative, abstract, and difficult if not impossible to prove. What *is* clear is that our focus on the past is not necessarily about the past per se, but rather about the present and future, about present needs and future ones. In other words, the importance of memory—what is "at stake" in the here and now—lies in its concrete social effects and political consequences.

There is an assumption, usually implicit, that Germans had and have a particular duty to remember the past, especially the crimes committed during the Third Reich.[36] More to the point, there is a wish to be assured that Germans have been "properly penitent"; that they have demonstrated "genuine" or "sufficient" remorse for past misdeeds; that, because they have "learned their lesson" from history, they have put their Nazi past behind them and no longer pose a threat. If articulated at all, the arguments in support of this mandate to remember usually fall into one or more of three categories: the moral, the psychological, and the practical. Scholars and statesmen, both in Germany and abroad, have frequently invoked the first, arguing that Germans had an ethical obligation and responsibility to remember and confront their country's past misdeeds because doing so not only provided valuable ethical lessons but also contributed to their moral well-being and "regeneration."[37] But is it possible to "prove" these arguments and suppositions?

A more compelling reason why Germans needed to face the past and learn its lessons looked to the supposedly practical benefits. The protracted process of remembering would prevent a repeat of Nazism by delegitimizing Hitler and the Third Reich, fostering democracy and civil society, combating extremism and aggression, promoting critical thought and the acceptance of certain duties, and, last but not least, making dangerous ideas and beliefs taboo. This was especially important for German youths, who needed to be carefully "immunized" against fascism and made resistant to any future siren call of Nazism. All of this, in turn, promoted the legitimacy and stability of the postwar political system, while enhancing the country's reputation among its neighbors and allies. In short, the argument went, an open confrontation with the past undergirded the durable move away from dictatorship. It also promoted postwar stability and "success"—at least in *West* Germany, where Auschwitz became an "amulet . . . to ward off evil."[38]

And in the GDR? If all this is true, East Germany's failure to deal as rigorously with that aspect of the past must have had deleterious consequences. Might it explain the higher incidence of xenophobic violence in the eastern half of Germany following unification? Did it account for the state's hostile policies toward Israel—or, for that matter, the repressive treatment of its own people?[39] Again, it is extremely difficult to prove any of this or establish clear causal connections. Those affected by the Federal Republic's Anti-Radical Decree of 1972, which banned members of "extremist" organizations from the West German civil service, would no doubt take issue with the claim that Willy Brandt's greater willingness to confront the past ushered in greater democratization and liberal reform. Foreigners who experienced rampant racism in West Germany would as well. After all, open xenophobic sentiment first emerged *after* 1968, and it even increased around the time West Germans "rediscovered" the Final Solution in the late 1970s. Racist incidents in the former GDR tended to grab headlines following unification, but there were equally spectacular cases of xenophobic violence in *both* halves of the formerly divided country. Finally, those who believe that East Germans had suppressed memories of the Final Solution might be hard pressed to explain why, in April 1990, the very first act of the first freely elected People's Chamber was to issue a declaration that explicitly accepted responsibility on behalf of the GDR for Nazi crimes against the Jews.[40]

Again, neither German state did a particularly good job during the first postwar decades of confronting the more violent and criminal— the genocidal—aspects of the Third Reich. Yet, whatever lingering admiration remained for certain aspects of Hitler's regime, few (openly) expressed any desire to return to the brutal, expansionist policies of the recent past. Regret or remorse no doubt played a role here, but that general sentiment was hardly the result of any real "memory work." The thoroughness of defeat, postwar material recovery, and eventual prosperity (especially in the West) were arguably more important for changed attitudes. The point is not that an honest acknowledgment of and open confrontation with historical misdeeds serve no purpose. Important work on the collective memory and commemoration of the American Civil War reminds us of the potential consequences for the present of selective or distorted memories—and that it is not just Germans who have a responsibility to confront the past. Distortion and silence can indeed have a "high cost."[41]

Still, we need to be cautious about drawing facile connections between morally admirable activities and pursuits, on the one hand, outlook, values, and actual behavior, on the other. It may be true that those who cannot remember the past are condemned to repeat it. Yet even those whose efforts to "deal" with their country's somber history have not been particularly impressive—the Japanese, say—have not been guilty of recidivism.[42] More to the point, even those well acquainted with the supposed lessons of the past run the same risk. Again, one thinks of the resurgence of xenophobia and the scapegoating of minorities in Germany since the 1960s and 1970s, at precisely the point in time that memory work on the Holocaust first got under way. Let us frame the issue another way: would Germans have pursued different policies at home or abroad if they had dealt less openly with its past? Would their responses to genocide have been different had there been no intensive reckoning with the Holocaust beginning in the late 1970s? Was *that* even the past that mattered most to them?

Most work on German memory focuses on what officials and other public figures have said, written, or otherwise expressed about the Third Reich, most literally in their speeches, statements, and essays, more figuratively in monuments, the arts, and the media. That approach is no doubt essential for getting at how *some* Germans ostensibly reckoned with the history of National Socialism.[43] But talk is cheap, as the saying goes, and public pronouncements are not necessarily the most reliable source for getting at internal values and beliefs, which, for most individuals, are often inscrutable, at best unstable and evolving. Still, they do provide some glimpse into what prominent Germans thought about the past and how they dealt with the more somber sides of their history. More important, they set a tone and gave voice to aspirations for society at large.

What Germans have thought and said about their past is indeed crucial for understanding how they have confronted their country's difficult history. But even more important are the *concrete* consequences and actions that flow from this. "To what contemporary uses are memories put?" Stanley Hoffmann asks in his foreword to Henry Rousso's pioneering study on French memories of the Vichy period. His response, that "the past never ceases to color and to disturb our behavior in the present," is likely true but still debatable.[44] And that brings us to the crux of this exploration of German responses to post-Holocaust genocides. If we wish to grasp how Germans reckoned with their past in practice—how and whether memories of the 1930s and 1940s not only shaped their values and beliefs, perceptions and mentalities, but also affected actual behavior—we must not focus solely on principled pronouncements and well-meant monuments. The focus here will be not just on what Germans said or wrote, but equally on the extent to which the lessons supposedly learned after 1945 guided concrete action at home and abroad—something Germans might call *Vergangenheitsbewältigung in der Tat:* reckoning with the past "in deed." To what extent, in short, were Germans indeed, and in deed, moved by the past to act on their convictions?

German responses to genocides in other countries since World War II help get at these issues. But which responses? And which genocides—and which Germans precisely? Let us begin with the last question. Our focus will be on those who occupied prominent positions in the public sphere: politicians, diplomats, and government officials; journalists, pundits, and public intellectuals; academics and human rights activists; novelists, filmmakers, and other cultural figures. Their voices, opinions, and rhetoric most readily left a trace in the historical record, but a focus on what they said and did is more than just a pragmatic choice. After all, they were the ones who molded popular discourse, shaped public opinion, and determined actual policy.[45] That is not to say that the attitudes and actions of "ordinary" Germans are unimportant or merely derivative. But they do tend to be more elusive, and getting at the extent to which individuals "bought into" the reigning "master narratives" of memory is challenging. Letters sent to politicians or the press, the results of public opinion surveys, and reports about various humanitarian activities at the grass roots nevertheless provide important clues. At the same time, they also help us get at whether popular opinion and attitudes had any effect on official policy—as a constraining force, for instance, when it came to the use of force, even for ostensibly humanitarian purposes.[46]

It is important, in any event, to distinguish between official statements, on the one hand, and popular perceptions about the past, on the other. A failure to do so only muddies the waters when making broad claims about "German" responses to genocide. And regardless of who said what and when, it is also important to pay close attention to language: to specific words and phrases, to recurring metaphors, images, and historical analogies. How they are used, their frequency, the extent to which this changed over time, and what they reveal about values and attitudes are all significant. As Richard Cobb sagely advised, historians must "show a willingness to *listen* to the wording of the document, to be governed by its every phrase and murmur, to explore behind every allusion . . . so as to hear what is actually being said, in what accent and in what tone."[47]

With that in mind, we will pay a good deal of attention to meaning, connotation, and the effects of language, to the "subtle undercurrents" that would have been especially "meaningful" to a German audience.[48] German politicians and officials who discussed the Federal Republic's accession to the Genocide Convention less than a decade after the horrors of the Holocaust were clearly sensitive to the importance and nuance of language in light of their country's recent past. But this was more than just a debate about "political correctness" and more than just an "academic" question. As Joschka Fischer rightly pointed out in 1995, invoking the term *genocide*—acknowledging that genocide was taking place somewhere in the world—brought with it certain responsibilities under international law. That alone justifies a focus on language and locution.

But did German responses to reports of this scourge go beyond mere words? Did they have "real-world" consequences? There is no shortage of pronouncements about the purported impact history and memory have had in the realm of foreign policy and humanitarianism: "Few countries have been as beholden to the past and the collective memories based on it as has the Federal Republic," where the lessons of the past have "loomed large" and had a "formidable influence" in the field of foreign affairs.[49] History writ large may shape precepts and principles; prescribe or proscribe certain actions, responses, and responsibilities; impose limits on freedom of maneuver and "acceptable" forms of behavior. That may all be true, but it is not self-evident—and it is not always precisely clear *how*. German responses to genocide elsewhere allow us to explore these intriguing suppositions. But first, it is important to trace the contours of postwar German foreign policy—especially that of the Federal Republic, a country that had far more leeway than the GDR, whose policies were slavishly tied to the whims of its patrons in Moscow.[50]

Several precepts governed West German foreign policy, beginning in the 1950s: predictability, reliability, and a commitment to working together with others in a multilateral framework. After the war, the country's unswerving dedication to the West, especially to erstwhile enemies in Europe and across the Atlantic, made Germany the "consummate team player" in international organizations. At the same time, the unspeakable suffering caused and experienced by Germans during World War II produced a robust aversion to militarism and highly ambivalent feelings about the use of force. For this reason, most officials preferred nonmilitary solutions and embraced deterrence: "total peace" in lieu of "total war," so to speak.[51] Both German states *did* rearm in the 1950s, but their leaders insisted this was purely for defensive purposes, something clearly set forth in their respective constitutions. The desire for "world peace" was a pillar of East German propaganda. Mainstream politicians in the West, for their part, eagerly embraced and took pride in the Federal Republic's "culture of restraint," a catchphrase that neatly captured the country's determined rejection of old-style power politics, its reluctance to resort to force, and its steady refusal to project power and throw its weight around aggressively—at least when it came to military action. (The economic and diplomatic spheres were a different matter.) As Willy Brandt once dryly observed, "There are worse things than pacifist Germans."[52]

Caution and modesty, deference and sometimes diffidence in the international arena were a far cry from Realpolitik—ironic given that Germans had coined the term in the late nineteenth century. But even if such policies ran counter to the expectations of self-styled "realists"— scholars who expect "normal" nations to act in their own "rational" self-interest—one should not assume that self-interest did not play a role in German decisions and deliberations. Many factors shape perceptions on this score, including a sense of the politically possible, tempered by historical experience, "cherished values," and collective memory.[53] In that sense, Germans were like the proverbial burnt child who now dreads fire.

If politics is indeed the "art of the possible," as Chancellor Otto von Bismarck put it in 1867, how did interpretations and memories of the past set the parameters of the possible? The crux of the matter for many Germans was this: how, in the shadow of past crimes, should their country act in the postwar world? More to the point, did the Nazi past oblige Germans to take action to prevent atrocities—or compel them to refrain from intervening at all?

Debates about these issues became especially toxic in the Federal Republic whenever the question of using force arose. During the Cold War, American nuclear protection and global policing rendered the issue of military engagement largely moot.[54] So, too, did a domestic political consensus that the West German constitution limited use of the country's armed forces to purely defensive purposes. Opinions evolved considerably on that score following unification, as we shall see. But the inconceivability before 1989 of German military involvement is an essential point. It is also an important reason why this book does not take a normative or prescriptive approach; it is not a j'accuse of Germans for what they "should" have done militarily or otherwise in the face of genocide. That is the thrust of Samantha Power's impassioned study of American responses to genocide in the twentieth century.[55] Her fierce indictment of America's failure—as the world's strongest military power and self-styled moral apostle—to act on the precept of "never again" is simply not applicable in the German case, at least not for the period before unification.

Few would have raised such expectations for Germany anyway, prior to the end of the Cold War. There were no UN requests for German peacekeeping forces (the "Blue Helmets") before 1990, even though it was a theoretical possibility. More to the point, such international missions remained infrequent into the 1980s, and the idea of "out-of-area" NATO missions—the deployment of combat forces beyond the territory of the member states—was rarely the topic of serious discussion.[56] One must, in short, consider actual circumstances and the realistically possible— as well as the possibility of "softer" responses to genocide and other human rights abuses that encompass more than just military deployment: engaging in feverish diplomatic activity, providing humanitarian aid, or hosting large number of refugees. These issues and themes lie at the heart of this book, and they are worth exploring in depth because they direct our attention to other important developments after 1945, from disturbing outbursts of xenophobia and bigotry to instances of remarkable largesse at the grass roots; from transnational efforts to alleviate suffering to the heated Cold War rivalry that played out between East and West Germany on the global stage. Before turning to them, it is necessary to make clear first which genocides we will explore, and why.

Since 1945, almost two dozen instances of state-sponsored mass murder have been regarded officially or unofficially as genocide. Three of them garnered the most international attention: the genocides carried out in Cambodia under Pol Pot in the late 1970s, and in Bosnia and Rwanda in the first half of the 1990s. These were not necessarily the "worst" genocides of the postwar period, in terms of the raw numbers of people killed, the percentage of the population murdered, or, more subjectively, the level of suffering and cruelty. But the high level of global attention they received at the time, and later among international scholars, means that the available source material on them is the richest—notwithstanding archival constraints that still restrict access to behind-the-scenes discussions and decisions about Bosnia and Rwanda.[57]

Geographic diversity is another consideration. Each of these genocides took place in a different part of the world: Asia, Africa, and Europe. Just as important, Germany's historical and contemporary relationships with each of the countries varied considerably. Rwanda had been part of the colony German East Africa until the end of World War I, German soldiers had brutally occupied the Balkans during World War II, and Cambodia played an important role in the Cold War diplomatic rivalry between East and West Germany in the 1960s. These and other differences allow us to explore the extent to which political, geopolitical, and diplomatic calculations, economic interests, racial and ethnic prejudices, and historical burdens shaped responses.

The timing of these three genocides is another reason to focus on them. A conspicuous spike in popular and scholarly interest in the fate of the European Jews coincided with the genocide in Cambodia. In fact, the genocidal Khmer Rouge regime was driven from power the very month the miniseries *Holocaust* first aired, in January 1979. We will explore how that chance confluence affected subsequent discussion of Germany's own genocidal past—not least during the infamous "historians' controversy" (*Historikerstreit*) of the mid-1980s, a fierce public debate about the uniqueness and causes of what was increasingly becoming known as the Holocaust.

But there are other reasons for beginning in the 1970s. It was the decade when global interest in human rights reemerged and the worldwide flow of refugees reached unprecedented proportions—developments that had a big impact on German reactions to foreign genocide.[58] This is not to suggest that Germans suddenly "discovered" these issues that decade. Soon after its founding in 1949, West Germany had signed nearly the entire gamut of international human rights treaties and obligations adopted during the heady years right after World War II. Along with other Soviet-bloc states, the GDR had also embraced the language and rhetoric of human rights following the death of Joseph Stalin, even if its record at home remained dismal. In terms of offering humanitarian assistance, both East and West Germany first became active in the 1950s, sponsoring various aid projects in Africa and Asia. A desire to win credibility and legitimacy at home and abroad drove such efforts, especially at a time when both German states were vying for diplomatic relations and trade ties beyond Europe.[59]

Human rights work and humanitarian "advocacy" really took off in the 1960s. GDR officials cultivated relationships with colonial independence movements, which also won the support of young progressives in the Federal Republic. This was, in short, the decade that Germans began to find a "moral voice in world affairs," largely in response to disturbing developments abroad.[60] The brutal French and American wars in Algeria and Vietnam, as well as the Biafran crisis of the late 1960s, were especially important in West Germany, where they not only stimulated grassroots activism, but also shifted attention from an earlier focus on human rights violations in the Soviet bloc to ones in the developing world. This is important context for understanding the reactions to the Cambodian genocide a decade later.[61]

At the same time Germans were becoming "citizens of the world" once again, those in the West began to face serious challenges at home, fueled in no small part by a worldwide refugee crisis that coincided with the Cambodian genocide of the late 1970s. Since that time, few issues have poisoned debate in the Federal Republic as much as immigration. A land of emigrants until World War I, Germany has had a difficult time coming to terms with the fact that, since 1945, it has become a "land of immigration" (*Einwanderungsland*)—a term mainstream officials across the political divide long rejected. Pressure to provide a haven for the victims of genocide fueled West German debates about the influx of foreigners—debates that revealed a great deal about racism, xenophobia, and "hierarchies of acceptability" in postwar Germany.[62]

There is a final reason for beginning with the Cambodian genocide: both postwar German states still existed in the 1970s and 1980s. That allows us to compare reactions, to gauge the extent to which divergent ideologies and experiences, differences in postwar memory work, and, finally, each state's international position, affected its responses to the increasingly harrowing reports about Cambodia. Those responses are important as well for what they reveal about the Cold War rivalry between the two German states.

A look at German reactions to the genocides in Bosnia and Rwanda during the first half of the 1990s takes our story into the period after the Cold War, and thus into a different era and geopolitical context—not least for Germany. Its unexpected unification in 1990 was a watershed moment that transformed the now united nation's position on the world stage. The restoration of full sovereignty meant that many of the country's major preoccupations of the postwar period belonged to the past and that it now had greater freedom to maneuver—as well as greater responsibilities—in the international arena. Its responses to the genocides in Bosnia and Rwanda allow us to explore how this affected the country's foreign policy *and* its relationship to an increasingly distant past—precisely at a time when most Germans had come to "internalize" and feel "deep . . . shame" for the extermination of the Jews, and the Holocaust had become *the* international "symbol" for all genocides and extreme forms of violence and racism.[63]

The Federal Republic's changed standing in the world gave rise to a great deal of anguish and hand-wringing, just as much at home as abroad.

Would unified Germany remain a "tamed power" or revert to its dangerous and destructive ways of yore? In other words, would the hoary "German question"—how to ensure that a powerful Germany would not pose a threat to its neighbors (or its own citizens)—once again rear its ugly head? That question seemed to have been settled in the late 1940s, at least provisionally, with the division of Germany into two states belonging to two rival blocs. But when the country regained full sovereignty, some German public figures began to speak of a "return to normality." What that meant in precise terms was unclear, but it led many to wonder whether their country would continue to be constrained by the collective memory of a dark past—or revert to its "old ways." Would there now be a dangerous resurgence of strident nationalism and a return of past aspirations to be a Great Power? Or had Germany truly "learned the lessons" of its history?[64]

There are other compelling reasons for taking our story into the 1990s. It was the decade when a post–Cold War "liberal consensus" emerged about a duty to defend human rights and use military force to "protect civilians from their own government." The 1990s also witnessed a veritable explosion of nongovernmental organizations (NGOs) dedicated to humanitarian work around the globe. Germans who wished to "make a difference" had expanded opportunities to work as activists on the front lines and participate in the "world of transnational networks and connections" to provide relief. Such grassroots activities grew in popularity in the 1990s, and this has spurred greater attention by scholars to the history of human rights, humanitarianism, and transnationalism, which poses pertinent questions about agency, motivation, and efficacy. Who acts, with what motivation, in which ways, and to what end? If it is true that only certain groups, types of events, and images "effectively galvanize collective outrage" and action, which ones are they and why?[65]

Humanitarian endeavors have given rise to a good deal of criticism as well. Were they being used to advance—or punish—particular political, ideological, or even economic agendas, often at the cost of those supposedly being assisted? Were humanitarian interventions mere "packaging" used to justify and legitimate the use of military force in the name of peace? Was such assistance used to create, in short, a world in one's own "civilizational" image?[66] At the same time, what do German humanitarian activities reveal about Germans' attitudes toward others, especially non-Westerners. Without diminishing the benefits that aid recipients enjoyed, questions like these help us avoid simplistic, laudatory narratives about purely noble altruism.

Our story begins, then, in the mid-1970s, at a time when the word *holocaust* was not yet widely in use and certainly not as ubiquitous as it is today, at a time when the Nazi genocide of the Jews did not yet occupy the emotional attention of most Germans in the way it soon would. Continuing past the fall of the Berlin Wall, it traces a twenty-year arc during a period of decisive and often drastic change in postwar Germany: from new forms of reckoning with the past to controversial decisions about committing German soldiers to trouble spots abroad. The evolution of a self-styled pacifist like Joschka Fischer in such matters was just one example, if a particularly striking one, of how feelings of guilt and responsibility were rekindled, recast, and reframed. Taking our story through the mid-1990s lets us explore the ways in which unification marked a genuine break in Germany's postwar history, not least with respect to dominant memories of a fraught past—*and* the effects of those memories. It was not at all self-evident that the Final Solution would remain a fixation after unification. After all, Germans now had to deal with the memory and crimes of yet another German dictatorship, the GDR.

East Germany's demise only reinforced a widespread tendency to see the Federal Republic as a "success story." There are good reasons for questioning that simple but uplifting narrative, not least because of its tendency to ignore or downplay the less sanguine aspects of West Germany's postwar history: endemic racism and sexism, for example, lingering wealth disparities and environmental degradation.[67] Still, even with those caveats in mind and even when not measured against the horrible foil of Nazi Germany, the Federal Republic was indeed a success story, a place where Germans had effectively put their violent, once genocidal past behind them. Their responses to organized mass slaughter in foreign lands are an untold aspect of that story. Those responses did not do much to prevent or punish genocide; they were more reactive than active. But they often went far beyond just high-sounding speeches meant to abjure or atone for past atrocities. And they reveal a great deal about German values, mentalities, and "lessons learned" after 1945.

Postwar "success," in the sense suggested here, is just as worthy of our interest as the topics in modern German history that receive the most attention: the Third Reich, World War II, and the Final Solution. That focus is understandable, of course. Yet the story of how Germans confronted their past and shaped a stable and prosperous democracy, of how their country rejoined the community of nations as a peaceful member reluctant to use force and dedicated to the rule of law, of how German leaders and ordinary citizens enthusiastically embraced human rights and energetically engaged in humanitarian activities in response to mass atrocities abroad—that, too, is an equally important and gripping story.

1

Pol Pot Is Like Hitler

From the very start of the Cambodian genocide, skepticism and denial went hand in hand, even on the part of foreign observers who were there at the time and might have known better. West German journalist Christoph Maria Fröhder and East German diplomat Erich Stange personally witnessed the fall of Phnom Penh to communist Khmer Rouge forces on April 17, 1975. That event marked the end of a bloody civil war that had begun five years earlier, following a successful coup by Cambodian prime minister Lon Nol against the country's longtime leader, Prince Norodom Sihanouk. Fröhder, the sole Western television journalist still in the city at the time, was later able to provide the rest of the world with the only visual record of the remarkable measures immediately introduced by the Khmer Rouge, namely, the mass evacuation of the capital city's two million inhabitants.

The young West German was no stranger to war or conflict. Born in 1942, roughly a year after Prince Sihanouk had ascended the Cambodian throne, Fröhder participated in the student protest movement of the 1960s. He began working as a freelance foreign correspondent at the end of that turbulent decade, apparently developing an affinity for war-torn regions in crisis. Fröhder accompanied both American and Vietcong units during the conflict in Vietnam, and he found himself on assignment in Uganda when Idi Amin came to power in 1971. But he first achieved international prominence thanks to the footage he took of the Khmer Rouge when they entered the Cambodian capital, which he later smuggled out of the country using a fake body cast.[1]

One of more than 600 foreigners who sought refuge in the French embassy in Phnom Penh, Fröhder was permitted to leave Cambodia in early May. By that point, the Khmer Rouge had moved almost all the city's inhabitants to the countryside. "Even the hospitals" had been "cleared out," with many patients rolling "along the streets in their beds." Phnom Penh was now a "ghost town," "eerily empty and silent," a "dead city."[2] In mid-May, the investigative weekly newsmagazine *Der Spiegel* quoted Fröhder in an article that seemed at pains to put to rest widespread claims that the Khmer Rouge had committed unspeakable atrocities. The piece acknowledged that there had been some shootings, but it also assured its readers there had not been any "bloodbath." Commenting on recent CIA reports about mass executions and even beheadings, Fröhder jauntily maintained that "such methods would completely contradict" the Khmer Rouge's usual "style."[3]

In a radio interview that same month, he similarly played down the many "horror stories" in circulation. The Khmer Rouge had entered the capital city in a "very disciplined" manner, he claimed. The "only truly brutal scenes" he had observed involved the evacuation of the hospitals, with some patients crawling through the streets on all fours—a "harrowing scene of human brutality" he had not "expected." The Khmer Rouge had otherwise behaved in a "very orderly" fashion. This elicited a skeptical response from the interviewer, who pressed Fröhder in vain about horrifying reports of mass atrocities across Cambodia, including the slitting of throats and even the ramming of broken bottles into the vaginas of rape victims.[4]

Erich Stange, the administrative attaché at the East German embassy in Phnom Penh, also wound up in the French embassy that April. According to an eyewitness account he submitted to his superiors in mid-May, Khmer Rouge forces had inspected the East German embassy "from top to bottom" on April 19, ostensibly looking for weapons. Three days later, an army unit evacuated the diplomat and his colleagues at gunpoint—despite their "common Communist worldview"—and drove them to the French embassy, where he "warmly embraced" their counterparts from Moscow, who were also there. The Soviets had gone through a "dramatic ordeal" at their own embassy, Stange said, and had been forced to "stand against the wall with their hands tied." Long-standing tensions between the Soviet bloc and China, the Khmer Rouge's staunchest ally, were no doubt behind such rude treatment. Regretting that he had taken the last flight back to Phnom Penh to celebrate the fall of the Lon Nol regime, Stange confided to a West German journalist that he "must have been crazy to come here."[5]

The diplomat later reported that Phnom Penh had been completely evacuated by April 22, "without consideration for old, sick, or wounded people, or even for babies and toddlers." Those stranded at the French embassy were removed a week later, when army trucks took them to the Thai border—a "brutal measure" that "attested" to the "true Chinese spirit" of the Khmer Rouge. In contrast to Fröhder, the East German diplomat vehemently criticized the undisciplined comportment of the plundering soldiers. He decried in particular the mass destruction of what was now "people's property," an instance of "un-Marxist behavior" that was "absolutely Chinese" in character. Apart from their different takes on the behavior of the Khmer Rouge, Stange and Fröhder did agree on one point: There had been no mass executions. The East German attaché nevertheless acknowledged that he saw "no people" in the countryside besides soldiers during his evacuation to Thailand. "Where are the many refugees and evacuees?"[6]

We now know that between 1.6 and 2.2 million people—roughly one-fifth of the population—perished in Cambodia between April 1975 and January 1979, the month the Khmer Rouge government was driven from power by invading Vietnamese forces. About half died as a result of violence, the rest from disease, exhaustion, and starvation. The dead included 19 percent of all ethnic Khmer, more than a third of the Muslim Cham minority, 30 to 40 percent of all Thais and Laotians, half of all Chinese, and almost all the Vietnamese people in Cambodia. That was the bitter price Cambodia paid for trying to create, Khmer Rouge leader Ieng Sary explained in a 1977 interview with *Der Spiegel,* "something that has never existed in history."[7]

For the first three years after the victory of the Khmer Rouge, there was not a single report in the East German media about any atrocities in

Cambodia. But that was not surprising. After all, stories about acts of violence committed by fellow communists would not have made for desirable headlines. The situation could not have been more different in the Federal Republic, where for some newspapers, they clearly did. The West German media's main story about Cambodia at this time was the mass expulsion from the capital, but other stories appeared as well, including news about acts of violence targeting specific social and political groups: the middle classes, as well as civil servants and members of the military who had supported Lon Nol and Prince Sihanouk. In one of the earliest intimations that a genocide was taking place, the *Stuttgarter Nachrichten,* a respected regional newspaper, reported in August 1975 that an "entire social stratum" was being "eliminated," including "city dwellers, the bourgeoisie, and landowners."[8]

The first explicit suggestions of genocide appeared around the first anniversary of the Khmer Rouge's ascension to power. A front-page editorial in the conservative *Frankfurter Allgemeine Zeitung (FAZ),* one of West Germany's leading daily newspapers, claimed that a "type of genocide [*Völkermord*]" was being committed by a "radical minority against its own people." It was also at this time that words like "exterminate" and "extermination" (*ausrotten, Ausrottung*) began to appear frequently in news stories and even headlines ("Communists in Phnom Penh Exterminate the Bourgeoisie"). Claims about "racially motivated" mass executions of ethnic Vietnamese and Chinese began appearing as well. Yet, the West German media still tended to place the word *Völkermord* in quotation marks because of continuing skepticism about the source of such stories: oral reports by Cambodian refugees who had fled to neighboring Thailand, where a staunchly anticommunist regime had come to power in the fall of 1976.[9]

The skeptical reaction was not entirely surprising, given the spate of shocking stories that appeared during the first year following the Khmer Rouge victory. Most painted a grisly portrait of entire villages and families being "exterminated," of large numbers of people being beaten to death with sticks, spades, hoes, and cudgels—to save bullets.[10] There were also reports that women, children, and babies were being beheaded and dismembered "like chickens," and that the members of the Khmer Rouge were even practicing cannibalism—the alleged fate of one of Lon Nol's soldiers, whose liver was "roasted" and then eaten.[11]

These stories met with disbelief. "Probably not every report from Cambodia corresponds with the complete truth," the *Stuttgarter Zeitung* delicately put it.[12] Foreign correspondent Carlos Widmann was more scathing in a piece he filed in mid-April 1976 from Aranyaprathet, a Thai border town where thousands of Cambodians had sought refuge: "A permanent ensemble of competing crown witnesses has emerged among the refugees, who relate again and again—and each time with more and more details—the kinds of horror that have taken place." A headline in the left-leaning *Frankfurter Rundschau* was even more cynical: "For a few dollars they'll tell you anything."[13] Revelations that some of the atrocity reports had been false only fortified such skepticism, especially on the political Left. Such "scare stories" had been "made up" and financed by the CIA, and "the right-wing press" eagerly embraced them, the *Rundschau* charged. *Unsere Zeit,* the newspaper of the (West) German Communist Party (Deutsche Kommunistische Partei, or DKP), similarly denounced the "bourgeois media"—above all the archconservative Springer press, which spread "factitious propaganda, crude falsifications, and hate-filled anticommunism."[14]

The Left's dismissal of reports that conservatives so eagerly embraced underscored the role Cold War politics and ideology played in the reception of such stories. The tales of atrocities coming out of Cambodia only confirmed what American hawks and the CIA had long predicted, namely, that a communist victory in Southeast Asia would result in a bloodbath. That in itself cast doubt on the veracity of the reports in the eyes of the Left—and not just in the Federal Republic. Still, most West German journalists had concluded by the time the new regime celebrated its first anniversary that the "horror stories" contained at least a kernel of truth. Even when applying the "strictest standards" in checking the refugee reports, the *Berliner Morgenpost* commented, it was "undeniable that . . . one of the most dreadful chapters since World War II" was "being written today in Cambodia."[15]

Whatever doubts remained, the shocking stories eventually had political consequences. On July 13, 1976, Dionys Jobst of the conservative Christian Social Union submitted the first formal query by a member of the Bundestag specifically asking the government to comment on such reports. He wanted to know how many murders had taken place in Cambodia since April 1975, and whether the government had issued a public statement expressing "the aversion of the German people toward such communist practices." Two months later, his colleague Hellmut Sieglerschmidt of the Social Democrats submitted a similar query, asking what information the government had concerning recent press reports about "mass murder and mass executions" in Cambodia and, if these claims were "accurate," what it had done or planned to do to end the suffering of the Cambodian people.[16]

Their colleagues in the Bundestag, often prompted by American press reports, would submit almost a dozen similar parliamentary queries over the next three years. Written in the main by members of the conservative opposition who hoped to score political points, they accused Chancellor Helmut Schmidt's SPD-led government of "passivity" in the face of communist aggression. What, they wanted to know, was the West German government doing to stop the "horror" and help the massive wave of refugees fleeing Cambodia?[17] The refugees' fate was of special interest to two members of the CDU who had themselves been refugees in the 1940s: Herbert Czaja and Herbert Hupka. As young men, both had been among the millions forced to abandon the eastern territories Germany lost after World War II. They later played prominent roles in the expellee community in West Germany, and the attention they paid to Cambodia surely owed as much to their anticommunist convictions as to their personal backgrounds.[18]

Prompted as well by the press reports, private citizens similarly demanded that Bonn respond to the alarming developments in Cambodia, and they usually did so in letters to West German politicians and officials.[19] In July 1976 a young man performing military service in Bavaria composed a handwritten letter to the West German Foreign Office asking about the "horrible situation" in Cambodia. He had recently heard reports that the Khmer Rouge had already killed a million people and that its leaders planned on killing millions more. "All actions" were "justified" when it came to stopping such misdeeds, he maintained, including military intervention by NATO. A year later, a concerned citizen from Stuttgart wrote to Foreign Minister Hans-Dietrich Genscher after seeing a television report in June 1977, declaring that people in the "'free world' should react with outrage" to developments in Cambodia, where the regime wanted to "outshine Hitler's henchmen in the concentration camps." He demanded, further, that the foreign minister raise this issue at the UN and do all he could "to put a stop to the killing of a defenseless population."[20]

These and similar inquiries received almost verbatim responses. The government had followed the stories "with concern," officials assured them, and it was working hard to determine their accuracy. But there was no "reliable information" apart from media reports based on refugee statements that were "not always free from contradictions." Still, the government had "hardly any doubts" that many had indeed been killed during the "ruthless resettlement" that came on the heels of the Khmer Rouge victory. But because the new Cambodian regime had cut itself off from the rest of the world and disappeared behind a "bamboo curtain," there was little Bonn could do.[21]

The politician pushing the hardest for the government to take a stronger stance on Cambodia came from within the ranks of the chancellor's own party—and his own cabinet. In January 1977, Minister of Justice Hans-Jochen Vogel of the SPD wrote to Foreign Minister Genscher asking whether the press reports were true. Genscher's evasive response reiterated the same familiar points.[22] Vogel pressed Genscher for more information a year later, following the publication in February 1978 of a harrowing eyewitness report about Cambodia in *Der Spiegel*. He now insisted that the "systematic genocide" be discussed at a cabinet meeting. Vogel kept up the pressure through the fall of 1978, and on October 4, Chancellor Schmidt finally requested that the Foreign Office draft a report about the "human rights situation" in Cambodia.[23]

The next day, Schmidt met in Bonn with Fang Yi, the deputy premier of China, one of only two countries with which the new Cambodian leaders maintained ties. (The other was North Korea.) The chancellor asked about the rumors of "large numbers of fatalities" in Cambodia. Fang Yi denied the accusations, but a week later Lee Kuan Yew, the leader of Singapore, confided to Schmidt that up to a million Cambodians had already been killed. "The West demands that the Soviet Union respect human rights," the chancellor complained to British prime minister James Callaghan and foreign secretary David Owen at a meeting on October 19, "[b]ut we haven't said a word about the complete disregard for human rights in China or Cambodia." Genscher was nonplussed.

Several weeks earlier, he had remarked with obvious exasperation to a high-level official in the Foreign Office that he did not understand why Vogel was placing "so much value on this issue anyway."[24]

What did account for the growing interest and sudden demands for action in 1977 and 1978? For one, these were banner years for the emergence of human rights as a guiding principle in international affairs. In 1977, Amnesty International received the Nobel Peace Prize and US president Jimmy Carter, in a series of major speeches, made the defense of human rights a cornerstone of his foreign policy.[25] Two years earlier, thirty-five states, including the Federal Republic, had signed the Final Act of the Helsinki Accords, which pledged respect for human rights at home and abroad. That provides important context for a letter that a local CDU youth group sent to Chancellor Schmidt in the spring of 1977, urging him to bring the "genocide" in Cambodia before the UN Security Council. It was the government's "responsibility to denounce all human rights violations and mass murder," regardless of whether they were committed by "left- or right-wing dictatorships," they wrote, especially in the wake of Helsinki. It is well known that the Final Act helped jump-start domestic dissident movements that later contributed to the demise of state socialism in Eastern Europe. That the Helsinki Accords also inspired grassroots activism in the West, if in a much different context, is a less familiar story. But at least some West Germans now believed that they should hold their own government to greater account and urge it to practice what it preached.[26]

There were other reasons for the noticeable growth of interest in Cambodia. The most obvious was the influence of the media, especially following the publication of a sensational book based on hundreds of refugee reports and filled with graphic descriptions of Khmer Rouge atrocities. John Barron and Anthony Paul's *Murder of a Gentle Land: The Untold Story of a Communist Genocide in Cambodia* was published in the United States in 1977 but attracted a great deal of attention abroad, including in the Federal Republic, where it later came out in translation.[27] Similar to the horrific stories recounted by Barron and Paul, a lengthy eyewitness account that appeared in *Der Spiegel* in early 1978 dramatically captured the brutal, indiscriminate nature of Khmer Rouge rule. This was, in fact, what had prompted Vogel's second letter to Genscher a month later. Written by a Cambodian refugee living in Austria, the two-part series provided firsthand details about the early months of the regime, including stories of "random shootings" and other dreadful crimes.[28]

Similarly disturbing reports appeared in the West German media throughout 1977 and 1978, often drawing on and sometimes adding new twists to those described by Barron and Paul. The popular tabloid *Bild am Sonntag* reported, for example, that anyone caught listening to the radio or practicing astrology or Buddhism risked the death penalty. Cambodians who held hands or flirted, had unmarried sex, copulated outside of official "mating seasons," or committed other seemingly minor infractions were summarily executed. The media also reported clear signs of cultural genocide: the destruction of libraries and other buildings, including Buddhist temples, pagodas, and statues.[29] Anything that seemed to be somehow "decadent" or "foreign"—that smacked of the "West," of "civilization," "capitalism," or "the past"—was banned or destroyed: money and private property, banks and other "colonial structures," public utilities and transportation, books and newspapers, schools and stores, cars and bars, religion and foreign languages, dancing, prostitutes, and even colorful clothing. In short, Cambodia had come to resemble a more murderous version of John Calvin's Geneva.

But the Khmer Rouge went even further in their radical wish to destroy all forms of private life and all existing social ties. Families were split up, men separated from women, children taken from their parents. Arranged marriages took place in mass ceremonies, and there were even reports that women were becoming infertile and ceasing to menstruate—not surprising under conditions supposedly similar to those in "concentration camps." In fact, the media reported, almost all Cambodians were forced to work up to sixteen hours a day on giant agricultural communes like the ones created in China during the Great Leap of the late 1950s. The sick, the infirm, and the elderly, children as young as age five, pregnant women—"even on the day after delivery"—all labored in rice fields or built canals and dams. There were no days off, no civil liberties, and no freedom of movement—only arbitrary repression.

Compared with Cambodia's rigid and compulsory corvée, *Der Spiegel* commented, Mao's China seemed like a "cheerful bourgeois society."[30]

Widespread doubts remained—and not just in the Federal Republic.[31] But by early 1978 in West Germany, much of the previous skepticism had more or less dissipated, even on the Left. Veteran foreign correspondent Winfried Scharlau, who had been covering Southeast Asia since the late 1960s, acknowledged in a televised report in June 1977 that the refugee accounts seemed "unbelievable," but said they had been "checked" repeatedly and confirmed by foreign correspondents and diplomats. It was "beyond any doubt," he reported, that "mass murder" was a "reality" in Cambodia, not something "invented by propagandists."[32]

Even the highly skeptical Carlos Widmann had a noticeable change of heart. In April 1978 he published an astonishingly frank if qualified mea culpa in the highly respected *Süddeutsche Zeitung*. The full-page report, which appeared in a prominent section of the paper reserved for major feature stories, began with a lurid description of a lynching by a group of Cambodian schoolchildren. "There is little reason to doubt the veracity of this story," Widmann continued:

> Certainly, many of the horror stories offered in the refugee camps . . . are exaggerated, grotesquely distorted, enhanced to apocalyptic proportions. The refugees must, of course, justify their flight, their request for asylum. . . . A permanent ensemble of well-practiced storytellers, each one outdoing the other, has formed, with CIA contractors and Thai generals serving as impresarios. The more vivid and gory these raconteurs describe conditions in Cambodia, the more benefits they receive.

But then Widmann's tone changes abruptly: "The fact that many of these horrors are made up does not mean that the horror in Cambodia is an invention." Outside observers of "every political stripe" had by now largely acknowledged the "inhuman methods" of Cambodia's "new masters." In an oblique reference to his own earlier reports, Widmann then poses a "self-critical question," asking whether "we reporters were blind? Have we failed? . . . Should we not have predicted the horror that

Cambodia is today suffering?" After all, many of their colleagues had been kidnapped and killed by the Khmer Rouge before 1975. The "horror stories" that had circulated during the civil war "should have given us pause for thought."[33]

Widmann was clearly distancing himself from his earlier, often sardonic dismissals of refugees' claims about Khmer Rouge brutality. But he did not abandon all skepticism, especially when it came to "fiercely controversial" claims of genocide: "Is a systematic extermination taking place in Cambodia? . . . Has class warfare degenerated into genocide? The quarrel among experts is already being carried out for more than a year with well-nigh theological subtlety." Widmann had little patience for claims that the killings were mere "excesses," as the regime's foreign defenders claimed, or a "cold-blooded reckoning" with old foes, as its critics insisted. Rather, it was an "indifferent, unsystematic, playful type of killing. The fury of the people was not running riot, but"—and then he added an important caveat—"there was no centrally directed execution apparatus. It was murder at will. . . . No, systematic extermination was *not* taking place."[34] Widmann was wrong, of course, and the number of deaths bandied about in the West German media certainly gave cause for thinking otherwise. The first figures that appeared in the press in April 1976 ranged from several hundred thousand to 1.5 million deaths. An increasing number of reports claimed in 1977 and 1978— accurately, it turned out—that the number of dead lay between one and two million.[35]

Whatever lingering doubts Widmann and others may have had, loaded terms like *Völkermord* and *Genozid, Ausrottung* and *Vernichtung* (annihilation), continued to appear in media reports—buttressed, no doubt, by new stories of Khmer Rouge atrocities against Vietnamese villagers living near the Cambodian border as nationalist tensions between the two countries ramped up in 1978. In an interview with the *Kölnische Rundschau,* a local daily in Cologne, Saigon's ambassador to West Germany claimed that "entire population groups" were being "exterminated" and even provided photographic evidence: "They cut open their bellies, hacked off their legs and hands, cut off their noses, gouged out their eyes . . . ripped out their livers . . . smashed their corpses."[36]

The leaders of the Khmer Rouge vehemently disputed such accusations. Ieng Sary, the Cambodian foreign minister, became the public face of such denials, claiming in his infamous *Spiegel* interview of May 1977 that "only" between two and three thousand people had died during the evacuation of Phnom Penh, and only "a few thousand" since then, on the rice fields. Chan Youran, Cambodian ambassador to the UN, made similar claims when he paid his first official visit to the West German Permanent Mission in New York in the fall of 1978. The foreign propaganda about internal developments in his country were "absurd," he insisted. "The people are happy and united, and they are dedicated to the peaceful reconstruction of the country."[37] Nothing could have been further from the truth.

We now know that the accusations of mass murder and genocide were indeed accurate. But what exactly did West German officials know for sure *at the time*? A great deal, it turns out, despite the absence of high-level diplomatic relations between the two countries since the late 1960s.[38] Foreign Minister Genscher may have found Hans-Jochen Vogel's repeated inquiries about Cambodia irksome, but in December 1978 his office finally sent the minister a five-page letter summing up what the government knew, based on reports by refugees, foreign diplomats, and journalists who had briefly visited Cambodia. The letter rehashed much of what the media had already reported: from the "radical, ruthless" evacuations that had led to the death of "thousands" in the spring of 1975, to the many domestic "reforms" introduced in Cambodia since then. It was impossible to accurately estimate the total number of victims, Genscher added.[39]

Much of what the foreign minister wrote was taken directly, often verbatim, from a string of in-house analyses, which all emphasized that much remained unclear because of the regime's self-isolation. But what was obvious, "beyond any doubt," was that serious human rights abuses were taking place and that many Cambodians had died—either as a result of severe malnourishment and widespread disease, or because of mass executions and other forms of brutality. One internal report speculated that the number lay between a hundred thousand and a million. Among the dead were loyalists of the old regime, including members of their family. This was reminiscent of the Nazi practice of *Sippenhaft* ("kin liability")—punishing family members for "crimes" committed by their relatives—and would have been familiar to Germans of a certain age. Monks and others caught practicing Buddhism were known to be among the victims as well.[40]

All of this made the charge of genocide applicable to Cambodia, according to the terms of the UN Convention of 1948. Yet West German diplomats made no such claims. In fact, the stories about Cambodia continued to meet with a great deal of disbelief behind closed doors, as they did in other Western capitals. But there were also less skeptical voices in the Foreign Office. Based on information supplied by the West German embassy in Hanoi, one in-house analysis from September 1976 acknowledged that the few reports that had made it out of Cambodia "convey horrific images that surpass the imagination" and were "only comparable to . . . the eyewitness testimonies at the Frankfurt Auschwitz Trial of 1964–1965."[41]

Leaving aside questions about the appropriateness of such comparisons, West German officials clearly had a good sense of the developments in the Southeast Asian country. And the East Germans: what did they know and think about what was going on in Cambodia, especially given their (marginally) closer ties to the regime? In contrast to the Federal Republic, the GDR still had formal diplomatic ties to Cambodia. In fact, its embassy in Phnom Penh had been the first one set up in a nonsocialist country after 1945. On April 23, 1975—one day after the Khmer Rouge had unceremoniously expelled the East German diplomats from that building—the Foreign Office sent a note to the Cambodian embassy in East Berlin, congratulating the National United Front (the anti–Lon Nol alliance of convenience formed by the Khmer Rouge and Prince Sihanouk during the civil war) on its recent success and expressing its "deep satisfaction about this historical victory." Two days earlier, Willi Stoph, the chair of the East German Council of Ministers, had personally received the Cambodian ambassador, Sisowath Methavi, who offered assurances that the new government planned to pursue "peaceful policies."[42]

Communication between the two capitals was, by contrast, almost nonexistent. In fact, the East German government received the first official communication from the new regime only in late February 1976, ten months after its victory. The country had a new constitution, the note revealed, and, in a rebuff to its colonial past, a new official name, Democratic Kampuchea. Relations remained otherwise nonexistent, apart from a semiannual exchange of formal greetings on major holidays. Repeated requests to reopen the GDR embassy in Phnom Penh went unanswered. In their dogged desire for independence, East German officials noted with displeasure, the country's new leaders were pursuing a rigorous policy of economic autarky and had rejected or ignored all offers of aid from the GDR and other Soviet-bloc states. So far as the East Germans knew, the only communist countries the regime had any contact with were Vietnam, North Korea, Yugoslavia, and, above all, China, which, GDR diplomats believed, was now calling the shots in Cambodia.[43]

East German authorities nevertheless had some sense of developments there, even if "fragmentary." Early reports, based primarily on the foreign press and on conversations with foreign diplomats, painted a surprisingly sanguine portrait. Local administrative committees had been created and staffed by "humble representatives of the people (peasants, workers)," who lived together with the "*Volk* and . . . participate[d] in the production process." Schools and lyceums had been reopened; free education and cultural opportunities had been introduced; gender and ethnic equality reigned supreme. Courses had been set up to eradicate illiteracy, and clerics were receiving "material and moral support."[44]

This was all false, of course, and such sanitized and highly misleading depictions quickly gave way to more critical analyses acknowledging that the unpopular policies of the new regime—essentially the same ones identified in the West—had prompted thousands of Cambodians to flee. Other reports mentioned the creation of "giant work armies" forced to harvest rice without pay and without the satisfaction of their basic needs "apart from eating and drinking." Evacuated city folk had been concentrated in "camps" and were now considered "second-class citizens" who did not enjoy the same rights as villagers. GDR diplomats learned from conversations with Cuban counterparts who had visited Cambodia in 1976 and 1977 that there were severe food and supply problems—even though rice was being exported to China in large quantities. As one

Cuban diplomat confided, with perhaps studied understatement, "Living conditions for those resettled from the cities are very complicated."[45]

Like the West Germans, East German officials clearly had some idea, then, of the actual situation in Cambodia, despite the regime's self-imposed isolation. But in contrast to the Federal Republic, in the GDR there were no suggestions or hints that a genocide was taking place. In fact, most reports tended to play down the level of Khmer Rouge violence. There was no "foundation" for reports about mass executions, they claimed, and Western stories about the mass murder of Lon Nol supporters were deemed simply untrue. They had been "overthrown, not wiped out."[46]

This suddenly changed in 1978. A report that fall claimed that the regime's methods involved "terror and savage oppression," and that disaffected members of the Khmer Rouge were being "physically anni-hilated."[47] The new tenor coincided with reports of violent border disputes between Cambodia and Vietnam, Moscow's closest ally in the region. East German media coverage now changed as well. The three-year ab-sence of any reports about Khmer Rouge atrocities came to a sudden end when, in mid-1978, several newspapers published responses to "reader letters" supposedly submitted by ordinary East Germans who wanted to know more about the current situation in Kampuchea. Their responses repeated much of what had already appeared in the Western press: there was little reliable information because the regime had shut itself off from the outside world; it was using "extreme brutality" against its own popu-lation; a variety of radical reforms had been introduced. As to the recent border attacks against Vietnam, they were a "safety valve" of sorts—a transparent attempt to "distract" the population from its own "oppres-sion."[48] Foreign aggression, in other words, wielded as the opium of the people.

Internal East German analyses from this later period were uniformly critical of the Khmer Rouge, with diplomats repeatedly emphasizing that the new regime was not truly communist but *Maoist*. The "Pol-Pot-Ieng-Sary clique" "misused" the hammer and sickle to "disguise" a "horror regime" (*Greuelregime*)—a common term for Cambodia in the West as well—that had "caused havoc under the guise of communism and thereby discredited socialism." It was "militant" and "nationalistic" and its "pseudo-revolutionary, repressive approach" had imposed a "farcical socialism on Kampuchea." Politically inexperienced and woefully unprepared, its "parochial" leaders, mere lackeys of the Chinese, had set an "un-Marxist" and "unrealistic" goal of immediately and independently establishing socialism in Cambodia. This was a lesson the East Germans had learned themselves the hard way, of course, two decades earlier during the mass uprising of June 17, 1953—the first of its kind in the Soviet bloc.[49]

The very language used by East German officials shows that their criticism was driven as much by ideological considerations and political infighting within the global communist community as by any sense of revulsion toward specific Cambodian policies, no matter how "radical." In fact, while the Khmer Rouge still held power, there was no sustained attempt in the GDR—at least not on paper, and apart from engaging in conventional communist clichés—to understand the nature or causes of this "deranged" form of extreme Maoism.

The situation was different in the Federal Republic, where journalists and pundits took a stab at offering just such an analysis—though this, too, often consisted of descriptive, hollow-sounding phraseology. The terms and phrases most commonly used to describe developments in Cambodia were "peasant revolution," "agrarian communism," and, last but not least, "stone-age socialism"—a term, coined by the French Catholic missionary François Ponchaud, that suggested the Khmer Rouge had managed to achieve what General William Westmoreland, commander of US forces in Vietnam, could not.[50] Regardless of the wording, there was general agreement that some sort of revolution was taking place and that the Khmer Rouge's paramount goal was to create a purely agrarian, completely classless and egalitarian society made up of "new human beings." Most journalists could not discern a clear ideology, however. These were "sui generis revolutionaries," and what was taking place there was not a "traditional" form of communism.[51] On that point East and West German observers agreed.

Stone-age socialism or not, this pithy catchphrase, like the others used in the Federal Republic and elsewhere, failed to capture the complexity of the Khmer Rouge and its program. The evolving explanations for the regime's motivation, policies, and violence were, in contrast, more sophisticated. One of the earliest and most popular focused on the "practical" aspects of Khmer Rouge policy. The excessively brutal actions, including the early evacuations of the urban populace from overcrowded cities, were seen as attempts to deal with supply problems, jump-start the war-ravaged economy, spur food production, and hinder possible opponents—especially the educated—from organizing against the new regime. "Whoever thinks," explained Christel Pilz in the *FAZ*, "is suspect." And because the Khmer Rouge were vastly "outnumbered," they ruled "even more brutally with terrorist force."[52]

The one-year anniversary of the communists' victory prompted the first systematic analyses in the West German media, and Carlos Widmann of the *Süddeutsche Zeitung* offered one of the most trenchant. The roots of the Cambodian terror were to be found, he claimed, in the process of brutalization experienced during the civil war and the American bombing campaign of 1969 and 1970. Equally significant, he averred, was the new leaders' need to satisfy a wild, raw, illiterate constituency—one obsessed by blind hatred and a desire for revenge against all who were in some way better off.[53] Many other journalists, and not just West Germans, similarly placed the blame squarely on the shoulders of the United States ("Not everything is Pol Pot's fault, mind you"), or on the supposedly "primitive" nature of poor peasants driven by class resentment—a "political form of vendetta." Journalist Michael Sontheimer revisited these political and sociocultural explanations in a book published a decade later, noting that the seemingly "soft" Khmer even had a special word for this: *kum,* a peculiar type of revenge mentality that gave rise to a "tradition" of "hate-filled brutality."[54]

Prince Sihanouk himself fueled but also pushed back against such interpretations. "Pol Pot and Ieng Sary have taught the children to hunt people," he explained during a lively interview with *Spiegel* publisher Rudolf Augstein and renowned Italian journalist Tiziano Terzani, who covered the region for the weekly newsmagazine:

Sihanouk: But the Khmer race (*Rasse*) is not responsible for that. Are you a bad race because you are a German? I'm certain that the German race is good. Hitler did not come to power because the German race is violent. Pol Pot is like Hitler. And you certainly don't want to claim that your race is a bad race, do you?

Der Spiegel: We aren't racists.

Sihanouk: I'm not a sociologist, but you have to understand, one can also create monsters among my race. Both races are very similar. We have experienced two Super Hitlers: Pol Pot and Ieng Sary. And just like you [in Germany], there were people who followed them.[55]

The interview was conducted in English, but language barriers aside, Sihanouk's understanding of the term *Rasse* was undoubtedly different from that of his European interlocutors, who cringed at his casual use of the word and were quick to assure the Cambodian prince that they were not "racists."

That may have been true, but many West German attempts to explain what was transpiring in Southeast Asia were unmistakably racist in tone, especially when it came to their ethnic characterizations. Commentators frequently praised the "brown" Cambodians, with their "almond-shaped eyes," as a highly "civilized people" that had once boasted of "more monks than soldiers." They were "loveable" and "fun-loving," "cheerful" and "friendly," "gentle" and "peaceful"—a "small, happy nation," in short. Equally frequent were condescending allusions to the "proverbial Far Eastern smile," the ubiquitous "Asian smile"—"*le sourire khmer*," as veteran Franco-German television journalist and author Peter Scholl-Latour put it, an "other-worldly, mysterious smile, inward-looking and horrible."[56]

There were more sinister allusions to the "Asian" character as well. The leaders of the Khmer Rouge had been educated in Paris but were "Asian thinking," whatever that meant—though it clearly had a negative connotation, given the popular notion of "Asian hordes" and of the Soviet Union as a menacing "Asian power."[57] In any event, just lurking below the friendly veneer of "formal Asian politeness" was a "dark side" characterized by a whole series of markedly less admirable attributes. The "diminutive" Cambodians were "indolent" and "primitive." Fascinated by modern technology, they nevertheless displayed a "childish naiveté" and even used amulets to ward off evil spirits. At the same time, Cambodians had an "unpredictable ferocity," which was why their history was blotted by "a great deal of savagery." It was this "other side of gentleness," which Westerners could "hardly imagine," that had made possible the recent atrocities in Cambodia—not to mention Indonesia, Malaysia, and the Philippines. "Sympathy" was a "foreign concept" in the region, which "hardly" had any "European-style" traditions in the realm of human or civil rights. Khmer Rouge atrocities simply "defied European under-standing," SPD politician Egon Bahr, the architect of Willy Brandt's Ostpolitik, later ventured—a curious comment by someone who had faced discrimination himself during the Third Reich as the son of a Jewish mother.[58]

Condescending claims about "civilizational" differences between Europeans and backward, brutal, and barbaric non-Westerners were not uncommon, of course.[59] And they were not a German peculiarity. But the conservative columnist Günter Zehm, who wrote a weekly column in *Die Welt* under the pseudonym "Pankraz," would have none of this:

> Many mavens of the . . . Southeast Asian ethnic soul ascribe the massacres to [its] dark side, which the Malayans call "Amuk." From this comes, not by chance, the phrase "running amok." . . . Visitors to Southeast Asia mainly experience the brown people there as true epitomes of naïve charm and a primordial zest for life. Then one day, as if out of the blue, the Night of the Long Knives arrives, and the friendly brown people murder each other with a thoroughness like nowhere else in the world. That's how it was in Indonesia in 1966 after the fall of Sukarno, and that's how it's supposed to be today in Timor—also in Cambodia, the ethnologists opine. Pankraz remains skeptical of this.[60]

Zehm instead attributed the atrocities of the Khmer Rouge, a clique of "trained communist career functionaries," to ideology and to the type of excessive utopian revolutionary practices described by Albert Camus in his 1951 essay, "L'homme révolté."[61] Other West Germans also focused on the utopian elements of Khmer Rouge policy: the desire to do away with socioeconomic iniquities, to bring about a "complete break" with their country's own history and social order, to destroy everything "old" in an attempt to create "new humans" who were "totally submissive." Or they suggested that the Khmer people suffered from some sort of "inferiority complex" because they lived in the shadow of the once-great civilization that had erected Angkor Wat, the majestic twelfth-century temple complex that symbolized Cambodia's glorious past. To compensate for their "miserable present-day reality," they declared, the Khmer emphasized their "racial and cultural superiority"—a simplistic idea that sounded suspiciously like a popular explanation for the early success of the Nazis.[62]

Veteran journalist and author Klaus Mehnert, an adviser to many West German chancellors on Asia, his area of expertise since the 1930s, touched on several of these themes in a lengthy radio commentary in mid-March 1978. A self-described friend of Prince Sihanouk, whom he had known for more than two decades since first visiting the country in the 1950s, Mehnert describes Cambodia as a "paradise on earth . . . an oasis of freedom and cheer" prior to the civil war that had begun in 1970, when the United States dragged the country into the "maelstrom of war." He begins with a disclaimer about what he will *not* discuss, namely, the recently reported "cruelties," because he did not like to speak about things "based on hearsay and propaganda. . . . Most of it is so awful I hope it's just exaggerations."[63]

Mehnert nevertheless concludes his report by doing just that—speculating about the reports of "incredible cruelties." Even if only "some of this is true," he declares, one had to wonder about the cause of such an "eruption." He then offers "a few conjectures," including the inability of the Cambodian people to fathom their fall to the level of a "politically insignificant ministate" under the control of foreign encroachers. After having been the masters of Indochina from the ninth to the fourteenth century, the "mighty temple of Angkor . . . must have weighed as crushingly on the Cambodians as the shadows of the pyramids" did on the Egyptians," he posits—a "silent rebuke of failure."

Perhaps, but Mehnert fails to explain why all their pent-up anger and frustration, more than a half millennium in the making, finally erupted when it did. His most persuasive explanation focused on the Khmer Rouge leadership—Marxist intellectuals who had spent more than a decade in the jungles of Cambodia practicing "intellectual incest" and dreaming about "ideological castles in the air" that they hoped to construct "with fanatic determination" once in power. They did this with a "clear conscience," just as Maximilien Robespierre had 200 years earlier during the French Terror.[64]

How East and West Germans talked and wrote about the causes of the Cambodian genocide is important because it helps us understand how and why they responded as they did to the harrowing reports about life and death under the Khmer Rouge—a point we shall return to. At the same time, it lay bare prevalent political, social, ethnic, and even racial prejudices that continued to have common purchase in the 1970s. The direct and indirect comparisons between Cambodia and what had transpired decades earlier during the Third Reich also offer hints about how Germans dealt with their own country's fraught past. Such comparisons became even more common—and more telling—following the fall of the Khmer Rouge in January 1979, when the dimensions of the Cambodian genocide became even clearer.

2

Asia's Auschwitz

In the fall of 1976, Walther Freiherr Marschall von Bieberstein, a West German diplomat who headed the Foreign Office's Department of International Law, sent an irate letter to Jürgen Wohlrabe, a prominent member of the Christian Democrats in Berlin. The Khmer Rouge had turned Cambodia into a "giant concentration camp," the diplomat fumed, and its leaders "hardly differed" from those who had run Auschwitz—a word and place long synonymous with the industrial mass murder of the Jews. Marschall von Bieberstein, a trained jurist descended from one of Germany's oldest noble families, had some familiarity with the country. After diplomatic ties between the Federal Republic and Cambodia had officially ended in 1969, he served as Bonn's representative in Phnom Penh, a position he held until 1974.[1]

The timing of the letter was no accident. Accusations of genocide had first surfaced in the West German media several months earlier in April 1976, on the first anniversary of the Khmer Rouge's victory in Cambodia. But it was not until 1979 that the use of language with clear genocidal connotations connected to the Third Reich first became widespread.[2] The sudden shift in language, which included the first use of the term *holocaust,* was also no accident. It was no doubt tied to two seemingly unrelated events that had taken place at the start of the year: the overthrow of the Khmer Rouge on January 7, and the airing on West

German television two weeks later of the popular American miniseries
Holocaust, a dramatized account of the Nazi genocide from the perspectives of a Jewish family and an "Aryan" one. Just weeks before the
broadcast, on December 25, 1978, a group of disaffected Khmer Rouge
leaders backed by Vietnamese armed forces had invaded Cambodia. This
marked the culmination of two developments: long-simmering ideological and territorial tensions between the two neighboring communist countries, and an ongoing, bloody crackdown on dissenters within
the Khmer Rouge. The invading forces captured the capital city in the
first week of January, and the Khmer Rouge fled to the western part of
the country. From there, they would fight an insurgency for the next
decade and a half against the new Cambodian regime headed by former
Khmer Rouge cadre Heng Samrin (and later by Hun Sen, another
former Khmer Rouge military commander).[3]

That was not the big story that month in the Federal Republic, however.
The media were mainly abuzz about *Holocaust,* which had first aired in
the United States eight months earlier. Nearly half of West Germany's
adult population watched the miniseries in late January, with some
twenty million people viewing at least one of the four episodes—despite
the withering criticism of West German pundits from across the political
spectrum, who dismissed the program as the typical melodramatic fare of
commercialized American popular culture: a manipulative soap opera
that trivialized and profited financially from past suffering.[4]

Whatever its stylistic or pedagogical demerits, *Holocaust* marked an
important shift in the way West Germans related to the Nazi genocide of the European Jews. They did not suddenly "discover" the Final
Solution in January 1979, of course. Marschall von Bieberstein's letter
from 1976, and its invocation of Auschwitz, make that clear. But it
brought about a "new level of awareness," a more emotional and personal connection to something now seen as *the* seminal event of the
twentieth century—the measure of all evil and the essence of Germany's
recent past.[5]

The broadcast of the American miniseries marked the beginning of
a new approach to history in the Federal Republic, one characterized by
a greater focus on victims, especially Jewish ones, and on the experiences

of ordinary individuals; by a "boom" in the study of memory; and, last but not least, by a greater sense of "moral responsibility" for past crimes committed in the name of Germans and Germany. Another consequence was a more popularized, more emotional, more commercialized treatment of history, which eventually brought in its wake a slew of public memorials, museums, and exhibitions—many focused on the genocide of the Jews. At the same time, the discussion provoked by the miniseries ushered in a dramatic increase in public education about the Final Solution, which now began to attract the attention of professional West German historians to a much greater degree than ever before. This was, in short, the moment in the history of the Federal Republic when the holocaust became the Holocaust.

This is a familiar narrative about how West Germans began to cope in new ways with their country's fraught past. Less well recognized is the impact the miniseries had on West (and East) German responses to the more recent genocide in Cambodia—especially as the new rulers in Phnom Penh released details and evidence of the ghastly atrocities committed there between 1975 and 1979, confirming the earlier reports that had met with so much skepticism. By the winter of 1979, even the highly skeptical *Frankfurter Rundschau* acknowledged the "terrible truth," namely, that the Khmer Rouge had "on their conscience" the deaths of at least two million Cambodians, and "likely more." When Prime Minister Moraji Desai of India told Helmut Schmidt at a meeting in June 1979 that the now deposed Khmer Rouge had murdered between one and a half and three million people, the chancellor gasped that it was a "disgrace" for humanity.[6]

Stories about individual victims put a more human, if not humane, face on such numbing numbers. These included a harrowing chronicle that appeared in *Der Spiegel* in March 1980. Reminiscent of the recent American television miniseries, it recounted the experiences of a single Cambodian family, the Keats, under the Khmer Rouge. The magazine's editors described the two-part report, written on-site near a refugee camp in Thailand by investigative journalist Ariane Barth, as a "lament and accusation." The first installment was accompanied by a two-page family tree titled "Cambodia: Fate of a Family," which provided a visual and almost visceral sense of the extent to which the family had been decimated. More than half the eighty-four names were printed in black to indicate those who had perished since the spring of 1975.[7]

Barth was in the region at the time, on vacation, when her editors asked her to do a story on the worsening refugee situation in Cambodia. She decided to find a single family whose "fate" would shed light on what had happened under the Khmer Rouge. The *Holocaust* miniseries had had "no influence" on her choice of topic—she had not yet seen it, she later explained—but Barth had long been interested in how "collective history was reflected in the history of an individual family." That interest had begun in the mid-1960s, she said, during the Frankfurt Auschwitz trials. In her early twenties at the time, Barth had been doing an internship with Deutsche Presse-Agentur (dpa), the West German news agency, and her task was to summarize the daily proceedings for the foreign press. This was when she first learned about what had happened to the Jews—the schools she attended had never addressed it—and what came to light during the trials greatly affected her. She "cried every night," she later revealed, and the topic refused to "let [her] go."[8]

Shortly after her arrival in Bangkok in the winter of 1980, Barth made her way to the Thai-Cambodian border, where she wound up living for three weeks in a house rented by a group of West German aid workers. Deliberately searching for a family in which all social and political "inclinations" were present, she eventually met the Keats at the Khao I-Dang refugee camp. Barth smuggled food into the camp for them each day and wrote her article at night. She found "all the horrors" they related to her "inconceivable," she said, so she made sure they reviewed a Khmer translation of her daily write-ups for accuracy. This partnership of sorts marked the beginning of a close personal relationship that would last for decades. Barth's main informant in the family, an economist who had been a government official before 1975, accompanied her back to the Federal Republic with his wife and their two young children—on a flight paid for by *Der Spiegel*. One of Barth's neighbors later took in other young members of the family, acting as a foster parent, and most of them remained in Germany. Most Germans did not ask them much about their experiences during the genocide, Barth ventured years later, but they were "infinitely helpful." After all,

FIG. 2.1. Journalist Ariane Barth of *Der Spiegel* with members of the Keat family at the Khao I-Dang refugee camp, Thailand, March 1980. Courtesy of Ariane Barth.

she offered by way of explanation, they could not "rectify" their own country's history, but they could, "by actively helping" others now, try to make up for it just "a little bit."[9]

Two years after her chronicle appeared, Barth and Tiziano Terzani, the newsweekly's main correspondent in Southeast Asia, republished it in book form, accompanied by shorter pieces each had written for *Der Spiegel*.[10] Its provocative title, *Holocaust in Cambodia*, would not have turned many heads by that point, in 1982. The word *holocaust* had already entered the popular lexicon. But at first the mainstream media had indeed used the term tentatively. Consider the following noteworthy editorial decisions. Two articles about Cambodia were published in early May 1979, one in the Swiss weekly *Die Weltwoche,* the other, two days later, in the West German conservative Christian daily, *Deutsche Zeitung.* Christel Pilz, who normally wrote about Cambodia for the *Frankfurter Allgemeine Zeitung,* appeared in the byline of the first article—"Olivia Wendt" in that of the second. The headlines were different, too. The Swiss article was called "Holocaust in the Land of the Khmer," the West German article "The Broken *Volk.*" But that was where the differences ended. The two articles were otherwise verbatim, apart from a single sentence. The final line in the Swiss version, referring to Pol Pot—"What he accomplished was destruction, was Holocaust"—was shortened in *Deutsche Zeitung* to "What he accomplished was destruction."[11] The omission of the word "Holocaust" may have been mere coincidence. But something else might have been at play here, namely, an inhibition—at least in West Germany—about using that loaded term to characterize what had just taken place in Cambodia. It might have also reflected editorial concerns about using a term with clear biblical connotations, or a reluctance to "equate" the two events for fear of accusations that the Christian daily was somehow "trivializing" the Final Solution.

If such inhibitions indeed existed, they had dissipated by the fall, when the term *holocaust*—which the government-sponsored Association for the German Language voted Word of the Year in 1979—appeared much more frequently in reports about Cambodia. That October, for example, *Der Spiegel* ran an article with the sensational headline "Asia's Auschwitz." This sea change was not peculiar to the Federal Republic. "As of ten days ago," a West German correspondent in Washington reported in early November, "no one had shown any interest in these people. Now all of a sudden everyone is speaking of a new Holocaust"— from members of Congress, including Senator Edward Kennedy, who called it "perhaps the greatest tragedy since the (Jewish) Holocaust," to folk singer Joan Baez, who commented, following a highly publicized visit to Thai refugee camps in February 1980, that she no longer had "any qualms about using the word *Holocaust*" now that she had been there.[12] Two hundred other celebrities had accompanied Baez, including Holocaust survivor Elie Wiesel and Norwegian actress Liv Ullmann. In a clip shown during a West German television broadcast about the group's "March for Survival" to the Thai-Cambodian border, Ullmann lamented that "our greatest excuse" earlier was that nobody had known what was happening to the Jews, that nobody had seen them being marched to their death: "I'm going [on] this road tomorrow because it is the same road that led to the gas chambers."[13]

That was a striking comparison. But the march was not just about what had taken place under the Khmer Rouge. According to a flood of accusations in the fall of 1979, including in the West German media, the Vietnamese and their new "puppet" government in Phnom Penh—the head of the "current genocidal regime"—were systematically starving the Cambodian people to make room for Vietnamese "settlers." More specifically, they were supposedly preventing foreign aid from reaching the needy. Communist leader Ho Chi Minh's erstwhile "dream" of a vast empire was heading toward another "genocidal end" in Cambodia, where the "Vietnamese occupiers were capitalizing on the thoroughness of Pol Pot's extermination experts." That was why the foreign celebrities were marching, West German journalist Rainer Kaufmann explained: to serve as the "world's conscience" and draw attention to the fact that the Cambodian genocide had not yet ended—even though it had been pushed out of the headlines by recent developments elsewhere: the sensational hostage situation that had begun at the American embassy in Tehran that November, and the Soviet invasion of Afghanistan a month later.[14]

The Cambodian genocide was "the most perfect destruction of human beings" since National Socialism, Kaufmann added, and it could only be "equated" with that of the Jews. Elie Wiesel explained, for his part, that he was participating in the march because he would be an "accomplice" if he were to do nothing. At the conclusion of the report, television moderator Franz Alt critically observed how "striking" it was that "no German" was among the march's two hundred participants.[15] Following directly on Wiesel's remarks, Alt's criticism seemed to imply that a sin of omission had somehow made Germans "accomplices" as well.

There were other accusations about supposed sins of omission, but those were directed mainly at the Left. Why had the leftist press published so little about communist atrocities in Cambodia, conservative commentators wanted to know. And why had those who had earlier demonstrated against American involvement in Vietnam, or who were now so concerned with human rights abuses in places like South Africa and Chile, not taken to the streets to protest the Khmer Rouge? Such criticisms were nothing new. In an editorial in April 1976, *Die Welt* had adopted a similar prong of attack, complaining that the "liberal world conscience" had said nothing at the time about the Soviet Gulag, "just as it remains silent today" about the "economically stingy" killing methods in Cambodia, like the use of bamboo sticks to save bullets. "The world conscience is also stingy—or, let us say, selective." In a similar vein, a letter to the editor published in *Der Spiegel* dismissively referred to the "deathly quiet" about Cambodia at German universities, and *Welt am Sonntag* launched a vehement diatribe against the "arrogance, blindness, and cynicism of the international Left": If its members were to "confront the communist murderers in Southeast Asia with the same united front, the same anger, and the same volume" as they had in their earlier protests, "they could perhaps again apply pressure—*this time* to the benefit of humanity."[16]

The *National Zeitung*, a far-right weekly, formulated similar criticisms but in an even more polemical fashion. In an article tellingly titled "The Great Silence: No Brouhaha about the 'Holocaust' in Cambodia," it argued that the

> persecution of the Jews during the Third Reich [has preoccupied] world opinion incessantly since the end of the war [*sic*], and even more so of late (one thinks of the US miniseries *Holocaust* . . .). But that a veritable genocide of tremendous magnitude is unfolding in the middle of this world—and right now!—hardly upsets anyone, least of all our opinion makers. . . . And why should it? They're still utterly busy coming to terms with the Jewish persecution that took place more than three decades ago. . . . Mass murder can range in the millions under communist regimes, but one . . . reserves one's revulsion for countries where blacks and whites use separate toilets.[17]

What is striking about this rant, apart from the extreme polemics and provocative language, is that it appeared in August 1978, months before the term *holocaust* began to gain traction in the Federal Republic.[18] Written in response to an earlier public discussion of the American miniseries, which had already aired in the United States, it makes clear that at least some West Germans already believed that their fellow citizens were too "obsessed" with the plight of the Jews.

A more frequent accusation at the time was that Khmer Rouge crimes followed in well-established *leftist* traditions. Pol Pot's "great model" was Mao's "peasant communism," wrote journalist and historian Karl-Heinz Janßen in *Die Zeit,* West Germany's most respected weekly newspaper. But the Cambodian leader also had a good deal in common with Stalin, he pointed out. After all, the "extermination of almost the entire upper class" in Cambodia was on par with the Soviet leader's "destruction of the kulaks." In fact, one television journalist averred, the "total revolution" in Cambodia was the "Gulag Archipelago's Final Solution."[19] The clear implication was that both fascism and communism were of a kind, with both ending in genocide. Such arguments jibed with the claims "totalitarian theorists" had been making since the 1950s. But they also foreshadowed the politicized debates that would rage in West Germany in the mid-1980s during the so-called *Historikerstreit,* or historians' quarrel, the controversy involving allegations that conservatives were "relativizing" the enormity of the Final Solution by placing it in a long line of other twentieth-century genocides.

The atrocities in Cambodia served, then, as an ideological Cold War cudgel—an opportunity to continue thrashing out the bitter political debates of previous decades.[20] But even on the Left, self-critical voices called into question their own lackluster response to developments in Cambodia under the Khmer Rouge. In a lengthy piece published in March 1978 in the alternative magazine *das da,* Wolfgang Röhl—the brother of *das da* editor Klaus-Rainer Röhl, founder of the influential leftist magazine *konkret,* and ex-husband of journalist and Red Army Faction leader Ulrike Meinhof—launched a stinging attack against fellow members of the West German Left:

> Myths last nowhere as long as they do in the leftist scene. When evidence mounted over the last year that inconceivable crimes were being committed in Cambodia, one read little about that in the leftist press. . . . Atrocity propaganda, many suggest[ed],

CIA rumors. . . . Only when the respected French leftist intellectual newspaper *Le Nouvel Observateur* published the first horror stories about the ghostly Khmer Rouge kingdom did one prick up one's ears here in [West Germany]. But some so-called leftists continued to act deaf. When DASDA [*sic*] published an article in 1977 titled "Auschwitz in Cambodia," we received indignant letters. . . .

Every attempt by the Left to play down or excuse the monstrous crimes against the civilian population is a declaration of moral bankruptcy. [Cambodia] is for many leftists an embarrassing chapter one does not speak about gladly. . . . But it's of no use to stick one's head in the sand. . . . One can no longer make the excuse not to have known anything.[21]

Years later, journalist Michael Sontheimer, a cofounder of the leftist *taz*, took a stab at explaining such willful amnesia. The "radical left" had "emotionally" made a choice—that there were "good guys and bad guys" in the conflict in Indochina—and after years of accepting this "David and Goliath image," it was simply "difficult to switch." The crimes were "so monstrous" and had led to so much "confusion and disappointment" that they were "best repressed."[22] Klaus von Dohnanyi, who had served as state secretary in the Foreign Office at the time, was less charitable. These were not "leftists," the SPD politician and former mayor of Hamburg remarked decades later, but rather "confused people" with "crazy ideas" about what the world should look like.[23] Dohnanyi clearly had in mind people like Joscha Schmierer, a West German Maoist who had traveled to Cambodia and even had a personal audience with none other than Pol Pot himself.

In December 1978, West German diplomats in Beijing met with the Swiss ambassador to China, Werner Sigg, who had just returned from a visit to Southeast Asia. During his travels, Sigg told them, he had several times run into Joscha Schmierer, a founding member of the Communist League of West Germany, the largest and most important of the Maoist "K-Groups" set up in the early 1970s. The young West German and his companions said they were there to show their "solidarity" with the Khmer Rouge, who had invited a select group of Westerners to visit Cambodia in late 1978.[24] Tensions with the Vietnamese regime were coming to a head, and the Khmer Rouge had decided to open their country to some foreigners in the hope of winning allies abroad. Other visitors included Elizabeth Becker of the *Washington Post* and the British journalist Malcolm Caldwell, a Marxist who was later murdered in Phnom Penh under mysterious circumstances.[25] Joscha Schmierer fared better and was able to leave with his life. But before doing so, he had the opportunity to meet with Pol Pot and the other Khmer Rouge leaders, whom he publicly praised on his return to the Federal Republic. Schmierer claimed not to have seen any violence or signs of terror. Two decades later, in an interview with the left-wing German weekly *Jungle World*, Schmierer was asked how that had been possible. "Because one couldn't see it," he explained, and because he had still believed in the regime's "propaganda" at the time.[26]

"They were shown the attractive things," journalist Christian Semler later surmised, "and they reported accordingly." A similar invitation had been extended to the rival K-Group Semler had cofounded in 1970, the Communist Party of Germany (KPD / AO), but its members decided not to go because of "inchoate misgivings" and "ideological uncertainty" about the Khmer Rouge. That did not stop Jürgen Horlemann, another cofounder of the party, from publishing an essay in 1979 that alternately denied and justified Khmer Rouge crimes. The regime had made some "mistakes," he acknowledged, but judging the regime by "European criteria" was not just "un-Marxist"; it also "smacked of arrogance." Even after unambiguous evidence of Khmer Rouge crimes emerged, Joscha Schmierer continued to defend and admire Pol Pot, even sending him an effusive message of support as late as the spring of 1980.[27]

Leftist "myths" about Cambodia remained tenacious, as Wolfgang Röhl bitterly remarked, even after the overthrow of the Khmer Rouge. That became especially clear during a lively discussion on West German radio in mid-March 1979. The participants included Swedish activist Jan Myrdal, an ardent Maoist, and professor of psychology Erich Wulff, an active member of the West German antiwar movement who had worked as a doctor in Vietnam in the mid-1960s. Myrdal, who had just returned from a trip to Cambodia, repeated the same justifications offered by the Khmer Rouge for their policies: for example, that there had been "rational arguments" for evacuating the cities in the spring of 1975. This proved too much for Wulff, who interrupted at this point: "Did the old, sick, and injured have to be sent off . . . to die a miserable death? That is no longer rational. . . . An abstract idea was to be translated into reality, regardless of whether it helped people." Most striking about the exchange was the absence of any real discussion about the atrocities committed by the Khmer Rouge. When the Swedish activist published a piece about Cambodia in *Die Welt* eight months later, former Southeast Asia correspondent Friedhelm Kemna criticized Myrdal for failing to mention the "mass murder" perpetrated by the Pol Pot regime—"the most rigorous, merciless, murderous 'purification' of a people since Stalin's purge and Hitler's Holocaust."[28]

That term must have resonated with German audiences, given the recent furor about the controversial American miniseries, and the same was true of other phrases commonly used in the media to describe the atrocities in Cambodia: "final solution" and "final battle," "pogrom" and "death march," "gas chambers" and "survivors," "seizure of power" and "Night of the Long Knives." Verbs like "exterminate" and "liquidate" were used to describe Khmer Rouge "atrocities"—*Greueltaten,* another popular term—and all would have hit close to home as well, by awakening similar historical associations. But the most common phrase, by far, was "concentration camp" (*Konzentrationslager,* or *KZ*)—in a literal sense (the giant communes established in the countryside) and in a more figurative one ("all of Cambodia was a *KZ*").

Accompanying photos of mass graves and countless skulls drove the point home—as did graphic descriptions of the "bestial tortures" that had taken place in Cambodia between 1975 and 1979. A three-part series that appeared in the *Süddeutsche Zeitung* in early 1981 revealed that the head of Tuol Sleng, the regime's most notorious prison and interrogation center, had supposedly had his "victims filled with water till they burst, had their livers cut out while still alive, had kerosene poured into the vaginas of women and then set aflame." Kang Kek Iew—a former teacher whose nom de guerre, "Duch," sounded uncannily like the German word for "German"—was described as one of the "most sadistic mass murderers in world history."[29] His methods were, in any case, eerily reminiscent of the experiments Josef Mengele had conducted decades earlier at Auschwitz.

Like "most sadistic," adjectives such as "brutal" and "fanatic," "gruesome" and "harrowing," "radical" and "relentless" were often used in the superlative to describe the Khmer Rouge, whose methods were "pitiless," "ruthless," "draconic," "merciless," "notorious," and "criminal"—"beyond all measure" and "without any scruples." The Khmer Rouge themselves were "barbaric" and "primitive," "bestial" and "inhuman"—"bare-footed cutthroats" who did not seem to be human. Such language was especially jarring in a place like West Germany, where biological, medical, and animalistic metaphors had gone out of style after the Third Reich.[30] The Khmer Rouge may have been "primitive," but their methods were "methodical" and "systematic," "thorough," "careful," and "calculated." Such locution became more common as the genocidal nature of the regime became increasingly clear, replacing earlier terms like "chaotic" and "arbitrary."

The language used to describe the Khmer Rouge and their atrocities evolved in other ways as well. Words and phrases with quasi-religious, almost biblical overtones became more widespread in the 1980s, for example. The fall of the "demonic," "satanic," "possessed" Khmer Rouge was a "salvation" for those Cambodians who had "arisen from the dead" in their own country or earlier embarked on an "exodus" to Thailand to escape Cambodia's "hell" on earth. All of this coincided with growing use of the term *holocaust,* and the biblical connotation of that very word—a burnt, sacrificial offering—may offer one clue for the noticeable shift toward more religious-sounding language.[31]

But what, if anything, did such words and phrases signify? And what was their significance? On the face of it, West German commentators were searching for language that would convey and elicit a sense of shock and horror about Cambodia. But some of the words they chose—like "fanatic" or "total," "systematic" or "extermination"—called attention to themselves for their obvious associations with National Socialism and the Final Solution.[32] Though not exclusively linked to Nazi crimes, such words were striking, given the genocidal context of what had occurred in Cambodia. What might have been the conscious—or subconscious—intent behind these language choices? Most Germans were surely not as sensitive to "historically burdened" language as trained linguists and other scholars, and one needs to be careful about reading too much into its almost casual use in the daily press and everyday politics. Still, there was an increase in sensitivity to this hyperbolic language in West Germany (and elsewhere) in the 1980s, accompanied by heightened criticism of those who used such terms either unthinkingly or for more nefarious reasons.[33]

Allusions to Nazi Germany were, in any event, usually indirect or implied. The vivid descriptions of the evacuation of Phnom Penh in April 1975, for example, recalled images of Jewish ghettos in World War II: "Children screamed for their parents, [but] were pushed forward by the soldiers. Those who hesitated were shot on the spot. Gripped by a deathly fear, the people allowed themselves to be driven forward like a never-ending herd of cattle." Equally evocative images accompanied a West German television report from early 1980, which began with footage of a path that resembled railroad tracks, leading to a Cambodian temple. With the reporter intoning that it had served for four years as a "transit camp," the camera scans the decomposing remains of the thousands of men, women, and children killed there—one of "innumerable death camps" spread across Cambodia.[34]

Reports of "mounds of corpses" must have awoken—were likely *intended* to awaken—similar associations. Descriptions of Tuol Sleng did so as well. After the ouster of the Khmer Rouge, this former girls' school turned prison was converted into a museum dedicated to memorializing the crimes committed there. Reminiscent of similar exhibits at Auschwitz and other Nazi extermination camps, one classroom was "stuffed from top to bottom" with the clothing of murdered victims. Headshots of former prisoners and photographs of cadavers were also prominently displayed on the walls of this "Asian Auschwitz," where the clothing of the thousands "brutishly" murdered there was "stacked in piles." The Khmer Rouge "proudly posed" before these "heaps of textiles," journalist Claus Happel noted—"a new edition of 'Holocaust.'"[35]

Direct comparisons like this in the German media sometimes included striking claims that Khmer Rouge atrocities were *even worse* than those committed by Hitler and his henchmen. Such declarations were almost always attributed to foreigners, like US senator George McGovern or American journalist Jack Anderson. But there were exceptions. "Not a single government," one West German journalist commented, had been able "to turn an entire country into a penal colony, terrorize an entire *Volk* like slave owners, and carry out the murder of [its] own countrymen with such brutality and perfection." According to others, Khmer Rouge massacres were "without precedent," even "more far-reaching" and "more horrible" than previous ones. "Humanity has likely never seen a more brutal form of rule."[36] In a book about Cambodia published a decade later in 1990, journalist Michael Sontheimer similarly referred to the "unprecedented brutality" of the Khmer Rouge—although he distanced himself from such language years later. That was mere "rhetoric," he explained in 2007, "a journalistic phrase" he would "not defend" today.[37]

Most West Germans were careful at the time not to make such loose assertions or comparisons. Instead, they claimed that these were the worst crimes committed *since* Hitler and Stalin—or that they were at least comparable. In a letter to the editor that appeared in the popular illustrated magazine *Quick*, FDP politician Jürgen W. Möllemann, chair of the West German Bundestag's Subcommittee on Humanitarian Assistance, wrote that he was "usually very cautious" about making comparisons to the Third Reich but could not think of anything to describe the "suffering" of the Cambodian people besides the "horror and misery" of those caught up in the Nazi "machinery of destruction."[38]

Indirect, wry comparisons to the Third Reich and to Hitler himself were another common device. "A satanical rabble of this sort lives only 'for the idea,'" commented the satirist Pankraz in a gloss in the *Süddeutsche Zeitung*, "It doesn't smoke, it doesn't drink, it's strictly monogamous . . . and when the time is ripe, it disappears for years into some earthen bunker to lead 'the people's war.'" Few readers would have missed the allusion to Hitler's asceticism or his final days. Or how might Germans have responded to this suggestive comment in the *Frankfurter Allgemeine*: Pol Pot "promised hope and thousands believed. How was it otherwise possible that he continued to have a significant following despite the brutality of his regime?"[39] The echoes of Germany's own history were unmistakable. Was this a way of "coming to terms" with the past—by proxy?

A searing account that appeared in *Der Spiegel* in early 1980 offers a clue. Written by theologian and activist Uta Ranke-Heinemann, who had just returned from an eight-day humanitarian trip to Cambodia, the piece emotively recounts the many atrocity stories she had heard from Cambodians she met—like Soum, a fifteen-year-old living at an orphanage. Its director explained that the boy was frightened because he was "the child of a Pol Pot soldier" and had heard from the other children that their parents had all been killed by Pol Pot. "I stroke Soum's head, but he just silently cries," wrote Ranke-Heinemann—a striking image of a *symbolic* "child" of perpetrators comforting the actual child of a perpetrator.[40] She also describes an encounter with an imprisoned Khmer Rouge soldier, who told her how he had performed mass executions. "It was men, women, and children," he admits, quickly adding that he was just "following orders." Such phrases—and excuses—were familiar to most Germans, and not just to those living in the Federal Republic.

Cambodia remained a nonstory in the GDR until mid-1978, when its border dispute with Vietnam became more intense and more public. The turning point came in late December, when the Vietnamese invaded and overthrew the Khmer Rouge. This prompted a flood of radio, television, and newspaper reports that, in terms of substance, were remarkably like the West German media coverage.[41] The East Germans described in similarly searing detail the many atrocities committed by the Khmer Rouge, invariably referred to, in typical socialist parlance, as the "Pol Pot / Ieng Sary clique." But they also used the very same language as the "bourgeois press" in the West. A "terror regime" that had adopted "barbaric," "bestial," and "tyrannical" methods, the Khmer Rouge had "exterminated entire population groups" and thus committed "genocide" (*Völkermord*). The large collective farms were "camouflaged *KZs*," Cambodia itself "one large penitentiary." Like many of their West German colleagues, East German journalists often spoke of Khmer Rouge crimes and atrocities in the superlative. Acting with "unparalleled savagery," these "deformed human beings" had carried out an "exterminatory campaign *without precedent*."[42] The similarities were almost uncanny—but not very surprising, given regional geopolitics. Vietnam was the Soviet bloc's closest collaborator there, whereas the Khmer Rouge were closely allied with China, Moscow's greatest foe.

A small number of East German journalists gained access to Cambodia shortly after the fall of the Khmer Rouge in January 1979, making them among the first foreigners allowed into the country. Over the next three months, veteran journalist Gerhard Leo and Klaus-Dieter Pflaum, a younger colleague stationed in Hanoi, filed a series of lengthy reports directly from Cambodia, where the blood of many victims was figuratively and sometimes literally still warm. In late January, Pflaum published his initial impressions of the carnage, including one of the first eyewitness accounts by a foreigner of Tuol Sleng prison: "Three buildings with barred windows behind thick barbed wire. . . . Pools of blood on the floor of 'House No. 1.' . . . The smell of corpses still permeates the air in the torture chambers. Fresh graves in the overgrown garden. . . . Seemingly medieval instruments of death all over the inner courtyard: axes, pliers, daggers, all covered with congealed blood." This full-page exposé, a solid piece of investigative journalism by any standard, appeared in the weekend edition of *Neues Deutschland,* the main newspaper of the ruling socialist party.[43]

Television reports on *Objektiv,* the GDR's foreign policy television magazine, presented East German viewers with similarly graphic footage of the prison: photos of mass graves filled with skulls and bones, images of dead men and even children, all with slit throats, arranged side by side in rows—an "exhortation" (*Mahnung*), reporter Lutz Herden told his audience, invoking a phrase closely associated with the Final Solution. As in the West, all of this must have brought to mind the liberation of the Nazi death camps at the end of World War II. References in the East German press to the Khmer Rouge's "fascist methods," as well as the use of words and phrases like "seizure of power" only reinforced the obvious historical associations.[44]

Gerhard Leo's reports from Cambodia were even more pointed in the parallels they drew between the Khmer Rouge and the Nazis—not very surprising, given his biography. Born in Berlin in 1923, Leo fled with his assimilated Jewish family to Paris after the Nazis came to power.[45] He joined the French Resistance during World War II, later becoming a member of the French Communist Party. Leo returned to Germany after the war, and in 1954 moved from the industrial Ruhr region in the West to the GDR, where he worked as a journalist. He covered the events of May 1968 in Paris for *Neues Deutschland,* as one of the few at the paper who spoke fluent French, and he traveled as a "special correspondent" to Cambodia a decade later. In February 1979 he visited an "extermination camp" in the Prey Veng province, where the "smell of decaying corpses" still emanated from the mass graves. The "most dreadful thing" he had seen there, he wrote, was a "giant clay vase filled with the bones and skulls of children. Whoever rebelled against the regime was punished with the annihilation of all family members, including children"—reminiscent once again of the Nazi practice known as *Sippenhaft.* Noting the "methodical extermination of workers," Leo rhetorically asked whether these "henchmen" had wanted to "get rid of witnesses, as the SS systematically did at the end of the World War."[46]

East German singer-songwriter Reinhold Andert also spoke publicly about the atrocities and the associations they awakened. After returning from a trip to Cambodia in June 1980, he revealed in an interview on GDR radio that he had been shown things there that he did not "gladly wish to speak about but probably must." Then, after a dramatic pause in which he apparently struggled to contain his emotions, Andert added that he had been "tremendously affected" by what he had seen—including a "*KZ.* . . . I have heard, read, seen a great deal about German fascism and the *KZ*s, about the destruction of the Jews and, and . . ."—with the last words delivered in a rushed, almost clipped tone of voice suggesting (misleadingly) that this was all somehow old hat, that one had heard all these things before, that everyone in the GDR was familiar with that gruesome chapter of history. There was, he continued, "no comparison" for the things "these criminals" had done in Cambodia—"torturing without expecting a confession, just out of pure delight in making others suffer." The interview touched, in short, on recurrent themes familiar in the West: bestial behavior supposedly devoid of reason, suggestive hints about uniqueness, comparability, and even the idea that what had just happened in Cambodia was somehow worse than what had happened decades earlier in Germany. Gerhard Leo drew more cautious conclusions. The "mass destruction" in Cambodia could be "compared" to the "crimes of the Hitlerian fascists."[47] But comparison was not equation, of course.

Leo conveyed his personal shock at what he had seen firsthand in Cambodia, and, like many in the Federal Republic, sought an explanation for this "outrageous savagery." To understand better who could be "capable of such acts," the veteran journalist interviewed two imprisoned Khmer Rouge "executioners" about their murderous activities. They admitted to him that they had also killed women and children, adding by way of excuse that they would have been beaten or even murdered themselves had they not complied. In short, they were just following "orders from above." This, Leo pointedly reminded his readers, was what the "mass murderer Eichmann" had told the Israeli court that sentenced him to death.[48]

Direct comparisons between the Nazis and the Khmer Rouge and even allusions to the Final Solution were not unheard of, then, in the GDR. Yet, most East German commentators tended not to dwell on that sort of historical parallel. They grappled instead with understanding how it had been possible for *communists* to have committed such crimes. Reflecting decades later about what he had witnessed in Cambodia, journalist Klaus-Dieter Pflaum said that he was still "shocked" that people who called themselves communists had been capable of committing such atrocities. Both his father and grandfather had been communists, and he had been socialized in a strictly communist milieu. "My God!" he wondered upon seeing the mass graves at Tuol Sleng, how could "communists . . . come up with such ideas?"[49]

Some East German authorities grappled with this conundrum by simply declaring that the policies of the Khmer Rouge were a "degeneracy" that had had "absolutely nothing" to do with socialism. Others took a more indirect approach, casting doubt on the bona fides of the Khmer Rouge leadership, whose social pedigree was somehow suspect. The "genuine" Cambodian communists had all been "exterminated" by Lon Nol in the early 1970s, they surmised, and replaced by "petit bourgeois elements"—like the term *clique,* another withering invective in the socialist lexicon. One communist ideologue even adopted racialist rhetoric to explain the atrocities, pointing to the "Chinese ancestry" of Khieu Samphan, the Khmer Rouge head of state. This, he argued, had had "an effect, after all."[50]

The social and "racial" background of the Khmer Rouge leadership was important, East German officials believed. But as the slur against Samphan's heritage insinuated, the real culprit in this drama was China. The Khmer Rouge were Chinese "puppets," and under their rule, Cambodia had become a "Chinese colony" used to advance Beijing's "chauvinistic, great-power policies." Maoism, "with its obedience to the 'Führer,'" was the "complete opposite of Marxism."[51] *Unsere Zeit,* the newspaper of the German Communist Party in West Germany, agreed. What had occurred in Cambodia was not communism but Maoism "carried out to the bitter end." It was not by chance that the "Maoist" Tuol Sleng prison was "tellingly" located on a street in Phnom Penh named for the deceased Chinese leader. But there was more than just an affinity between Maoism and the atrocities in Cambodia. East Germans went a step further, implicitly blaming Beijing for the Cambodian genocide. The "iron logic of the Maoist model" had called for it.[52]

A trial in absentia of Pol Pot and Ieng Sary, held in Phnom Penh in August 1979, took up these themes.[53] Its goal, according to internal East German reports, was to "denounce and condemn" Beijing, whose policies were the root cause of the "suffering" endured by the "Kampuchean people." The reports revealed something equally important about the trial, namely, the central role GDR officials played in its preparation. It was the East German attorney general's Department of International Relations that drew up plans to charge the Chinese for their "complicity" in the genocide, explicitly citing the relevant articles of the UN Genocide Convention, which the GDR had signed onto six years earlier. A wanted poster was to be designed using an East German model—the very same one printed in the early 1960s for the trial in absentia of West German state secretary Hans Globke, one of Chancellor Adenauer's closest advisers and one of the jurists who had written the legal commentary for the antisemitic Nuremberg Laws of 1935.[54]

Carlos Foth, the head of the Department of International Relations and a leading figure in the prosecution of German war criminals, provided remarkable details about a "controversial and fierce discussion" he had had with the Vietnamese official in charge of preparing the spectacle, during the lead-up to the trial. It mainly had to do with Vietnamese characterizations of Cambodian atrocities as "the gravest crimes in the history of humanity," carried out by a "fascist government" using "fascist methods" that, in terms of their "extent and savagery," had "greatly exceeded those of the Nazi regime."[55]

Foth, who had been involved in the GDR campaign against Globke, "most vigorously" contradicted these provocative assertions. For one, he argued, the term *fascist* did "not apply to Kampuchea" under the "Pol Pot regime" because the "only valid and undisputed definition" of the term among Marxist-Leninists was still that of Bulgarian theorist Georgi Dimitroff, the interwar leader of the Comintern. Foth also took issue with other "careless" comparisons. "Since the 1920s, the European bourgeoisie spreads the [anticommunist] claim . . . that a state ruled by the hammer and sickle is worse than one ruled by the swastika." Such accusations should not be "aided and abetted," and that, Foth charged, was precisely what the Vietnamese were doing. Finally, he pointed out to them that "many more people" had been "insidiously and agonizingly murdered *industrially* with Zyklon B and other gruesome methods" in Nazi Germany.[56]

Foth's protestations were no doubt sincere, but they rang hollow. After all, the government-controlled East German media had itself referred to the Khmer Rouge's "fascist methods." His objections nevertheless showed just how concerned East Germans were about the *image* of communism, especially when compared unfavorably with fascism. But Foth's comments were important for another reason. They underscored, just like Gerhard Leo's articles in *Neues Deutschland,* that the Final Solution was indeed a theme in the GDR, despite the usual silence there about Nazi crimes against the Jews—whom, it is worth noting, Foth did not specifically mention when he spoke about Zyklon B. Still, the allusion to the Final Solution was evident.

That was probably no coincidence, given Foth's previous prosecutorial activities. Just as important, no doubt, were explicit comparisons at the time between the Nazis and the Khmer Rouge across the border in West Germany, especially following the American miniseries *Holocaust.* East Germans did not use that term—perhaps because of its association with the West, perhaps because of its biblical connotations, perhaps because of its emphasis on Jewish suffering. Besides, using that precise word would have been a tacit admission that East Germans were watching West German television, an activity frowned on by the regime.[57] Regardless, Foth's remarkable comments did suggest some sensitivity, a sense of responsibility, and perhaps even guilt about the genocide of the Jews.

Almost all these themes surfaced in a series of poignant films that the famed East German documentary filmmakers Walter Heynowski and Gerhard Scheumann made about Cambodia after spending two weeks there in February and March 1979: *Kampuchea—Death and Resurrection, The Angkar,* and a short film called *Exercises.* Another full-length documentary, *The Jungle War,* was made but never shown in public because of the changing international climate and because of the filmmakers' political downfall—for reasons intimately tied to their films about Cambodia.[58]

The internationally renowned Heynowski and Scheumann were the GDR's best known and most prolific documentary filmmakers. During a partnership that lasted a quarter century, they made more than seventy films, including popular "cycles" about Cambodia, Vietnam, and Chile. The content and style of their films, which combined investigative reporting with hard-hitting political propaganda, reflected their training as journalists and as committed socialists. Both were members of the ruling Socialist Unity Party (Sozialistische Einheitspartei Deutschlands, or SED), and both enjoyed close connections with its upper echelons. Their early collaborations enjoyed so much success that they were able to persuade Politburo member Erich Honecker to back their request to form a private company independent from the "stifling" bureaucracy of DEFA, the central East German film studio. Studio H&S was founded in 1967—and abruptly dissolved in 1982.[59]

One theme dominated much of their work: a passionate critique of the Federal Republic and American "imperialism." Heynowski and Scheumann nod to this in the documentaries about the Khmer Rouge, although their primary focus is on two other, closely related issues:

China's alleged role in the Cambodian genocide, and the fact that communists had committed such atrocities. Early in *The Angkar* ("The Organization," the name the Khmer Rouge used early on), the camera pans to a large portrait of Pol Pot, who, in posture, face, and garb, bears a striking resemblance to Mao. Above him hangs a large red flag adorned with a hammer and sickle and an image of Cambodia's national symbol, Angkor Wat. The narrator asks why this man called himself the secretary of a *communist* party: "Why does he adorn himself with a hammer and sickle," symbols that are "personally dear to us communists?" The film keeps returning to these questions, finally reaching the conclusion that Pol Pot and the other Khmer Rouge leaders were not true communists. They had misused those symbols to deceive the Cambodian masses, who had been fighting for communism since the 1930s. The genuine communists, the film suggests, were those who had joined the resistance movement against the Pol Pot regime—disaffected Khmer Rouge officials and Cambodian peasants who wanted "real" agricultural cooperatives, not "forced" communes. It was they who embodied the country's "authentic revolutionary movement."

Toward the end of the documentary, the filmmakers include extended excerpts from an interview with former foreign minister Ieng Sary, who flatly denies that the Khmer Rouge had ever adopted the hammer and sickle as their symbol. "Of course not," the narrator intones. "They were never communists," but stood "instead for a special variety of *anti*-communism." There is then a quick cut to footage of Adolf Hitler, gesticulating wildly during a speech: "Or was this one here perhaps also a socialist?" the narrator asks rhetorically, just because he called *his* political doctrine National Socialism? The film concludes with footage taken at the ceremonial refounding of the Cambodian Communist Party in 1981, where a large hammer-and-sickle flag hangs prominently in the background.

If the Khmer Rouge were not really communists, what were they? Echoing other East German commentators, Heynowski and Scheumann claim that they were Maoists completely subservient to Beijing. To make that point, *The Angkar* includes a "group portrait" of Tuol Sleng "interrogators," with their Chinese "counselors . . . clearly labeled." Juxtaposing photographs of the carnage that took place in two Vietnamese villages—one purportedly attacked by the Khmer Rouge, the other by Chinese forces during the Sino-Vietnamese border conflict of early 1979—the film asserts that both bore the same "handwriting," implying that the Khmer Rouge had merely followed the example set by their masters in Beijing.

But the root cause of the genocide lay elsewhere: in the great disparities, the film suggests, between the urban and rural populations—the product of a century of Western imperialist exploitation. The resentment that such disparities had produced was what eventually allowed Pol Pot to "put the pseudo-revolutionary teachings of Mao Zedong into gruesome practice." Footage of Cambodians, a "musical *Volk*," singing a song lamenting the plundering of their country by China reinforces the indictment. What might have crossed the minds of East German viewers during this scene? Did some think about the way the Soviet Union had exploited their own country after the war? And what reaction might the pointed criticism of the large Cambodian communes have elicited among East Germans who still chafed at collective agriculture in their own country? When asked years later whether some sequences had been intended as a roundabout criticism of the GDR itself, Heynowski vigorously (and perhaps self-servingly) nodded, "Yes, of course!"[60]

The genocide of the Jews was not a focus of these films. But in a related and especially memorable sequence in *The Angkar,* Heynowski and Scheumann present excerpts from a Chinese propaganda film about life on the Cambodian communes. The narrator explains, with images in the background of singing farmers happily performing choreographed dance numbers while swinging giant red flags, that "everything here is phony." He then compares the footage to *The Führer Gives a City to the Jews,* a 1944 Nazi propaganda film about Theresienstadt—an elaborately staged hoax that misrepresented life in that concentration camp, produced for foreign consumption. Only "stubborn Maoists deny" what happened in Cambodia, the narrator concludes, just as only "stubborn fascists deny" the gas chambers of Auschwitz and the "systematic extermination of the Jews" by the Nazis.

This kind of direct and public comparison between the two genocides was as rare in the GDR as invocations of the Holocaust itself. Even in Heynowski and Scheumann's films, they are usually only indirect. Yet, frequent images of skulls and mass graves, of discarded items heaped together—photographs of the dead, of clothes, shoes, and even scrap metal, which would be used to make statues and busts of Pol Pot—must have evoked recollections of the Nazi death camps for many East German viewers (not to mention the personality cults of Stalin and Mao). In a scene reminiscent of the Jewish ghettos of Eastern Europe after their evacuation in the early 1940s, the filmmakers enter an empty room in an apartment in Phnom Penh and the camera alights upon a black-and-white photograph of an old woman, hanging on the wall: "Where are these people who look at us as if they wanted to ask us questions?" the narrator sorrowfully asks in *Kampuchea—Death and Resurrection.* The camera then cuts to an image of abandoned shoes haphazardly strewn on the floor: "Who once wore these shoes?" Several minutes later, a photo of a gate at the entrance to one of the "compulsory communes" underscores the obvious allusion. Those who worked there were reduced to "skin and bones," the narrator says. There was "just a way in but no way out."

The association is even more explicit in *The Angkar,* which, at one point, juxtaposes photographs of the entrances to Auschwitz and Tuol Sleng, referred to as a "Gestapo headquarters." After showing an image of the "Arbeit macht frei" (Work sets you free) gate at the former death camp in Poland, the narrator poses a rhetorical question: "And what did *they* have to read, those arrested by Pol Pot and his Angkar, and then brought through this gate?" A similarly sardonic exhortation: "Fortify the spirit of the revolution." Officials in both places, the narrator continues, kept detailed records of all prisoners and their fates. They also took photographs of each one, including the women and children—images that later adorned the interior walls of the two prisons after they were reconsecrated as museums. To drive the point home, the film includes accompanying shots of an English-language sign hanging at Tuol Sleng's entrance: "Tuol Sleng Extermination Camp." None of this was by chance. East Germans, who had had experience designing concentration camp memorials in the GDR, advised the Cambodians on the design of the museum.[61]

All of these images would have been familiar to East Germans who had, perhaps as schoolchildren, visited local concentration camps in the

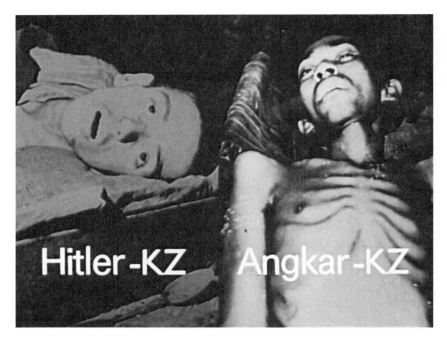

FIG. 2.2. Image from the documentary film *The Angkar*. Studio H&S (Berlin), 1981.

GDR, such as Buchenwald or Sachsenhausen. Lurid descriptions of the brutal methods used to murder the prisoners would have resonated as well. After presenting a series of extremely graphic photographs of dead women, children, and the elderly—whose throats and stomachs had been slashed open before they were thrown into cold water to see how their bodies would respond—the filmmakers show an image in *The Angkar* of a live human "medical" experiment at a German death camp. This is followed by a split-screen series of harrowing stills of dead prisoners: those who perished at the "Hitler-*KZ*" on the left, those at the "Angkar-*KZ*" on the right. "Blood and soil . . . went together, yet again." Subtlety was clearly not the forte of Heynowski and Scheumann—nor their intention.

In another memorable sequence in *The Angkar*, we see a photograph of Duch, the chief interrogator at Tuol Sleng, surrounded by his extended family: "The men who beat to death children of all ages were fathers themselves. And they saw no contradiction there." Some viewers may have recalled similar photographs of Rudolf Höss, the commandant of Auschwitz, standing with his family at their house, a stone's throw from the crematoria. But the East German filmmakers take a different tack. "The killers had no sense of guilt," the narrator intones, "and, in that sense, Pol Pot's Black Guards were like the mobile killing units [Einsatzgruppen] of Hitler, who declared entire peoples to be *Untermenschen* and approved their extermination. Once someone internalizes the theory of the master race, he feels no sense of remorse." A quick cut follows to an infamous photograph from World War II showing a member of one such unit shooting a civilian above a ditch.

The direct comparisons and indirect allusions to the Third Reich mirror East (and West) German media reports from the time. The language and frequent use of superlatives in the films do as well. What had occurred in Phnom Penh had "no comparable precedent in history." It was "barely comprehensible"—the "bloodiest regime" the world had known "up to now."[62] What did Heynowski and Scheumann hope to convey with such assertions? That what had transpired in Cambodia had been even more heinous than the crimes committed during the Third Reich? Reflecting three decades later about these films, Walter Heynowski acknowledged that Germany's "fascist past" had been his "lifelong theme," and that this had indeed colored his portrayal of the Cambodian genocide. In fact, he confided, he no longer wanted to belong to the German *Volk* after seeing "in the flesh" Jews who had just survived the death camps.[63] This was not someone who wished to relativize Nazi crimes.

Heynowski was born in 1927 in Bavarian Ingolstadt, and he grew up in a middle-class milieu. He fought as a young man in World War II, and after the war studied briefly at the University in Tübingen before moving to East Berlin, where he began work as a journalist. His entire family remained in West Germany. Long after the demise of the GDR, Heynowski said he believed that East Germany had indeed been "different" from the Federal Republic. He pointed to the treatment of Jews, who were "better off" in the East. Not a single Jew had held a ministerial position in West Germany, he noted, and Hans Globke had even served in Adenauer's government. By contrast, Albert Norden, whose father had been a rabbi, sat on the SED Politburo and had led the GDR's campaign against Globke.[64] Heynowski's attachment to the socialist project remained intact—one reason he still refused to accept the idea that the Khmer Rouge were genuine communists: "If those were communists, then my entire life was a mistake."[65]

At an internal screening of *The Angkar* at the East German Academy of the Arts, a high-level party official confided to his comrades that the Khmer Rouge were "our flesh," and that what the two filmmakers had shown in their film was "abnormal, but us"—truly a stunning admission. Heynowski realized he had made a film that raised difficult questions East German "society did not wish to answer"—above all, how communists could be capable of such crimes and atrocities.[66] The films inadvertently raised other questions, too, about East German media policies, ones that elicited strident public criticisms by Heynowski's partner, Gerhard Scheumann, about how the GDR had earlier dealt with the Cambodian genocide.

The context was the growing rapprochement in the early 1980s between China and the Soviet bloc following Mao's death. In 1978 Mao's successor, Deng Xiaoping, introduced a series of radical new policies intended to make the Chinese economy more dynamic. Both sides launched diplomatic feelers, and in early 1981, Soviet leader Leonid Brezhnev and Erich Honecker, by now head of the GDR, gave major speeches signaling their interest in improved relations with China. That same year, a series of visits took place between East German and Chinese diplomats and economic officials. Contact intensified in 1982, the same year SED officials halted all East German media attacks against China.[67]

It was during this rapprochement that Heynowski and Scheumann were completing the Cambodian cycle. Suddenly their heavy-handed criticism of Beijing's role in Cambodia was highly undesirable. The change in political climate resulted in a bitter behind-the-scenes clash over the anti-Chinese tenor of the films, eventually leading to the dissolution of Studio H&S and the subsequent revoking of the special privileges Heynowski and Scheumann had long enjoyed. But the real catalyst of their downfall came on September 16, 1982, several months after a high-level decision not to show *The Angkar* on East German television—a galling affront for the two men, who insisted on having their documentaries also shown on television because of its greater "impact" on the "masses."[68] That day, in a fateful speech given at the Fourth Congress of the East German Association of Film and Television Workers, Gerhard Scheumann openly criticized official media policy. Angered by the criticism and censorship of his films, Scheumann declared that if documentary films were "only supposed to be used as a vehicle for everyday media policies, they will go to rack and ruin [*verkommen*]." His larger point was that documentaries should remain above the normal political fray and not be held captive—like other forms of media in the GDR, such as the press—to the everyday whims of evolving political considerations.[69]

Scheumann became even more specific in his critique of East German media policy, openly questioning, for example, the public praise recently heaped on the autocratic shah of Iran and the brutal Ugandan dictator Idi Amin. There must have been "some sort of diplomatic or economic reasons" for this, he suggested. Scheumann then turned to Cambodia itself and to the public reaction to his most recent film with Heynowski. After seeing *The Angkar,* he said, viewers asked them "why our media had remained silent about Kampuchea" from 1975 to 1978—a question that took "aim" at the very "trustworthiness" of the GDR's media.

That was a stunning speech, and the fallout was immediate. Those in attendance quickly distanced themselves from Scheumann's remarks during the ensuing discussion, which was abruptly cut short. Honecker, who promptly received a copy of the speech, highlighted the most "offensive" passages in the margins. Four days later, Scheumann met with his contact at the Ministry for State Security—he had worked as an unofficial informant for the Stasi since 1957—and recanted the criticisms he had made. But the damage was already done. On September 24—two days after Scheumann, in a desperate act, had tried in vain to leave the GDR via a border crossing in Berlin—Minister of Culture Hans-Joachim Hoffmann formally dissolved Studio H&S. The two filmmakers lost all their artistic and financial privileges, and DEFA was charged with overseeing the themes and content of their future films. Heynowski and Scheumann had been effectively muzzled.[70]

The third documentary in the Cambodian series, *The Jungle War,* was never released as a film; it was issued only in book form, in 1983. In contrast to the first two full-length films in the Cambodian cycle, genocide is not the focal point of *The Jungle War,* which focuses instead on the civil war that erupted after the fall of the Khmer Rouge. There are nevertheless occasional images of skulls and other evidence of Khmer Rouge atrocities. Their policies are again referred to as "genocide" and "extermination," and the same language describes their rule as a "terror regime" run by a "clique of mass murderers" and "barbarians." Clear allusions to the Nazis appear as well. Khmer Rouge soldiers perform a "goose step" in one scene; the communes are called "concentration camps."[71]

Allusions to Nazi Germany and the Holocaust are present, then, in all the films in the Cambodia cycle. But what is striking about the one never shown in public are its silences. Most conspicuously, it barely mentions the Chinese. The film does revisit one sensitive issue, though: the fact that people who called themselves communists had carried out such atrocities. During one remarkable sequence, several refugees explain that they will not return to Cambodia because it is still controlled by communists: "I left Kampuchea under Heng Samrin because that regime is also communist, just like Pol Pot's. No real difference. There may be a little freedom, but it is a communist regime, and that is why I'm scared." Others declare that they want to go to the United States, but a Cambodian pediatrician dismisses this "venal" desire as a wish for mere "convenience." He nevertheless attempts to explain the widespread fear and hatred of communism: "The Pol Pot regime produced in us a fear of communism because it claimed to be communist [but] then negated the teachings of socialism." The point, once again, is that Pol Pot and his followers were not *genuine* communists: "After the liberation of January 7, 1979, hope nevertheless came alive in us once again," the doctor continues, "the hope for true socialism. And that is what we are now achieving under the leadership of Comrade Heng Samrin."[72] China may have no longer been a topic, but the other major themes—the parallels between the Khmer Rouge and the Nazis, the difficulty of coming to grips with ostensibly communist crimes—remained the same.

3

Why Don't *We* Act?

Angela Warnecke had just started working at a hospital in Hamburg when she heard from colleagues in the winter of 1979 that a humanitarian aid organization was searching for medical volunteers to go to Cambodia. After doing some research and speaking with journalist Rupert Neudeck, the dynamic organizer of the new initiative, the young West German physician decided to take six weeks of "vacation" to volunteer with German Committee: Doctors for Cambodia. Warnecke was on the first team Neudeck sent that November to provide medical assistance to refugees on the Thai-Cambodian border. A year later, she returned to the region aboard a Dutch freighter Neudeck's organization had chartered, thanks to donations from thousands of other West Germans. The now legendary ship, the *Cap Anamur,* would rescue almost ten thousand "boat people" from Indochina over the next three years.

Reflecting decades later, Angela Warnecke recalled the Khmer Rouge soldiers she encountered in the refugee camps, recognizable by their trademark black clothes. She also remembered sewing up injuries caused by the mines they had laid. There were other grave dangers, including the many pirates on the South China Sea who raided the *Cap Anamur* and stole from those on board. Warnecke felt little fear at the time, she says, despite the many risks. But why did she become a volunteer in the first place, and why did she continue her humanitarian activities later on, taking a course on tropical medicine in 1981, for example, so she could provide relief to suffering Somalis and Afghanis?

"German history certainly played a role," Warnecke explained, but added that her country's past had been more likely an "unconscious" factor. That was also true, she suspects, for the other German volunteers—among whom was a Jewish man who showed them his tattoo from Auschwitz. Warnecke was too young to have been a member of the sixty-eight generation of student radicals, but she did participate in Vietnam War protests in the early 1970s, likely a greater source of motivation for her later activities. That "they all continued to wipe each other out" after the American withdrawal "really shook me to the bone." Violence leads to violence, Warnecke concludes, and such horrors happen everywhere—though that did not in any way relativize what had earlier happened in Germany, she quickly adds.[1]

Just as Warnecke was preparing to leave for Southeast Asia in late 1979, a rank-and-file member of the Social Democratic Party was organizing a "silent march" in her city to "draw attention" to the "mass death" taking place in Cambodia. Since mid-September, West German diplomats and the media had been accusing the new regime of deliberately starving the Cambodian people by refusing to accept Western help, or by giving food and medical supplies to Vietnamese soldiers, not needy Cambodians. Searing images of starving and "emaciated" children, a media mainstay since the Biafra crisis of the late 1960s, accompanied dire reports about calamitous food shortages, acute malnourishment, and widespread starvation. West Germans learned that because of this "deadly famine," Cambodian women had become infertile and could not nurse their babies. "The 'land of fruit,' as the Khmer empire was once called, has become fruitless" and this was its "final struggle"—an apocalyptic term associated with the Nazis. The glossy weekly newsmagazine *Stern* also warned that the Khmer would soon "only be able to be marveled at by our children in one place alone: in the 'extinct peoples' section of an ethnology museum."[2]

In response to these reports on nightly television and in the press, the protesters in Hamburg planned to demonstrate in front of the Soviet consulate and the Chinese trade mission. Assisted by a Lutheran minister, they drafted a resolution calling on Beijing and Moscow "to do all in their power, in the name of humanity, to bring an *immediate* end to the mass murder in Cambodia." The population could be helped only if the new regime allowed in humanitarian aid. Prominent members of the SPD, including human rights activist Freimut Duve, along with representatives from a variety of organizations—the Confederation of German Trade Unions, the Free Democratic Party, the Christian Democratic Union, churches, and humanitarian groups like the Red Cross and the Gesellschaft für bedrohte Völker (Society for Threatened Peoples)—all agreed to participate in the event, which the organizers stressed was "nonpartisan."[3]

West Germans across the political spectrum warned that the Cambodian people faced a choice between "two executioners": the Khmer Rouge and the new regime in Phnom Penh. This charge of genocidal equivalency jibed with claims by the ousted Khmer Rouge, whose leaders had launched a media counterattack in response to details released by Heng Samrin's regime about the "earlier" genocide. In an interview that July, so-called Minister of Social Action Ieng Thirith, Pol Pot's sister-in-law and wife of Foreign Minister Ieng Sary, told a West German journalist in Rome that a genocide was indeed "under way" in Cambodia—this time, one the *Vietnamese* were organizing, with Soviet assistance. The "almond-shaped eyes of the diminutive woman sparkled with fire," the journalist noted, drawing on racial stereotypes, "and the proverbial Far Eastern smile disappeared from her ochre-colored face."[4]

In a bizarre twist, many West German conservatives, no doubt motivated by anticommunism, eagerly embraced these accusations—as did prominent figures on the "undogmatic" political Left, including former student radicals like Joschka Fischer, because of their growing disillusionment with Vietnam following America's withdrawal. The East Germans, by contrast, vigorously denied the allegations about a Vietnamese "holocaust" in Cambodia, as did *Unsere Zeit,* the organ of the (West) German Communist Party, which defended the Samrin regime against such "slander." "The Great Powers of the West—including Bonn—were joining in unison in the chorus of hatred against Vietnam," charged

West German leftist Jutta von Freyberg. "But the truth is that Bonn is refusing to provide aid to the survivors of the Pol Pot regime."[5]

The claims about a Vietnamese-backed genocide came to an abrupt halt in December 1979, following the publication of an impassioned exposé by Erhard Haubold, the *FAZ*'s new Southeast Asia correspondent. Relying on reports from international aid organizations, Haubold disputed claims that the Vietnamese and the Samrin regime were purposely starving Cambodians. A decade of warfare and destruction had caused logistical problems that were hindering the distribution of food, he acknowledged, but the shortages were not a "political decision." It was simply not true that a "new form of genocide" was taking place "through systematic starvation"—an assessment *Neues Deutschland* later cited with undisguised satisfaction.[6]

Further confirmation came a month later when Catholic theologian Uta Ranke-Heinemann, the eldest daughter of Gustav Heinemann, president of the Federal Republic from 1969 to 1974, published a lengthy report in *Der Spiegel* about her recent humanitarian mission in Cambodia.[7] In December 1979, at the height of media reports about the hunger crisis, Ranke-Heinemann personally delivered eight tons of medicine to the country, purchased through private donations. "The catalyst for me," she recalled decades later, was a remark by Cardinal Josef Höffner of Cologne. Cambodia was "starving," he claimed on television, but its leaders refused to accept any aid. "I wanted to get to the bottom of this, since it simply could not be true. And indeed it was not true. So, I brought assistance—not just to refute the cardinal but [mainly] to help."[8]

Ranke-Heinemann's passionate piece in *Der Spiegel* further documented the many horror stories about the reign of the Khmer Rouge. She also used the article to counter the recent criticisms by Cardinal Höffner and others. There was no truth whatsoever to Western rumors that Phnom Penh was not accepting humanitarian aid, she declared, drawing on conversations she had had with representatives from German aid organizations. In an interview on East German radio, she similarly rejected assertions in the West German media that Vietnam and the Heng Samrin government were preventing necessary goods from getting to Cambodians—a "completely bald and unbelievably dangerous lie."[9]

Two days after her exposé appeared, an official from the West German Foreign Office confirmed behind closed doors what Ranke-Heinemann and Eberhard Haubold were claiming. Cambodian civil servants were trying "in good faith" to help those in need, but poor infrastructure, insufficient supplies, and inadequate security were impeding the distribution of aid.[10] There was a noticeable change in tone in the West German media following the reports in the *FAZ* and *Der Spiegel.* A segment that aired in February 1980 on *Tagesthemen,* the most popular daily evening news program in West Germany, offered a surprisingly positive portrayal of Vietnamese occupation troops. "One thing is clear," the report concluded. "There would no longer be a Cambodian *Volk*" without the Vietnamese and their "assistance."[11]

"A human tragedy of unimaginable dimensions" was how Chancellor Helmut Schmidt described Cambodia in a private conversation with visiting Chinese leader Hua Guofeng in October 1979. Comments like this, as well as the flood of reports in the West German media about the hunger catastrophe, refute widespread complaints at the time that the Federal Republic was ignoring or indifferent to the plight of the Cambodians—a common refrain even before the fall of the Khmer Rouge. The lament grew louder once reports of a famine began appearing in the fall of 1979. Millions were dying in post–Pol Pot Cambodia, Rupert Neudeck complained, and "we just observe . . . from the European loge."[12]

Why this supposed indifference? For one, the focus at the time was on the Vietnamese boat people and the American hostage crisis in Iran. But some suspected there were other reasons, too. After so many years of tragedy in Indochina and other parts of the developing world, the West had become inured to "terms like *hunger, refugee, genocide*" and could now react only with "fatalism and resignation."[13] Only that could explain the seemingly heartless behavior of foreign journalists who took "sightseeing tours" to this "Disneyland of suffering." With obvious disdain, one German journalist recounted the behavior of a "throng" of American correspondents he had encountered in a refugee camp in Thailand: "The US invasion rolled over the speechless Khmers for an hour. Stage directions were hollered out so that American viewers could be presented with photogenic images of Cambodian suffering: '*Jack, come here, that's a great shot.*'[14]

Foreign media coverage was a two-edged sword. It was important for drawing attention to Cambodia, but, critics insisted, it needed to be done in a "proper" way, without exploiting the victims. Similar arguments would later be made about media coverage of mass rapes in Bosnia. Whatever its shortcomings, the fierce coverage of the hunger crisis was clearly at odds with continuing complaints that the country was being ignored. Those who made such claims were not necessarily being disingenuous or (just) assuming the moral high ground. It was also a rhetorical strategy to draw attention to Cambodia. And it worked. Major public figures began to demand immediate action, including West German president Karl Carstens and former chancellor Willy Brandt.[15] One of the most energetic voices was once again Jürgen Möllemann of the FDP, chair of the Bundestag's Subcommittee on Humanitarian Aid. In a series of press interviews and letters to the editor, Möllemann called for an end to the "polite silence" that had greeted this "genocide of gigantic proportions." He even demanded that the UN dispatch peacekeeping forces to prevent further "mass death" in Cambodia.[16]

That did take place, but only a decade later, in the early 1990s, when unified Germany participated in just such a mission in Cambodia. For the time being, German public and private involvement remained limited to humanitarian assistance. The situation in Cambodia was "extensively discussed" at a cabinet meeting on October 24, and a government spokesperson announced shortly thereafter that Bonn would provide 20 to 30 million of the 90 million DM earmarked by the European Community (EC) for Cambodian refugees; a month later, the Ministry of Finance announced it would provide an additional 10 million DM. From mid-October, when the EC began to send the first food and medical supplies to the region via airlift—a term with special meaning for West Germans since the Berlin *Luftbrücke* of the late 1940s—to late February 1980, the West German Foreign Office donated some 24.5 million DM in aid. The Ministry for Economic Cooperation provided another 32 million DM, making the Federal Republic the fifth largest Western supplier of aid after the United States, France, Canada, and Australia.

This was, a member of the West German branch of UNICEF effusively declared, "one of the greatest humanitarian actions in the history of humanity."[17]

Public pressure was clearly having an effect, with money also pouring in from private citizens encouraged by the media to donate. Special bank accounts were set up, and concerned citizens responded with alacrity. German charities with ties to the Catholic and Protestant churches, like Caritas, Misereor, and Brot für die Welt, collected tens of millions of deutsch marks, and the West German section of the Red Cross raised almost 32 million DM by February 1980. Major news outlets, such as *Der Spiegel* and *Die Zeit,* organized their own fundraising activities and even sponsored the entry of hundreds of refugees, including fourteen Cambodians who wound up in Hamburg, headquarters of the West German press. The CDU was equally active in its efforts—*and* equally unrelenting in its demands that the refugees receive greater assistance.[18]

Political considerations played a role here, to be sure. The situation in Cambodia was grist for the mill of anticommunist Cold Warriors in the CDU. But humanitarian and even religious motivations also came into play, as one conservative parliamentarian from Lower Saxony learned in a heartfelt appeal from a constituent. Together with friends, the man had collected signatures urging the federal government to do all it could to assist Cambodia:

> There is clearly a discrepancy when a society, whose major parties use the adjectives Christian and Social in their official names, hardly take notice when an entire *Volk* dies. The citizens who have signed this appeal are of the opinion that everything must be done, ideological barriers aside, to put an end to this mass death.[19]

West Germany also had a duty to act, he added, as one of the world's wealthy industrial nations. But the silences here are just as striking. After all, there is no mention of Germany's own genocidal past. "Very few would have reached the conclusion back then," suspected diplomat Berthold Freiherr von Pfetten-Arnbach years later, that Germans had some sort of "special responsibility" to act or condemn the Khmer Rouge because of their own past.[20]

Whatever the motivations of those who called for more assistance, the plight of the Cambodians continued to attract a great deal of attention in West Germany, eliciting comparisons to what had happened in Biafra a decade earlier and prompting more than just token expressions of concern. Efforts to help had begun even before any suspicions of genocide had surfaced. At a cabinet meeting held shortly after the fall of Phnom Penh and Saigon in April 1975, the Schmidt government announced its "fundamental willingness" to take in refugees from Indochina "for humanitarian reasons." The federal states (*Länder*) agreed at a gathering that November to accept 1,000 refugees from the region, but three years later fewer than 150 had reached West Germany. That was only a drop in the bucket, given that tens of thousands were living in desolate, makeshift camps in Vietnam and Thailand.[21]

At the request of the federal government, the *Länder* agreed in the second half of 1977 to raise the number of spots to 1,200, and a series of incremental hikes brought the number to almost 5,300 by the spring of 1979.[22] News of the hunger crisis elicited increasing pressure from the media, concerned citizens, and the conservative opposition to accept even more refugees. In late September, the *Länder* raised the refugee quota to 20,000, and by April 1980, almost 14,000 refugees from Indochina were living in West Germany—a sizable number but still not a particularly high figure considering the total number of refugees at the time.[23] Estimates fluctuated wildly on that score. In June 1979 the Thai prime minister told Foreign Minister Hans-Dietrich Genscher that 250,000 refugees had entered Thailand since 1975, 80,000 that month alone. Whatever the actual figures, they jumped again following Vietnamese military offensives in the spring and fall of 1979, and by the winter, there were reports of more than a half million Cambodian refugees on the Thai side of the border. Most were housed in large refugee camps such as Aranyaprathet and Sa Kaeo, "microcosm[s] of the Cambodian tragedy."[24]

Conditions in these "helplessly" overfilled and unsanitary camps were horrendous, the suffering "indescribable," in the words of the *General-Anzeiger*, the Bonn daily read by most federal officials. Sa Kaeo was a "city of misery," a "refuge of unimaginable horror" that elicited an "overwhelming feeling of deep empathy [and] tears. . . . Skeletons covered by leathered skin. Bodies bent in agony. . . . A little child, just a few months old, with the face of an old person, the skull of a dead person, even though the heart still beats. . . . Mothers bent over their apathetic children, death written in their faces."[25] Other, similarly emotional reports mentioned the "lethargy" of these "vegetating," "gaunt figures" who were being treated "like worthless cattle." After a visit to Aranyaprathet, one journalist rhetorically asked, "Are those still human beings?"—a phrase eerily, and perhaps purposefully, reminiscent of Primo Levi's famous memoir about Auschwitz. "Motionless . . . dull gray skin," the reporter continued. "Empty eyes. . . . It is a like a cemetery where one forgot to bury the corpses."[26]

The packed camps lacked adequate medical facilities, food, and fresh water. To make matters worse, there were reports of stealing and rapes by Thai soldiers, as well as violence on the part of the tens of thousands of Khmer Rouge soldiers also in the camps. Easily recognizable by their distinctive dress and superior physical condition, the Khmer Rouge lived side by side with the "old bourgeoisie" of Phnom Penh and other civilian refugees—"executioners next to their victims," not unlike the many Jews forced to live in "displaced persons" camps after World War II alongside their earlier tormentors. The Khmer Rouge acted "as if they were back at home in Cambodia," taking the best provisions for themselves and behaving as if they were still in control. There were reports in the summer of 1979 that they had horrifically crucified one young boy for stealing food, and the *Westdeutsche Allgemeine*, a regional paper in the industrial Ruhr district, even published a photograph supposedly depicting the brutal punishment.[27]

Such stark imagery elicited expressions of horror and outrage in West Germany, as well as frenzied demands for more assistance. Under pressure from the conservative opposition, Genscher called on the EC that October to take in more refugees. Some of the loudest demands for more aid came from within the foreign minister's own party, the FDP, which adopted a set of new foreign policy guidelines that winter calling for the "generous acceptance" of refugees. Genscher, who had fled East Germany in the early 1950s, mentioned the political and personal reasons for this commitment when he met with the prime minister of Thailand: "The expulsion of hundreds of thousands is taking place once again under Communist auspices. We ourselves had bitter experiences after World War II as refugees. That is why we can appreciate the magnitude of the problem."[28]

Genscher's younger colleague and party protégé, Jürgen Möllemann, continued to be a dogged advocate of the sorely afflicted Cambodians. Behind closed doors and in a series of public statements, he echoed similar themes of duty and historical experience, calling specifically on West Germany, one of the "richest countries on Earth," to take in more refugees from Southeast Asia: "The citizens of our country experienced the free world's willingness to help during the dark hours after 1945. Today we have the opportunity and duty to show . . . that we have the same ability to provide practical and humane assistance."[29] FDP politicians received many letters of support for their efforts, including one appeal by Catholic clergy from the Rhineland who believed the country should take in more refugees: "[We] ask you to set a clear example for peace by generously accepting helpless people into our country. . . . Assistance for defenseless expellees should have priority over political sanctions against communist strongmen, even if their policy deserves to be condemned by the entire world."[30]

Members of the conservative CDU also expressed unstinting concern for the plight of the refugees, whom they also insisted on referring to as "expellees" (*Vertriebene*). This semantic choice, which connoted deportation by force, was a pointed allusion to the fate of millions of ethnic Germans expelled from Eastern Europe after World War II, and it hinted at the political motivations underlying ostensibly humanitarian concerns: from staunch anticommunism to continuing resentment about the post-1945 territorial losses.

One of the most outspoken advocates for the refugees was, in fact, Herbert Czaja, a member of the CDU from Stuttgart who already enjoyed a solid reputation for defending the rights of those forced to flee their homes—including and above all ethnic Germans. Czaja was born in Eastern Silesia shortly after the outbreak of World War I, a region that belonged at the time to the Austro-Hungarian Empire and became a part of Poland after 1914. Raised in a middle-class Catholic family, Czaja studied to be a teacher and earned his doctorate at the University of Kraków in 1939. No fascist, he refused to join the Nazi Party after the German invasion of Poland because of his political and religious beliefs. He lost his position at the university as a result.

Czaja fought in World War II after being drafted in 1942 and was wounded on the Eastern Front. Following his release from an American prisoner-of-war camp, he returned to his hometown but was expelled in 1946. He eventually settled in Stuttgart, where he later entered local politics and became heavily involved in the work of expellee organizations that vigorously represented the interests of those from the East. A year after becoming head of the Union of Expellees of North Württemberg, Czaja entered the West German Bundestag in 1952 and remained a member until 1990. He was elected president of the West German Federation of Expellees in 1970, a position he held until 1994.[31]

Because of his association with expellee organizations; his staunch opposition to Willy Brandt's *Ostpolitik,* West Germany's contribution to détente; and his increasingly revisionist agitation, Czaja earned a reputation as a conservative firebrand. But he was also a steadfast defender of human rights, dedicated to the plight of refugees around the globe. Czaja became a member of the Bundestag's Committee for Foreign Affairs in 1964 and was especially active on its Subcommittee for Humanitarian Assistance. During the Biafra crisis of the late 1960s, he called on the West German government to provide aid to the Christian Igbo people of the war-torn African region and even flew there with other members of parliament on a fact-finding mission. In the late 1970s, Czaja turned his attention to refugees from Indochina. He was especially interested in reuniting families, and to make that happen, he even arranged for the behind-the-scenes payment of "bribes"—a West German practice used to secure the release of East German dissidents.[32]

Czaja's efforts were impressive, but the CDU member who did the most for the Southeast Asian refugees was Minister-President Ernst Albrecht of Lower Saxony, which took in more displaced persons from the region than any other West German state. Albrecht recalls in his memoirs precisely when and why he decided to help. In November 1978, West German television broadcast heartrending images of 2,000 people stranded aboard a steamer near the Malaysian coast. They had no food and hardly any water, and the "entire . . . world" saw their "affliction and desperation . . . but no one did anything. I said to myself: Why don't *we* act, we Lower Saxons?" Albrecht's state subsequently took in half the refugees aboard the steamer, and thousands more boat people later.[33]

Politics were surely a factor here. Since the Left was already focused on other humanitarian issues, like apartheid in South Africa and human rights violations in Latin America, supporting the Southeast Asian refugees allowed West German conservatives to take the moral high ground, too, as defenders of human rights. At a national conference in 1979, one CDU delegate admonished his colleagues that their party could "only persist" by realizing "our ideals. . . . Ernst Albrecht's acceptance of a thousand refugees in Lower Saxony was just such a signal for young voters. We must set further benchmarks in this regard."[34] It was a bid for political capital, to be sure, but it was more than that. Other factors were at play, including a profound sense of Christian duty. "Only Lower Saxony . . . helped truly out of conviction," Ernst Albrecht fervently believed, especially the many "engaged Christians" who volunteered their assistance. They were, he claimed, motivated by a belief that solidarity, the "secular form of charity," must not "remain limited to people from one's own nation."[35]

At the same time that some conservatives were advocating energetically on behalf of Southeast Asian refugees, others cautioned against taking in "too many." Their main concern was the supposed difficulty of integrating so many refugees into West German society and the labor force. Even Herbert Czaja believed that the "entire problem" could be solved not in the Federal Republic and the Western industrial states but instead in "thinly populated" regions without "excessively racist barriers." Dieter Graf Landsberg-Velen, another prominent member of the CDU, argued along similar lines. It was "utterly wrong to transplant these people from their *Heimat* [homeland] to America or the European continent.

The acclimatization will be tremendously difficult given their lifestyle habits and education levels."[36]

Politicians from the governing SPD made strikingly similar arguments, warning that the Federal Republic could not absorb so many refugees. Besides, Chancellor Helmut Schmidt confided to China's leader Hua Guofeng in October 1979, they would not be "happy in foreign surroundings." His predecessor, Willy Brandt, chimed in a month later, telling reporters that there had been "no more awful challenge" than Cambodia since Auschwitz *and* Hiroshima, a notable juxtaposition. But the "main response," he said, could not be that faraway regions accept these refugees—a remarkable statement from someone who had himself fled Nazi Germany and sought political refuge abroad a half century earlier. The SPD was divided on the issue of immigration, but its parliamentary caucus nevertheless declared in the spring of 1979 that "when it comes to accepting large numbers of refugees from some trouble spot in the world, humanitarian or emotional considerations . . . stand at the forefront." The "hard reality," it warned, comes after their admission.[37]

Leading German politicians believed, then, that the West had a responsibility to help the refugees, but by helping other countries in Southeast Asia to absorb them, not by bringing them en masse to Western Europe. The government preferred to "pay instead of play," to increase foreign aid rather than accept more refugees. Not all agreed with that approach: "Even if the climate and lifestyle are much different from their *Heimat*, even if the acclimatization will be very difficult, and even if they will always remain strangers here . . . they will be able to *live* here"—"without fear" and "without being helplessly exposed to hunger and sickness."[38] That this heartfelt appeal appeared in the *Bayernkurier*, the newspaper of the conservative Christian Social Union, makes one thing clear: there were no clear-cut party lines on the issue.

Those who urged a more cautious approach offered other reasons why it would be difficult to take in large numbers of refugees. The arrival each year of thousands of so-called *Aussiedler* (persons of German ethnic descent who migrated from Eastern Europe and the Soviet Union to the Federal Republic) was the most popular one, as it had been since the 1950s. Almost 60,000 arrived in 1978 alone, on top of more than 30,000 asylum seekers from other parts of the world.[39] Stressing his country's "special legal and moral responsibility" toward the *Aussiedler,* State Secretary Klaus von Dohnanyi of the SPD argued that West Germany's "absorption capacities" were "limited." He also emphasized the high financial costs involved. Besides, he added, among those countries that were not "classic immigration countries" or that had no "special links" to Indochina—as the United States and France did—the Federal Republic had accepted the largest number of refugees from the region "by far."[40]

Claims that West Germany was not an "immigration country" were common. A month after formally declaring in November 1981 that the country was not and "should not" become one, Helmut Schmidt's cabinet adopted measures to curb further immigration—all part of a general backlash against refugees and asylum seekers, especially following the second global oil shock, in 1979. The resulting economic downturn and growing unemployment rate made foreigners, in theory, unwelcome rivals for increasingly scarce jobs—no doubt an important reason why the SPD, traditionally a working-class party, had qualms about letting in more. To make matters worse, the downturn coincided with a significant spike in the raw number of West Germany's asylum seekers, which jumped to more than 200,000 between 1979 and 1981— up from roughly 178,000 *altogether* between 1953 and 1978. This went hand in hand with a huge spike in the total number of refugees worldwide: between 12 and 15 million in 1979.[41]

The new challenge was one of West Germany's own making, at least in part. In 1973 the government had decided to halt the recruitment of so-called guest workers (*Gastarbeiter*), manual workers recruited— through a series of bilateral agreements signed in the 1950s and 1960s with poorer countries like Italy, Portugal, and Yugoslavia—to satisfy the country's voracious appetite for labor. That decision had been part of a conscious attempt to integrate foreigners already living in the Federal Republic instead of recruiting new ones. But it now meant that asylum one of the few ways to gain residency. The country was a popular refugee destination because of its material wealth and generous social welfare policies—and also for another reason: it had one of the world's most liberal asylum policies. As a form of "atonement" for the crimes of the Nazi era, Article 16 of the West German constitution guaranteed refuge to any "persons persecuted for political reasons," wording that gave immigration authorities a good deal of leeway when deciding who could stay.[42]

The subsequent surge in applicants did not become a major issue until the late 1970s, when the main regions of origin shifted from Eastern Europe to the developing world. That, coupled with the economic downturn, created a shrill backlash against asylum applicants, who became a partisan wedge issue in West German electoral politics. Conservatives obsessed more and more about a "foreigner problem," and they increasingly spoke in metaphoric language about a "flood" of bogus asylum seekers, or *Scheinasylanten,* a term first used in the late 1970s. That word, and similar ones like *Wirtschaftsflüchtlinge* (economic refugees), had strong negative connotations. In contrast to earlier asylum seekers, these charlatans were supposedly coming under false pretenses: not because of political persecution per se, but to "abuse the system."[43]

Such fears and resentment spurred an increase in xenophobic violence. In 1980, two Vietnamese refugees in Hamburg were killed in a Molotov cocktail attack—the first time in West Germany that an assault on refugee housing had resulted in death. This marked the beginning of an uptick in xenophobic violence that lasted through the 1990s. Some politicians and intellectuals began to claim that certain groups of foreigners, especially from Asia and Africa, could not be assimilated because of their vastly different cultural practices and values. The first anti-immigrant grassroots organizations were founded during this period, including the Citizens' Initiative to Stop Asian Immigration and Other Foreign Infiltration (*Überfremdung*)—an unpleasant term, first used in German nationalist circles in the late nineteenth century, that had become taboo after 1945. In 1981, a group of West German professors signed the so-called Heidelberg Manifesto, which espoused racist and *völkisch* arguments condemning the *Überfremdung,* or "foreignization," of West Germany. The document drew particular attention to immigration's "Asian component"—at a time when the 200,000 Asians living in West Germany made up only 5 percent of all foreigners.[44]

The idea that German prosperity, identity, and culture were "under siege" was especially popular in publications from the conservative Springer press. But it was by no means limited to the right—and it was also nothing new. Still, one should be careful not to draw facile conclusions about German "continuities" across the 1945 divide. The abominable claims about immigrants were racially inflected, to be sure, but the emphasis was now on ethnic and cultural differences, not biological ones. And these claims were by no means limited to the Federal Republic. Other Western European countries witnessed a surge in xenophobia, too, at the time. But there is another point worth emphasizing. Foreigners were not the only ones who bore the brunt of rising xenophobia. There was also a conspicuous increase in discrimination against ethnic Germans in the 1980s, at a time when it had become easier for *Aussiedler* to leave the Soviet bloc. The point is that resentment and prejudice were not "just" about race, and that had long been the case—as unwelcome *German* refugees from the East learned firsthand during the first postwar decade.[45] The prejudices of the 1980s were, in a sense, little more than old wine in new bottles.

Whatever the causes and character, the tide had indeed turned against "economic refugees" and "bogus asylum seekers" by the start of the decade. Franz Josef Strauss, the flamboyant leader of the conservative CSU, captured the new mood in a blistering speech at a meeting of the party caucus in early March 1980, just months before unsuccessfully running for the chancellorship:

> After what we experienced in the Third Reich, the term *political asylum* is just as holy as it was in antiquity. . . . But the fact that whole planeloads now arrive, that there are several large syndicates—smugglers, haulage contractors who charter airplanes, groups of lawyers who have the necessary forms ready at hand when the planes touch down—that has . . . nothing to do with *political asylum*. (Applause.) I think of the persecuted Jews in the Third Reich, who tried in the dead of night to flee across the Swiss border. . . . One should be liberal [but only] when it comes to *true* cases of asylum.[46]

The FDP was the sole party whose members consistently played down such concerns. "Because of our history," commented an editorial in the party magazine *Neue Bonner Depesche* a month after Strauss's remarks, "we have a duty to act liberally toward asylum seekers." But, the prescient piece warned, the "stylized dramatizing" of the "new challenge" West Germany was facing meant, "for the first time" since 1945, that "one could blatantly appeal to national instincts, to fear of foreign infiltration, to xenophobia. A fuse is being lit."[47]

Resentment toward immigrants and refugees increased over the course of the 1980s, as the editorial predicted. Global hunger catastrophes in the developing world and the collapse of communism in Eastern Europe at the close of the decade only heightened tensions, leading to further bureaucratic efforts to discourage asylum requests. They also fueled the rise of xenophobic political parties like the Republikaner, cofounded by a former member of the Waffen-SS in 1983. The initial willingness to take in refugees and the eventual backlash were harbingers of the intense political disputes that would wrack Germany more than three decades later. But there were more encouraging developments as well, including a backlash against the backlash. Pro Asyl, an organization that acted on behalf of asylum seekers, was founded in 1986, for example, and between 1981 and 1991 the Federal Republic wound up accepting more refugees than the rest of Western Europe combined. The media gushed about the "never-ending" willingness of many ordinary West Germans to assist refugees, including those from Indochina.[48]

Rupert Neudeck, the humanitarian activist, was less effusive. "German society doles out its charity in fine doses," he carped in his memoir. "On the one hand, it has become an integral part of television entertainment. . . . On the other, the Germans' happiness to donate is tax deductible."[49] Such prickliness did little to defuse the hefty disputes he had with politicians and other public figures in West Germany because of his humanitarian efforts. But even Neudeck could not help quoting with palpable pride from a letter he received from one Cambodian woman who had served as a translator for German medical personnel he had sent to the region: "We knew your land under the name of Hitler, the Führer, and the Gestapo. These names reminded us of the concentration camps and the terror against the Jewish population. We made the mistake of thinking that all Germans are just as evil as Hitler. . . . That was why your arrival was such a pleasant surprise for us. We thought of Hitler a great deal under the Pol Pot regime."[50]

Germany's past was indeed always present, even in the minds of many foreigners. But expressions of gratitude like this also gave Germans cause to feel good about themselves. "When we escaped from this tyrannical system," the translator continued in her letter to Neudeck, "we thought we would first receive help from those who had once been our protectors, the French and Americans. But not a single Frenchman has yet come to this camp. . . . Nobody besides you has had the courage to come to us and distribute goods with their own hands."[51]

Neudeck, the West German most closely associated with helping refugees from former Indochina, represents a particularly instructive case of private initiative from this period. Born in Danzig on the eve of World War II, Neudeck fled westward with his mother and young siblings, away from the Red Army, in the waning months of the war. He studied law as a young man and served as a Jesuit novice, but then decided to change course and write a doctoral thesis on the "political ethics" of Sartre and Camus. After completing his degree, Neudeck took a different career path once again, beginning work in 1977 as a journalist and editor at West Germany's premier public radio station. He and his wife, Christel, were leading a "perfectly bourgeois life" at the time.[52]

That all changed in February 1979 during a trip he took to Paris to collect material for a new book on Jean-Paul Sartre. Neudeck met with renowned French philosopher André Glucksmann, who was the first to speak with him at length about the dire situation of the boat people in Southeast Asia. Their plight had broken as a major news story several months earlier. "Que faites-vous?" Glucksmann asked Neudeck in the café where they met: what was *he* personally going to do about the refugees? Neudeck had similarly memorable meetings with Sartre himself, and with Bernard Kouchner, the future French foreign minister who had founded Doctors Without Borders in 1971. At the time of Neudeck's visit, Kouchner was active with Un Bateau pour le Vietnam, an organization that had several months earlier sent a ship to rescue the boat people. Neudeck later recalled "how encouraged" he felt by this and by Sartre's "Catholic stimulus." Knowing that one must act when one can, and then acting, was the very "essence of Christianity," he declared.

It is worth noting, since Neudeck does not, that Glucksmann and Kouchner had a different stimulus. Both had Central European Jewish backgrounds, and both had lost family members during the Holocaust.[53]

Inspired by the three men, Neudeck returned to Germany intent on doing his part to help the refugees. Because most humanitarian efforts at the time focused on the refugees still living on land, Neudeck decided to focus on those who were stranded and dying on the high seas. Like Herbert Czaja's efforts at the time, this decision had a great deal to do with his personal history. On January 30, 1945, during their flight from Danzig, he and his family had arrived in the Baltic port city of Goten-hafen (today Gdynia, in Poland), where they saw a large cruise ship in the harbor, the *Wilhelm Gustloff*. Originally built in the mid-1930s as a passenger ship for the Nazi leisure movement Strength through Joy, the ship was now being used to evacuate German officials, civilians, and ref-ugees from the advancing Soviet army. Neudeck's mother did not have tickets for the *Gustloff* (she would not have taken a "luxury ship for Nazi bigwigs" anyway, he later insisted), and they wound up on a coal steamer instead. Later that day, a Soviet submarine sank the *Gustloff*, and thou-sands of its passengers drowned in the freezing waters of the Baltic—the greatest loss of life involving the sinking of a single ship. Horrific im-ages of the disaster left an indelible impression on the five-year-old. This was why, Neudeck believed, death by drowning became such an important "archetype" in his life—and a major motivation for his later relief efforts.[54]

In July 1979 a West German announcement at a UN conference on the refugee crisis in Southeast Asia reinforced Neudeck's decision to help the boat people: every refugee saved by a ship "flying under the German flag" would be allowed into the Federal Republic. Neudeck appealed to German novelist and Nobel Prize recipient Heinrich Böll for support, and the two men held a joint press conference in Bonn, where they an-nounced plans to provide humanitarian assistance to the region.[55] Besides rescuing Vietnamese boat people, Neudeck's organization also sent hundreds of German doctors and nurses to the region to assist Cambodian refugees who had survived the recent genocide. That initia-tive came about at the urging of Gisela Sperling, a pediatrician from Bochum and a volunteer on the *Cap Anamur* who, during a visit to the

FIG. 3.1. Rupert Neudeck posting a sign for the West German organization Doctors for Cambodia at a refugee camp in Thailand. Rupert Neudeck Collection / DOMiD Archive, Cologne, Germany.

Thai border, had come upon two refugee camps previously unknown in the West. Sperling phoned Neudeck from Bangkok to let him know that Cambodians were arriving "in droves" at the border and that medical assistance was urgently needed. Soforthilfe, a charity established by a group of attorneys in Munich with personal connections to high-level Thai military commanders and German businesspeople in Bangkok, quickly raised 750,000 DM in donations in support of Neudeck's new initiative, the German Committee: Doctors for Cambodia.[56]

Millions of marks in private donations, as well as logistical assistance from employees at the Bangkok bureau of Henkell, a German sparkling wine company, allowed Neudeck to send additional medical teams to the border. Just as essential was the engagement of more than four hundred West German doctors and nurses who volunteered for stints of four to eight weeks. Among them was Ursula Bruch, a nurse from Bonn who decided to volunteer instead of taking a ski vacation that year. Working for five weeks "under the most primitive conditions . . . and every day, from 9 to 5, without any breaks," Bruch received no remuneration apart from her flight and lodging. Neither did Neudeck, who used his own vacation time for his various humanitarian pursuits. He later recalled with a chuckle that Deutschlandfunk, his employer, was "sympathetic" to his efforts but could not simply give him time off, owing to the strict rules and regulations of "German officialdom." He and his wife did all their humanitarian work "on the side," during vacations and on nights and weekends in their modest townhouse on the outskirts of Cologne.[57]

Their work in Cambodia and elsewhere was made possible by a flood of donations from private citizens—and from German celebrities, including rock-and-roll singer Udo Lindenberg, who donated the proceeds from a benefit concert in Dortmund. Journalist Franz Alt televised a fundraiser that brought in more than a million marks in late July, and a group of newspaper publishers in Westphalia did their part by donating a million marks of their own to a foundation that then raised additional hundreds of thousands of marks. All in all, Neudeck's organization received some 4 million DM by mid-December 1979: "More and more people in the Federal Republic feel responsible for these poorest of the poor," he wrote approvingly.[58]

Neudeck's voluntary efforts initially met with a positive response in West Germany. But they also led to a series of disputes with government officials, other aid organizations, and neighboring countries in the region that were worried the group's activities could cause political problems.[59] Thai officials were especially ill-disposed to his organization's efforts on the Cambodian border and wanted them to leave. They placed many obstacles in the group's path, Neudeck believed, such as forbidding volunteers to live in the refugee camps. As a result, they lost a good deal of time each day driving for several hours back and forth, often through mine-infested territory. There was another disadvantage. To be effective, Neudeck believed, volunteers needed to live together "with the people," without any showers or other niceties. "Experiencing hardship is crucial for aid work[,] . . . as is physically sharing [the refugees'] everyday reality."[60] One detects here the Christian impulse behind this former Jesuit novice's activities—and, perhaps, his scholarly interest in existential philosophy as well.

Critics in the Federal Republic of Germany charged that the very presence of the ship *Cap Anamur* was encouraging refugees to take to the seas in a desperate attempt to come to the Federal Republic—and also that aid to the refugee camps was "unwittingly" helping the Khmer Rouge maintain its strength. But that was only the tip of the iceberg. One government spokesperson claimed that the rescue ship suffered from poor hygiene and lack of security, that Neudeck's "main concern" was "publicity," and that his people always "wanted to be the first ones [to arrive] everywhere!"[61] Hans-Jürgen Schilling, general secretary of the German Red Cross, voiced similar "concerns" about what he called an "amateur" aid organization. Neudeck, for his part, mordantly referred to the Red Cross as a "gluttonous and bureaucratically inert institution." Personal "jealousies" and antagonisms became so fraught that Schilling, who was attracting attention for his public statements about the perils of *Überfremdung* and the dangers of "blending Germans with extremely foreign minorities," refused to attend meetings with the head of Cap Anamur.[62]

Neudeck dismissed the criticism, as well as complaints that he did not "play by the established rules." He simply wanted to help "where relief was most necessary." And in response to critics on the Left who accused the Social Democrat of being anticommunist—because he was saving the "wrong" people (that is, those fleeing communism)—he stressed that his work was above any political or economic interests, an approach he christened "radical humanism." Clearly inspired by his philosophical role models, Neudeck believed that actions and deeds were what counted, not words, though he was certainly adept at advancing his agenda in the media.[63]

Rupert Neudeck eventually made peace with his critics, and with German "society" as a whole. Sitting in a living room filled to the brim with foreign art and other artifacts collected over the years, Neudeck—who cut a dashing figure, with a gaunt, weathered face, neatly trimmed white beard, and the air of a sea captain—reflected decades later on the earlier frictions. All in all, he said, he was more "content than critical" of Germany and his fellow Germans. He "gladly" lived in a place where one could count on the state to abide by established legal rules and procedures. The West German government may not have always welcomed his efforts, but Neudeck admired its "complete reliability" and commitment to the rule of law. He was also glad to live in a country where people *acted*—that is, where people supported and even personally carried out concrete humanitarian actions. Neudeck prudently refused to speak with any certainty about why his volunteers did what they did. They had "endless motivations," he surmised. But there was "most certainly a very great collective willingness" on the part of his fellow Germans "to do more for humanitarian issues than all other European nationalities [did]. And that most certainly has to do with the past."[64]

But which past exactly? His own main motivation, he readily acknowledged, had been his traumatic experiences as a child refugee. But what about the suffering that Germans had caused, not the suffering they had experienced themselves? Nazi crimes against humanity, and against the Jews in particular, had played a "powerful role," he believed, adding that his organization's activities were a "semiconscious attempt to compensate somehow for this past"—to portray Germany "a little bit differently" in the world. And when it came to humanitarian actions, German volunteers always did more than other Europeans because they did not want to be "surpassed" in their efforts. This was, after all, one area where they were "allowed to be on top of the world."

A childhood trauma, a Catholic upbringing, and a fortuitous visit to Paris—these were the three main influences that first spurred Rupert Neudeck into action. The journalist's prickly zealotry may have made him some enemies along the way, but the number of Cambodian and Vietnamese refugees West Germany was willing to accept steadily increased because of the public pressure—or "moral blackmail," as his critics charged and as Neudeck later conceded—he placed on prominent politicians. In the end, he and his volunteers could point to the thousands of lives saved in Southeast Asia—and later, as we shall see, in places like Rwanda and Bosnia.

Uta Ranke-Heinemann, the Catholic theologian who paid a humanitarian visit of her own to Cambodia in the late winter of 1979, encountered similar difficulties with West German authorities. "All sides rebuked" her, she later recalled, "except for the communists."[65] West

German officials did indeed express misgivings about her planned trip, in part because it had not been coordinated with the Foreign Office. Taking a swipe at both Ranke-Heinemann and Neudeck, one SPD parliamentarian disdainfully complained about the recent "tide of touristic assistance" that was supposedly hindering the work of established charity organizations in Cambodia. Ranke-Heinemann, for her part, insisted that Bonn had deliberately placed obstacles in her path. The Ministry of Defense refused to supply her with a plane to deliver the aid, she told reporters, which was why she had to fly instead with Interflug, the East German airline.[66]

GDR officials were indeed more supportive of her efforts. They noted approvingly that the progressive theologian wished to use her visit to Cambodia "to draw attention to the mendacious chatter about Western aid efforts." But Ranke-Heinemann experienced frictions with the East Germans as well on the eve of her departure, largely because of her wish to bring along a West German television team led by well-known foreign correspondent Peter Scholl-Latour. The problem, from the perspective of the East Germans, was that Scholl-Latour had "repeatedly . . . attracted attention" because of his unfavorable reporting about Vietnam.[67] A linguistically gifted Franco-German journalist who headed the Paris studio of ZDF, a West German public television network, Scholl-Latour was well known as an expert on the Middle East, Africa, and Southeast Asia. He had recently published a memoir, evocatively titled *Der Tod im Reisfeld* (Death in the Rice Field), that consisted of vignettes recounting his three decades of personal experience in Indochina.[68]

Scholl-Latour's reporting was indeed highly critical of the Vietnamese, whose "storm troopers" had overthrown the Khmer Rouge "terror regime" in a "Blitzkrieg"—and "yet, the killing and dying continue," he wrote. Condemning Hanoi's "hegemonial policies" in the region, he further claimed that Cambodia's leader Heng Samrin was a puppet of the Vietnamese, who were continuing an "old Vietnamese tradition of ousting foreign races" and sending "soldier peasants" as settlers to Cambodia. Ranke-Heinemann defied the pressure from East Berlin, insisting that Scholl-Latour accompany her. But, for unknown reasons, the controversial journalist did not travel along with her in the end. He did somehow manage, several months later, to spend time with the "soldiers of the apocalypse," his cutting term for the Khmer Rouge leadership, over a four-course meal served with whiskey and coke, making him the first Western journalist to meet with them after their fall from power.[69]

On her return to the Federal Republic, Ranke-Heinemann took to the press and airways to emphasize how much humanitarian assistance the Cambodians were receiving from the GDR. She praised in particular the efforts of Rolf Dach, the first East German ambassador to Cambodia following the ouster of the Khmer Rouge. In a piece in *Der Spiegel,* she highlighted the imminent arrival in the region of teams of doctors from the GDR and Cuba, and specifically mentioned Dach's efforts to provide medical assistance in Phnom Penh. In an interview on East German radio, Ranke-Heinemann praised the ambassador for all the assistance he had given during her stay, noting that they had "worked well together." West German journalist Michael Sontheimer, who later met Dach during a visit to Cambodia in 1989, also spoke highly of the ambassador, who did not have the "arrogant attitude" cultivated by many West German diplomats.[70]

Rolf Dach would indeed have been an oddity among his West German counterparts, many of whom, like their prewar predecessors, were members of the old German nobility. Born in 1934 to a working-class family, he grew up poor in a small village near Eisleben, the hometown of Martin Luther.[71] The son of a miner, Dach attended vocational school, working first as a railroad repairman before training to be a truck mechanic. Because of volunteer work he did with youths in his spare time, he was invited to attend a training college for teachers. In 1959, after teaching for many years, he was encouraged to enroll at the GDR's training academy for diplomats. Reflecting decades later on how he, a manual worker, had eventually become ambassador to Cambodia, Dach wistfully responded, in a thick Saxon accent, that it was a "typical German story"—though he likely meant a typical *East* German one. Because so many diplomats had fled to the West, and because of years of international isolation, there was a shortage of professionals in the foreign service when the GDR finally began to establish diplomatic relations with the nonsocialist world in the 1960s.

Dach was assigned to francophone Africa at the training academy, which meant he had to learn French, he said—"such a complicated language!" After spending several years training in Africa, he returned to the GDR and was assigned to a youth academy near Berlin, where, for ten years, he was responsible for hosting foreign students. Dach made it clear to his supervisors in the Foreign Office that he would not accept any assignments abroad unless his family received an apartment in the GDR—a typical East German pressure tactic to acquire something that was in short supply.[72] After the regime finally found an apartment for his family in 1972—a "*beautiful* one" in Marzahn, the future site of vast, prefab housing estates in northeastern Berlin—Dach was assigned to the East German embassy in Brazzaville, Congo. There, he said, he "learned by doing" what diplomatic work entailed. Though criticized for his "chummy way of behaving" and for not exerting "sufficient authority," Dach received subsequent assignments to Mali and Angola.

Two months after the GDR had recognized the new Cambodian regime in January 1979, Dach received word that he would be transferred to Phnom Penh. His knowledge of French, as well as contacts he had established with visiting youth delegations from Cambodia in the 1960s, were important reasons for the assignment, his first as ambassador. Dach later explained that he had never expected or wanted to become an ambassador, that he felt he was not "cut out" for such work and had always been a "realist" about his own capabilities. But he accepted the position because he wanted to help those who had just survived the "bloody reign" of terror.

Dach landed in Phnom Penh in March 1979. There were no signs of life at the airport, apart from hordes of scurrying rats and feral dogs, until a white Mercedes adorned with an East German flag suddenly appeared, driven by a Cambodian who, it turned out, had just been appointed head of diplomatic protocol that very morning. Like most Cambodian officials, the new diplomat was a military man with no prior experience as a civil servant—but that was "convenient," Dach drolly commented years later, because he had had no experience himself as an ambassador.

Conditions at the East German embassy were not much better than those at the airport. Vietnamese soldiers had defecated inside the "completely devastated" building when they had marched into the capital two months earlier—a parting shot at the North Koreans, who had used the building after the last East German diplomats had been forced to leave in

April 1975. Dach's main task was to determine what "practical" assistance was needed right away. He flew back to Berlin a month later to deliver his assessment and, thanks to his reports, the GDR would eventually send millions of marks' worth of essential goods to Cambodia—"free of charge," East German leader Erich Honecker emphasized on many occasions. Besides pharmaceuticals and medical devices, East Germany also sent along medical personnel to provide health care and train new doctors, whose ranks had been decimated under the Khmer Rouge. They were later joined by naval engineers, who helped rebuild the infrastructure used to cross the Mekong River, and by German-language teachers charged with preparing Cambodians for study and training in the GDR.[73]

There were occasional hiccups. The East German Ministry of Health balked at sending more medical personnel because Cambodia was "unable to create the requisite working and living conditions for GDR citizens." After a visit to the country in October 1980, a delegation from the ministry complained that four East German doctors and a nurse had already been living for three months in "unacceptable housing" in a hotel without air-conditioning or a steady supply of electricity. "This situation must be remedied as soon as possible . . . because of the heavy psychological and physical strain."[74] That demand was a far cry from Rupert Neudeck's wish for his volunteers to live directly among those whom they were helping.

But there were others who had more positive experiences. One East German doctor extended his stay three times and worked in Cambodia for four years. Waldemar Pickard, a "very nice East German bloke" whom West German journalist Michael Sontheimer met during a visit to Cambodia in 1989, was another example. A thirty-five-year-old engineer from Thuringia, Pickard had been working in the country with UNICEF for four years, traveling to remote villages to help the inhabitants dig wells for fresh water. (The old wells had been contaminated by the corpses dumped in them by the Khmer Rouge.) Pickard, who extended his stay several times and even spoke "passable" Khmer, told Sontheimer that he preferred working with the "absolutely honest" and "highly motivated" Cambodians. Besides, he added, "you had the feeling you were doing something worthwhile . . . that you could really help people."[75]

The East German media dutifully reported on the various forms of humanitarian assistance provided by the GDR and other Soviet-bloc states, praising in solemn terms this "eloquent expression of working-class solidarity" with the "sorely afflicted Kampuchean *Volk*." But the goal was not to awaken overly sentimental feelings of pity, recalled journalist Klaus-Dieter Pflaum and his wife, Hannelore, also stationed in Southeast Asia at the time. In fact, they were specifically instructed not to report in a "tear-jerk manner" about the many horrors that had taken place in Cambodia. The goal was to encourage the Cambodians to work hard to rebuild the country themselves—*Hilfe zur Selbsthilfe,* as the saying went ("Helping people to help themselves"). In other words, GDR officials wanted to make sure their financial assistance would be put to good use, so that they would not have to keep pouring money for reconstruction down the proverbial drain.[76] Their assistance was not pure charity, however. The Cambodians worked to repay their debts—by exporting black pepper and rubber to the GDR, for example. Such attitudes nevertheless reflected condescending attitudes toward the "Third World," where, when humanitarian projects went amiss, East German officials and aid workers were quick to blame the so-called natives—a habit of many West Germans as well.[77]

Shortly before being recalled to Berlin in 1990, Ambassador Dach confided to Michael Sontheimer that working together with the Cambodians was "often not easy." Inexperienced Cambodian officials sometimes made absurd requests that could not be fulfilled—like the time the minister of industry asked the GDR to ship his country several million kilowatts of electricity. "They had the simplest conception of what was possible," Dach explained. Besides making "unrealistic demands," they also suffered from what he referred to as a "subventionist mentality." And there were "communications problems," too. In contrast to Africans, who were "open" and "poured out their hearts," Dach remarked, it was difficult to know what the Cambodians were "really thinking" behind the ubiquitous "Asian smile."[78]

Whatever reservations East Germans may have had, various forms of aid—and explicit Cambodian requests for assistance—continued to flow throughout the 1980s. Most aid requests were personally approved by Honecker himself, to the tune of roughly $5 million annually.[79] And when something went amiss, Dach would sometimes help out personally—as he did when dozens of East German trucks stopped working one month after their arrival. The ambassador, a trained mechanic, responded to this "public-relations disaster" by driving out to investigate the problem himself. He hopped into one of the vehicles, popped the hood, and discovered that the drivers had forgotten to clean the oil filter, so he showed them how to do that and how to repair the damaged cooling system.

Erhard Haubold, the *FAZ*'s Southeast Asia correspondent, recalled this story years later. Like Michael Sontheimer, he was able to establish close contact with Dach, an "agreeable figure" who, in contrast to other East Germans, could "speak relatively openly." Haubold suspected that the ambassador had gotten into some "trouble" for meeting "so often" with Western journalists, but he said Dach "couldn't care less because he was an authentic member of the working classes."[80] In any event, such contacts were rare moments of German-German harmony at the height of the Cold War, including in Cambodia, where humanitarian aid remained a source of competition and mutual recrimination, with each side accusing the other of not doing enough.

Aid continued to flow to Cambodia throughout the decade, but not from the West, which sent relief instead to the refugees in Thailand. This angered some visiting West Germans, like Sontheimer. "Whenever I visit the miserable hospitals in Cambodia or walk through the run-down parts of Phnom Penh," he wrote in 1990, "I am overcome by a feeling of shame—and anger. It is simply a disgrace that 'my' government—one of the richest in the world, mind you—boycotts this poor land out of ignorance and anticommunist solidarity."[81] That was not the only source of tension. The Cold War competition between the two German states spilled over into the diplomatic arena as well. As we shall see, this culminated in a protracted struggle over who had the right to represent Cambodia at the United Nations—the new government or the deposed Khmer Rouge—with the Federal Republic grudgingly giving its support to the perpetrators of the recent genocide.

4

No One Can Say They Didn't Know

In the fall of 1979, just as stories of the Cambodian hunger catastrophe were filling the news, the West German Foreign Office received a series of letters from concerned citizens disturbed by a recent decision at the UN General Assembly. On September 21, the Federal Republic had voted with a majority of Western states to continue recognizing the deposed Khmer Rouge as the legal representative of Cambodia.[1] "Are the representatives of the Federal Republic who did this the same ones who otherwise claim at every official ceremony that their highest principles are freedom and respect for human beings around the globe?" one man from the Ruhr industrial region wrote indignantly to Foreign Minister Hans-Dietrich Genscher. "Are they perhaps also the same ones who proclaim that the Holocaust . . . was the German people's greatest shame?" A literature professor at the University of Münster wrote to Genscher in a similar vein, holding the government to its own professed standards and asking it to practice what it preached:

> It's been known for years that the so-called Pol Pot government in Cambodia wiped out probably 1 million of its own people and may have thus surpassed the bestiality of Nazism. . . . Despite that, Mr. Minister, you have instructed our representative at the UN, [Rüdiger Freiherr] von Wechmar . . . , to recognize the gangs that directly carried out organized genocide. . . . This [is]

like jurists conferring before the gates of Auschwitz about whether the SA or SS have the right to administer the death ovens. If the federal government's position here is supposed to be realpolitik, then realpolitik has become a form of insanity.[2]

The mainstream media joined in the chorus of criticism, with one commentary in *Die Zeit* calling the vote a "macabre spectacle." Another wryly observed that Ambassador von Wechmar—who, two years earlier, had refused to applaud for Pol Pot at a ceremony in China, saying he did not "clap for mass murderers"—had now voted for the Khmer Rouge at the UN: "Once again, moral principles have become victim to interests." A series of letters to the editor in *Der Spiegel* were equally damning. It was "amazing" that the federal government, "despite the experiences we Germans have with dictators," gave political recognition to Pol Pot's "genocidal system." Another was even more pointed: The recognition of the Khmer Rouge made West Germany itself "an accessory to genocide." The government was attacked from all sides of the political spectrum—from *Unsere Zeit,* the organ of the (West) German Communist Party, which accused Bonn of pure "hypocrisy," to a group of Christian Democrats in Lower Saxony who wrote to their local parliamentarian that they "could not fathom" how the government could recognize a regime "responsible for the death of some three million people."[3]

Domestic criticism did not let up, and explicit, no doubt instrumental comparisons to National Socialism continued apace. Another letter to the editor in *Der Spiegel* in April 1980 angrily declared that the "photos from Phnom Sampeau and Buchenwald, from Dachau and Kampong Cham" were all similar: "Do foreign policy officials in Bonn have a modicum of decorum and dignity left?" Another claimed that the recognition of the "Pol Pot mass murder regime" was analogous to condemning the Allied invasion and then recognizing Hitler's government as the legal head of Germany.[4]

Those who appealed directly to Genscher about the vote at the UN, including the members of a high school senior class in Hessen, received almost verbatim responses from the Foreign Office. The government, they were assured, "shares" their concern about the "fate of the Cambodian people," had publicly and "utterly condemned" the "murderous"

Pol Pot regime, and was now doing all in its power to assure the "survival" of the Cambodians by providing humanitarian aid to the region. The Federal Republic had voted as it had, the official responses continued, for two main reasons. The first touched on procedural issues of a technical nature. One had to respect the decision of the UN Credentials Committee, which had earlier recognized the Khmer Rouge as Cambodia's legitimate representative and just reaffirmed that decision a day before the vote on September 21. But there were geopolitical considerations as well. A vote against the Khmer Rouge would have signaled approval of the Vietnamese invasion of Cambodia, an "act contrary to international law" that had caused "new misery" in the region. In short, officials claimed, the main issue at stake was the inviolability of state sovereignty. But the issue was not that clear-cut, given fundamental tensions in the UN Charter between those sections that promoted respect for human rights and those that defended the principle of state sovereignty. In any event, Helmut Schmidt privately told French president Valéry Giscard d'Estaing, one could not "convey the impression" that one "tolerates a Great Power taking punitive action against a neighbor."[5]

That line of argumentation found support among some influential voices in the media. Foreign correspondent Peter Scholl-Latour agreed that recognition of the Heng Samrin regime would amount to an "ex post facto justification of Vietnamese aggression." Connecting this to the Soviet invasion of Afghanistan in December 1979, he warned about the "disastrous psychological effects of such 'appeasement.'" The *Frankfurter Allgemeine Zeitung* similarly argued that the primary issues at stake were the sanctity of state sovereignty and the halting of Soviet expansion: "The unpleasant thing about principles is that they usually also must be adhered to, [even] when they benefit nasty people and [even] in rotten situations" like this one. The conservative daily then took a gratuitous swipe at the German Left for its past positions on the Khmer Rouge: "There are no panegyrists for the Khmer Rouge and their atrocities. They only existed between 1974 and 1978—precisely among those who now, to cover up [Vietnamese] aggression . . . , cannot place the number of Pol Pot's murder victims high enough."[6]

That same day, the more liberal *Süddeutsche Zeitung* took the opposite tack, caustically commenting that "the world's conscience has found a permanent disposal site in the glass house on the East River," where everyone agrees that "'interference" in the internal affairs of a sovereign state is the "cardinal sin of our century." This doctrine makes the outside "removal of mass murderers" like Idi Amin or Pol Pot "a greater crime than their misdeeds." In fact, other journalists pointed out, the Federal Republic and other Western countries had recently adopted a double standard, essentially turning a blind eye to Tanzania's invasion of Uganda and violent deposition of its brutal dictator in April 1979. The seeming difference, *Der Spiegel* explained, was that Tanzania, in contrast to Vietnam, was not a political ally of the Soviet Union. Pol Pot was "too important a chess piece" for the West and the Chinese, in their global "games" with the USSR, "to do without him." Geopolitical considerations and the Cold War evidently trumped all else.[7]

Years later, former chancellor Schmidt showed little understanding for such criticism. He did not specifically recall the decision to recognize the Khmer Rouge, but he strongly doubted that "morals" would have influenced his government's course of action. The Federal Republic's "vital interests" eclipsed such considerations, he said, and in the realm of foreign affairs, those interests consisted almost exclusively back then of the existential threat posed by Soviet nuclear weapons. Developments in Cambodia "didn't concern us," and what happened tens of thousands of miles away in Southeast Asia did not threaten West Germany "in any way." Almost all Asian countries committed acts that "violated morality," he added, but that was simply not "our affair." Schmidt said he suspected that Washington's position on the matter was likely determinative in the end. "We had enough difficulties with [President] Jimmy Carter, especially I did personally," and there had been no need to create additional tensions, given West Germany's dependence on American nuclear protection. Assuring that protection was, in a nutshell, *the* "fundamental interest" of his country and government.[8] Klaus von Dohnanyi of the Social Democratic Party, a minister of state in the Foreign Office at the time, confirmed Schmidt's recollections. The chancellor "really hated" Carter, whom he considered a "naive do-gooder" whose focus on human rights endangered détente. Besides, Dohnanyi pointed out, West Germany was not an "independent country" at that time but merely a US "satellite." There was a clear "tradition" of going along with Washington's political wishes. A less generous way of putting this was that the Germans were "just following orders."[9]

The Federal Republic's position on the recognition issue was not as clear as West German officials suggested at the time. Until just days before the vote in the General Assembly, the Foreign Office still had been seriously considering alternatives, like abstaining from the vote or—as Prince Sihanouk urged Genscher to do in a private letter—voting against both parties. An "empty chair" solution would not have been a stretch, one internal analysis reasoned, given the choice between a "*regime mauvais*" (bad regime) and a "*regime encore plus affreux*" (an even more dreadful one). West German officials sat on the fence until the last minute because they preferred that the European Community speak "with a single voice" on major issues. But on the eve of the vote, the West Europeans were almost equally divided between supporting the Khmer Rouge and abstaining altogether. In the end, five of its nine members abstained. The Federal Republic, by contrast, joined the majority of the General Assembly, including China and the United States, and cast its ballot in favor of the deposed communists.[10]

On the day of the vote, State Secretary Günther van Well instructed the West German delegation by telegram how to proceed. It was to issue a statement explaining that the decision signaled support only for "correctly observing" the UN's own established rules on accreditation. The last-minute nature of the directive strongly suggested that the decision had not been made lightly or with an entirely clear conscience. But in the end Bonn essentially accepted British and American arguments, which were shared in private on the eve of the vote. An "empty chair" solution would set a dangerous precedent, so the seat should go to the representative whose credentials had last been accepted by the General Assembly. That did not signal, van Well insisted, any "sympathy" for the Pol Pot government, "whose serious violations of the most elementary human rights we utterly condemn."[11] The decision was guided solely by *procedural* considerations.

But that was not the whole story. Just as important in the decision to recognize the Khmer Rouge were fears that a vote against the recommendation of the UN Credentials Committee might "alienate" moderate countries in the region, especially the Association of Southeast Asian Nations (ASEAN), a bloc of staunchly anticommunist states founded in 1967 with the goal of promoting regional cooperation and economic development. Its members emphasized the dangers of Vietnamese—and, by proxy, Soviet—expansion in the region, which was why it was exerting great pressure on the West to vote in favor of the Khmer Rouge.

There were several reasons why the West Germans and especially Foreign Minister Genscher were so concerned not to alienate ASEAN. For one, its members were considered an important counterweight to the Soviet Union in Asia, and thus important for regional stability. Economic considerations were just as significant. Like other industrial nations, the Federal Republic was greatly interested in increasing trade with these emerging economic powerhouses—and the gamble paid off. An EC-ASEAN Cooperation Agreement was signed in March 1980, just six months after the vote at the UN, and annual trade between nations in the EC and ASEAN would increase almost eightfold over the next two decades.[12]

Political and economic relations with China played an equally important role, as much for Bonn as for Washington. Both capitals had resumed diplomatic relations with China in the 1970s, and both were extremely interested in expanding trade in the wake of major economic reforms announced by Chinese premier Deng Xiaoping in late 1978. Beijing's alliance with ASEAN on the recognition issue therefore made the choice even clearer. "We support ASEAN, too, even if we don't like Pol Pot," Helmut Schmidt privately assured Chinese leader Hua Guofeng during his state visit to Bonn in October 1979—a visit that marked, incidentally, the start of intensive economic cooperation between the two countries.[13]

ASEAN's decisive influence was made clear at a closed meeting of the Bundestag's Foreign Affairs Committee that November, when Lenelotte von Bothmer of the SPD asked why the government had decided "for" Pol Pot. They were "certainly not happy" about the decision, State Secretary van Well assured Bothmer, and it had not been a vote "*for*" the Khmer Rouge. But a decision had to be made, "one way or another," he said, because the other members of the EC were "waiting" for West Germany's decision. "It is no longer the case that we can simply issue a directive to join the [EC] majority because they're now all waiting for us. Things have reversed themselves a little bit in that respect." This attested to West Germany's increased stature among its allies—or at least its self-perception on that score. But then the minister of state came to the crux of the matter: "*First and foremost, naturally,* we also positioned ourselves politically" with the ASEAN states, which had "implored us . . . not to abandon them on this question." It was important to have allies at the UN who would show their support when it came to matters vital to the Federal Republic, a high-ranking West German diplomat based at the UN at the time later explained: One hand washed the other, and it was important to make compromises.[14]

Whatever the reasons, the weekly newsmagazine *Stern* was not far from the mark when it later accused the Schmidt government of "kowtowing" to Beijing. Geopolitics and economics had indeed played a decisive role in the recognition issue—not just lofty "principles."[15] That cut both ways. The constellation of Cold War alliances and antagonisms meant that the GDR immediately recognized the new Cambodian regime installed by Vietnam, which was a close ally of the USSR and an archfoe of the Chinese. Peter Florin, the GDR's permanent representative at the UN, even took a leading role in behind-the-scenes maneuvering to win recognition for the Samrin regime, pursuing the matter in a series of letters to UN secretary-general Kurt Waldheim. The Khmer Rouge could not represent Cambodia at the UN, Florin argued, because it was "guilty of the crime of genocide." There was a certain irony here, given later revelations that Waldheim—who observed at the time that the situation in Cambodia may have had "no parallel in history"—had himself been implicated in Nazi atrocities in the 1940s.[16]

The East Germans took another tack as well, effectively turning arguments about the sanctity of state sovereignty on their head. A refusal to recognize the new Cambodian regime constituted a violation of state sovereignty and the UN Charter because it involved "clear interference in the internal affairs" of a member state. Besides, the Vietnamese incursion had been not an act of aggression but a defensive response to unprovoked border attacks by the Khmer Rouge. These arguments were not entirely erroneous, but they failed to persuade a majority in the General Assembly. The outcome of the recognition vote was, the East Germans believed, a serious diplomatic setback.[17]

But there was also disappointment, and even voices of dissension, within the West German diplomatic corps. In June 1980, the Permanent Mission to the UN sent an eight-page letter to the Foreign Office in which it pleaded for a rethinking of the Federal Republic's position: "Even the . . . mere appearance of support for this regime seems no longer sustainable." The report alluded to the West's tacit acceptance of Tanzania's invasion of Uganda but pointed above all to moral considerations. It had initially made sense to support ASEAN, the letter acknowledged, but the situation had changed as more and more details emerged about Khmer Rouge atrocities and their bloody cross-border attacks against Vietnam— and as it became clear that life inside Cambodia had greatly improved since their ouster.[18]

The arguments fell on deaf ears in Bonn—as did an open letter sent to Chancellor Schmidt by four dozen journalists, social workers, and medical personnel several weeks later. The cosigners, who had all recently spent time in Cambodia, argued that recognizing the Samrin regime would make it easier for humanitarian aid to reach the country.[19] But the government stubbornly refused to modify its stance on the credentials issue—and it was even less inclined to do so after the Soviet invasion of Afghanistan in December 1979, which made Vietnam's presence in Cambodia appear to be part of a new and aggressive wave of Soviet global expansion.

Foreign Minister Genscher formally decided in August 1980 that West Germany's position would remain unchanged in a second, upcoming vote, and ordered his diplomats to "work" on the country's allies to ensure a unified West European stance on the issue. Those efforts paid off, and on October 13, 1980, the Khmer Rouge received even more votes than it had a year earlier. Diplomats in Bonn crowed that "our position . . . was conducive" to Great Britain's and Denmark's decisions not to abstain this time. Whatever misgivings the members of West Germany's Permanent Mission in New York may have had before seemed to have dissipated by this point—or been shut down. In fact, the diplomats were at pains to stress West Germany's leading role in the result, claiming that within the EC, the Federal Republic was among those that had come out *most clearly* for Pol Pot's continuing right to be seated." Ambassador von Wechmar's address nevertheless acknowledged the controversial nature of their position: "I want to emphasize that we have no sympathy of any kind with the abominable regime of Pol Pot, whose infamous record of atrocities is known worldwide. Yet, we do not recognize [Vietnam's] flagrant violation of international law." Two days later, Wechmar laconically, almost cynically, wrote to the Foreign Office that his speech should satisfy "our domestic political needs."[20]

That turned out not to be the case. One week later, *Der Spiegel* published a scathing piece highly critical of the Federal Republic's vote. It quoted Ernst-Jörg von Studnitz, head of the UN mission's political department, who claimed that the votes for the Khmer Rouge had meant "'the opposite of friendship.'" But what did *that* mean? The "convoluted line of thought," explained *Der Spiegel,* was this: "Had the Federal Government or the United States voted, say, to throw out [the Khmer Rouge], it would have established under international law, according to Studnitz, that 'a regime can be chased out through use of external force, and another installed by bayonets.' Contradiction upon contradiction." A quarter century later, Studnitz was still upset about this "personal attack." A lawyer by training who later served as Germany's ambassador to Russia, he described the decision as a choice between "the plague and cholera." Since one had to choose between two "awful" contenders, he reasoned, it was better to pick the one that at least had the "veneer of legality."[21]

Even one clearly guilty of mass murder? The decision was not made, Studnitz explained, from a "moral viewpoint," with the genocide in mind. The "sole determining consideration" was international law and the principle of state sovereignty. No one "shed any tears" about the fall of the Khmer Rouge, of course, but Vietnam had invaded a sovereign country. Looking back years later, the diplomat nevertheless acknowledged that the credentials vote had been a "real balancing act." Bonn had acted correctly, he still believed, for the reasons offered at the time. But even if he and his colleagues in New York had felt differently, they would have had little choice. They received their instructions directly from the

Foreign Office in Bonn, and they had to follow those guidelines—
"whether we liked it or not."[22]

Interest in the recognition issue quickly diminished, but Germans in the
East and West did not entirely forget Cambodia in the 1980s. In major
policy speeches to the Bundestag following federal elections in 1983 and
1987, Helmut Kohl of the CDU, who succeeded Helmut Schmidt as chancellor in 1982, included short but symbolic statements demanding the
withdrawal of Soviet soldiers from Afghanistan—and of Vietnamese soldiers from Cambodia. Members of his party posed pointed questions
about Cambodia at least once a year throughout the decade, including
ones about the GDR's supposed military presence there. Herbert Hupka,
who had asked repeatedly about the plight of Cambodian refugees in the
second half of the 1970s, became the Bundestag's most dogged interrogator of developments in Cambodia the following decade, submitting
more than a half dozen written queries to the government.[23] Like Herbert Czaja, Hupka was interested in Cambodia because of his own
background as a refugee from Silesia. A former radio journalist, Hupka
was a Social Democrat who had broken with his party over *Ostpolitik*.
He joined the CDU in 1972 and was active in expellee politics, serving
for more than thirty years as the president of a Silesian expellees'
organization. His Jewish mother had survived Theresienstadt, which
may have played a role as well.[24]

Public interest in Cambodia briefly resurfaced in the middle years of
the decade following the success of *The Killing Fields* (1984), a popular
British film about Cambodia under the Khmer Rouge regime, released
in German theaters in early 1985. A year later, *Die Wochenpost* published
a remarkable report by Horst Szeponik, the East German author of a
recent biography about Vietnamese leader Ho Chi Minh. The lengthy
article, which covered two full pages in the GDR's most popular weekly,
described Szeponik's recent visit to the former Tuol Sleng prison and
Choeung Ek, one of the most infamous of Cambodia's killing fields:
"One may not forget them, as little as [one may forget] Auschwitz or
Buchenwald"—a sentiment that underscored the attention the Final
Solution was receiving in the GDR by the 1980s, even if the popular

refrain "never forget" remained much more common on the other side of the Berlin Wall.[25]

Less than six months after Szeponik's article appeared, the West German historian and philosopher Ernst Nolte published a provocative piece in the *Frankfurter Allgemeine Zeitung* focusing on the recent fixation on the Holocaust. "The Past That Will Not Pass" ignited a sharp exchange among Germany's leading historians and intellectuals. Dubbed the *Historikerstreit* (historians' quarrel), the debate raged in the pages of the West German press and generally pitted conservatives against progressives over the origins and singularity of the Holocaust. Nolte and others argued that the genocide of the European Jews was one in a long series of state-sponsored atrocities punctuating the modern era. A more controversial point of contention was Nolte's claim that Nazi crimes had been a *response* to the perceived threat of Bolshevism in the East. The backlash was immediate. The renowned sociologist and philosopher Jürgen Habermas condemned Nolte and his defenders for trying to "trivialize" National Socialist crimes and "relativize" the Final Solution.[26]

The exchange quickly became a fundamental struggle over how to interpret the past. But Nolte's 1986 commentary in the *FAZ* had a less well-known precursor. Six years earlier, the Berlin-based academic had delivered a lecture in Munich that presented in embryonic form some of the main ideas that would cause so much controversy later in the decade. His 1980 lecture is important in the context of German responses to the Cambodian genocide because it included a lengthy excerpt from a Cambodian proclamation recently published in *Neues Deutschland,* the official organ of East Germany's ruling party. In its statement, the new regime described Khmer Rouge crimes in searing detail, including the creation of "camouflaged concentration camps." That "awakens all kinds of memories," Nolte commented: the "bellicose communism" of 1917–1918 and the forced collectivization in the Soviet Union a decade later, which had led to the deaths of millions. The proclamation also recalled "memories of far older times," he continued, going back to Europe's incipient socialist movements of the nineteenth century and even earlier to the French Revolution, which had, "for the first time in European history, made the concept of annihilating classes and social groups a reality."[27]

Other memories the statement might have awoken—namely, *German* crimes in the twentieth century—were conspicuously absent from Nolte's analysis. That was not surprising. After all, he was trying to make a larger point: the Khmer Rouge followed in established *leftist* traditions, a common argument at the time in conservative circles. In fact, Nolte added, recent events in Indochina should have "made clear what, in terms of annihilating classes, nationalities, and social groups, was the original and what was the copy"—the "copy" being Auschwitz, the "fear-borne reaction to the acts of annihilation that took place during the Russian Revolution." The disturbing and intentionally provocative suggestion that the Left was ultimately responsible for Auschwitz was as much a political statement as a scholarly argument, a point Nolte made even clearer in the 1986 article that set off the *Historikerstreit*—and that referred, incidentally, to "'Asiatic' deeds": "All the attention devoted to the Final Solution . . . diverts attention away from pressing questions of the present—for example, the question of 'unborn life' or the presence of genocide yesterday in Vietnam and today in Afghanistan." In 1980, Nolte even described the exodus of the boat people as a "holocaust on water," a jarring mixed metaphor.[28]

Emerging details about the Cambodian genocide had clearly influenced his thinking on these matters, though Nolte later denied any connection.[29] The prominent place he gave to the Khmer Rouge in his 1980 lecture was telling in itself but must be seen in conjunction with something else: the shift in West German thinking about the Final Solution following the popular *Holocaust* miniseries. The 1980 lecture specifically begins, in fact, by alluding to that spectacular media event, which is significant because it suggests that the roots of the *Historikerstreit* went back to at least January 1979, when two seemingly unrelated events coincided: the fall of the Khmer Rouge and the airing of the American miniseries.

Ernst Nolte may have been the "loser" of the *Historikerstreit* in terms of mainstream public and scholarly opinion, but his ideas resurfaced in a piece about Cambodia that German journalist Mourad Kusserow published in the summer of 1989 in *Der Tagesspiegel,* a centrist West Berlin daily. That "Holocaust," Kusserow wrote, "falls in a continuous line of persecution and destruction in our century, from the extermination of the Armenian people in Turkey (1915) to the gas chambers of the 'Third Reich,' the Stalinist deportation and extermination of the people in the Soviet Caucasus, all the way to the mass murder of Biafrans, Bengalis, Eritreans, and Kurds."[30] Nolte could not have put it much better himself, which suggests just how "mainstream" some of his views had become in West Germany on the eve of unification.

All of this must be seen in the context of larger shifts in German efforts to "come to terms" with the past (*Vergangenheitsbewältigung*) in the 1980s. The decade witnessed a veritable explosion of public memory—a "memory revolution" that produced a "new infrastructure of institutional memory." It found expression in memorials, speeches, and assorted cultural products, as well as in a noticeable uptick in research by younger West German historians about the Final Solution, long a neglected scholarly topic in their country.[31] A spectacular turning point came in the spring of 1985, when President Richard von Weizsäcker delivered a much remarked upon speech commemorating the fortieth anniversary of the end of World War II. Breaking with past taboos, the president, who belonged to the more liberal wing of the conservative CDU, referred to May 8, 1945, as a day of "liberation," not defeat. He placed the blame for the war squarely on German shoulders, spoke self-critically of a "responsibility" toward the past, and described the genocide of the Jews as "unparalleled in history."[32]

The speech sent shock waves through the country, fueling, no doubt, the conservative pushback a year later by Nolte and others. But again, the groundwork for the "historians' controversy" had been laid even earlier. It was part of a larger struggle about the meaning of the past, one that was revived when Helmut Kohl became chancellor in the fall of 1982. Kohl, a historian turned politician, fervently believed that the interpretation of the past was the "key" to Germany's future, its standing in the world, and the very identity of its people. To that end, he and his advisers hoped to foster a "healthier," more "self-confident historical consciousness" that did not reduce German history to the twelve years of Hitler's thousand-year Reich, a focus they found "debilitating," especially for young Germans. Many of the chancellor's public statements may have "displayed considerable moral complexity and sensibility," but his political foes focused instead on his more questionable remarks and decisions, including a highly controversial visit with President Ronald Reagan to a German military cemetery in Bitburg in 1985.[33]

Cambodia played a subsidiary role in all this, to be sure. In fact, the story that attracted the most attention in Germany in the 1980s was the civil war that had erupted there right after the Khmer Rouge were ousted from power. The protracted military conflict pitted the new regime in Phnom Penh against three main opposition groups: the Khmer Rouge, Prince Sihanouk and his supporters, and the followers of Son Sann, a former prime minister and leader of the anticommunist resistance. Despite their mutual antipathy, the three groups put aside their political differences to create the Coalition Government of Democratic Kampuchea in 1982. International recognition was transferred to the new coalition, which made the recognition issue at the UN somewhat more palatable to critics.[34]

Tensions remained rife among the three partners, but Prince Sihanouk steadfastly defended his controversial decision to work with his former enemies. The Khmer Rouge were preferable to the Vietnamese and the Soviets, he told a West German correspondent, adding, "with an enigmatic smile," that they were "now very nice." The former rulers did indeed make several gestures to "brighten" their "dismal image." They officially distanced themselves from communism, claimed to have put their old policies behind them, and now supposedly approved of schools, families, religion, money, and even the free market. *Die Welt* reported that they were even helping to build pagodas for Buddhist monks, whom they had earlier slaughtered en masse. But these changes were seen as cosmetic in both German states, and there were good grounds for such skepticism. Pol Pot was relieved of his official positions but continued to maintain control behind the scenes. And Khieu Samphan, his successor, publicly promised to turn a small border town into a "mass grave of Vietnamese," a stark image that clearly called to mind past genocidal atrocities.[35]

Statements like these made rampant speculation about the possibility of the Khmer Rouge's return to power especially frightening to many Germans. A recurrent theme throughout the 1980s, the prospect became increasingly credible at the close of the decade, as the global Cold War wound down. A steady stream of stories about the seemingly inexorable advance of the Khmer Rouge toward the capital—reminiscent of reports from the mid-1970s—reinforced the drama, and a string of military successes made their imminent return seem likely.[36] That eventuality was met with resignation and a palpable sense of foreboding, even if the fall of the Berlin Wall and the demise of the Soviet bloc meant that most eyes in Germany were turned elsewhere at the time. The dire possibility nevertheless attracted the attention of some leading West Germans—none more so than Petra Kelly, the "symbolic figure," "undisputed star," and public face of the West German Green Party and peace movement.[37]

Petra Karin Lehmann was born in 1947 to a devout Catholic family in Günzburg, a small Bavarian market town on the Danube—and the birthplace, incidentally, of Josef Mengele, something the future Green politician often alluded to later in life. Her father, a Pole from Dresden, abandoned the family when she was a young girl, and she was primarily raised by her maternal grandmother, who, unlike the rest of the family, had refused to have any truck with the Nazis. It was from her *Omi* that Kelly first learned the progressive politics—and from the Englishes Institut, a local Catholic school run by nuns, the discipline and hard work—for which she would later become renowned.

A member of the postwar baby boom generation, Kelly grew up in the US zone of occupation. Her mother married John Kelly, an Irish American lieutenant colonel stationed in Germany, and the entire family left for the United States a year later, in 1959. Petra, who took her stepfather's last name, attended high school in Georgia and Virginia, where the young woman who had once planned on becoming a Dominican nun became a cheerleader. Kelly attended American University's School of International Service in Washington, DC, where she protested the war in Vietnam and cultivated ties to prominent progressive politicians, including Bobby Kennedy and Hubert Humphrey, before graduating cum laude.

Kelly returned to Europe shortly after graduation. She became heavily engaged in various peace and environmental activities in the 1970s and was a founding member of the West German Greens. In 1983 she served as one of the new party's first members in the Bundestag. Human rights

FIG. 4.1. Petra Kelly (*second from right*) in the Bundestag. Like Kelly, Hans-Jochen Vogel of the SPD (*far left*) also pressured Foreign Minister Genscher for more information about Cambodia. Former chancellor Willy Brandt sits between them; Marieluise Beck of the Greens is on the far right. Bonn, May 1983. dpa picture alliance / Alamy Stock Photo.

became the centerpiece of Kelly's parliamentary pursuits, and one of her pet issues was human rights abuse by the Chinese, especially in Tibet—an interest that had begun in the early 1970s shortly after the untimely loss of her ten-year-old half sister to cancer. It was at this time that Kelly began to sponsor an orphaned Tibetan girl of the same age, whose parents had died while fleeing the Chinese. Her campaign on behalf of Tibet became the one "nearest to her heart"—an issue she saw as the "touchstone of morality in international politics."[38]

Cambodia was not exactly on Kelly's radar when, in the summer of 1988, she received a letter from Xing-Hu Kuo, a Cambodian journalist living in the Federal Republic. Kuo invited Kelly to publish a statement about human rights abuses in a German-language periodical he edited, but Frieder Wolf, Kelly's assistant, counseled her not to comply because the organization seemed to lean "more to the right." In the end, Kelly decided not to submit a statement but for a different reason. A one-time declaration, she thought, would not be of much use to the Cambodian cause.[39]

Kelly nevertheless began to express an interest in the Cambodian situation several months later, just as fears began to mount that the Khmer Rouge might soon return to power. On January 6, 1989, she sent a two-page letter to Foreign Minister Genscher voicing her concern about the Federal Republic's "stance" toward a country that had experienced "one of the most horrible and brutal events in history." The Khmer Rouge, she reminded him, had committed "atrocities that are often compared to Hitler's destruction of the Jews and Stalin's mass murders." She also repeated the common complaint that Cambodia was "practically not a topic of public interest." That was a squandered opportunity, she argued, since "China's most important friends and trading partners" could influence Beijing by publicly criticizing its diplomatic and military support of the Khmer Rouge. Could the German government's lack of interest be, she asked, feigning ignorance, because the Federal Republic had voted "*repeatedly*" in favor of the Khmer Rouge at the United Nations?

> I would be grateful to you if you could . . . describe to me the political and moral reasons for such a vote. The position of the Federal Government and the Foreign Office is very depressing, and I simply cannot imagine what the political and tactical considerations were or could be that led to such an implausible policy. . . . Is it in any way consistent with the positions that you represent in the realm of human rights policy? And why has the Federal Republic not spoken a clear word in public up to now about Cambodia to the People's Republic of China? I already dread the evasive diplomatic response to this question![40]

Without waiting for a response, Kelly submitted a formal inquiry to the Bundestag four days later, essentially restating her points. She received a written reply on February 9 from Minister of State Helmut Schäfer, who sent along West German declarations made at the UN that forcefully condemned the Khmer Rouge's "gruesome" violations of the "most basic human rights." That "Pol Pot's genocidal practices can never again—may never again" repeat themselves was a point, he emphasized, that Bonn had "clearly stated . . . on every occasion," including in talks with China and ASEAN.[41]

Kelly received a handwritten letter a month later from the journalist Michael Sontheimer, an old acquaintance, who was in Cambodia working on a book. "Good to see that my research about such a remote topic like Kampuchea has had a small parliamentary echo," he wrote, alluding to a piece he had published in *Die Zeit* in December 1988 about recent developments in Cambodia. "Also good that you go to bat for the terribly afflicted Khmer."[42] Sontheimer's recent reportage was indeed an important spark for Kelly's increasing engagement. In fact, the multilingual politician was assiduously collecting newspaper clippings from the German, American, and French press about developments in Cambodia—and making copious comments in the margins, often in English. This prepared her for her next public statement on Cambodia a half year later, following the failure of peace talks among the warring factions in Paris. At a press conference in early September 1989, she blamed the disappointing outcome on the participation of the Khmer Rouge: "Who would have thought of allowing the NSDAP to participate in political discussions about Germany's future in 1945?" she demanded to know. She also used the occasion to take a jab at the Chinese. The recent "massacre" at Tiananmen Square in China's capital had made it clear, she said, why Beijing supported "precisely these criminals."[43] The East Germans could not have put it any better themselves.

At this point Kelly came out in full force on Cambodia. At a press conference on October 20, she vehemently criticized the West, especially the United States and the Federal Republic, for its position on the UN credentials issue. "How can it be that Pol Pot's ambassador still represents Cambodia at the United Nations—the same Pol Pot, under whose rule at least 1.5 million Cambodians died, beaten and starved to death, mortally oppressed by slave labor?" Kelly reminded her audience that the Vietnamese had "ended the genocide" while the West stood by and did nothing. She also censured the European and German Left for its initial response to reports about the Cambodian genocide in the 1970s. What the Khmer Rouge had done "in the name of Marx, Lenin, and Mao was, for most leftists, so unbearable that it simply had to be ignored."

This blistering attack was familiar. Conservatives and a handful of critics on the Left had made similar accusations a decade earlier. But there was a specific context for Kelly's angry outburst. She was sorely disappointed about the lackadaisical response of the West German Left to the recent events in Tiananmen Square, and about its failure to devote more attention to Tibet and other human rights issues close to her heart.[44]

Kelly concluded the press conference by calling for a Bundestag debate about Cambodia's future. And, in a press statement released on November 8—one day before the fall of the Berlin Wall—she once again attacked the "cynical policies" of the West and the Chinese. "From 1975 to 1979, the world did *not* want to see what was occurring in Cambodia, and afterward there were many who could say, 'We didn't know.' This time, however, everyone must know who the Khmer Rouge are. When they now stand once again before the gates of Phnom Penh, no one can say they didn't know"—a phrase with heavy meaning for most Germans. The implication was clear: They had a duty to act this time *because* of their own history.[45]

Several weeks later, Kelly filed a formal parliamentary inquiry that incorporated verbatim suggestions she had earlier solicited from the Cambodian journalist Kuo. She specifically asked what the Federal Republic was doing to prevent a "new seizure of power" in Cambodia. Minister of State Schäfer responded in writing on December 13, reiterating the government's staunch rejection of the Khmer Rouge, who had been "guilty of serious crimes, right up through genocide" during its "reign of terror"—the first time a government official had characterized the atrocities as genocide.[46] The two politicians would have a chance to hash out these issues face-to-face at two Bundestag debates in January and March 1990.

Petra Kelly and the entire Green caucus submitted a formal motion on January 17, calling on the government to take concrete steps that would exclude the Khmer Rouge from power. They had turned Cambodia into an "indescribable hell," the caucus declared, and their "brutal Stone Age communism" had led to the death of more than a million people. The petition placed the blame "above all" on China and the United States, but also on America's allies—"and thus also the Federal Republic." This "obliged" Bonn to do everything it could to prevent the Khmer Rouge from seizing power once again.[47]

Kelly explained her reasons for championing this issue at a press conference two days before the debate on January 25. "I have always tried to act on behalf of those who have no lobby in Bonn—never earning a headline, just derision—for example, children with cancer, Tibet, . . . Indians and today Cambodia! (The Khmer Rouge is again on the march.) Cambodia—possibly a second killing fields—that disturbs hardly anyone in Bonn." The self-righteous tone and the almost self-pitying complaint that the press and public ignored or made light of the issues she adopted were familiar fare. But it was simply disingenuous of Kelly to suggest that Cambodia had been a nonissue in West Germany. Her comments, which again included comparisons of Pol Pot to Hitler and Stalin, foreshadowed what she would say in the Bundestag two days later. China had "disqualified itself as a civilized government" for supporting the Khmer Rouge, "*docile students of Mao Zedong*" who had "systematically carried out his policies." She may not have explicitly blamed the Chinese for the Cambodian genocide, as GDR officials had a decade earlier, yet the sentiment and implications were of a kind.[48]

But "what does all of this have to do with the Federal Government?" she asked rhetorically. Chancellor Kohl and Foreign Minister Genscher should match their lofty "words" about the "struggle for human rights" with "deeds." Kelly also criticized Bonn's stance on the recognition issue—its insistence on the inviolability of state sovereignty—asking whether it was not obvious that mass murder was "much more contrary" to international law. Besides, she insisted once again, it was the Vietnamese invasion that had stopped the genocide in the first place. And that was not all. Kelly accused the government of "*never*" having said a "*plain word*" about any of this to China, out of "consideration" for economic interests and trade. She then took the Left to task once again for being so "dishonest" on this issue: "no protests, no political passion."

Her petition made it to the Bundestag's agenda on January 25— not as a motion, as she had hoped, but as the theme of a so-called *Aktuelle Stunde,* a roughly hour-long discussion that limited each speaker to five minutes.[49] Thanks to Kelly, this was the first time the Cambodian genocide was the topic of a major debate in the Bundestag. In her opening statement she began by emphasizing the likely return to power of the "murderous Khmer Rouge," whose "killing fields," she admonished once again in suggestive language usually reserved for the Final Solution, "the world should not forget." Much of what followed was a re-hashing of what she had said two days earlier at the press conference, but she added a new twist: "The Khmer Rouge also proudly point of late to weapons produced in West Germany, like, for example, the 'Armbrust' anti-tank weapon. A Khmer Rouge commander calls it the most important weapon they've ever received."[50]

The exchange that followed focused on four main issues: UN recognition, humanitarian aid, weapons deliveries, and leftist inaction. The first to respond to Kelly's remarks was Winfried Pinger of the CDU, who began by taking a characteristic swipe at those who "marched through the streets with red flags and demonstrated for the 'liberation' of Kampuchea, but didn't want to acknowledge the kind of murderous regime they supported." Those same people, he continued, then "erupted in joy when Pol Pot finally took power"—prompting CDU parliamentarian Michael Glos to call out, "That's true! That must also be said for once!" It had been said, of course, by many on the right and left, including Kelly herself at her recent press conferences. Pinger's other remarks were more conciliatory. He criticized the international community for acting according to the axiom "'the enemy of my enemy is my friend,' even when he is a mass murderer"—a clear dig at the diplomatic recognition of the Khmer Rouge, including by West Germany.

The next speaker, Hartmut Soell of the SPD, took up a few of these themes. A professor of history at the University of Heidelberg, Soell agreed with Pinger that Cambodia represented a "good example of the selective perception of human rights violations by certain segments of the public, also on the Left. That must be admitted." Soell called for an immediate moratorium on all arms shipments to the region, and, like Pinger, spoke in favor of supplying direct humanitarian aid to Cambodia. It was "high time" for the international community to "atone for its grave failures" there.

The major parties were essentially in agreement on Cambodia. Minister of State Schäfer of the Free Democratic Party was given the final word, and he, too, agreed that the Khmer Rouge should not return to power, that China bore a "heavy responsibility" for the situation in Cambodia, and that all arms shipments to Cambodia should stop. The minister of state then dropped the first of two proverbial bombs. The Federal Republic, he announced, would provide *direct* aid to Cambodia— an important policy shift related, no doubt, to the ongoing peace talks in Paris. And just as it seemed that the discussion would contain few other surprises, Schäfer made a series of equally remarkable statements about the recognition issue: "That that was an unfortunate decision is clear to us all here, and I have . . . repeatedly pointed out that [recognition] was not a very fortunate solution." It was the first time a government official had made such a concession in public. Petra Kelly must have had good reason at this point to feel satisfied about the direction the discussion had taken.

Schäfer's final point responded to Kelly's remarks about the antitank weaponry. The government had never received or approved a request for the sale of this weapon, he said, but if the Khmer Rouge had indeed received the Armbrust, this needed to be investigated. In any event, it "did not occur with the approval or knowledge of the Federal Government." It was this issue that apparently attracted the most public attention. In late February, Kelly received a letter from a man in Schleswig-Holstein asking if she could provide any evidence about West German arms deliveries to the Khmer Rouge. That would, he believed, spark enormous public "outrage. . . . You would find great support for your motion, since *nobody in this country can forget* . . . the *unbelievable massacre*" the "Chinese-backed" Khmer Rouge had committed "against *their own population.*" The next month, she received a letter from a young woman in North-Rhine Westphalia, who, along with a dozen friends, had written to their CDU representative in the Bundestag demanding to know whether he believed that arms shipments to the Khmer Rouge were "justified." After all, this was a "terror organization of mass murderers" who were "in no way inferior" to the Nazis.[51]

The second discussion of Kelly's petition took place on March 15, 1990—just three days before the first free elections were scheduled to take place in the GDR.[52] Kelly dismissed Minister of State Helmut Schäfer's explanation for the government's recognition policy as mere "wordplay"—a reading that singularly failed to acknowledge the important concession he had made at the last debate. Kelly then rehashed her criticisms of Washington, Peking, and Bonn, lambasting the German government for caving in to American leaders like Henry Kissinger and George Bush, who "openly admit to following the Chinese line completely" on Cambodia. "Their Vietnam trauma apparently weighs more heavily" on them than the "disgust" anyone with "normal sensibilities" would feel about the Cambodian genocide. "Without Chinese arms deliveries," she continued, "the notorious 'killing fields' . . . would have never existed."

Freimut Duve of the SPD came out strongly in support of Kelly, who worked with him on the Foreign Affairs Subcommittee. He began his comments with a characteristic flourish, calling the genocide in Cambodia "the second greatest crime against humanity after Auschwitz." In a confusing soliloquy in which he compared a current Khmer Rouge officer to Heinrich Himmler, Duve—the illegitimate son of journalist Bruno Herzl, a Croatian Jew and the great-nephew of Theodor Herzl—then lambasted the international community for having failed "to put an end to this mass murder." He also lectured Schäfer, saying that Cambodia could "no longer be treated like a side issue. . . . We will no longer allow the federal government to deal with the topic of Kampuchea as casually" as it had in the past. This was curious coming from a member of the SPD. After all, Helmut Schmidt had been chancellor when West Germany's policy toward Cambodia was first formulated. "We, as the opposition party, will probe here much more deeply," he ominously warned, concluding with a "personal" nod to Petra Kelly "for being the only one among us who has stuck to her guns" on Cambodia.[53]

The next speaker, Hildegard Hamm-Brücher of the FDP, also called for greater attention to Cambodia, wondering aloud whether their country's "entire foreign policy [was], at present, too Germany- or Europe-centered" and whether West Germany did not, as a member of the United Nations, have a "global responsibility" to act. There was "no excuse" for observing human rights violations in Cambodia "from the sidelines" and only issuing "verbal statements"—an astonishing declaration from someone who had herself temporized on the Cambodia issue as state secretary in the Foreign Office in the late 1970s.[54]

The hypocrisy did not go unnoticed by Helmut Schäfer, who delivered a withering response. "One acts here as if Frau Kelly had personally discovered the Cambodia conflict." If that were the case, he demanded to know, why had others not broached the topic earlier? Acting as if the government's critics had "alone grasped global morality" and suggesting that "the rest of the world had done nothing" was simply "intolerable." This "moralistic posturing"—a common conservative criticism of Kelly and the Left—was getting "on his nerves," Schäfer continued. He then turned to the specific issues at hand. "You say we should try to get China to stop supporting the Khmer Rouge. Excuse me, but *you* try to achieve that with China! We're also trying, but it's not so simple."[55] Schäfer then huffed that one should "not act" as if the UN seat had been assigned to the Khmer Rouge because of some "unbelievable failure to recognize the situation" there. At the conclusion of his speech, Annemarie Renger, vice president of the Bundestag, commented dryly that the minister of state had been "very feisty today."

Kelly's motion was sent to the parliament's Foreign Affairs Committee for further consideration, and the Bundestag received its recommendations three months later. They were essentially a watered-down version of Kelly's original motion, full of vague formulations and without the intense rhetoric—in essence, the lowest common denominator of what she had called for. A large parliamentary majority accepted the recommendation on June 22, and Kelly spoke briefly following the vote, expressing her satisfaction with the outcome. She reiterated her provocative points about German responsibility for developments in Cambodia and concluded with pointed language clearly intended to evoke memories of Germany's own genocidal past. The "survivors of the Cambodian holocaust," she ominously warned her colleagues, were facing another "seizure of power."[56] Kelly's pet foreign policy issue may have been China and Tibet, but she clearly knew which themes hit closest to home.

5

Even Angels Live Perilously

A bitter tribute appeared in the popular *Bild-Zeitung* in October 1993 to honor Alexander Arndt, one of several hundred German combat medics deployed to Cambodia after the signing of a peace treaty that finally ended the decade-long civil war:

> *We grieve. It is* the first German soldier to fall on a military mission since World War II. *Fallen*—for what? *For the promise* of a new, peaceful world? Dutifully carrying out Germany's contribution to the UN? *Dying*—for an idea? *Soldiers have,* in German history, already died for too many ideas.[1]

Sergeant Arndt had been fatally shot in downtown Phnom Penh with a bullet to the heart, just weeks before he and his colleagues were scheduled to return home.

The exact details of what transpired on the evening of October 14 were unclear, but it seemed that Arndt and a companion had driven their jeep through a puddle and inadvertently splashed a group of young Cambodian men. They wanted to "hurt my feelings," one of the arrested men later protested.[2] There was a good deal of speculation in the German media about the motive for the killing, but also general agreement that it was not political in nature: neither the work of the Khmer Rouge nor a "targeted attack" against Germans qua Germans. That last point seemed to be a serious preoccupation, underscoring just how concerned the country still was about its image abroad, decades after the end of World War II. There was little cause for concern on that score. The vehicle displayed UN insignia, but it was impossible to identify the nationality of the occupants. Besides, the weekly newsmagazine *Focus* commented, "The German combat medics are well-liked." Rather than being political in nature, the media speculated that the shooting was alcohol related. The following day was a major holiday in Cambodia and thus the occasion for excessive drinking. Others suggested a different motive—namely, a "delight in killing," an explanation some Germans had proffered in the late 1970s to explain the wanton behavior of the Khmer Rouge.[3]

The disproportionate reaction of the young men who, "filled with rage" and firing gunshots, had chased the jeep aboard a moped was not altogether surprising. There was a good deal of anger in Phnom Penh about UN personnel, whose reckless driving had supposedly caused many accidents there. They "act in a morally corrupt way in our city, behave boorishly, and adopt a rough tone" in their everyday interactions with the local people, one young Cambodian complained to a German journalist shortly after Arndt's murder—a charge many Germans themselves had leveled at foreign occupation forces in their own country during the Cold War.[4] By all reports, that was *not* true of Sergeant Arndt and the other German medics. Arndt, twenty-six years old at the time of his death and engaged to be married, had arrived in Cambodia that June. Originally from a village in Lower Saxony, the state that had taken in so many refugees from the region a decade earlier, he had joined the armed forces, the Bundeswehr, in the mid-1980s and was in Phnom Penh mainly tending to babies in the intensive care station of a German-staffed hospital, the Federal Republic's main contribution to the mission.[5] Arndt was the seventy-first member of the UN deputation to die in Cambodia but the first—and last—German fatality. That his senseless death occurred just weeks before the mission was scheduled to end only heightened its poignancy.

Given the increased attention to the Holocaust since the close of the 1970s, it is tempting to ascribe united Germany's participation in the

Cambodia peacekeeping mission to the ongoing efforts to "come to terms with" and somehow "make up for" the darkest aspects of the Nazi past. After all, what could be more fitting than the scene of arguably the most horrific genocide since the mass murder of European Jewry now serving, for humanitarian reasons, as the stage for the first large-scale, foreign deployment of German soldiers since 1945? Just two years after national unification, it would have made for a fairy-tale ending for the land of (sometimes morbid) fairy tales. But memories of the Holocaust do not seem to have played much of a direct role in the decision to send medics and border guards to Cambodia in late 1991. Officials offered different reasons: their country's duty to the international community, and its greater global responsibility following unification and the recovery of full national sovereignty; the belief that a successful deployment would burnish Germany's international reputation and prepare the path to participation in future operations of a more expansive nature. And that was precisely what worried opponents of the mission.

The mission was the product of an October 1991 peace treaty that had capped years of feverish negotiation between the Vietnamese-backed regime in Phnom Penh and the rebel groups that made up the Coalition Government of Democratic Kampuchea. The Federal Republic eventually joined and signed the agreements in April 1994—just as another genocide, this time in Rwanda, was getting under way. The warring factions had come together for talks for the first time in Indonesia in July 1988, when the international situation was evolving dramatically. As the Cold War wound down, China and the Soviet Union had begun to withdraw from regional conflicts like this one, and Vietnam announced the removal of its own soldiers from Cambodia in January 1989. Six months later, a major international conference convened in Paris, with representatives from all the Khmer factions, the permanent members of the UN Security Council, and more than a dozen foreign ministers. Negotiations focused on a peace proposal similar to one adopted several years earlier to end a protracted conflict in Namibia—former German South West Africa. After another year and a half of intense negotiation, a peace plan was finally signed in Paris on October 23, 1991. One of its most important features was the deployment of UN peacekeepers—so-called Blue Helmets or Blue Berets—to the war-torn country. Their primary task was to oversee a cease-fire and the holding of democratic elections.[6]

The German government formally decided at a cabinet meeting in April 1992 to participate in the United Nations Transitional Authority in Cambodia (UNTAC), the largest full-scale UN mission of its kind up to that point. Secretary-General Boutros Boutros-Ghali had specifically invited the Federal Republic to participate, and the first German detachment arrived in Cambodia in November 1991 as part of an advance medical mission. The main contingent eventually included hundreds of emergency medical personnel and border guards from the Federal Republic. Rudolf Seiters, the minister of the interior, emphasized that the request had come "not least" because of the "positive impression" West German border guards had made during the recent UN mission in Namibia. A German physician, Peter Fraps, was even placed in charge of the entire UNTAC emergency medical team—a "sign of great confidence in 'Germany,'" he later crowed, and "a great honor for me personally."[7]

The unarmed German combat medics worked together with 400 medical personnel from other countries. Their main task was to provide care for UNTAC's 22,000 soldiers, police, and civilian officials. The mission's 75 German border guards belonged, for their part, to an international "civil police" force consisting of 3,500 officers from more than thirty nations. Their responsibilities were twofold: training and overseeing local police and political parties to ensure that national elections, scheduled for May 1993, would be "peaceful and fair," and helping to oversee the safe repatriation of some 370,000 refugees still living on the Thai-Cambodian border.[8] The first contingent of 140 German combat medics included 30 doctors. All were volunteers and all were men, except for one "delicate" female administrative assistant, as the *Süddeutsche Zeitung* indelicately put it. They left Munich for Cambodia in the early spring of 1992—just as another war was getting under way, this time in Bosnia—and were later replaced by fresh teams. Altogether, some 450 German medics served in Cambodia between November 1991 and October 1993.[9]

This was the first time the Federal Republic had participated in a peacekeeping mission. But it was not the Bundeswehr's first mission beyond NATO territory. It had been involved in bilateral, humanitarian assistance operations since the 1960s, and, after joining the UN in 1973, had participated in a supporting role in a half dozen relatively uncontroversial ventures: in the Middle East and the Persian Gulf, in Africa and Central America. But, as Minister of Defense Volker Rühe pointed out, UNTAC represented a "new caliber" of German participation. It was not only the largest military contingent ever involved in a UN mission, but also the Bundeswehr's largest "out-of-area" assignment to date involving more than just logistics. The German Blue Berets were "writing history" in Indochina—at a time when only a minority of Germans supported such missions.[10]

The novel and controversial nature of the deployment was one reason why the Bundeswehr decided to send only volunteers to Cambodia. By late May 1992, more than 1,200 active soldiers and reservists, men and women of all ranks and ages, had volunteered for the mission, most from former West Germany. The volunteers claimed that they were not doing it "just for the money" (they received an additional 4,000 DM in monthly wages). "I want to take part," one radio operator explained, because the mission was "something new, an adventure." But for those eager and willing to serve, Cambodia was more than just another outlet for the modern "thrill-seeking society," *Welt am Sonntag* believed. "I wanted to help rebuild this country," a private first class explained to a reporter. "That's a real responsibility."[11]

Some were apparently so taken with Cambodia that they extended their stays. This included one man who had married a Cambodian and found himself in "no hurry" to return to Munich: "I like this country. The people are warmhearted and open." Like those West Germans who had worked with Rupert Neudeck a decade earlier, one reservist, an eye-ear-and-nose specialist from Bavaria, closed his practice for three months to volunteer—and "to show the international public that our Bundeswehr also acts responsibly." He was joined by Vata Leng, a twenty-three-year-old Cambodian conscript who had received political asylum in the Federal Republic in 1980 and later trained as an automobile mechanic in the Bavarian town of Grafing. Leng and the other volunteers, who referred to him as "the little one," all insisted on the "usefulness" of their assignment—in any event more "useful," Leng added in

FIG. 5.1. Minister of Defense Volker Rühe visits German Blue Berets. Phnom Penh, May 1992. dpa picture alliance / Alamy Stock Photo.

"perfect German, with a slight Munich accent," than repairing tanks in the Bavarian capital.[12]

The primary task of the German contingent was to provide medical care for UNTAC personnel, but its members were also permitted to help injured or sick Cambodians in emergency situations. News quickly spread about the excellent care they provided, at no cost, and soon there were several dozen Cambodians lined up every morning in front of the German field hospital located in the northern part of Phnom Penh. Chief Medical Officer Fraps boasted that the four-story, sixty-bed clinic—dubbed by locals the "German Hospital" and later the "House of Angels"—would one day become the "most modern" ever seen in Cambodia.[13]

During a "lightning visit" to Cambodia in late May 1992, Minister of Defense Rühe insisted that the mood of the German Blue Berets was "brilliant." That was not entirely accurate. Some of the medics were already making "critical noises" about UN guidelines stipulating that local patients were to be handled as a lower priority than UNTAC personnel. This was not how they had pictured a humanitarian mission, several complained, especially since many members of UNTAC were being treated for venereal diseases and traffic accidents caused by their own reckless behavior. They act "like occupiers," one disillusioned German private confided to a journalist, echoing the criticism voiced by many of the city's inhabitants.[14]

Relations between the Cambodians and the medics, whom locals took to calling the "Angels of Phnom Penh," were idyllic, by contrast—at least according to the German media. The medics expressed "astonishment" at the Cambodians' "friendliness and beauty," their "impressive hospitality and cooperativeness." In turn, the medics were extremely "popular" among the locals. Small wonder. They were known to distribute chocolate bars and other food from their rations to local children, a practice reminiscent of Germany's own occupation right after World War II. Many even spent their free weekends providing care for the sick in nearby villages. "We can't just close our eyes to the suffering," one dental surgeon explained. A physician from Hamburg even threatened to "go back home" if they were forced to stop helping "the natives."[15]

The medics continued to provide treatment for large numbers of civilians, at first with tacit and eventually explicit approval from officials in Germany. Over the course of the seventeen-month mission, about a quarter of the almost 100,000 patients who received treatment were Cambodians. But because this cost time and money, it led to growing frictions with UNTAC officials, who complained that it was a waste of limited resources. The German government tried to defuse tensions by increasing the number of hospital beds and paying out of pocket for care provided to the local population.[16] But there were other sources of discontent among the medics: about pay levels and insurance coverage, about poor hygienic conditions and the lack of necessities like running water, mosquito nets, and proper uniforms suitable for Cambodia's tropical clime. "You're housed worse than asylum seekers in Germany," quipped Alfred Biehle, the Bundeswehr's ombudsman, who accompanied Minister of Defense Rühe during his 1992 visit. The German military was simply not prepared for "out-of-area" missions, concluded *Die Welt*. But they were "better off than the Australians, who live—without complaint—on bare floors in tents."[17]

Fraps blamed these assorted shortages and mishaps on UN bureaucracy, and many medics heartily agreed: "Of all people," they supposedly "sigh[ed] with new-German uninhibitedness, the Poles are responsible for logistics: 'Polish economics!'"—a reference to a negative stereotype popular since the late eighteenth century. One young staff doctor similarly confided to a visiting journalist that he would have preferred to have *German* "pioneers" (the soldiers responsible for engineering and construction tasks) because one could not rely on "what the other countries provided." In the future, he added, "Germans should man the key positions." National pride and prejudice were clearly alive and well, and some UN officials responded in kind. "This time it is the Germans who lag behind their legendary efficiency," groused one Japanese member of UNTAC.[18]

Such tensions were a source of concern to German officials, who were at pains to make sure that the medics and border guards did not give offense, attract too much attention to themselves, or behave in a way that might have given rise to stereotypical complaints about the German "national character." The Germans stationed in Cambodia wanted to do well during their "UN premier," Matthias Naß reported in *Die Zeit*—"as is their custom." But, he added, officials worried about the impression this might make. That was why Dr. Fraps, who was "surely familiar with the talent of his countrymen to make themselves unpopular through their demonstrative efficiency," immediately proclaimed, "Eyes up, ears open, mouth closed whenever possible."[19] German officials had taken this injunction to heart even before the soldiers arrived. In an article revealingly titled, "As Inconspicuous as Possible," *Der Spiegel* reported that Bonn had "restrained itself" at the UN during a month-long "tug-of-war" over the distribution of tasks in Cambodia, with other countries wrestling for a "part of the action that was as conspicuous and important as possible." National differences in style continued once the mission began. Other countries used their air force to transport troops and material to Cambodia, for example, but the Germans relied on civilian aircraft. That was not all: "Right after their arrival, the French christened their neighborhood the 'Quartier français,' and the Australians hung flags and pictures of kangaroos from their barracks. All the armies wear the name of their country on the epaulets of their uniform—only the Bundeswehr does not. The word 'Deutschland' is not seen anywhere."[20]

Within months, many Germans apparently became less cautious about national displays and less concerned about acting with the requisite "modesty" expected by their superiors. "They self-confidently display flags on the road to the Pochentong airport," Matthias Naß reported in a follow-up story in *Die Zeit,* and the "black-red-gold [the German flag] waves next to the blue of the UN" atop the field hospital. There were "no historical qualms about the mission there," Naß added by way of explanation, because the "bloody trail of German conquering expeditions" did not "reach all the way to Indochina." The Germans nevertheless had a "special status" in Cambodia, and that apparently rankled. For that reason, Klaus Naumann, general inspector of the Bundeswehr, suggested to Rühe that a special medal be given to those who served in Cambodia. "That's good," one medic commented approvingly. "Then our chests are no longer so empty, compared to soldiers from other nations."[21] Having a special status did offer certain advantages, of course. For one, it meant that they would not be sent on combat missions and thus come in harm's way.

Whatever anger and resentment, whatever feelings of inferiority existed, the mood was positive, by and large, and most of the medics were reportedly "proud" to be among the first Germans to participate in such a large, multinational affair. "We are pioneers," one nurse explained, adding that humanitarian work was personally "satisfying"—a sentiment that accorded nicely with how officials were trying to sell the mission, namely, as a humanitarian one. That was important in a country still wary of military engagement abroad, no matter what its nature. But the mission in Cambodia was intended just as much for international as for domestic consumption. Such humanitarian activities were "tremendous capital" for Germany's image abroad, Minister of Defense Rühe acknowledged. And because government officials wanted their country to be seen as a "reliable partner" for future missions, they wanted to make sure that the current one ran as smoothly as possible—a likely reason they anted up the money for treating Cambodian civilians, rather than haggling with the UN over medical costs. The Federal Republic paid 280 million DM for the mission in toto, covering approximately 9 percent of UNTAC's entire budget.[22]

Germany generosity did not meet with universal acclaim back home, where the high costs of unification were imposing serious financial strains.[23] Sending UN peacekeepers to Cambodia nevertheless enjoyed widespread domestic support in the Federal Republic, costs aside. The decision to send *German* ones quickly became a major source of controversy, however. The dispute focused on the legality of German military participation in out-of-area assignments. Government officials had "no qualms" about this. The Cambodia mission, they argued, fell within the parameters set by the relevant passages of the German constitution; it was a position legal scholars and a handful of conservative politicians had embraced since the 1970s.[24] According to an editorial in the *FAZ*, the constitutional "prohibition" of out-of-area missions was an "invention" of Hans-Dietrich Genscher. The foreign minister had "cultivated that invention for so long" that many politicians now "recognized it as useful and convenient." But the issue was not always so clear-cut. Prodded by Washington, West German leaders on both sides of the aisle had countenanced such missions in the 1960s. In a sense, the debates of the early 1990s—about Cambodia, later about Bosnia—were throwbacks to ones that had taken place decades earlier.[25]

The Social Democratic Party, the Greens, and even the union that represented the members of the Bundeswehr were much more skeptical about the government's current position on the matter. Any military deployment to Cambodia was in a constitutional "gray zone," their representatives believed, and that made its legality unclear. The Social Democrats nevertheless voted in favor of the deployment, but they demanded, at the same time, that the constitution be amended to allow for future peacekeeping missions. This was the "last time" they would allow themselves to be "eased into this 'legal gray zone,'" they warned Minister of Defense Rühe, because the "next instance would create customary law." Even though a member of the governing coalition, the FDP joined the oppositional SPD in calling for a constitutional amendment—a position both parties had also made clear during the Gulf War of 1990–1991. Party whip Werner Hoyer, echoing concerns about a constitutional fait accompli, cautioned the Ministry of Defense not to act as if such a change had already been made. "In the interest of the Bundeswehr soldiers," he declared, "we Liberals won't tolerate such salami tactics."[26]

The SPD and Free Democratic Party were thus open to German soldiers serving as Blue Berets in humanitarian peacekeeping missions organized by the United Nations, but only after the constitution had been modified. This was a position Chancellor Kohl initially supported, but not the members of his own party, who did not believe an amendment was necessary and who generally opposed any restrictions on Bundeswehr missions abroad.[27] Leaving aside the delicate constitutional issue, the Christian Democrats, the FDP, and the SPD were all largely in agreement about *why* Germany should participate in such missions. Its duties and responsibilities as a member of the UN were one important reason, even more so with the acquisition of full national sovereignty following unification in October 1990. The government and most conservatives even argued that, as a signatory to the UN Charter, the Federal Republic was *required* to engage in missions like the Cambodian one. The SPD did not disagree per se. "Precisely by supporting and participating in UN peacekeeping measures," SPD chair Björn Engholm allowed, the country "can demonstrate that the new, unified Germany acts cautiously and responsibly with its power." But, he added, that did not mean that Germany's new "global responsibility" was "best demonstrated by participating in global combat missions."[28] No one seemed to be suggesting otherwise, for the time being. Even the leftist *Frankfurter Rundschau* agreed that the mission in Cambodia was a "recognition of German responsibility to the community of nations" and that the country's altered international status meant that it was "no longer" stuck in the "wake of world history," as it had been during the Cold War.[29]

The new consensus seemed to be, then, that Germany could no longer be content to be an "economic giant" but a "security-policy dwarf," and that a failure to step up on this issue would only hurt Germany's reputation abroad. Others put a more positive spin on it. The FDP's Klaus Kinkel, who succeeded Hans-Dietrich Genscher as foreign minister in May 1992, argued that Blue Beret missions were important for "burnishing" Germany's international credibility. "Wherever our soldiers are on a humanitarian mission, they are . . . also German ambassadors for peace," his colleague Jürgen Koppelin agreed. "And with that," he added, "they render a great service to Germany abroad" in light of its history.[30]

German leaders well understood the challenges their country faced because of its dark past. The "misfortune" that "our country" caused in Europe and the world was simply "too great," FDP party chair Otto Graf Lambsdorff argued in a carefully worded editorial in the *Passauer Neue Presse.* That was why "our neighbors' memories reach beyond Germany's democratic traditions." But it was not a question now of "more power but rather greater responsibility," he wrote. The old policy of "paying" instead of "playing"—that is, of providing financial but not military support, of expecting others "to step up" instead—would only lead to resentment, to angry accusations that the country was trying to "buy its way out of responsibility." In a similar vein, Minister of Defense Rühe told the Bundestag that, in the past, "we have frequently marched ahead militarily and grievously isolated ourselves and committed crimes. But the reverse situation must not come to pass," namely, that Germany fails to fulfill its responsibilities to its partners in Europe and the international community. It was, in short, a question of solidarity and especially responsibility—*Verantwortung,* the buzzword of the early 1990s in the realm of German foreign affairs.[31]

Other politicians also spoke to the burden of German history but drew vastly different conclusions from it—none more so than those in the Party of Democratic Socialism (PDS), the legal successor to East Germany's ruling Socialist Unity Party. The PDS uncompromisingly opposed on principle any type of German military involvement abroad. In a parliamentary resolution submitted in April 1993, it called on the government to withdraw all military personnel from Cambodia and replace them with civilians. The willingness to participate in such missions was not just unconstitutional, the party argued. It undermined the "existing social and political consensus" that "war may never proceed from German territory." The military "self-restraint" anchored in the Federal Republic's constitution, the Basic Law, was the "lesson" from the two world wars that "Germany had provoked this century. By participating in such actions, the federal government wants to rid itself step-by-step of [that] special historical responsibility." For the PDS, self-restraint and a commitment solely to humanitarian endeavors had to remain the sine qua non of German foreign policy.[32]

Andrea Lederer, a communist lawyer originally from West Germany, was the party's most energetic proponent of these principles in the Bundestag. "Who or what compels us" to participate, she rhetorically asked her colleagues in June 1992. "Nothing and nobody besides our political will, much less the people of the world. They luckily have no need for German soldiers." The PDS was not demanding that the Federal Republic halt all assistance to Cambodia. But why could the field hospital in Phnom Penh not be run instead by German civilians, a suggestion the pacifist Greens also made? The reason was simple, Lederer ventured. The government chose this path because it was paving the way to military participation, "under combat conditions," in the future.[33]

Was there any basis for such fears? In an interview a month earlier, Minister of Defense Rühe had made it clear that the Federal Republic would not participate in a military conflict like the recent Gulf War. For one, there was "no majority" in parliament, "at the moment," that would allow for the necessary constitutional change. Just as important, he said, the German people were not "prepared . . . psychologically" for this. The "instincts" the Germans had developed over the previous forty years regarding "our restraint" in military matters could not simply be "commandeered away from above" overnight. And he was correct. A survey from the summer of 1990 found that three-quarters of Germans opposed the participation of the Bundeswehr in out-of-area NATO missions— even to stop a dictator who was breaking international law. But what one could "surely expect from us," Rühe continued, was a willingness to participate in "completely normal" Blue Helmet deployments, or *Blauhelmeinsätze*—crowned "word of the year" by one German language organization in 1992. It was unclear what "completely normal" meant precisely, but it seemed that Germany was taking a "first step" in that direction in Cambodia.[34]

Rühe and other conservatives clearly hoped to acclimate the German public to the idea of participating in future missions, eventually in a more expansive capacity. Yet, with a nod to Germany's "culture of restraint"

(*Kultur der Zurückhaltung*), and hoping to get the SPD on board, the defense minister spoke in favor only of humanitarian missions—at least for the time being: "We will not play global policeman everywhere in the world," he promised. Rühe nevertheless made it clear that he also envisioned a more expansive role for the Bundeswehr down the road, one that included combat missions. Cambodia was, in a sense, a "precursor" for "unlimited" participation in a variety of future UN missions.[35]

The policy lines were clearly drawn in a political and constitutional debate in Germany that would only intensify as the conflict in former Yugoslavia heated up. But questions about the propriety of the Cambodian mission were not the only source of controversy. Critics also complained that officials had made misleading claims about the nature of the deployment to Cambodia by claiming that it was "exclusively" limited to humanitarian assistance. Prominent public figures, including Major General Volker Grabarek, the head of the Armed Forces Medical Office, called this a "sham" and accused the government of acting with "duplicity." The medics may have some sort of "special status," commented the *Frankfurter Rundschau*, "yet, they carry small arms . . . and do what the political and military leadership of the UN mission desires."[36]

During his brief visit to Cambodia in May 1992, Rühe declared reassuringly that there was "no danger" because most of the fighting was taking place in the western region of the country and the German medical personnel were stationed in the capital. But the minister of defense sang a different tune several weeks later, when he acknowledged in an interview with *Bild am Sonntag*, a popular tabloid, that the German volunteers were surrounded by millions of land mines. "The rifles carry ammunition, not flowers, even on UN peace missions," he added, and it was possible that German soldiers could "also shoot in self-defense and even die like other Blue Helmets." A month later, Rühe informed the Bundestag that he had agreed to a UN request to deploy German combat medics outside of Phnom Penh, "in the jungle, to render medical care to a French battalion." Anticipating objections, he asked how they were supposed to "build" a unified Europe if they were "not prepared to support French soldiers in such situations?" That assignment made the mission clearly unconstitutional, SPD defense expert Horst Jungmann charged. "Despite previous guarantees," Jungmann reported after a visit to Cambodia in late August 1992, the medics were routinely flying into combat areas, where they came under fire, to rescue and treat wounded UN soldiers.[37]

The situation became more deadly the following year. More than a dozen members of UNTAC were violently killed and several dozen injured in Khmer Rouge attacks in the spring of 1993, leading to growing concern back home about the safety of the German contingent. Sergeant Arndt's killing took place several months later, in mid-October—just weeks after the infamous Battle of Mogadishu in Somalia. The reaction in Germany was remarkably placid if not fatalistic: "It has happened!" the *Bild-Zeitung* announced, while other newspapers acknowledged that dangerous missions like this always involved the risk of death. "What was to be expected has now occurred," a local paper in the eastern city of Chemnitz commented. "Even angels live perilously." Arndt's death was "disturbing but not surprising," and the appellation "humanitarian" had led to the "erroneous conclusion" that the mission was "harmless." Wolfgang Lerke, Germany's top diplomat in Cambodia, acknowledged that Arndt's death was a "very high" price to pay, but insisted it was "Germany's moral duty to support other peoples in difficult times."[38]

"I Had a Comrade," the traditional dirge of the German armed forces, was played at a ceremony accompanying the departure of Arndt's body from Cambodia, and again at his funeral back home. Officials in attendance stressed that his "self-sacrificing" death had not been in vain: "He died . . . on behalf of his fatherland and in the service of the international community," Minister of Defense Rühe remarked with diplomatic finesse. Just a few weeks earlier, the young sergeant had supposedly commented himself that "if everything goes smoothly till the end," the mission will have "served its purpose."[39]

That question—whether UNTAC had been successful—was a source of intense debate. Critics argued that the 1991 Paris Peace Agreements ending the war in Cambodia had not been strictly enforced, which was why the Khmer Rouge remained in control of large swathes of territory.[40] Government officials pushed back against accusations of failure. Addressing the last group of returning border guards, State Secretary Eduard Linter assured his audience that UNTAC had been a "great

FIG. 5.2. The funeral of Sergeant Alexander Arndt, the first German soldier to die on a military mission since World War II. Ministers Rühe and Kinkel stand in the background, to the left of the coffin. Note the UN blue helmet atop the Bundeswehr flag draping the coffin. Wunstorf, October 1993. IMAGO/localpic.

success." An "unexpectedly calm" election had just taken place in late May 1993, with a participation rate of almost 90 percent.[41] But the holding of free and fair elections was only part of the story. The Khmer Rouge had boycotted the vote and refused to demobilize, and the possibility of a new civil war loomed on the horizon.

Whatever the shortcomings of UNTAC and the peace process, Germany's relationship with Cambodia had normalized once again by this point. Full diplomatic relations resumed on February 14, 1992, and the last German medics left Cambodia on November 12, 1993. A month later, Bonn dispatched diplomat Wiprecht von Treskow to Phnom Penh to serve as ambassador there—the Federal Republic's first in nearly a quarter century.[42]

"No tyrant anywhere had ever executed a *fifth* of his own people, and yet the Khmer Rouge leader Pol Pot did precisely that in the aftermath of the Vietnam War. The future will surely remember that atrocity when it has forgotten much else about the Cold War, yet hardly anyone out-side of Cambodia noticed at the time."[43] John Lewis Gaddis's poignant assessment of the Cambodian genocide is remarkable on several levels: its personification of responsibility for that tragic event in a single indi-vidual; its implicit suggestion that the atrocities committed by Pol Pot against his own people had a special quality that distinguished them from (and seemingly made them worse than?) previous instances of state-sponsored mass murder; its bold claim about future memories of the Cold War. Each of his points is debatable, but Gaddis's final one is surely inaccurate. Many people outside of Cambodia had indeed taken notice of the atrocities, and they had done so from the very be-ginning.[44] That was certainly true for West Germany, where even the regional press reported regularly on Cambodia, and it was also true for East German officials. But, like the rest of the world, neither country took any concrete steps to end the mass slaughter. Why?

For one, a great deal of skepticism had persisted about the extent of the carnage, and the idea that a genocide was taking place had not meet with universal acceptance—far from it, in fact, and not just in Germany. The "natural, human incapacity to take their imaginations" where the refugees reports "demanded they go" was, Samantha Power has argued, one reason why American political elites adopted a policy of "nonen-gagement, noncondemnation, and noninterest."[45] Perhaps. But given Germany's *own* genocidal past and given increasing German efforts to confront that past since the 1960s, "imagining" genocide could not have been that great a leap—the use of recurrent tropes like *unimaginable* notwithstanding.

There are more plausible explanations for the German response. In the first place, officials and other observers had strong suspicions of genocide but no definitive proof. As one West German diplomat declared in May 1977, there was "hardly . . . sufficient evidence" to justify "inter-national measures." Ongoing, politically motivated skepticism about the refugee reports and an inability to verify them firsthand "blurred clarity and conviction" and allowed Bonn, like Washington, to "seek shelter in a fog of plausible deniability."[46] Besides, Phnom Penh had cut itself off almost completely from the rest of the world. Diplomatic pressure was not a possibility, which meant that "concrete possibilities" to influence

Phnom Penh were "extremely meager."[47] Cutting off trade or military aid was also a nonstarter, given the regime's strict autarchic policies.

The absence of any real interest in Cambodia, economic or otherwise, explains Bonn's passivity as well—though ties to other players in the region would play an important role in West German policy *following* the ouster of the Khmer Rouge, especially when it came to the delicate issue of diplomatic recognition. After a decade of heated domestic disputes about America's bloody conflict in the region, Indochina "fatigue" was also a factor. More to the point, most West Germans were preoccupied with pressing issues closer to home—not least, domestic terrorism. Just a week after the Khmer Rouge had come to power in April 1975, a group affiliated with the far-left Red Army Faction took (and later executed) hostages at the West German embassy in Stockholm. And just as skepticism about the refugee reports began to dissipate, the Federal Republic found itself in the midst of the long "German Autumn" of 1977, when a sensational series of kidnappings, assassinations, and even a hijacking dominated the headlines.[48]

But what could West Germans have realistically done in response to the reports of atrocities and speculation about genocide? Officials might have formally labeled it *Völkermord,* but that would have opened the government to demands that it take concrete action. Taking action was not really a concern to men like Helmut Schmidt and Hans-Dietrich Genscher, though a number of citizens and politicians did indeed call on them to act, even in the absence of a formal declaration. In any event, unilateral military intervention was not a realistic option, given the country's constitution and circumscribed global standing. No one expected the Federal Republic to get involved, least of all the West Germans, and there was no external pressure to do so either, since Washington and the other major allies were all sitting on their hands themselves.

There was another possibility. The West Germans could have filed charges in the International Court of Justice. That would have been a largely symbolic act, and in fact that is precisely what the government wound up doing: limiting itself to largely symbolic acts, like issuing critical statements; supporting an investigation by the UN; and signing off on condemnatory international declarations that had no teeth. In the end, West Germans merely looked on in horror, like the rest of the world, acknowledging the atrocities but remaining "mere bystanders"—even if some West Germans did indeed wish to do *something*.[49]

Doing something was never a consideration in the GDR. The East German government kept tabs on the brutal policies of the Khmer Rouge while keeping its own citizens in the dark from 1975 to 1978—not surprising, given the ostensible ideological affinities between the two regimes. The Khmer Rouge may have denied being traditional communists, but their atrocities were still an awkward source of consternation and embarrassment that would not have made for desirable press. In a sense, more was at stake for the East German regime. However, once it publicly acknowledged the crimes carried out by the Khmer Rouge, true believers and others who assiduously toed the party line argued that they were not really communists, because *true* communists were incapable of committing such atrocities.

That communists had indeed committed horrendous crimes was self-evident for many West Germans, who believed that Pol Pot and his ilk had simply followed long-established leftist traditions going all the way back to the French Revolution and, more recently, to the mass communist crimes of the twentieth century. That theme would resurface during the *Historikerstreit* of the mid-1980s, the intemperate debate that had partial roots in the Cambodian genocide. For journalists and politicians in the Federal Republic, the atrocities were a recurrent theme from the start, except for those on the (hard) left of the political spectrum. They, like the East Germans, had a difficult time admitting that their political brethren were capable of committing such crimes, that the dire predictions of conservative Cassandras and the CIA had been correct after all. Their silence aroused the ire of West German conservatives, who used it as an ideological cudgel to continue the acerbic political debates of the previous decade—just as the East Germans later used the Cambodian genocide against the Chinese. The main interest, for many in both East and West Germany, lay in scoring ideological points against their political foes, not in "preventing or punishing" genocide.

There were self-critical voices on the West German Left that denounced the failure in their own ranks to confront Khmer Rouge crimes more forthrightly. By contrast, almost no one in the GDR openly decried the deafening silence at home. How could they have, given the muzzling of the media and other restrictions on free speech? There was at least one exception, but it came after the fact, when the disgruntled documentary filmmaker Gerhard Scheumann took the East German government to task for ignoring the plight of Cambodians prior to the fall of the Khmer Rouge. Even if primarily a product of professional frustration, that courageous criticism cost Scheumann his career.

For all the differences, there was at least one striking similarity between responses to Cambodia in the GDR and the Federal Republic. Once the East Germans acknowledged what the Khmer Rouge had done, the suggestive language and imagery used on both sides of the Wall were remarkably alike, not least in their implicit and explicit comparisons to crimes of the Third Reich. The word *Holocaust* may not have been used in the GDR, but East German media coverage—as well as observations made behind closed doors—strongly indicate the extent to which the Final Solution had become a theme there as well. That is worth emphasizing, given the widespread perception that East Germans ignored or downplayed the mass murder of European Jewry. Their efforts to "cope" with that particular aspect of Germany's past certainly paled in comparison with those of their counterparts in the West. But even if it assumed less visible forms in the East, greater engagement in the 1980s with the genocide of the Jews points to at least one area of "convergence" between the two German states—one that may very well explain why, in April 1990, the first act of the first freely elected East German People's Chamber was to issue a declaration that explicitly accepted responsibility on behalf of the GDR for Nazi crimes against the Jews.[50]

By this point, Germans of all political stripes in the West agreed that their country had an obligation to help the Cambodians, and also thereby attempt to "atone" for past inaction. This need to atone, to "never forget," marked a significant shift in the way Germans talked about Cambodia, no doubt connected to the increased focus on what was now commonly known as the Holocaust. The growing sense of responsibility for the past would become even more pronounced and have even greater repercussions just a few years later in response to another genocide—one closer to home, in the Balkans. But the systematic murder of the Jews was not necessarily foremost in the minds of those who came to the aid of

Cambodian survivors. Their motivation was more complex than a wish to atone somehow for the past. West Germany's intense preoccupation with that aspect of their history was only just beginning; it had not yet become *the* moral litmus test for historical and political sensibilities.

A mix of humanitarian, religious, and other intensely personal factors played a role, as we have seen, but they were just part of the equation. Political considerations were more important for some, and they, too, were often related to personal experiences. Resentment about the loss of *Heimat* decades earlier, coupled with strong anticommunist sentiments, clearly influenced the political proclivities and humanitarian activities of politicians like Genscher and Herbert Czaja. For them, German history weighed heavily—although not necessarily in the way foreign observers may have assumed or wished. The dire descriptions from Cambodia elicited other historical associations besides the genocide of the Jews. Images of destroyed towns and cities, of long columns of Cambodian refugees carrying the little they possessed on rickety wooden wagons, recalled the suffering and experiences of many *non-Jewish* Germans during and after World War II. Reports that almost every Cambodian family had lost one or more members, and later claims that many Cambodians were now suppressing all memory of these events—this, too, must have resonated with German audiences.

It was this profound and often personal sense of recent history—be it the Holocaust, the mass expulsion of Germans from the East, the challenges of German postwar reconstruction, or the protracted war in Indochina—that inspired so many West Germans to come to the aid of the Cambodians. The emotive nature of media coverage, with its searing images of mass misery and starving children, only reinforced such historical associations and the widespread willingness to help. At the same time, providing aid and hands-on help stimulated a sense of pride in many Germans—*as* Germans, given their country's dark past—about their humanitarian endeavors. This translated into thousands of hours of volunteer work and millions of marks in private donations.

The compulsory nature of donation drives for humanitarian purposes makes it difficult to assess attitudes and grassroots support in the GDR. There were no East German Rupert Neudecks or Uta Ranke-Heinemanns, but of course the controlling nature of the regime made such private initiatives a nonstarter. That does not detract from the humanitarian activities of people like Ambassador Rolf Dach or the many doctors, nurses, and engineers sent by the regime to Southeast Asia, even if political and pragmatic considerations appear to have been foremost in the minds of high-level GDR officials. In the end, the "why" of such assistance—and the various ways in which the GDR and the Federal Republic both politicized the aid—mattered little to the beneficiaries, although it does explain why East German aid went to Cambodia directly, whereas West German assistance focused almost exclusively on helping those stranded in Thailand. This made the mutual recriminations that the other side was not doing enough, or anything at all, beside the point—a mere by-product of increasingly stale Cold War rivalries.

Those in West Germany who demanded that more be done frequently appealed to a sense of duty, to their society's cherished values and principles. They not only stressed the responsibility of the wealthy Federal Republic to help the less fortunate and defend human rights, but also recalled the massive amount of aid West Germans had received from their erstwhile enemies after 1945. In a similar way, GDR leaders reminded ordinary East Germans of their duty to help struggling peoples on *their* march to socialism. In short, there were demands on both sides of the Wall for each country to live up to its core values—demands that intensified after unification in 1990, when new genocides occurred, this time in nearby Bosnia and faraway Rwanda.

6

It Is Genocide and Must Be
Designated as Such

When war came to Bosnia and Herzegovina in the spring of 1992, few Germans who had followed recent developments in the Balkans were surprised. Tensions had been on the rise there since the spring of 1980, following the death of Marshal Tito, Yugoslavia's communist leader since the end of World War II—but they were also nothing new. Great regional disparities in wealth and political power had created frictions among the country's almost two dozen national, ethnic, and religious groups in the years following the founding of the Kingdom of Serbs, Croats, and Slovenes in 1918. The new country, renamed the Kingdom of Yugoslavia in 1929, may have united the southern Slavs into a single political unit, thereby fulfilling a century-old nationalist dream. But it did not herald, by any measure, a period of lasting harmony.

Tito's multiethnic partisans successfully tied down the Wehrmacht after the German invasion of Yugoslavia in the spring of 1941, but internal tensions nevertheless exploded during World War II. Almost all major sides committed unspeakable atrocities, beginning with the systematic murder and persecution of Serbs and Jews by the Ustaše, the fascist organization that called the shots in the newly independent Croatian state created by Germany and Italy. Tito's postwar communist regime cultivated a deceptive myth of partisan unity during World War II, hoping to keep a lid on memories of the many wartime crimes, including genocide. But the violence of those traumatic years left "deep traces" in the country's collective memory that fueled persistent regional and ethnic conflicts.[1]

An important turning point came in the spring of 1986, when Slobodan Milošević became head of the Communist Party in Serbia, one of the six republics that—along with Bosnia and Herzegovina, Croatia, Macedonia, Montenegro, and Slovenia—made up the Yugoslav state. During a period of waxing economic insecurity and crisis, Milošević increasingly played the nationalist card. His statements and policies eventually prompted the Slovenes and Croats to declare independence from Yugoslavia in late June 1991, a fateful decision that brought two wars in its wake, the first in Europe since 1945: one that pitted the Yugoslav Army against Slovenian forces in a ten-day skirmish, and another, against Croatian soldiers, in a much bloodier conflict that lasted seven months.

The West Europeans attempted to end hostilities by persuading the two states to delay independence, but those efforts failed—in no small part thanks to German foreign minister Hans-Dietrich Genscher, who not only insisted on recognizing Slovenia and Croatia but also exerted considerable pressure on Germany's West European allies to follow suit. His actions during this period would remain a source of vigorous debate and controversy, with critics at home and abroad blaming him for the deteriorating situation in the Balkans. Journalist Michael Thumann, who covered the region for *Die Zeit,* would later call this "unified Germany's first major foreign policy mistake."[2]

Attention in Germany first turned to Bosnia, by chance, in the very same month the warring factions in Cambodia signed a peace treaty ending their decade-long civil war. On October 15, 1991, the Bosnian parliament's Croat-Muslim majority adopted a motion effectively declaring independence, following in the footsteps of Croatia and Slovenia. But the European Community now made recognition dependent on the outcome of a referendum. Muslim and Croat leaders eagerly accepted this condition, but the minority Serbs, who wished to remain a part of Yugoslavia, rejected it, fearing the expected outcome. Their leader, Radovan Karadžić—a

trained psychiatrist and practicing poet—warned that Bosnian independence was a threat to "Serb identity" and thus a "declaration of war."
The German media was indeed full of dire warnings about a looming
armed conflict. "War is on everyone's mind," screamed one headline
in *Der Spiegel,* and all sides were "armed to the teeth." Another foreign
correspondent reported that there was "one soldier for every eight inhabitants" and that the conflict would soon be a matter of not just
"political but also physical survival."[3] Those were prophetic words.

The referendum on independence took place in late February and
early March and passed by an overwhelming majority, thanks to a boy-
cott by the Bosnian Serbs. Karadžić had warned beforehand that his
supporters would "set fire" to Bosnia if the referendum took place, and
he remained true to his word. Violence broke out during the vote and
continued after the results were announced. The spark appeared to
have been an altercation at an ethnically mixed wedding in Sarajevo,
where a Muslim man murdered the Serb father of the groom. "The
death inflamed passions beyond all measure," *Die Tageszeitung* (*taz*)
reported, and Serb forces threw up dozens of barricades across the
city—"melodramatically" using the incident as a pretext, wrote Viktor
Meier, a Swiss-born journalist and vehement critic of the Serbs who
had been covering developments in Southeastern Europe for the *Frankfurter Allgemeine Zeitung* since 1975.[4]

Isolated voices in Germany warned against recognizing Bosnian independence, but the overwhelming consensus was in favor—no surprise,
given the widespread political and emotional attachment to the principle
of self-determination, especially in the wake of Germany's own recent
unification. Support was greatest among conservatives. On returning
from Sarajevo, where he had been "trapped" for several days after serving
on an international team monitoring the referendum, the young parliamentarian Stefan Schwarz of the Christian Democratic Union commented during a television interview that the Serbs had to be brought
to "reason by force." But even the leftist *Frankfurter Rundschau* opined
that any hesitation at this point would only "encourage the aggressive
elements and provoke senseless bloodshed."[5]

Apart from the far left, Germans across the political spectrum were
banging the drum for recognition, but the Federal Republic did not take

the lead this time. The EC recognized Bosnia as an independent state on April 6, 1992, an especially poor choice of date for at least two symbolic reasons: one religious and one historical. It was the end of the Muslim holiday Ramadan that year—and the date on which Nazi Germany had launched air attacks against Belgrade fifty-one years earlier, killing thousands of civilians. No doubt more sensitive to the poor symbolism, German officials waited three days before announcing their own recognition of Bosnian independence on April 9.[6]

Whatever the validity of the arguments for and against recognition, the fighting escalated, and the first stream of reports reached Germany that spring and summer about systematic atrocities: from mass shootings and mass rapes to mass expulsion and mass imprisonment in what were quickly referred to as "concentration camps"—*Konzentrationslager,* or *KZ.* The first atrocity reports appeared in Germany on the very day Bosnia was first recognized as an independent state, April 6. Serb forces had ran amok in the town of Bijeljina, where they entered a mosque and supposedly "shot indiscriminately at believers," killing an imam. Reports about the "bloodbath" claimed that fathers had been lined up against a wall and told to pull down their pants. Those who were circumcised and thus recognized as Muslims—a procedure familiar to persecuted Jews during the Third Reich—were supposedly shot "on the spot," along with their families.[7]

Increasingly graphic descriptions of Serb atrocities appeared with great regularity in the German media that June. One married couple who had survived a massacre in the city of Zvornik described in gruesome detail what they had witnessed there in an interview that appeared in the *taz.* An accompanying photograph showed a dismembered arm, one of several "cut-off limbs" lying around on the ground: "They slashed the throats of many people and hanged them on trees in the city [while the] children looked on. . . . There is a hospital in Višegrad where handicapped children also lived. The Serbs killed all the children, raping the girls beforehand." The murder of handicapped children had obvious associations for a German audience: the euthanasia program ordered by Hitler during the earliest stage of World War II.[8]

Another story might have awoken similar associations for German readers—at least those familiar with the horrific decision the Polish protagonist of the 1979 novel (and 1982 film) *Sophie's Choice* is forced to make about the fate of her two young children in Auschwitz. The report provided details of a Muslim woman's ordeal at the Manjača prison camp. "They did everything," she explained, "tortured, raped, cut off limbs, beat, killed." She focused on an exchange with a guard about her twelve-year-old daughter and younger son. The Serbs, she claimed, had raped the former, threatened to cut off the genitals of the latter, and then forced her to choose between them:

> "Which child do you love more?"
> "I love both."
> "Then we'll slaughter both and throw them in the Sava River."
> "You'll do what you want to do anyway."
> "So, you agree . . ."

They did not follow through on their threats, and the woman and her children were later exchanged for sixty Serb prisoners, but before being released, she was branded with a "red-hot iron rod on the thigh and buttocks . . . like an animal."[9]

The Society for Threatened Peoples, a human rights organization founded by activist Tilman Zülch in the wake of the Biafra crisis of the late 1960s, organized a two-day hearing in Frankfurt that September, at which other "survivors" had an opportunity to describe the atrocities they had witnessed at a different internment camp.[10] In contrast to the response to reports about Cambodia in the late 1970s, there was little skepticism this time about the veracity of these eyewitness accounts. But, also in contrast to Cambodia, German journalists had almost full access to Bosnia and could therefore report directly from the front lines, where they personally witnessed the carnage, spoke with victims, and saw physical evidence of the atrocities. Wilhelm Höynk, the German ambassador to the Organization for Security and Cooperation in Europe, dispelled any lingering doubts during a radio interview in mid-September. More than twenty camps had already been visited, Höynk said, where civilians were being kept "under inhuman conditions . . . some in stables, which speaks for itself." The discovery later of mass graves filled with the remains of hundreds, sometimes thousands, of victims put to rest any lingering doubts.[11]

Certain themes and images dominated the media coverage. The most familiar one was Serb snipers firing "at everything that moved," including women and children fleeing war-torn cities and villages.[12] The Serb siege of Sarajevo that began in early April 1992 quickly became a mainstay of media coverage as well. That foreign journalists, including Germans, were also victims of these sniper attacks was no doubt one reason they received so much media attention—and why the tenor of most media reports was so inimical to the Serbs. There were even rumors that Serbs were offering "bounties" for journalists, a story that first surfaced after the capture and release of a German cameraman and television correspondent Christoph-Maria Fröhder, the last foreign journalist to have left the Cambodian capital in the spring of 1975.[13]

Slit throats and cut-off noses, mutilated ears and male genitals were other images ubiquitous in the media—something Stefan Schwarz memorably conveyed in an impassioned maiden speech he gave in the Bundestag on global Human Rights Day in December 1992. He offered harrowing descriptions of these and other atrocities, from mass rape to castration, from a man supposedly forced to consume his own dismembered ear to the "use of gas"—a practice that had obviously chilling associations. "Allow me to conclude with the most brutal [act], because I find, unfortunately, that this is probably necessary in Germany," a direct allusion to his country's own dark past. "On the first day they threw fifteen children, from the very smallest to five-year-olds, into the oven . . . [and] closed it" in a way that made the children "roast" instead of quickly burn.[14]

Two days earlier, Schwarz had delivered an impromptu but similarly impassioned speech about Bosnia at a closed meeting of the CDU's parliamentary caucus. When the discussion turned to the upcoming commemoration of Human Rights Day in the Bundestag, Schwarz had raised his hand and begun to summarize and quote from recent accounts in the press. "I wanted to read them the riot act," he later recalled. In his early thirties at the time, Schwarz was one of the youngest persons in the room. "What happened to the values you raised us with if we don't

FIG. 6.1. CDU parliamentarian Stefan Schwarz admonishes his Bundestag colleagues: "No one sitting here can say after this genocide ends . . . we didn't know." Bonn, December 10, 1992. Bundestag/YouTube.

get this right?" he demanded of his much elder colleagues—if, for all the talk of human rights and "never again," they were not prepared to do anything when push came to shove. It was "so quiet you could hear a pin drop" when he concluded his remarks. An hour-long discussion ensued, and at its conclusion, Wolfgang Schäuble, the caucus chair, asked Schwarz to address the Bundestag two days later—his first speech in that assembly.[15]

As a rule, Schwarz later maintained, such speeches were "incredibly unimportant"—something he knew as the son of Hans Schwarz, who had served in the 1970s as minister of the interior of the Rhineland-Palatinate under Minister-President Helmut Kohl, a close friend of the family since the late 1940s. But in this case, his speech had an explosive effect—like "a tsunami," according to Schwarz. Schäuble had alerted journalists beforehand, and the *Rheinische Merkur* reprinted his remarks in full. His office "drowned in faxes," including messages from teachers who had discussed it in class with their pupils. A gynecologist congratulated him for "finally saying what needed to be said," adding that the government's "silence" was a "disgrace" that filled him with "deep shame." Schwarz even received a letter from a pastor who had read the speech to his congregation that Sunday instead of delivering a sermon.[16]

Delivering the speech had not been easy for Schwarz, who said he had to "force his lip muscles" to read certain passages—including one about a Muslim man being forced to bite off the testicles of a fellow prisoner. He had "purposefully" included that disturbing detail, he later explained, because "80 percent" of the Bundestag was composed of "lads" (*Jungs*). They would all "grab themselves in the crotch" when they heard that, he suspected, and he wanted them to "feel" as much of the "pain" as possible. One colleague later wrote him, in fact, that the speech had moved him to tears. But it also inadvertently encouraged some in the German media to seek out the most extreme footage it could find. To the chagrin of Schwarz and his assistants, his office even received a request for images of allegedly "crucified babies."[17]

Schwarz's interest in the Balkans was relatively recent. He had never been to the region and had no ties there. That changed in late 1991 following the fall of the Croatian city of Vukovar to Serb forces, who committed a series of massacres while "ethnically cleansing" the baroque city. A Croatian woman living in the Federal Republic had provided him with graphic details of what transpired there, and that was when he decided that "something had to be done." Reflecting decades later on his subsequent activities, Schwarz pointed to his upbringing in a politically engaged, "liberal" Catholic family, where the precept "never again" played an "enormous role." What took place in Vukovar and later Bosnia was, "in principle, 'again.'" The son of a prominent politician and a devout mother who had "almost vomited" when she first heard the reports about the Nazi death camps in 1945, he and his siblings were driven by a "sense of urgency and social responsibility." And that was why, he explains, the Balkans became such an obsession. He wanted to make sure at least one politician in Germany did not "look away" and that the atrocities became part of the public record.[18]

Schwarz made Bosnia his primary focus in the coming months and years. Working together with politicians from other parties, including the Social Democrats and the Greens, he initiated a public appeal calling for armed intervention in Bosnia. He also passed along urgent requests for assistance from Bosnian officials to German authorities, including Helmut Kohl, and frequently appeared at rallies and on television talk shows and nightly news reports—which, he believed, did more to "shape" Germany's stance toward Bosnia than any parliamentary speeches. Schwarz became widely known for his "straight talk," as well as for his casual appearance, often wearing sneakers, never a tie—even when he addressed the Bundestag in December 1992. At the same time, Schwarz was heavily criticized by those opposed to armed intervention. Peter Glotz of the SPD accused him of being "in love" with the topic of Bosnia because it had suddenly transformed him from a completely "unknown politician into a relatively better known" one. Schwarz responded in kind, characterizing the position of his critics and those who merely looked on as practicing a form of "genocidal pacifism."[19]

But Schwarz was by no means the only German politician who spoke out about the "gruesome crimes"—a phrase Chancellor Kohl had used in an address to the German diplomatic corps just two days before Schwarz gave his speech.[20] Reports of small children blown apart by grenades and cluster bombs, burned by napalm or white phosphorous, beheaded in front of their mothers; stories of pregnant women with bellies that had been slashed open, of Serb forces supposedly burying victims while still alive, or placing mines under the bodies of the dead in order to kill those who tried to collect and bury the corpses. A striking photograph by the young American photojournalist Ron Haviv appeared in *Der Spiegel* of a "bloke in combat fatigues, designer eyeglasses pushed up into his stylishly cut hair, a cigarette in the left hand and a Kalashnikov rifle in the right," using his boot to kick in the skull of an old woman lying on the ground after being shot.[21] These and other shocking images, which Germans read and heard about in the press and radio and saw day after day on nightly television newscasts, provoked understandable outrage that, in turn, indelibly shaped their responses to the Bosnian conflict. These were not the sanitized videos shown by the US military during the recent Gulf War.

One of the most appalling descriptions of the atrocities was a lengthy, firsthand account by a Polish mercenary named "Tomek," whose story appeared that September in the *General-Anzeiger*, the regional paper read by government officials in Bonn. The man claimed to have been a member of a unit made up of other Eastern Europeans, including a "slew" of former East Germans who acted "like Rambo." Describing in chilling detail their "daily routine" of "murder, rape, and plunder"—as the headline put it—Tomek also related his experiences at one of the infamous "concentration camps," where he had seen "bored, half-drunk guards . . . slice open one fellow's hands and strew salt and pepper on [the wounds] to see whether he becomes unconscious. . . . I've seen them ram a Johnny Walker bottle into a young girl's vagina. For them that was a form of fun."[22]

The first sporadic reports that specifically referred to "concentration camps" had appeared three months earlier, in June 1992. But the story really exploded in early August, when the German media picked up an exposé published in the United States by Roy Gutman, stationed in Bonn as the European correspondent for *Newsday*. Based on interviews with former camp inmates—and accompanied by photographs surreptitiously taken by Andree Kaiser, a former East German who had learned in the GDR how to make himself as "inconspicuous" as possible—Gutman's reports, especially their effect, were reminiscent of John Barron and Anthony Paul's book fourteen years earlier about Khmer Rouge atrocities in Cambodia. Shortly after it appeared, setting off a flurry of reports in Germany and elsewhere, British journalists filmed prisoners behind barbed wire at a camp in the mining town of Omarska. The footage of their "emaciated, starved bodies," their "evasive, fearful glances," was broadcast around the world. This, along with reports that the prisoners were being transported in packed freight cars, prompted *Die Welt* to publish a story on August 6 under the sensational headline, "Are the Serbs Operating Extermination Camps?"[23]

There was some initial uncertainty and skepticism in Germany and elsewhere in the West—not dissimilar to the early reactions to reports about Cambodia, especially on the Left. Many of the accounts were based on "hearsay" and were "often not entirely consistent," the *taz* pointed out. "But too much dovetails, too much is precisely and consistently described, too much is being experienced firsthand" to allow for any "rational doubt" about the existence of the camps: "Whoever has seen all the misery of the refugees [and] the faces of these people knows that the camps are no fiction."[24]

Subsequent reports continued to include graphic details of the many atrocities supposedly being committed there, from systematic torture to mass executions. Interviews with released prisoners appeared in the German press that October and confirmed the "rumors of medieval cruelties," including ones about guard dogs biting off penises.[25] The most common words used to describe the prisoners—*abgemagert* (emaciated) and *ausgemergelt* (gaunt)—were the same adjectives used to describe Cambodians a decade earlier, and European Jews almost four decades before that. The prisoners at Omarska, the "most infamous" of the camps, were "so emaciated that their skin spanned their cheekbones like parchment paper." They were kept in "metal cages," *Der Spiegel* reported in mid-August: hundreds standing "squeezed together . . . shoulder to shoulder" without access to toilets. In another striking parallel reminiscent of earlier reports about the Khmer Rouge, one Serb guard claimed that he and his comrades did "not even waste bullets." Because the prisoners had no roof over their heads, "sun, rain, cold nights, and twice daily beatings suffice. We give them neither water nor food. They starve to death like cattle."[26]

German officials confirmed the existence of the camps and called in late August for an international court to prosecute these crimes, at a time when international interest was already turning elsewhere, to a bloody civil war in Somalia. The "appalling conditions" in Bosnia, Press Secretary Hanns Heinrich Schumacher of the Foreign Office told reporters, make one's "hair stand on end." The same was true of stories about the systematic removal of targeted ethnic groups—above all, Muslims—from territories claimed by the Serbs. By June, the German media had already begun to refer to this as "ethnic cleansing" (*ethnische Säuberung*), a "brutal" process that involved violence and terror against not just men but also women and children, invalids and the elderly. The goal for the Serbs was to make certain villages, towns, or regions entirely "free of Muslims"—a phrase reminiscent, of course, of the Nazi term *judenfrei*.[27]

Approximately three-quarters of all the "ethnic cleansing" had taken place by August 1992, resulting in the dramatic demographic transformation of hundreds of villages and towns. When journalist Walter Mayr visited the Bosnian town of Olovo in the winter of 1993, only four Muslims were left from a prewar population amounting to 80 percent of the town's residents.[28] Human upheavals like these had a long pedigree in

Europe and elsewhere, going back not just to the two world wars but also to earlier efforts in the nineteenth century to create ethnically homogeneous nation-states. Klaus Kinkel, who had succeeded Hans-Dietrich Genscher as German foreign minister in April, alluded to such inglorious traditions at a major international conference in London dedicated to the Balkans crisis. The Serbs, he claimed, were trying to create a *Groß-serbien* ("Greater Serbia") that was as "ethnically pure as possible."[29]

Media reports nevertheless pointed out that it was not just Bosnian Serbs who were carrying out "ethnic cleansing." Croats and Muslims were doing so as well, and all sides had set up internment camps. But as a rule, German officials and the media focused most heavily on Serb atrocities, especially during the earliest phase of the war. This eventually led to blowback by some critics, especially on the far left, who claimed that the mainstream media, following well-established traditions going back to the nineteenth century, was inherently biased against the Serbs.

A series of polemical essays made just that case in a volume that appeared in 1994, titled *Serbien muß sterbien* (Serbia Must Die), a popular slogan from the World War I era because of the role Serbia had played in sparking that conflict. *Neues Deutschland,* the former daily newspaper of the East German Communist Party, was especially fond of emphasizing that atrocities were being committed on all sides, that the "cruelties are the same" everywhere.[30] All of this anticipated a heated controversy in the second half of the 1990s surrounding Austrian author Peter Handke, who, in a series of publications, criticized the supposedly one-sided coverage of the conflict by the mainstream German (and French) media. Handke, who later received the Nobel Prize in Literature, was accused of relativizing Serb guilt and of being an apologist for the Serbs, who, like the Khmer Rouge a decade earlier, issued stark denials of any wrongdoing. "The Muslims are moving away," Karadžić was quoted as saying with studied understatement in *Die Zeit,* "because they don't feel at ease." That was no doubt true for the Muslim man forced to carry his pregnant wife ten kilometers to safety—even across a mine field.[31]

Systematic mass rape was one reason why so many Muslims did not "feel at ease." The horrific practice was a constituent part of the ethnic cleansing, Edith Niehuis of the SPD told her colleagues during an impassioned Bundestag debate about Bosnia in December 1992. The fear it instilled was intended to drive Muslims from their homes and villages and "save many grenades" in the process.[32] The first reports about rape surfaced in the German media that summer, but the stories began to appear with great frequency in late October, when journalist Alexandra Stiglmayer—who, as a young girl, had emigrated from Croatia to the Federal Republic with her Croatian mother and ethnic German father—published a deeply disturbing report in the *Deutsches Allgemeines Sonntagsblatt,* a Protestant weekly. Her article, "The Men's War against Women," began with the story of Marijana, a pregnant, half-Muslim, half-Croatian seventeen-year-old she had met at a women's clinic in Zagreb:

> Marijana's unborn child is the product of an estimated 1,350 rapes. She spent four and a half months in a Serb women's camp. . . . The camp's only purpose was rape, and, according to her own testimony, she was raped at least ten time[s] daily by different men. . . . All the girls and women were raped day and night by different men . . . sometimes by several men at the same time.[33]

Stiglmayer and other journalists published similarly horrifying details in other, more prominent media outlets with larger readerships, including the popular weekly *Stern.* All the stories were largely consistent: women and girls—some pregnant, some only twelve years old and even younger—were being raped, sometimes together with their mothers, sometimes in front of both parents, frequently by neighbors or colleagues they knew by name.[34] The Serbs reportedly "bragged" during the rapes that the women would now "'give birth to little Chetniks'"—a term, rich in historical meaning, that referred to nationalist Serb fighters who, during World War II, had resisted the Germans, fought the fascist Ustaše, and massacred Croat and Muslim civilians en masse. Those rape victims who became pregnant were supposedly held in captivity in special camps set up to prevent them from having an abortion. That way, they were told, "more Serbs come into the world" and "Serb blood increases." The camps represented their very own "Topography of

Terror," one journalist commented in an allusion to a well-known memorial in Berlin located on the former site of the Gestapo and SS headquarters.[35]

The story really took off on November 15, when *Mona Lisa,* the first "magazine" program on German television dedicated to women's issues, aired a special forty-three-minute report about the rapes. Journalist Maria von Welser, who had created *Mona Lisa* in 1988, decided to do the show after reading one of Stiglmayer's accounts in a local Munich newspaper. The segment began with a short film, shot a week earlier, created from interviews with thirty women, age fourteen to sixty, housed at four refugee camps in Zagreb. This was the first time that any Muslim women or girls had spoken about their experiences in front of a camera. They provided extremely graphic details—of forced oral sex, of a seven-year-old who died shortly after being raped in front of her mother—and claimed that the rapes were being "ordered from on high." The Serbs, they concluded, want to "exterminate all of us."[36]

Welser moderated the program, which included a live roundtable discussion with two women—German politicians Herta Däubler-Gmelin, deputy chair of the SPD, and Uta Werfel of the Free Democratic Party, an expert on women's issues—and three men: former minister of defense Rupert Scholz of the CDU, American journalist Roy Gutman, who had first broken the story about the Serb camps, and Rupert Neudeck, who, since founding the organization Cap Anamur in 1979 to help rescue Vietnamese boat people, had become active in humanitarian crises around the globe. Representatives from the UN and the Red Cross declined invitations to participate, the moderator explained, making the excuse that none of the claims had been "proven" and that it could all just be "wartime propaganda." Anticipating similar objections by viewers, Welser began the report by declaring that *Mona Lisa* had indeed obtained "authentic" proof of what was happening just "an hour away from Munich by plane." That very skepticism, she added, was "a little reminiscent" of the Third Reich—or, more precisely, of Allied doubts about wartime atrocity reports during the early 1940s. Instead, she reminded viewers, "one kept one's eyes shut." But after this show, Welser asserted, nobody could claim that these were "just isolated cases. It really seems to be a planned effort."[37]

The report struck a chord. The television network received hundreds of calls and the German government "drowned in a flood of letters," including petitions to Chancellor Kohl signed by thousands. There were also benefit concerts and donation drives, including one set up by Welser and the two female politicians who had taken part in the roundtable discussion. Their initiative raised almost 1.8 million DM within days, and *Mona Lisa* would go on to produce seven more shows about the war in Bosnia.[38]

The major newspapers and magazines now all ran stories about the rapes. Their reports met with "sheer horror," produced a "wave of indignation," and sparked a variety of efforts by German officials and private citizens.[39] Foreign Minister Kinkel sent a medical doctor from the Foreign Office to carry out an investigation in Zagreb, and women's groups organized hundreds of protests outside public buildings, including silent ones at which the participants dressed all in black, inspired by an ongoing protest movement by women in Belgrade. "Engaged Christians" appear to have been especially moved by the reports. One Protestant women's organization called on its members to collect signatures and write letters to the German government, and its Brunswick branch organized shows of solidarity with the victims by ringing church bells and placing candles in windows on the final day of Advent that year. The German Evangelical Church, for its part, published a statement condemning rape as an "especially perfidious" form of ethnic cleansing. Sigrid Häfner, the church's representative responsible for women's issues, reported she had "never experienced . . . such a sizable public reaction" to a church declaration on human rights: Protestant men were equally "indignant" and "shocked," and had "shown solidarity" by writing hundreds of "protest letters" to the Foreign Office and UN refugee officials.[40]

The *Mona Lisa* segment led to a public hearing three weeks later, on December 7, conducted by the Bundestag's Committee for Women and Youth Affairs. Minister for Women and Youth (and future chancellor) Angela Merkel was in attendance, and Rupert Neudeck was again one of the speakers. A representative from Amnesty International wanted to know why the "outrage" was so great this time, given that her organization had long been reporting about mass rape in other countries and regions. She suspected that visual images and live eyewitness accounts "bring home the horrors to a much sharper extent than sober reports that rely on emotions and facts." She had a point, and it is no doubt true that television coverage played a major role in setting the tone for German responses to the carnage in Bosnia.[41]

The rapes received further media attention that February following a conference in Zagreb organized by German media personality Lea Rosh, the granddaughter of a German Jewish baritone and head of Norddeutscher Rundfunk studio in Hannover. One of the first women in charge of a German broadcasting studio, Rosh was no stranger to controversy. In 1988 she had initiated a drive, along with historian Eberhard Jäckel, to create a massive Holocaust Monument in Berlin. The goal of the Zagreb conference was to draw even greater attention to the "deliberate genocide" in the Balkans, raise money for the victims, and prepare a set of demands, including the creation of an international tribunal to prosecute the perpetrators. In a statement released prior to the conference, Rosh alluded specifically to the Third Reich: "Back then everyone said, we didn't know. Nobody can say that today. We know [what is happening] and that is why we are going to Zagreb."[42]

Six hundred women from across Europe attended the conference, which took place on February 7. Many prominent German politicians and public figures were in attendance, including Hamburg's evangelical bishop Maria Jepsen. In her own statements, Rosh emphasized that the Serb militia were guilty of genocide, though not the "Serbs as a whole," a claim that must have been positively received in Germany, given the enduring sensitivity there to any suggestions of "collective guilt." She echoed earlier comments about the Allied failure to respond during World War II to reports about Nazi extermination camps but acknowledged that they could not "march into the rape camps and liberate the women" themselves—an idea previously floated by Tilman Zülch, who said this should have happened at Dachau in 1934, and by Rupert Neudeck, who later wrote that his "good old pacifism" had dissipated after witnessing so many massacres in Bosnia. This "giant women's spectacle"—in the words of *taz* reporter Erica Fischer—created a good deal of controversy, but it did achieve its primary goal of drawing more global attention to the rapes in Bosnia. That winter, Eva Quistorp of the

German Greens was instrumental in pushing through a statement in the European Parliament that condemned the rapes.[43]

The reasons for the rapes and their precise number generated a great deal of public discussion and speculation. But whatever the exact figures and causes, a consensus quickly emerged that, just like the policy of ethnic cleansing, this "systematic practice" was part and parcel of a greater criminal act: genocide. The first media reports to use that crucial term appeared in the spring of 1992, usually quoting Bosnian officials. But by the summer, German journalists and politicians on all sides of the political spectrum—from Chancellor Kohl of the CDU and Foreign Minister Kinkel of the FDP, to leading members of the SPD and the Greens—were also widely invoking the term to describe, in Kinkel's words, the "inhuman war of destruction and expulsion" in Bosnia. "What has taken place is genocide," he added unequivocally.[44]

Among government officials, the Germans were the only major European leaders to use that weighty term, and they had already done so in August 1992 in London at the International Conference on the Former Yugoslavia, which adopted a set of principles aimed at finding a diplomatic and political solution to the conflict.[45] In contrast to the United States, which witnessed the "most wide-ranging, most vocal, and most decisive debate ever held on whether [Rafael] Lemkin's term should apply," there was no similar debate in Germany, where, as we shall see, the focus was instead on whether comparisons to the Holocaust were appropriate.[46] Still, one of the earliest and most forceful statements to make the case appeared in mid-July in the *taz*. Writing under a sensational headline—"It Is Genocide and Must Be Designated as Such"— Bundestag member and publicist Freimut Duve of the SPD, the illegitimate son of a German mother and a Croatian Jewish father murdered by the Ustaše, strenuously argued in favor of using the term, just as he had two years earlier during the Bundestag debates Petra Kelly had initiated about Cambodia: "A genocide against Muslims has been taking place for months in Bosnia. They are murdered, terrorized, expelled, with a single, clearly recognizable goal: to make Bosnia 'free' of Bosnians with Muslim background. And precisely that is genocide, according to the definition of the United Nations."[47]

There were important reasons to call a fig a fig, Duve argued. For one, only this would permit the perpetrators to be brought to justice before an international tribunal:

> With genocide, there are no excuses related to "acts of war," civil war chaos, political conflicts. The perpetrators of genocide cannot look forward to a statute of limitations. But, since 1948, the Genocide Convention has not been used. It was created to define the crimes of Auschwitz, but it has never been used to act as a deterrent against future genocides. Not in the case of southern Sudan, not in Cambodia, not [for] the Indians in northern Guatemala. Of course, one can argue about what constituted mass murder and genocide [but] the "Convention" of December 9, 1948, provides a fairly unambiguous formulation. . . . Precisely that is taking place right now in Bosnia. . . . The goal is the extinction of the Bosnian Muslim people—be it through death or disappearance![48]

Duve revisited these arguments during a passionate Bundestag debate on October 15. The Serb army was "destroying an entire people," whose only "error," he insisted, was to believe, "just as we had believed," that there could not be any genocide again "after Auschwitz and Cambodia. . . . Mass murder has a place in European history again . . . not in March and April 1945, but now, day for day, these past months."[49]

Duve, who had lost thirty-five family members during the Holocaust, later explained that his position on Bosnia had "everything to do with his ancestry."[50] But he was preaching to the choir. Neither the German government nor the major political parties denied that a genocide was taking place or doubted the applicability of the 1948 Convention. Nor did they dismiss, for that matter, the claim that mass rape was tantamount to genocide, or that Serb perpetrators were raping "on orders from on-high." In December 1992, State Minister Ursula Seiler-Albring of the FDP acknowledged in the Bundestag that *if* the reports about the systematic rape of mainly Muslim women and girls were confirmed, this would indeed "satisfy" the terms of the UN Convention.[51] Yet the Federal

Republic never invoked the Genocide Convention at the UN or anywhere else. Why that was the case is one of the most perplexing questions about German responses to genocide since 1945.

"What is going on in the minds of people who sexually debase and torture others in the most horrible way," Joachim Geiger wondered in a piece about Bosnia that appeared in the *Deutsches Allgemeines Sonntagsblatt*, "only to slaughter them like cattle in the end? What kind of men nonchalantly go through destroyed villages with machine guns, cigarettes hanging from the corners of their mouths, to murder the elderly, women, and children?" Such passages must have reminded at least some readers of their country's own inglorious past. After all, Germans knew exactly what "kind of men" did such things. They were sometimes older family members—ones who bore an uncanny resemblance, perhaps, to the Serb perpetrator who later defended his actions by explaining that he had to "obey my orders."[52]

It is doubtful that Geiger was acting coy about Germany's sordid past, rather than simply expressing genuine shock and outrage. Regardless, it would not have been surprising if this and similar reports about Bosnia reminded Germans of their country's own sadistic history—especially given the language frequently used to describe what was taking place in the Balkans. Terms like *concentration camps, ethnic cleansing,* and *genocide* led to the use of other evocative words and imagery similarly—and unmistakably—reminiscent of the 1930s and 1940s. "If the Serbs don't come 'back home to the Reich,'" journalist Josef Joffe quipped about Serb land grabs, for example, "then the Reich must come to them"—a pointed reference to a foreign policy initiative from the late 1930s ("Heim ins Reich") that encouraged so-called *Volksdeutsche* (ethnic Germans) living outside Germany to relocate to areas under German control. Others referred to Serb efforts to obtain more *Lebensraum* (living space), to the "blood-and-soil language" of Serb "fanatics" and *Schreibtischtäter* (desk murderers) who "glorify . . . violence" as they struggle to achieve an *Endsieg* (final victory) or an *Endlösung* (final solution) in a "total war"—a "racial war" aimed at constructing a "'racially' pure" state.[53]

Similarly shocking stories in the media reported that Muslim prisoners were being "slaughtered like sheep" by "death squads." Inmates from one internment camp had been forced to "kneel down so that their blood could flow into the Sava River" after their throats were "sliced open." The Serbs then burned the bodies in a cattle feed factory, making the air "so bad one could not open the windows." Evocative olfactory imagery like this was not uncommon, also in later reporting about the genocide in Rwanda. Peasants living near one internment camp complained about the "stench" of decaying corpses. According to one eyewitness, it was "as bright as day in the middle of the night" when the Serbs set his entire village aflame: "There was this smell of burned human flesh," he added. "I will never forget that smell."[54]

German readers stumbling across such phrases, images, and innuendos must have perforce thought of the Nazi genocide, of the persecution and mass murder of the Jews and other groups. More direct allusions underscored the point. The future Nobel Prize–winning novelist Herta Müller, an ethnic German born in the Banat region of Romania, argued, for example, that the "fascist anti-Jewish laws" had served as the "model" for similar Serb decrees, such as one she had read about in a newspaper proclaiming that "'those who are not of Serb descent may neither sit in city cafés, nor swim in rivers or use cars.'" In Banja Luka, the second largest Bosnian city, Serbs were supposedly wearing a "specially imprinted white armband" for protection. "Whoever doesn't wear it," eyewitnesses told the politician Freimut Duve, "becomes a victim of terror"—a perverse "reversal of the Nazi Star of David."[55]

Disturbing similarities between contemporary Serb and *past* German behavior were obliquely remarked upon in other ways as well, either in the offhand use of the term *fascist* or in more deliberate decisions to use it. In August 1992, following the initial flurry of reports about the internment camps, two leading Green politicians declared in a public statement that "ethnic corrections" and "archaic violence" like this were "clear components of fascism." Their colleagues on the party's executive board also spoke at the time about the "hallmarks" and "horror of Serb fascism," and the "fascist brood of murderers" in Serbia.[56] The term was also used to describe the behavior of extreme Croat nationalists: their open adulation, for example, of Ustaše wartime leader Ante Pavelić, who had once benefited from Hitler's "grace"; their black uniforms adorned with fascist insignia—including SS runes (which some Serb paramilitaries also wore); the slogans they adopted, such as "Western Herzegovina *über alles*"—graffiti written in German, of course, to emphasize the message. "It shocked us," wrote veteran journalist Peter Scholl-Latour after a visit to the Balkans, that, on seeing the German license plate on his vehicle, uniformed Croat guards clad in black had repeatedly "raised their arms in a fascist greeting . . . even the children at the wayside repeated this embarrassing gesture."[57] Try as they might, Germans could not escape their country's ignominious past.

Whatever affinities Croat extremists may have had with earlier fascists, the Serbs' policies and behavior, as well as shocking statements by Serb leaders, were what prompted the most direct comparisons to Nazi Germany and the genocidal horrors of the Third Reich.[58] The German media frequently noted that foreigners, especially Jewish ones, were making similar comparisons. *Bild am Sonntag,* the tabloid with the highest circulation in Europe, reported that the first televised images of the Serb prison camps—of "emaciated men with shaved skulls" and rib cages that "protruded so strongly that a crater formed in the middle"—had reminded the new Israeli prime minister, Yitzak Rabin, of the "Nazi Holocaust." Art Spiegelman, the Jewish American cartoonist whose book *Maus* had just won the Pulitzer Prize, drew similar conclusions in an essay published in the *taz* in late 1992: The "hunted, empty eyes" of the camp inmates he had seen on television were "those of my parents fifty years ago" following the liberation of the death camps.[59] Invocations of the Warsaw Ghetto were also common, especially when it came to reports about the siege of Sarajevo. "We've reached the end of the line," Bosnia's Muslim president Alija Izetbegović wrote in a dramatic appeal to French president François Mitterrand. "We have no food, no weapons, no hope. It's like the Warsaw Ghetto. . . . Will the world allow the Warsaw Ghetto to die once again?" Such references were not coincidental, especially on the eve of the fiftieth anniversary of the Warsaw Ghetto Uprising by Jewish resistance forces.[60]

Other references to the Final Solution were more oblique. In a speech at the UN in September 1992, Foreign Minister Kinkel warned about the need to "Wehret den Anfängen!" (Beware of the beginnings), a famous Latin saying by Ovid (*Principiis obsta*) that had become closely associated in Germany with the Holocaust—an exhortation to take action before things careened out of control, as they had so catastrophically under the Nazis. Tilman Zülch's Society for Threatened Peoples feared, for its part, that a Serb victory could lead to "up to six million" victims (a figure not likely chosen by chance), and readers of the *taz* learned that parking lots were being built in Serb-controlled towns on spots where mosques had once stood—a reminder perhaps of Joseph Goebbels's nasty quip right after the burning of Jewish synagogues on Crystal Night in November 1938: "We shall build parking lots in their place."[61] In an essay in *Der Spiegel,* two sociologists wondered whether Muslim children would later remember how they had been separated from their mothers, or

> that adults in uniform [had] confined them like cattle in freight cars without roofs, and sent them off without food, without water, without toilets for three days to an unknown fate. . . . Or will it become branded in their memory how the adults rejoiced when [it] then suddenly began to rain—because the mothers, who had baby bottles, could now collect a little rainwater and give it to the children to drink?[62]

German readers with good memories may have recalled this passage if they were among the millions who went to see the 1993 Hollywood film *Schindler's List* later that year, especially during one memorable scene in which Oskar Schindler hoses down cattle cars carrying parched Jews to Auschwitz. Intentional or not, other reports—of "special trains" (*Sonderzüge*), of Muslims being forced to sell all their belongings "for a song" before expulsion, of Serb neighbors walking past those waiting to be deported "as if nothing were happening"—all drove home the same point.[63]

The appropriateness of drawing such disturbing, "undeniable parallels to Hitler" and the Third Reich were at the heart of a heated exchange in the German parliament in the spring of 1993, just as commemorations marking the fiftieth anniversary of the Warsaw Ghetto Uprising were getting under way.[64] It began when Vera Wollenberger of the Greens opened her speech with a quote by Dr. Marek Edelmann, the last living ghetto survivor: "Mass destruction is taking place in Bosnia, and Europe acts the same way it did back then. . . . Our children and grand-children" will ask "us" the same questions "we posed to our parents and grandparents," Wollenberger continued: Why did the world just look on when the Warsaw Ghetto was destroyed, why did it not supply any arms to the fighters there (an allusion to the international arms embargo imposed on the Balkans since the fall of 1991), and

> why were the supply routes used to transport people to Auschwitz not destroyed at least—which, in the summer of 1944, could have saved 200,000 Hungarian Jews from gassing? . . . In the past year, at least 200,000 Bosnians have died. They were killed in concentration camps, as a result of rape, starvation, in enclosed train cars, during massacres [and] shootings—we are familiar with similar images from history.

Instead of acting, "excuses" were being offered—for example, that what was taking place in Bosnia was "not comparable with Nazi crimes. Really not?" Wollenberger demanded.[65]

Freimut Duve applauded repeatedly during Wollenberger's speech, but her last comment drew a sharp rebuke from Duve's colleague in the SPD, the well-known leftist politician and political commentator Peter Glotz: "No, really not! Do you want a new *Historikerstreit*?"—a direct reference to the controversy that had roiled the German historical profession in the 1980s. Wollenberger responded with a list of Serb "special conditions" forbidding Muslims to enter public buildings or use public transportation, to go on the street at certain times or have more than two persons present at burials—which drew another sharp intervention from Glotz: "The Nazi murder of the Jews is incomparable. Just stop already!"[66]

Glotz returned to the theme later in the debate, cautioning his colleagues not to make such comparisons or "dispute" the "uniqueness" of the Holocaust because it risked "a definitive break with the postwar consensus." Wollenberger interjected at one point that Glotz's comments were "revolting," but Freimut Duve responded at length to his arguments:

> For as long as I could think in political terms, I have always considered the matter of the uniqueness of the genocide of the Jews by Germany to be a mandate to prevent future genocide. . . . The uniqueness of the Holocaust also demands that one ask whether genocide took place in Cambodia . . . whether the [International] Court [of Justice] in The Hague was correct when it declared the actions against Muslim Europeans in Yugoslavia to be acts of genocide in the sense of the Genocide Convention of 1948. I do this, and I will continue to do this. I see that as my task. I fundamentally disagree in this matter with the assertion that there was the Shoah, and nothing else can be compared with it.[67]

The exchange was the continuation of a debate that had played out in the press a month earlier, when Glotz similarly warned in *Der Spiegel* against a "downplaying" (*Verharmlosung*) of the Nazi genocide (though he apparently had no qualms later that year comparing Serb "atrocity propaganda" with that of Joseph Goebbels, an "equally ruthless and brilliant propaganda artist"). Duve responded with an essay in the *taz* in which he worried about the lesson his colleague had taken from the Holocaust, namely, that its alleged "uniqueness . . . relativized" all "post-Holocaust crimes." That tendency had "bothered" him during the genocides in Cambodia, East Timor, and Guatemala, and now in Bosnia.[68]

Duve developed his ideas a year later in the *Süddeutsche Zeitung*, acknowledging that some may find "every association with Nazi crimes" to be "troubling." But, he asserted, words like *ghetto* and *genocide* were entirely appropriate for describing the current situation in Bosnia. Those like himself who had visited besieged cities like Mostar or Srebrenica had witnessed firsthand "ghetto-like situations," where people "defend themselves like the Jews of Warsaw had defended themselves." The word *Völkermord*, he continued, "may not be made taboo. The Genocide Convention . . . wanted to prevent this sort of tabooing from the very beginning." Marieluise Beck of the Greens strongly concurred. It was "precisely" her generation (she was born in 1952) and "political milieu" that claimed to have done so much to confront the Nazi past. But they now had to ask "what it means to be a historical witness" and consider the responsibilities this entailed. Serb and Nazi crimes were "not comparable in their totality" because there was "no industrial mass murder" of a people, but "a deliberate genocide" was taking place, Beck asserted—"just like fifty years ago."[69]

Balkans correspondent Erich Rathfelder of the *taz,* a vigorous proponent of outside military intervention to stop the carnage, wrote along similar lines that the "principle questions of this century" had renewed urgency because of the searing images of the Serb internment camps. One had thought that "systematic incarceration" in "*KZ*-like camps" had become "a thing of the past *in Europe*" after the "convulsions of the Nazi genocide and the Gulag Archipelago." That the French had used similar methods in Algeria in the 1950s, that "uninhibited soldiers" in Africa and places like Cambodia continued to commit such atrocities, showed that the "lessons from Hitler's and Stalin's death camps" were "only drawn" when they served "current political interests. . . . Despite all the resolutions affirming that this horrible history must never repeat itself, a new Auschwitz is beginning now and today in Bosnia."[70]

Reflecting on these assertions years later, Rathfelder recognized that he "sometimes" wrote his articles "too fast." He had lived in Bosnia throughout the entire war, "out of a suitcase," and would sit "in some rundown pub . . . trying to get across" what he had just witnessed. "That was very difficult. You don't have days to write, just a couple of hours or even minutes." Under less "extreme" circumstances, he normally "attached great importance" to maintaining a strict separation between news reports and editorials. But the revelations about the Serb internment camps had an enormous effect on his thinking. In fact, he had opposed outside intervention up to that point. But it now became difficult to maintain a "psychological" distance, especially after conducting interviews with survivors and perpetrators. "One had to take a stance." Many letters to the editor complained about Rathfelder's partisan reporting and, he recalls with palpable emotion, he was even booed at a teach-in about Bosnia he attended in Germany. That was not easy for a former sixty-eighter whose "entire life had revolved around fascism."

No, he later acknowledged, the internment camps were not the same as Auschwitz, but "the thinking was the same." In the end, he said, there was "not much" he had written at the time that he would "take back."[71]

Joschka Fischer and Daniel Cohn-Bendit of the Greens similarly invoked the specter of Auschwitz, and Bosiljka Schedlich, the Croatian-born director of the Süd-Ost-Zentrum in Berlin, spoke of similarities as well. She wondered if, "in fifty years," they would be erecting monuments to the victims of Serb aggression and making films about the "Schindlers of today."[72] Was all of this, as Glotz feared, a relativization of the Holocaust? Seeking guidance abroad, the leftist *taz* conducted interviews about these very issues with two prominent American Jews: Robert Goldman, a representative of the Anti-Defamation League in Europe, and Henry Siegman, the director of the American Jewish Congress and a Holocaust survivor. Both acknowledged what they saw as "upsetting" or "unmistakable" parallels with the earlier persecution and murder of the Jews. The treatment of Muslim women was reminiscent of Josef Mengele's "insane methods," Goldman claimed, while Siegman spoke of a "deep moral duty" not to look away again. The Austrian-born Holocaust survivor and famed "Nazi hunter" Simon Wiesenthal had a different take: Such comparisons were a "*Verharmlosung*" (downplaying), he believed, a "*Verniedlichung*" (minimization) of "real" concentration camps.[73]

Peter Glotz was not the only German who objected to analogies between Bosnia and the Third Reich. Robert Leicht, the editor in chief of *Die Zeit*, argued that facile comparisons with the Nazis were "misguided" because Hitler had wanted to "conquer the world" and—unlike Milošević and the Serbs—had the "means to do so." But it was especially those on the Left who balked at what they saw as reckless analogies, especially ones involving the use of historically charged words and phrases like *pogrom* and *concentration camp*. The inflationary use of the term *KZ*—to describe conditions in Sarajevo or Bosnia as a whole, for instance—must have done little to calm the skeptics and the cautious.[74] "When characterizing these crimes . . . ," declared journalist and former Maoist Christian Semler in the *taz*, it was necessary "to refrain from using terms that only whip up emotions and suggest false historical analogies . . . to the SS state [and its] bureaucratically driven mass murder." The crimes being committed in Bosnia by a "marauding soldiery often no longer responsive to their own official command structures" were qualitatively different, he believed, even if that difference did not "mitigate their crimes."[75] SPD politician Egon Bahr, the son of a German Jewish mother, strongly concurred. Auschwitz was "unique" because of its industrial nature, he maintained years later, and such comparisons "terribly upset" him. They were the "product of a guilty conscience," he added, "misused" to influence policy toward former Yugoslavia.[76]

That was a provocative statement, but his final point about *intent* was no doubt a valid one, also for other countries where Auschwitz and the specter of the Holocaust were frequently invoked. That included France, Britain, and especially the United States, where "television producers often accompanied their daily Bosnia coverage with scenes from Holocaust newsreels." That had earlier been the case for Cambodia in the United States—and even in the GDR, as we know from Walter Heynowski's documentaries about the Khmer Rouge. The parallel nevertheless "resonated" in a much different way when it came to Bosnia, likely because it was in Europe. That was true on both sides of the Atlantic. There was a difference, however. "In most countries," Paul Berman writes, describing one's "enemies as Nazis . . . was a figure of speech." In Germany, it went "beyond metaphor."[77] To be sure, it had a different quality there, and that, in turn, had vastly different political ramifications.

Debates about the nature of the camps and about ethnic cleansing were not just charged with "emotion, selective perception, and partiality."[78] They were also highly politicized, to a much greater extent in Germany than elsewhere in the West—a crucial difference when gauging the peculiarities of German responses. The Left was especially sensitive to Holocaust comparisons because of a recent shift in the tenor of political discourse in the Federal Republic. Beginning in the 1980s, conservative politicians felt less compunction about using labels to smear political opponents as Nazis. During the early postwar years, West Germans had reserved such slurs mainly for their counterparts in the GDR (and vice versa). But by the 1960s, such smears were increasingly used to score points in domestic political disputes, with the Left loosely and almost ritualistically accusing conservatives of having "fascist tendencies"—common parlance among the sixty-eighters. In the 1980s, prominent conservative politicians began to draw on the legacy of the Third Reich as well, to discredit foreign *and* domestic foes. Heiner Geißler, secretary-general of the CDU, suggested during a Bundestag debate in 1983 that leftist pacifism in the 1930s had "first made Auschwitz possible"—a stinging indictment not soon forgotten on the Left. Later that decade, Helmut Kohl would compare Mikhail Gorbachev to Goebbels and refer to the GDR as a "*KZ.*" Even though Chancellor Willy Brandt, the father of *Ostpolitik,* had made comparable claims about East Germany in the early 1960s (under much different geopolitical circumstances), politicians in his party, like Peter Glotz, were now quick to condemn such aspersions as a "trivialization" of Nazi crimes.[79] How accurate were such allegations?

German conservatives were certainly not shy about drawing historical parallels between the Third Reich and Bosnia. Carl Gustaf Ströhm, a veteran Eastern Europe correspondent at *Die Welt,* addressed the issue head-on in reference to a television moderator who had recently called for caution when using the term *concentration camp.* Ströhm wanted to know why: "A *KZ* is a *KZ,* regardless of whether German Nazis, Russian Bolsheviks, or Serb fanatics go on a rampage there." An editorial in the conservative *FAZ* addressed the issue more delicately, with a nod to the crucial distinction between concentration camps and death camps. "There are camps once again on European soil that reach a dimension of horror akin to the Dachau concentration camp at the start of the Nazi regime. . . . The ethnic-religious criteria of selection of the camp inmates . . . recall the dark period of six decades ago. One should not compare, but one cannot keep the recollection at bay."[80]

More troublesome was the notion that Serb crimes were "just as bad" as, or even worse than, those committed by the Nazis. Such assertions, which had also surfaced during and after the Cambodian genocide, were usually oblique and normally attributed to foreigners—for example, the Croat doctor who told a German correspondent that this war was "unique. Never had something similar taken place, never again will something comparable occur." Carl Gustaf Ströhm described a similar conversation he had with a Croatian civil servant, who confided that the

Serbs were behaving "worse there than any sort of occupation power. . . . Neither the Turks nor Napoleon, *nor the Germans in World War II,* had ever caused such depredation." Ströhm himself, who later moved from *Die Welt* to *Junge Freiheit,* an extreme right-wing daily, reminded readers that the Wehrmacht had to "intervene repeatedly" during World War II to prevent the Serbs from committing "mass murder" against the Muslims. Were such statements indicative of some sort of exculpatory undercurrent in German discourse? Another one of Ströhm's comments certainly seemed to veer in that direction—or at least flirt with national self-exoneration for past German misdeeds: "One should certainly not make the Serb people collectively responsible for these crimes. But . . . it gives pause for thought that Serbia is not under the thumb of a dictator whom one must obey at the risk of one's life, that there are indeed elections there and the possibility to express one's opinions."[81] Ströhm might have added: as opposed to Nazi Germany. But he did not need to. The message was clear enough.

Still, as German responses to the reports of mass rape in Bosnia reveal, things were not that clear-cut, even for someone like Ströhm. Just as the refugee crisis in Cambodia had conjured up painful memories of German flight from Eastern Europe after World War II, the Bosnian atrocities did not just recall Nazi crimes but also other aspects of the past that, for many Germans, hit just as close to home. This was especially true of the suffering endured by German women at the close of World War II, a theme long taboo in West Germany and the GDR, but one that received greater public attention after unification in 1990.[82] Increased interest in this painful subject came at a time when Germans were becoming more prone, once again, to expressing their own sense of past victimhood. That makes the claim that the crimes in Bosnia against women were qualitatively different and, in some ways, worse than the ones fifty years earlier in Germany especially striking—a notable reversal of the notion that foreign atrocities were sometimes on par with or "somehow worse" than those perpetrated by the Nazis. There was an instrumental element to all this, of course. Those who made such claims were banging the drum for outside military intervention.

In any event, Ströhm made precisely that point in a December 1992 editorial in *Die Welt.* "As terrible as it was," even the Red Army's "hunt for women" in 1945 did not "smack" of the same "bestial systematization" as in Bosnia, which "surpasses everything that seemed to be imaginable in Europe from time immemorial"—a curious comment, of course, in the wake of Auschwitz.[83] Like Ströhm, Marieluise Beck of the Greens also spoke of the "systematic" nature of the Serb atrocities, adding that there were "no historical examples." Uta Würfel of the FDP acknowledged, however, that rape as a wartime tactic was nothing new. Mass rape had been carried out in previous conflicts, including by German soldiers fighting in Belgium during World War I. There was wide agreement, in fact, that rape had long belonged to the repertoire of military "victors," and that male behavior was largely consistent across time and cultures. But what was "new for all of us" in Bosnia, Würfel added, was the "phenomenon of mass rape in camps" specifically set up for that purpose. The Serbs had not "invented" wartime bordellos, of course. The Wehrmacht had also set them up in occupied territories during World War II. But purposefully bringing the resulting pregnancies to term made these rapes, as sociologists Cheryl Benard and Edit Schlaffer put it, "a little different."[84]

Those Germans who had experienced the horrors of wartime rape firsthand, either as victims or observers, made similar distinctions. "The Russians raped and hideously abused . . . out of lust and a desire for revenge," Rupert Neudeck remarked after a recent visit to Bosnia, where he had just been exposed to such atrocities for a second time. (The first instance had been at age six, during his flight from Danzig with his mother, sister, aunt, and grandmother.) The Serbs, by contrast, "rape, murder, and abuse to the point of conception to humiliate" and to create a "time bomb" of "Chetnik babies" among the Muslim population.[85]

Filmmaker Helke Sander, who had just completed *BeFreier und Be-Freite* (Liberators Take Liberties), a controversial documentary about the rape of German women in the 1940s, pointed out another crucial difference. In Bosnia, the "'vanquished' often personally knew the 'victors.'" Whatever the differences, German women clearly had one thing in common with Bosnian Muslims. Both experienced the same sort of social disgrace that came in the wake of sexual violation. Many German women told Sander, in fact, that the reactions of their closest relatives had been often "worse than the rape itself"—something powerfully captured in a common German adage from the 1940s: "Nobody wants a broken cup."[86] Referring to this distasteful but suggestive saying, an early article on the mass rapes in Bosnia acknowledged that the "code of honor" that made rape tantamount to a sexual "death blow" in the Balkans "apparently exists among us as well." It related the story of a German officer who remarked, after witnessing the rape of German women in Berlin in 1945, "If that were to happen to my wife, I'd shoot her."

In late May 1992, *Spiegel* correspondent Erich Wiedemann filed a human-interest story on "enemy stereotypes" in Bosnia. It began by describing a remarkable encounter he had recently had with several Serb women at a marketplace in Sarajevo: "Listen here," one of them told him, "we Serbs are a friendly nation, we fulfilled the Bosnian Muslims' every wish, and they now want to destroy our people as thanks." She admitted that she had only heard of alleged Muslim massacres of Serbs "at third hand" and that her "assessment" of the Bosnian Muslims' "national character" was "just six weeks old." In fact, she insisted, they had, "up till last month, all lived together as tolerably good neighbors." But schoolchildren were now wearing armbands so that their ethnic background was "easier to recognize." What had led to such sudden hostility, Wiedemann wanted to know.[87]

That question preoccupied many Germans, who wished to understand how and why such terrible things were happening—completely understandable, given their own history. Some threw up their hands in disgust and outrage, claiming that the "unprecedented brutality" in a place many considered a favorite vacation spot was simply "inexplicable" and "unimaginable." That was a common response. But like the women in the marketplace, others resorted to cultural and ethnic stereotypes, not unlike earlier speculation in Germany about the underlying causes of the Cambodian genocide. Some referred to the people of the Balkans as "traditionally wild and cruel," with a penchant for "patriarchal customs," "militaristic traditions," and epic poems that "glorified violence." A more common explanation looked to Bosnia's explosive ethnic dimension—a major theme in the existing literature most journalists would have consulted.[88] All agreed that the region was an ethnic "patchwork rug," a "pied leopard skin"—Yugoslavia's "multiethnic mixture par excellence." The population, which was divided into three main groups (approximately 45 percent Sunni Muslim, 30 percent Orthodox Serb, and 18 percent Catholic Croat), all lived "jumbled together"—and that, it was claimed, was the very source of this "problem from hell," in the words of US secretary of state Warren Christopher. Living in such proximity, in many areas without a clear ethnic majority, made it extremely difficult to separate the increasingly hostile groups, whose members were often "hopelessly intermarried."[89]

What made the spiraling conflict so inexplicable for many Germans was the equally widespread notion that these groups had lived together more or less peacefully for centuries—or at the very least in "tolerable harmony," as the Serb woman at the marketplace in Sarajevo had intimated. For many, especially on the Left, the capital city embodied the prewar ethnic harmony supposedly characteristic of the Bosnian "model of coexistence." It was a "bastion of multiculturalism" that represented a "unique symbiosis of different cultures," with mosques and synagogues, Orthodox and Roman Catholic churches, one next to the other. Even the Bosnian Serb leader Radovan Karadžić, it was noted, had before the war frequented Sarajevo's many literary cafés, where Muslims, Serbs, and Croats gathered together. In fact, his friends from that time could not understand how this "literary figure," known for his "wild curly hair" and "gnawed off fingernails," had become a "Serb radical overnight."[90]

Most eyes focused on the "cosmopolitan" and "tolerant" capital city, not least because of the spectacular siege taking place. Yet not all Germans embraced such rosy visions of past harmony. Carl Gustaf Ströhm drew on his expertise of Eastern Europe to argue that Bosnian "reality" actually consisted of "centuries-old, pent-up hatred" that had been "swept simply under the rug" during four decades of communist rule. Tito's suppression of ethnic and national tensions, coupled with simmering resentment against Serb political and economic dominance, was precisely what had fomented anti-Serb agitation and a Serb nationalist backlash in the 1980s following the charismatic dictator's death.[91] German politicians adopted similar arguments. Foreign Minister Kinkel alluded on more than one occasion to "the breaking of ice"—in a negative sense— in a troubled region where ethnic conflicts had been "frozen" since 1945.

What had taken place in Yugoslavia during World War II had been "repressed" under Tito and must "now be dearly paid. . . . The past exacts vengeance."[92]

But which past? Most observers agreed that the origins of the conflict were to be found in the history of the region. The most common historical point of reference was World War II, because of the bloody, interethnic fighting that had taken place following the German invasion. "The genocide of yesterday incites the ethnic hatred of today," commented *Der Spiegel,* and the "wounds from back then" were now being "ripped open again," the "ghosts of the past" indeed returning. Gregor Gysi, head of the leftist Party of Democratic Socialism, the successor of East Germany's ruling Socialist Unity Party, would have none of this. The West was to blame for artificially "fomenting" and "fueling" the ethnic dimension of the conflict, he later claimed, "so that no socialist country remained in Europe. To that end, they accepted the destruction of Yugoslavia."[93]

Other analyses traced the roots of the conflict much further back in time, all the way to injuries suffered centuries earlier, beginning with the Serb-led army's loss to the Ottoman Empire at the Battle of Kosovo in 1389—a defeat that would become a mainstay of Serb nationalism centuries later. The "dogged national pride of many Serbs, their understanding of themselves as a victim nation," began a lengthy *Spiegel* report about the historical antecedents of the current conflict, "originated in the Middle Ages." Religious frictions were not much of a theme in the German media, but this pent-up hatred and anger, especially about centuries of oppression under the Ottomans, had first been "discharged" during World War II, culminating in bloody massacres of Muslims, disdainfully referred to by Serb Chetniks as "Turks."[94]

Muslim actions during World War II supposedly served as a further pretext. Most had joined Tito's partisans in the fight against the Germans, but a minority, under the tutelage of the grand mufti in Jerusalem, had indeed supported the Axis powers. Much was made in the media about a "Muslim SS" unit that had "rampaged" with the Ustaše against the Serbs, which was why the latter now wanted to "hit" back at their enemies "so devastatingly"—to "correct history." Bosnian Serbs made such arguments to justify both their opposition to independence and the aggressive actions they had taken since the 1992 referendum. They saw themselves as a minority facing extinction, and feared becoming victims of genocide, just like in the 1940s. "If we stop fighting," Karadžić was quoted in the *FAZ* as saying, "we will all be killed."[95]

That distinct sense of victimhood was the very same sentiment expressed by the Serb woman at the marketplace in Sarajevo. It was one that all the main ethnic groups in Bosnia shared—and one with which many in the Federal Republic could identify. In fact, atrocities in foreign lands only rekindled Germans' own sense of past victimhood. As we have seen, the harrowing reports from the Balkans dredged up painful memories of the mass rape of German women by Red Army soldiers—just as the plight of Southeast Asian refugees had brought to mind the mass flight of Germans from the East in the 1940s. Bosnia and Cambodia compelled many Germans to reflect on their own country's history, in short, conjuring up memories of not just past German misdeeds but also past German suffering. But that did not mean that Germans played down the pain and sorrow of others to their own "historical" benefit, as the discussion of rape in Bosnia made clear.

There was, of course, an instrumental element to all this. Besides allowing Germans to give voice to their shock and outrage, portraying developments in Bosnia in the worst possible light only fortified the case of those calling for decisive steps to stop the bloodshed. It was precisely the perceived affinities to Nazism that made so many Germans demand that their own country, its allies, and the international community take immediate action. Those affinities were self-evident for those with a high degree of historical (and perhaps moral) sensitivity, and that is precisely why the very *way* in which Germans talked about developments in Bosnia was so significant—even if their many words did not lead immediately to any concrete action. For many, the weight of the German past, coupled with the realization and acknowledgment early on that a genocide was indeed taking place in the Balkans, meant only one thing: more was required than mere words.

7

Our Revulsion against Military
Force Is Understandable

A marathon debate took place in the Bundestag on July 22, 1992, just two weeks before the story broke about the Serb internment camps. The focus was on German participation in international measures meant to stop the bloodletting in the Balkans. One week earlier, Chancellor Kohl's cabinet had announced that the government was sending three reconnaissance planes and a naval destroyer to help enforce a UN-sanctioned trade embargo against Serbia. A majority voted by acclamation for a resolution supporting the government's decision. It stated that the actions of the Serb army in Bosnia constituted "attempted genocide" and called on the government to "investigate" how the UN should respond.[1]

At a press conference one day later, a journalist pointedly asked Kohl why he had not spoken during the lengthy, five-hour session. The chancellor offered a coy response: "I don't have to raise my hand at every Bundestag gathering, do I?" His subsequent comments suggested a more plausible reason for his uncustomary silence. He agreed with the arguments made by the members of his own coalition *and* by the opposition— at least on one fundamental issue. Germany could not participate *militarily* in the Balkans "for all sorts of reasons," the chancellor explained, not least because of what the country had done there during World War II. And that was why, Kohl argued, "we Germans should hold back from doling out advice" to others, adding, "I'm leaving aside for now the constitutional aspect"—a reference to the fraught question of whether the Basic Law allowed for the deployment of the Bundeswehr to regions outside North Atlantic Treaty Organization (NATO) territory. Even if that issue were now "unanimously resolved ..., nobody could seriously say that the Germans—of all people the Germans!" should participate in a military mission in the Balkans.[2] The chancellor's remarks were eminently reasonable, especially for someone whose government, just a day earlier, had been accused by a handful of parliamentarians of harboring ambitions to create a resurgent German *Großmacht*.

Talk of sending German soldiers to Bosnia or engaging in combat there was putting the cart before the horse. No one—least of all in Germany—was seriously considering military intervention in the Balkans at the time.[3] Such talk intensified, however, when it became clear that the initial flurry of international actions—ranging from economic sanctions and a weapons embargo to a series of diplomatic initiatives by high-level European and American officials—had failed to defuse the conflict or stop the violence from escalating. Over the next three years, various foreign dignities, as well as German officials and pundits, would bandy about the possibility of a military response or plead for one directly. The earliest and most insistent calls came, not surprisingly, from top officials in Bosnia, who also made their case in Germany directly. NATO, its sister military alliance the Western European Union (WEU), and the UN Security Council were all speaking openly about long-distance attacks by air and sea in the summer of 1992. Yet for all the talk about possible military intervention, no intervention occurred during the first three years of the conflict. The conservative *Frankfurter Allgemeine Zeitung,* whose opinion writers all supported a forceful response, succinctly summarized the situation: "Actions are announced again and again, and then quickly discarded."[4]

Despite the absence of concrete military action in Bosnia, its very possibility became a source of vigorous debate in the Federal Republic. There was a largely sober exchange of ideas about the desirability and practicability of any outside intervention whatsoever. And there was a more heated discussion about the role Germany should play in the event an intervention should take place, what Germany's contribution should be to armed efforts to enforce international sanctions, and, finally, whether such participation was even constitutionally permissible. This quickly turned into a more general debate—in the media, the Bundestag, and elsewhere—about Germany's "proper" place in the international arena since unification, and, more ominously, whether the nation was once again striving to become a global military power. The Third Reich loomed large over such discussions. That the past should play a role in the present was a point on which almost all Germans could agree—even if they drew diametrically opposed lessons from their country's fraught history.[5]

History was important, but the extremely graphic media coverage of the war in Bosnia played an equally significant role in shaping German responses. It was why so many spoke out in favor of foreign military intervention in principle, and why they frequently resorted to humanitarian, moral, and even emotional arguments to make their case. Perceptions dictated reactions, even if those reactions remained largely limited to verbal hand-wringing—like that of journalist Pierre Simonitsch, who had also covered Cambodia more than a decade earlier. He admonished early on that the world community could not simply "stand idly by" as a part of Europe was "reduced to rubble" and as international law and "moral values" were "trampled underfoot." Too many people had already died in Bosnia because of global inaction, he insisted, the time for back-and-forth discussions about the relative merits of intervention was over, and the choice was thus a simple one. Peter Meyer-Ranke, the Middle East correspondent for *Bild-Zeitung,* similarly argued that political pressure and economic sanctions were not enough to stop the Serbs because "war criminals only understand force." These comments *preceded* the shocking revelations about Serb internment camps in early August 1992, and the tone became even more urgent after the first images were published. "Enough with the palaver," the popular tabloid *Bild am Sonntag* implored. "It is high time somebody confronts the Serb butchers. . . . Stop the killing in the Balkans now!"[6]

Even those who had strong reservations about the wisdom of military intervention expressed sympathy for such arguments. Ulrich Irmer, the Free Democratic Party's spokesperson on foreign policy, acknowledged that there were situations in which—"as a last resort," after all economic and diplomatic means had been attempted—there was no other choice besides force. What else could one do in a "hopeless situation" against "bloodthirsty aggressors" such as Slobodan Milošević—or, for that matter, Adolf Hitler? Jürgen Maier of the pacifist Greens strongly concurred, even as he expanded the list of historical precedents for military intervention: "The prevention of genocide and the protection of human rights have never alone been a cause for intervention, and that is why there will be no intervention in Bosnia. *Unfortunately,* I'd like to add . . . Hitler's armies, the US Army in Vietnam, Saddam's genocide campaigns [in Iraq], and the Khmer Rouge . . . could not have been overcome by pacifist means, but only through armed self-defense."[7]

Practical considerations were just as important as humanitarian and moral concerns for those who supported military intervention in Bosnia. Unchecked Serb aggression would set a dangerous precedent and serve as a "fatal model" for other states in Eastern Europe and elsewhere in the post–Cold War world.[8] And, they argued, there was another issue at stake—namely, Western credibility in the face of despotic behavior. "Conflict prevention and crisis management hinge on the readiness of the international community to apply military means as well, if necessary," Helmut Kohl remarked at an international security conference in Munich. The setting could not have been more appropriate, given the city's indelible association with the policy of appeasement toward Hitler in the 1930s. On a related note—and with an eye to the Gulf War of 1990–1991—others argued that inaction would open up the West to accusations of hypocrisy for imposing a double standard, for supposedly acting only when its own material interests were involved. Would the West, journalist (and former Maoist) Helga Hirsch mordantly asked in *Die Zeit,* really "die" for Sarajevo, where it was "not about oil . . . but just human lives?"[9]

There was another practical reason to use force. It was the only way to ensure the distribution of humanitarian aid—an argument even those with misgivings about a military response found plausible. The Social Democrat Freimut Duve pointedly asked how it would be possible to deliver food, medicine, and other assistance to the 800,000 people trapped in the besieged city of Tuzla *without* taking forceful measures. Duve had just visited the city in the spring of 1993, and its mayor had personally asked him to speak in the Bundestag about "militarily securing" the only access road to the city.[10]

That was an eminently pragmatic argument for taking some form of military action. But those opposed to using force in Bosnia argued in equally practical terms. They pointed, for example, to the dangers foreign personnel would face. If airstrikes were to commence, Foreign Minister Kinkel and others warned, all humanitarian aid workers and UN personnel would have to be withdrawn because of Serb threats to "hunt" them down "when the first bombs fall." Others contended that military intervention would lead to "uncontrollable escalation" and an even greater "bloodbath."[11] Instead of bringing ordinary Serbs "to reason," the newsmagazine *Stern* argued, airstrikes would "drive them deeper into nationalist insanity" and thus prolong the conflict. Such attacks would undermine any willingness to compromise, leftist politicians like Barbara Höll of the Party of Democratic Socialists (PDS) and Oskar Lafontaine of the SPD similarly warned, and a solution could not be "bombed into existence" by outside forces. They may have had in mind their own country's experiences during World War II, when aerial bombardment had not only failed to break morale but even strengthened the resolve of many Germans—including those who had not been among Hitler's most ardent supporters. Even Duve, a steadfast advocate of military intervention, rejected this tactic because of the "painful memories" associated with Dresden and Hamburg, his hometown.[12]

More important, critics argued, airstrikes would pose unacceptable dangers to innocent Bosnian civilians. Because of the country's complex demographic makeup, it would be almost impossible to attack Serb targets without hitting Muslims—a point underscored by the military in Germany and elsewhere. This "spiritual kinship" between the condemnation of military intervention by political progressives and the warnings of the military was "remarkable," Klaus Hartung commented in *Die Zeit*. In fact, at a public debate about Bosnia organized by the Greens in Hamburg, "excitement first erupted" when one of the discussants dared to express doubt about the "expert knowledge" of the military— underscoring the curious alliances and affinities being forged in the ongoing debate.[13]

The SPD's Margitta Terbourg, born in Lower Silesia in 1941, was simply "appalled" by the "insensitivity" of those arguing for targeted bombing: "I experienced such bombardments as a very small child. I'll never forget [them]. . . . And I think of all the small children, the mothers, the old people who will suffer under our bombs."[14] These were deeply personal reasons to which all Germans of a certain age could relate. But the possibility of aerial warfare in the Balkans did not just awaken painful memories of German suffering during World War II. It also gave rise to resentful arguments tinged at times by anti-American sentiment—not unlike the ones that had surfaced during the Cambodian genocide. This time, however, the jabs were usually cloaked in purely strategic considerations. Theo Sommer, the politically moderate publisher of *Die Zeit* and a teenager during the war, decried airstrikes as the "traditional *American way of war,*" a form of bombing intended to mitigate "pangs of conscience." But it had not been decisive during World War II, he reminded his readers, nor had it prevented defeat in Vietnam.[15]

Sommer's remarks touched on the most common argument against foreign intervention: the manifold military challenges it would face. Those on the Left, and even prominent German military leaders like Gerd Schmückle, a four-star general and former Deputy Supreme Allied Commander Europe, did not tire of evoking the specter of another Lebanon or a "European" Vietnam. Pessimists offered a variety of reasons why Bosnia would not be the same cakewalk that, for instance, Kuwait had been in the recent Gulf War.[16] They pointed above all to the local terrain, ideal for the type of partisan warfare that had proven so successful against the Wehrmacht during World War II. Not "even forty divisions" had been able to "pacify" Tito's followers, recalled Hermann Otto Solms, head of the FDP caucus in the Bundestag, during the lengthy debate of July 1992. The comment drew a sharp reproach from Gregor Gysi, the colorful and quick-witted head of the PDS: "What's the point— that we Germans had no military success at the time, and *that* is why we shouldn't intervene again in Yugoslavia today?" That was perhaps unfair, even if Solms had opened himself up to such a rebuke. Still, those favoring outside intervention would have none of it. With barely disguised admiration for German military prowess, conservative commentator Carl Gustaf Ströhm rejected popular claims that Serbs were "born partisans" and a "regular" army could not defeat them, dismissing such ideas as pure "legend" and "myth." In fact, he continued, the Wehrmacht had had only a "very few real fighting units" in the Balkans because the "elite divisions" had all been on the Eastern Front.[17]

Military experts speculated it would take up to a quarter of a million soldiers on the ground to restore peace in Bosnia. But, Foreign Minister Kinkel made clear, because of the geographic situation and the experiences of World War II, "no one" in the West was "prepared to do that."[18] There was an alternative, of course: lifting the arms embargo imposed on the entire region since the fall of 1991. That highly controversial policy had put the Muslims at a strong disadvantage because Serb forces controlled almost all the armaments. Washington and most Islamic states were sympathetic to Muslim demands that this "license to kill" be lifted, but the UN and the European Community remained just as vigorously opposed, fearing it would escalate fighting. German leaders were more or less of the same opinion—at first. But Kohl and Kinkel began to change their tune by the end of 1992. "We indeed support and, in my opinion, must support the weapons embargo," Kinkel announced that winter. But "these wrongfully attacked people" also had a right to self-defense. One could "at least help them to protect themselves." It was a "moral-ethical responsibility"—even if it ran the risk, he warned, of being "massively counterproductive."[19]

Kohl shared Kinkel's ambivalence, emphasizing the "unusually intensive moral dimension" of the entire matter. At a press conference in June 1993, the chancellor candidly acknowledged that almost all of Germany's European allies had reservations about lifting the arms blockade, especially those with soldiers in the region, like France and Britain. But the situation was different in Germany, where tens of thousands of Bosnian refugees were now living. Their horrific accounts about the cruelties taking place back home had elicited an "extremely . . . emotional response" in the Federal Republic, one reason Kohl now believed lifting the embargo was the "right step." Another was behind-the-scenes pressure from the new American president, Bill Clinton. Hewing to their country's strong attachment, since 1945, to multilateralism, Kohl and Kinkel emphasized that there would be no "German solo action" on this score; instead they would try to coordinate—in vain, it turned out—a joint measure with European allies.[20]

Prominent politicians in the chancellor's own party had begun calling for an end to the embargo long before Kohl publicly changed course. Ten days after Stefan Schwarz's maiden speech in the Bundestag on December 10, 1992, Claus Jäger of the Christian Democratic Union called on the government to send armor-piercing antitank weaponry to the Muslims and Croats defending Sarajevo. Christian Schwarz-Schilling vigorously denounced Bonn's position as well, becoming one of the party's most outspoken members on this issue after hearing Schwarz's remarks at the closed meeting of the party's parliamentary caucus on December 8. If the international community would not intervene militarily, he reasoned, not allowing the Muslims to defend themselves was tantamount to "massive interference" in favor of the Serbs: "Nobody will declare us innocent of this, also not history." Schwarz-Schilling was so incensed he dramatically resigned his position as minister for post and communication several days later, "ashamed" to be part of such a government, he told the chancellor after a fiery cabinet session. After all, he later explained, he had first entered politics to make sure that barbarities like those committed by the Nazis would "never happen again."[21]

The devout Catholic politician had first heard about the atrocities in Bosnia while on a family vacation in southern France in early August 1992. Like Stefan Schwarz, he was "left speechless" by Roy Gutman's graphic reports in *Die Welt* and could not believe "such catastrophes" were taking place again "in the middle of Europe," almost a half century after the end of World War II. Schwarz-Schilling had suffered personally during the Third Reich. The Gestapo had repeatedly interrogated his parents and even imprisoned his sister because of their opposition to the regime. He later found out, after her death, that his mother had been Jewish.[22]

Following his departure from Kohl's cabinet, Schwarz-Schilling quickly became an advocate for decisive action. He did not support sending German soldiers but did believe that aerial attacks were "the least" the international community could do—something of an irony given his earlier opposition to America's bombing of Vietnam.[23] Hawks in the German media agreed. They also accused the West of making it impossible for the Muslims to defend themselves after giving them false hope of support. "And when things became serious," Carl Gustaf Ströhm fumed, the West did not "lift a finger" to help. From such accusations followed hackneyed historical analogies about the failed policy of appeasement in the 1930s. Western diplomacy could sigh a "gasp of relief" at having avoided war, Herbert Kremp editorialized in *Die Welt*. But this had come at the expense of Bosnia, whose sovereignty was being "smashed" like that of Czechoslovakia in 1938 and 1939. The UN and the European Community, Kremp concluded, have "learned nothing from history," an accusation made in the United States as well.[24]

Journalist Josef Joffe similarly reached back in time to make a case for lifting the embargo, noting that the Western Allies had had "no problems" providing munitions to Tito's partisans in the 1940s. Like Kohl and Kinkel, Joffe alluded to the "moral" dimension of the weapons issue. The West found itself in the position of a "well-intentioned" citizen who witnesses a "muscle-bound, well-armed thug" attacking a weaker person. Given the risks to life and limb, the citizen's "moral responsibility" was "not entirely clear" in this situation. "But whoever . . . does not intervene at least has the duty to . . . throw a cudgel to the oppressed." Western inaction was, in short, a sin of omission bordering on one of commission. Johannes Gerster of the CDU, a longtime member and later president of the German-Israeli Society, was even more blunt: "Those who now do nothing are complicit in genocide."[25]

The arguments against any form of outside military intervention and ending the arms embargo were just as vigorous as those for it. Still, they tended to be primarily pragmatic in nature, and with some exceptions, debate about these issues proceeded in a largely sober manner. By contrast, the question of *German* participation in some type of military action was discussed much more fiercely, as it had been during the recent Gulf War. That earlier conflict also inspired frequent allusions to the Holocaust, especially after it was revealed that German firms had provided

Iraq with the technology to produce chemical weapons—technology the Iraqis threatened to use, after they began launching dozens of missiles into Israel.[26]

Most striking, in any event, was the focus by all sides on the "lessons of history" as a guide for current policy decisions. The substance of those lessons nevertheless remained a matter of spirited dissension. "Our revulsion against military force is understandable," acknowledged Karl Lamers, speaker of the CDU/CSU caucus on foreign affairs, at the July 1992 Bundestag debate. It was also "reassuring" for Germany's neighbors and "indeed even for us ourselves," given the events of World War II. But, he continued, the desire to participate in some way in Yugoslavia and in other troubled regions did not reflect some sort of "rampant interventionism." It was a desire to defend others, defend peace, and draw the "right lessons" from the past. Lamers's parliamentary counterpart in the FDP, Ulrich Irmer, concurred:

> It is always said that the German past prohibits us from participating in such missions. It is correct that German soldiers were misused in the past by a shameful terrorist regime to break international law and disrupt peace. But can that mean that we, as a democratic country dedicated to human rights, offer excuses today by saying we are not prepared to defend international law and secure and serve the cause of peace? That, I believe, is a completely erroneous interpretation of our history.

It was "*precisely* our past," Irmer forcefully added, that "obliges us *not* to shirk from such missions."[27]

Lamers and Irmer were pushing back hard against insinuations by leftist politicians in the chamber, like Gregor Gysi of the PDS. After two world wars had begun "on German soil this century," Gysi admonished, it was "completely ahistorical and dangerous" for the country to become militarily active again and to try, "in this way, to forget the past." Rejecting the use of force was not a form of "shirking" one's duty, as his conservative opponents maintained, but "precisely the opposite, namely, accepting real political responsibility . . . and, in that way, not negating history." Like Gysi, Norbert Gansel, chair of the SPD's parliamentary working group on foreign and security issues—and, incidentally, a former naval officer who had supported the recognition of Croatia and Slovenia—insinuated that the government's call for some sort of "return to foreign-policy normality" laid bare its "great power" pretensions and a desire to repress the Nazi past. "What does 'normality' actually mean" in light of Germany's history, he demanded to know.[28]

Like others opposed to any German involvement in military measures, Gysi and Gansel were making a larger statement about the use of force that went well beyond Bosnia. But was there any substance to their dramatic remarks? Conservative politicians repeatedly emphasized their categorical opposition to sending German combat soldiers to Yugoslavia. At the same time, they affirmed again and again that evading the past was not at all their intention—much less preparing for a war of aggression. Rather, they argued, Germany's past imposed a duty on them to act in the present. "As a postwar German," the young CDU parliamentarian Stefan Schwarz told his colleagues, "I believe it is antifascist to say, 'Precisely because we experienced it, we must do something against it.'" Ursula Männle of the Christian Social Union echoed the point: "Precisely this historical legacy obliges us to demand that human rights be respected around the globe [and to] help those who are victims of brutal violence." Männle then took aim at her colleagues on the left side of the aisle. Germany's role in all this could not "amount to nothing more than just moral judgment [and] condemnation." Instead, it required active engagement in humanitarian endeavors—and "unfortunately, as paradoxical as it sounds, with armed force as well."[29]

Several German pundits and public intellectuals drew similar lessons. "Our most recent history demands of us special restraint," commented Christoph Bertram, the diplomatic correspondent for *Die Zeit*. "But must one who makes use of our history not instead derive from that just the opposite conclusion, that the Germans may not stand aside with folded arms when people are once again herded into camps, transported in cattle cars, and selected for death according to ethnic criteria?"[30] Jürgen Maier of the Greens concurred, rejecting the argument that the country had to show special restraint because of Germany's involvement in the "mass murder of Serbs" a half century before: "This convinces me just as little as the argument that Germans should be restrained in their criticism of Israeli crimes against Palestinians and of Israeli wars of aggression. Why did nobody suggest, after the Nazis had massacred 20 million Russians and Ukrainians, that Germans had to be especially restrained when it came to criticizing the Soviet Union?" Two other leading Greens, Helmut Lippelt and Claudia Roth, expressed similar misgivings after a visit to Bosnia in August 1992, shortly after the claims about "concentration camps" had first surfaced. Germans had a "special historical responsibility . . . to speak up against every form of fascism and National Socialism." They vigorously opposed the indiscriminate use of force but nevertheless acknowledged that those twin scourges had to be "resisted and fought . . . *by force, if necessary.*"[31]

That was a major concession for the leaders of a pacifist party—one that Joschka Fischer, the popular Hessian minister of the environment, echoed a day later in an interview with the *taz.* Acknowledging his own "internal strife" on the matter, Fischer, a so-called *realo* (political realist) since the 1980s, explained that he opposed military intervention in Bosnia because it would lead to an escalation of the war. But the larger question, to his mind, was how a pacifist party like the Greens should act in a situation involving "extreme nationalism" that "veered in the direction of National Socialism." He had been politicized by two historical experiences. One was the "mandate that Auschwitz never repeat itself," that one could not remain "silent and inactive" if that ever became a possibility. The other was that "Germany must never again start a war." Pacifism could not have "prevented" Auschwitz, he conceded, and he was "energetically opposed" to anything that might once again lead to German "imperialist politics." But he was "enough of a realist to know that, at some point, some scoundrel will come to power in Europe and want to maintain power using horrible means. And one will have to put a stop to his activities. One will not be able to escape this, also as a German."[32] This all foreshadowed debates that, in just a few years, would shake his party to the core.

Those willing to support some form of German military participation in Bosnia—if called on by the international community to do so, and short of sending ground troops—did not just invoke the legacy of the Third Reich. Many focused as well on Germany's experiences *after* 1945. Vera Wollenberger of the Greens, a former GDR dissident who vigorously supported lifting the arms embargo and would later join the CDU, believed that the country now had a "special responsibility"—as a formerly divided nation that had enjoyed the "solidarity of the free world"—to oppose the forced separation of Bosnia along ethnic lines. There were other, more indirect allusions to German division. In a speech rhetorically reminiscent of Ronald Reagan's famed comments at the Berlin Wall in 1987, Klaus Kinkel admonished the mutually belligerent Muslim and Croat inhabitants of Mostar to "draw the right lessons from history" and "rip down the invisible wall" dividing the city and "build bridges instead—not just over the Neretva River, but also in your minds and hearts."[33]

Such sentiments must have resonated in eastern and western Germany during the heady but difficult years following unification. But an equally important argument for international solidarity and an expanded international role for Germany focused on how much had changed since 1989 in a different way. In the wake of regaining complete national sovereignty, Germany now had greater global responsibilities. Being a signatory of the UN Charter entailed not only certain "rights" but also "duties"—including a willingness to provide support during military actions ordered by the Security Council.[34]

Kohl, Kinkel, and others also emphasized Germany's responsibilities to its allies and neighbors, who expected the Federal Republic to do its "fair share" in Bosnia. A failure to comply, they feared, would severely damage Germany's reputation. Besides, Karl Lamers of the CDU asserted, their allies did not believe that it was "just noble motives" underlying German hesitation. They suspected that Germany's reluctance was "fundamentally" about letting others "perform the heavy work . . . [and] not wanting our own tranquility disturbed." The country's trustworthiness and reliability were on the line, and international isolation on this issue was, in Helmut Kohl's words, the "last thing" the country needed. The matter was "incredibly important" for Germany's "global reputation." But what was also at stake, the chancellor added, was an "appreciation of the country's dignity"—not least "on the part of its own people." That sentiment underscored the chancellor's firm belief that Germans, especially younger ones, needed to develop a "healthier," more positive relationship with their country and its history.[35]

For all these reasons, Germany could no longer follow a "special path" (*Sonderweg*) in the international arena. "That historical period is now over," Hermann Otto Solms of the Free Democrats declared during the July 1992 debate. Foreign Minister Kinkel wholeheartedly agreed: "Yes, we wish to and must keep in mind our history, but we may not hunker down behind it. . . . There is really only one lesson from that history: Never again break rank with the West, no more special paths. . . . Have we forgotten that only armed force—not peace marches—finally put an end to Hitler's crimes in 1945?" The reference to a *special path* was a clever inversion of its conventional meaning among historians of modern Germany. For them, it referred to the country's authoritarian, militarist past, when Germany's supposed deviation from the political path of its West European neighbors had led inexorably to the "German catastrophe" of the early twentieth century.[36]

What did the opposition make of all this? For all his reservations about a "return to 'normality,'" Norbert Gansel of the SPD concurred with his more conservative colleagues. Germans had "no more excuses" after 1990, and a sense of a "duty toward German history" should not lead to a "flight from responsibility"—though what precisely that responsibility entailed remained a matter of debate. Those further to the Left vehemently rejected such arguments, with Gregor Gysi making the strongest case. In the first place, the head of the PDS countered, the UN Charter did not make military participation a duty. It was a voluntary choice. And in response to arguments about Germany's "heightened political responsibility" since 1989, Gysi demanded to know why this had to assume a military dimension: "We have many other means and methods of helping . . . in a way that promotes peace. We do not need to send German soldiers out into the world for that."[37] Peter Glotz of the SPD strongly agreed. Germans had fought "enough" wars that century, and the Federal Republic could "sooner satisfy" the expectations of the international community if it were to double its foreign aid rather than participate in military operations. After all, he added, if his fellow citizens had learned anything from the 1930s and 1940s, it was that "skepticism and caution" were the "most important virtues for the once so reckless Germans. . . . We have the right to say that we will help in humanitarian terms, we'll help with money . . . but, when it comes to war, kindly leave us in peace for a couple of decades!"[38]

Foreign Minister Kinkel firmly rejected the idea that Germany should continue to "pay" and not "play," that is, provide only financial support and logistical assistance. "In the long run," he declared in a speech to the American Chamber of Commerce in Stuttgart in July 1992, Germany could not "just stand there with a checkbook" while others sent soldiers. That it was highly hypocritical to call for some form of military intervention in Bosnia but then refuse to join in oneself was, in fact, one of the most powerful and frequent arguments made by those advocating some form of German military participation. It would damage the country's reputation, Minister of State Helmut Schäfer lectured the Bundestag, if Germans were to ask others to intervene in Bosnia and then not be willing to participate themselves. The SPD's Norbert Gansel more or less agreed ("Never demand of others what you are not prepared to do yourself"), and Ulrich Irmer of the FDP wanted to know if it were more permissible to put at risk the lives of young American or French soldiers, Danes, or Nigerians. The German *Volk,* he believed, would not be "so selfish."[39]

Advocates and opponents of German participation in some sort of military intervention in Bosnia both spoke, then, of various duties: to the victims, to the international community, to the West because of its steadfast support during the Cold War, and, last but not least, to German history. But since it was clear to almost everyone that German soldiers could not be deployed to the region, for historical and probably constitutional reasons, much of the debate may have seemed academic. It was not, in fact, because of another issue that quickly became an important source of discord: whether the country could participate in international military actions aimed at bringing the warring parties to heel when those actions remained *below* the threshold of actual combat. More concretely, could the Bundeswehr provide logistical support to other forces sent to establish and maintain peace in Bosnia, or provide protection to aid convoys en route to besieged cities? Could German forces participate in measures to enforce economic sanctions against the Serbs or a "no-fly zone" over Bosnia? Could German Blue Helmets be sent to Bosnia on a UN peacekeeping mission at some point?

The last issue did not become acute until late 1995, following the signing of the peace agreement that ended the conflict, but the other two came to a head in late 1992 and early 1993, when NATO and the WEU started to enforce a series of UN Security Council resolutions intended to pressure the Serbs. The first, Resolution 757 of May 30, 1992, instituted a trade embargo and other measures aimed at isolating the Serbs internationally, reaffirming more than a half dozen other resolutions adopted since fall 1991, including an arms embargo on the entire region.[40]

Economic and diplomatic sanctions were something almost everyone in Germany could agree on. Most Germans believed, in fact, that this should be the international community's primary focus. That was clearly the government's position. It preferred to wait and see what sanctions achieved, Kinkel commented during a radio interview in the spring of 1992, "Then we'll see further"—carefully alluding to the possible use of more forceful measures later on. It was no surprise that political progressives, including Joschka Fischer, strongly supported sanctions over military intervention. As Fischer argued that summer, an embargo would force "all combatants . . . to their knees"—curious language for the leader of a pacifist party but revealing of his future position on military intervention and, perhaps, of his life as a militant activist and street fighter in the early 1970s.[41]

The German government not only welcomed such measures but also claimed to have been instrumental in bringing them about. One day before the embargo was passed, Kinkel had boasted on German radio that he had been the "main driving force" behind calls for concrete action at a recent international gathering in Lisbon. He was also "pleased," he added, that the Americans had now "fully adopted our position" in this matter.[42] Drawing attention to Germany's role served several purposes. For one, it underscored the government's unwavering commitment to a nonmilitary solution. At the same time, it emphasized Germany's increased stature on the world stage—at least in the eyes of high-ranking German officials. This was partly for domestic consumption. But it must also be seen in the context of other efforts to increase the country's global standing after unification—such as lobbying for a permanent seat on the UN Security Council.[43] One detected a growing sense of pride, at least among German elites, about their country's new role in the world. Whereas German diplomats had boasted *internally* about their part in securing recognition of the Khmer Rouge at the UN a decade earlier, authorities now seemed more comfortable drawing public attention to Germany's growing stature, providing ammunition for those who feared the country might be getting a bit too big for its britches.

Whatever the motivation for supporting sanctions, the goal was clear: to pressure the Serbs into ending their bloody campaign in Bosnia. Striking an optimistic note, German politicians and pundits religiously maintained that the measures had indeed forced Belgrade and the Bosnian Serbs to make important concessions. However, it was also widely acknowledged that the sanctions were largely ineffective because they were not strictly enforced. Through various "tricks" and "loopholes," Belgrade was able to circumvent the embargo, which was "as full of holes as a Swiss cheese," and receive clandestine overland shipments of essential items like weapons and oil from many countries, including Germany. There were also reports that the Muslims were buying weapons on the black market in the Federal Republic, and that German-built weapons were being used in the conflict. Officials vigorously denied such claims—as they had when similar charges surfaced about the Khmer Rouge. Such rumors did not become "any truer through repetition," a spokesman for the Ministry of Defense sniped at reporters.[44]

Circumvention of the embargo was why NATO and the WEU decided to give it real teeth at a meeting in Helsinki in early July 1992. Concretely, that meant adopting more robust monitoring measures. The German cabinet decided to do its share at a meeting on July 15, and later that month the government sent three reconnaissance planes and a destroyer, the *Bayern,* to the Adriatic. German officials were at pains to emphasize that the action involved only monitoring and was not a blockade. Yet the actual character of the mission—and Germany's role in it—remained ambiguous, an impression Kohl and Kinkel only reinforced at a joint press conference they held in the Finnish capital. In his opening statement, the chancellor emphasized that these were not "coercive military measures." Then, just a few minutes later, the foreign minister backtracked, admitting it was "naturally a military mission" because it involved the deployment of a destroyer. Both Kinkel and Minister of

Defense Volker Rühe subsequently made it clear that the *Bayern* had the right to defend itself if attacked.[45]

The exact nature of Germany's participation was quickly and hotly contested, with critics charging that the decision was unconstitutional—or, at the very least, in a constitutional "gray zone." Whether that was the case hinged on how one interpreted two key articles in the Basic Law: Article 87a, which stated that the armed forces were to be used solely "for purposes of defense," and Article 24, which said that Germany could join "a system of mutual collective security" to achieve peaceful goals. The SPD considered taking the issue to the Federal Constitutional Court in Karlsruhe but decided to go a different route. In a formal parliamentary motion, the main opposition party accused the government of violating the Basic Law. The country "owes it to its history and its constitution, and to the members of the Bundeswehr, that an armed mission involves no legal gray zones." The PDS had gone even further in a motion filed a day earlier. Relying on "threatening military gestures" that did nothing to calm the situation or help those affected by the war, the government, it said, was trying to make out-of-area missions politically and "morally" acceptable. In an emotional editorial in *Die Welt,* a clearly exasperated Carl Gustaf Ströhm called the opposition's objections "shameful" and demanded to know whether its members had seen the most recent photographs from Sarajevo of "the mutilated children, the murdered civilians."[46]

The various motions, including a joint one submitted by the governing coalition parties backing the mission, were the focus of the July 22 debate. German participation provided "proof . . . of our reliability as allies," Foreign Minister Kinkel averred in his opening statement. But to calm his critics, he quickly added that the Bundeswehr was participating *without* the use of any armed force. It would serve "merely" as an observer, he insisted, and only provide information to international monitoring agencies. The "experience of our most recent history"—not just the "inhuman and destructive" Nazi dictatorship but also the "rogue regime" in East Germany—bestowed a "special duty" on Germany "to engage actively in an international framework for peace and human rights"—"Just like 1941!" interjected Uwe-Jens Heuer of the PDS, a tone-deaf historical comparison to be sure.[47]

The other members of the opposition reiterated their constitutional objections in a more measured manner. But there were exceptions. It was a "helpless gesture" that would not do anything to lessen the suffering in Bosnia, charged Hans-Ulrich Klose, head of the SPD caucus. Instead, it was a "demonstration" of Germany's new position in the world that said, "We are emerging from the shadow of the past." Konrad Weiß of the Greens offered a more cynical explanation. Sending a destroyer to the Adriatic was an effort to "divert attention" from the government's "disastrous" unification policies—at the cost of young and innocent German soldiers. And what *did* the German military think of the mission? Andrea Lederer of the PDS addressed that issue head-on, alluding to what she described as the "front-like," jingoistic tenor of recent media coverage. One television report claimed that "the lads" on the *Bayern* were going to Yugoslavia "in lockstep," confirming her worst suspicions.[48]

All sides had an opportunity to air their views, but in the end the government motion before the Bundestag passed, the opposition's motions were defeated, and German participation proceeded as planned. Nine months later, Kinkel announced that the Federal Republic was providing the "largest contribution" to the embargo in terms of personnel and matériel.[49]

On August 13, 1992, a week after dramatic footage of the Serb internment camps had sent shock waves across the globe, the UN Security Council passed another resolution, this time calling for military protection to assure the delivery of humanitarian assistance to Bosnia. High-level German officials, including Kohl, Kinkel, and Rühe, made it clear that German combat troops would not be involved. Those "familiar" with his country's history, the chancellor explained once again, must have "special understanding" for its unwillingness to send soldiers. By this point, his aversion to sending soldiers to areas previously occupied by the Wehrmacht had become known as the Kohl doctrine. Still, he added almost laconically, "We do not make it easy for ourselves in this matter."[50]

Two months later the international community took an even firmer stance against the Serbs. On October 9, the Security Council announced that a "no-fly zone" would be imposed over Bosnia, but it was not until late March 1993 that the international body gave the ban real teeth by adopting yet another resolution, this time permitting "all necessary measures . . . to ensure compliance." It went into effect in mid-April, with the full support of the German government. "A small gesture must always be backed up with an iron fist," journalist Josef Joffe commented approvingly.[51]

Public figures on the left and right supported the new measures, but that consensus quickly and characteristically fell apart when the question of *German* participation arose. On April 2, the cabinet announced that Germans would participate in monitoring activities aboard the AWACS military surveillance aircraft deployed by NATO. Their task would be to enforce the no-fly zone and monitor the delivery of aid. This represented a major step in the history of the alliance: it would be NATO's first "out-of-area" mission as well as the first time its forces were used to support a UN peacekeeping operation in a military role. But Germany's decision to join the mission also had important domestic reverberations in the Federal Republic, where it almost led to the collapse of the governing coalition.[52]

The opposition parties predictably protested the move, branding it an unconstitutional break with the "prevailing postwar consensus." The SPD filed a motion making a familiar case about the historical "burden" of World War II. More surprising was the reaction of the FDP as a member of the governing coalition. Its renitent ministers had voted *against* specifically permitting German participation on board the AWACS planes.[53] Klaus Kinkel, who would become chair of the party a month later, was conspicuously absent from the April cabinet meeting. The FDP subsequently filed a formal act of protest, objecting to any German presence on the surveillance aircraft as unconstitutional. The Ministry of the Interior, under Rudolf Seiters of the CDU, rejected those claims. Not only was German participation "literally and figuratively" compatible with the constitution but, just as important, the absence of a German crew would impede the mission's "operational capability" to such an extent that the no-fly ban would be only "partially enforced." In a groundbreaking five-to-three decision announced later that week, the Federal Constitutional Court rejected the FDP's case, as well as a similar one filed by the SPD. Essentially adopting the government's arguments, the court ruled that the absence of German soldiers on the AWACS planes would not only severely impede enforcement of the no-fly zone but also lead to a serious loss of trust on the part of Germany's allies. Minister of Defense Rühe celebrated the decision and acknowledged that it had great foreign-policy consequences, but he emphasized once again that it had nothing to do with sending soldiers or flying fighter aircraft, both of which he objected to—for the usual "historical reasons."[54]

Kinkel was in a delicate situation. His own party had filed a lawsuit against the government's decision, but he had to balance his party loyalties with his duties as foreign minister. The FDP would "obviously" respect the court's decision, he announced at a press conference alongside Rühe, despite the party's continuing "legal concerns." He then clarified his own position as Germany's top diplomat. He was "grateful" that the foreign-policy arguments had won out because a different decision would have led to severe "foreign-policy damage." Still, the fact that the court's decision had been so close demonstrated, the trained lawyer and former justice minister could not help adding, that the "legal considerations" had not been "so simple."[55]

All of this set the stage for another vigorous, hour-long debate in the Bundestag on April 21, 1993. This one focused on German participation aboard the NATO aircraft. In an opening statement, the foreign minister reiterated the argument that "our reliability as an ally" was at stake, but quickly added that the government's recent decision did not provide "carte blanche for all types of missions"—just those approved by the UN Security Council. "Solo actions" were "ruled out," he added, and any future decisions about participating in such actions rested in the hands of the Bundestag, as the court had explicitly stated in its ruling. Hermann Otto Solms, head of the FDP caucus, accepted the decision to put Germans on the AWACS planes but ominously warned that Germany had now "crossed a Rubicon."[56]

The opposition was predictably outraged by the court's ruling, calling it a "definitive break with the postwar consensus" and a slippery slope to future German militarization. Gerd Poppe of the Greens dramatically argued that the government was taking advantage of the dire situation in Bosnia "to legitimize the Bundeswehr's first combat mission."[57]

Roughly three-fifths of the Bundestag's delegates nevertheless voted for German participation aboard the planes. With only a few exceptions, including a handful of abstentions (mainly by members of the FDP), almost every member of parliament voted along party lines.[58] The outcome was therefore a foregone conclusion. However, the discussion, like the one in July 1992, was by no means superfluous. Important issues had come to a head during the first year of the Bosnian conflict: whether some form of foreign military intervention was desirable, and, more controversially, what Germany's role should be if foreign intervention came to pass. This, in turn, gave politicians and pundits the opportunity to express their ideas about the "proper" response, *as Germans,* to the bloodshed in Bosnia. Once the government decided to send military ships, planes, and personnel to the region, those debates left the realm of speculation. Push had come to shove.

For all their points of contention, there was fundamental agreement among German politicians on at least three major issues: international sanctions were the best course of action for the time being; the burden of the past weighed heavily on Germany's *present* actions and decisions; and, following from that, German combat troops had no business in the region, at that time or in the future. Germans may not have been able or willing to use forceful measures to put a stop to what many considered an ongoing genocide, but there were other ways they could help. That was why most officials and politicians, along with human-rights activists and other civilians, focused their immediate attention elsewhere: on the provision of humanitarian assistance to the victims—including, once again, the large number of refugees fleeing from yet another war-torn region.

8

Humanity in Action

The Federal Republic did not need to "hide behind anyone" when it came to the "humanitarian realm," Klaus Kinkel remarked with great self-assurance during a radio interview in late June 1992. "We've done much there, very much, knowing that in the other realm"—namely, armed assistance—"we cannot exactly help as we'd perhaps wish." The new foreign minister was referring specifically to the dire refugee situation in former Yugoslavia—the "greatest human and political tragedy" to plague Europe since the end of World War II. By the spring of 1994, just as another genocide was beginning, this time in faraway Rwanda, the Federal Republic would take in between 350,000 and 400,000 persons from the Balkans—more than half of all who had fled. That was, Kinkel told the Bundestag "with pride" at the time, "more than twice as many as all the other European countries put together . . . an astonishing achievement."[1]

Kinkel's remarks solemnly celebrated German humanitarian engagement in the Balkans, but they also drew attention to the ways his country's hands were tied. The Federal Republic's military options were limited in Bosnia, for constitutional and historical reasons—though no one else in the international community was rushing to send combat troops. At the same time, the foreign minister's remarks reminded his audience that force was not the only possible response to genocide and other mass atrocities—or, if efforts to prevent or halt them came up dry, to their aftermath. The failure of the international community to put a stop to the carnage and suffering in Bosnia generated a great deal of hand-wringing in the Federal Republic. And it prompted both officials and ordinary Germans to search for other, nonlethal ways to help.

Humanitarian assistance once again became the default response. It also became a source of anger and resentment—on the part of German officials who complained that their European allies were not doing enough, and on the part of ordinary Germans who believed that the Federal Republic should be doing even more to help the victims and refugees. A high level of civic engagement was, in fact, a direct response to such criticisms. But it was motivated by other concerns as well—humanitarian in nature, and also related to Germany's own troubled past.

Estimates of the number of Bosnian refugees who fled their homes varied widely, from 1.5 to 3 million out of a prewar population of 4.5 million. German politicians, humanitarian groups, and the media spoke incessantly of their "indescribable suffering" and "wretched" living conditions. They pointed in particular to severe shortages of food, clean water, and medicine, as well as to overcrowding and poor hygienic conditions in makeshift shelters, where the refugees were "herded tightly together" in some places "like animal transports on barges."[2] Just as during the Cambodian crisis, their words and media images of the refugees' "emaciated" bodies, of the "pale, bloated faces" of undernourished children, once again struck an empathetic chord. Minister of the Interior Rudolf Seiters explained at an international refugee conference in Geneva in the summer of 1992 that Germany was "at the forefront" of ongoing efforts to help the refugees because Germans knew "better than most people in the world what it means to lose one's *Heimat* and have to flee." By February 1993, more than a third of the more than 700,000 refugees who had left the Balkans and fled abroad had wound up in the Federal Republic. German prosperity and social largesse drew them, but there was another reason as well. Many had family members who had been living there as so-called guest workers since the 1960s—some 700,000 when the Bosnian war began.[3]

All of this took place at a time when Germany, Europe, and the world were experiencing the greatest demographic upheaval since 1945. In the wake of unification, the western half of Germany had gained approximately three million people: more than a million from former East Germany and nearly a million ethnic Germans from other former communist countries in Eastern Europe. On top of this, the Federal Republic received 1.4 million applications for asylum between 1983 and 1992—almost three times as many as France or Sweden, the two European countries with the next highest numbers.[4]

For all this largesse, or perhaps because of it, the treatment of Bosnian refugees quickly became a hotly disputed issue. At a heated press conference in early May 1992, government representatives fielded increasingly aggressive questions about why Bosnian refugees were being unceremoniously turned away at the German-Austrian border. After all, one journalist quipped, they were not coming for a "summer holiday"—an especially ironic comment, given that many Germans considered the Balkans a favorite vacation destination. Others were blunter. Human rights activists and members of the political opposition referred to these "scandalous" and "cynical" policies as "callous and inhuman," "shameful and profoundly unchristian." In a letter to the editor in *Neues Deutschland,* one reader likened government officials to "desk murderers" (*Schreibtischtäter*) for adopting policies that "aided and abetted genocide." Bavarian guards who "chased back" refugees at the border, the letter added gratuitously, gave a "new dimension" to the old East German "shoot-to-kill order" at the Berlin Wall. While some critics insinuated that the treatment of the refugees embodied prevailing prejudices against Muslims, others warned that the Bosnians were becoming the "new European Jews"—a telling metaphor. Jewish visitors to Bremen remarked, in fact, that the difficulties the refugees faced reminded them of the Holocaust.[5]

Whatever the validity of such claims and comparisons, there was a simple bureaucratic reason for the border denials. Since late April, Bosnians had been the sole group from former Yugoslavia required to obtain visas for entry. Chancellor Kohl's cabinet had originally decided to do away with the requirement but then reversed its decision at the behest of the Ministry of the Interior. What did the Bosnians need to do to make their reason for coming to Germany more "credible," one journalist angrily asked, if flight from "terror and massacres" did not suffice? "Those who have seen . . . the television images of mutilated people . . . know that hundreds of thousands must have good reason to fear being shot, raped, blinded, or castrated because of their nationality—and so they flee." Hanns Heinrich Schumacher, press secretary of the German Foreign Office, lamented the "contradictory" nature of this absurd bureaucratic situation and even assured critics that the strange "state of affairs" would be "remedied as quickly as possible."[6] Yet in subsequent months, government officials steadfastly refused to budge on the issue, and thousands of refugees continued to be denied entry at the border.

The representative of the UN High Commissioner for Refugees (UNHCR) in Germany similarly called on Bonn to lift the visa requirement and offer refugees a more stable legal status than mere *Duldung* (toleration)—"a supercilious term" from the Aliens Act of 1965. It meant they could not be deported, for the time being, but also that they had no right to work, receive professional training, attend university, or even travel outside their delegated federal state. They were forced to rely on welfare, as a result, and could not visit relatives or friends living elsewhere in the Federal Republic. "Damned to doing nothing" but watch television all day, to live in limbo and languish, slowly "going to rack and ruin."[7]

For all his sympathy for the plight of the refugees, Minister of the Interior Seiters tirelessly justified the government's position by arguing that an abolition of the visa requirement would not be responsible, because it would send a "false signal" and prompt an "uncontrolled wave of immigration"—a "bursting of the dam." The best solution for those wishing to leave was to remain "on site" in the Balkans, he insisted.[8] Similar arguments had been made a decade earlier about German efforts to rescue boat people fleeing former Indochina. The knowledge that Rupert Neudeck and the *Cap Anamur* were waiting on the high seas, the argument went at the time, only encouraged more to leave. It made more sense, Seiters argued, to ensure that the Bosnians already in Germany were receiving proper and humane treatment. Walter Zittelsberger, of the Bavarian Ministry of the Interior, similarly warned about the danger of an uncontrollable "immigration flood"—a popular metaphor.

Local authorities were already overburdened, said Zittelsberger, and so long as lodging and upkeep were "not secured" for those who had already arrived, the "gate" should remain "shut." Munich no longer had any more shelter available, he added by way of clarification, which was why the city was sending "homeless people" and "tramps" (*Penner*) to sleep under bridges or in nearby fields.[9]

The Bavarian response was not surprising. Most of the refugees were drawn there because of its geographic proximity and robust economy. But Bavaria was not alone in opposing changes to the existing visa requirements. As federal officials repeatedly explained, they could not modify the procedures without the express permission of the German states. And, with some exceptions, most remained opposed. At a meeting in May 1992, all the interior ministers of the *Länder* agreed to uphold the visa requirement, and they further stipulated that only those who had found a sponsor willing to sign a declaration promising to cover all the expenses of their upkeep would be allowed into the country.[10]

Such non-tax-deductible outlays, which included medical insurance as well as any costs incurred in the event of later deportation, understandably made many think twice before making a commitment. To make matters worse, many insurance companies refused to offer refugees coverage because of the financial risks. "What's a genocide," one journalist acerbically commented, "compared to the problems of German insurance companies." As a result, one host had to pay 17,000 DM for two operations on a Bosnian refugee who had injured himself riding a bicycle. According to another report, a dentist in Hamburg suddenly stopped an emergency extraction when he learned his Bosnian patient was uninsured. Torture and humiliation at the hands of Serb Chetniks was "not much better," *Neues Deutschland* remarked, with more than a touch of hyperbole.[11]

Those willing to offer sponsorship, despite the obstacles, sometimes faced further bureaucratic hurdles, like proving to fastidious officials their willingness to assume all financial responsibility. This prompted some proactive German Samaritans to journey directly to the Austrian border to bring back stranded refugees after signing a sponsorship pledge in person—like Birgit Prosker, a businesswoman from Munich who drove to Salzburg to pick up a mother and her two young children after seeing a harrowing report about them on television. Over the next three years, roughly 40,000 refugees from Bosnia would be sponsored by strangers like Prosker, by aid organizations and churches, and, most commonly, by Yugoslav relatives already living in Germany.[12]

Those trying to obtain a visa faced additional challenges: a mad rush followed by long waits and considerable costs at German embassies and consulates. There, critics charged, they frequently had to deal with "heartless" officials who did everything only by the book—behavior, *Der Spiegel* tartly commented, that recalled the "bureaucratic practices" of the former GDR. Following the "traumatic experiences" of war came the "trauma of German bureaucracy." Some frustrated Bosnians, referred to in officialese as *Einreisebegehrer* ("those covetous of entry"), even complained that the Germans they encountered were treating them "like a lower race."[13] Remarks like these appear less exaggerated in light of comments attributed to the deputy general consul at the German consulate in Salzburg. Droves of Bosnians had descended on Mozart's birthplace when it was announced that visas could be obtained in Austria. "I don't want to say that these people are unclean," he groused, lamenting the damage the refugees were supposedly causing to the walls and carpeting of the consulate. "But should I repaint the stairwell every two weeks?" This attitude only confirmed the negative reputation of "ugly Germans," squawked the Party of Democratic Socialists in an official parliamentary motion.[14]

Resentment about Germany's strict visa policy was especially pronounced in Austria, where officials repeatedly called on Bonn to change its guidelines—while sharply recalling the role former foreign minister Hans-Dietrich Genscher's diplomacy had played in the current crisis. One local official in Salzburg even described the German entry restrictions as "inhuman" and "lacking in solidarity"—a charge German leaders would later make, usually in more diplomatic terms, against other European governments.[15] Arguments about lifting the visa requirements fell on deaf ears, although officials did make one important concession. Deportations were suspended in May 1992, and all Bosnians already living in Germany were granted the "right to remain" until September 30, 1992. This *Bleiberecht*, which was later extended to March 31, 1993, and again several times after that, came partly in response to public pressure from the German states more open to taking in Bosnian refugees—including Lower Saxony, which had done so much a decade earlier to help refugees from Indochina. The more magnanimous states announced an end to deportations even before it became federal policy, and the interior ministers of the Rhineland-Palatinate, North Rhine–Westphalia, and Hamburg—all members of the Social Democratic Party—even called for a temporary end to the visa requirement, which soon became their party's official position. The Greens and the PDS demanded, for their part, that the Bosnians simply be allowed in for the duration of the war.[16]

Such largesse was not limited to political progressives. Erwin Teufel, the conservative Christian Democrat and minister-president of Baden-Württemberg, called on the *Länder* to take in thousands more and threatened to "go it alone" if they did not comply. Even the conservative *FAZ* argued that "war refugees" should be granted sanctuary, "not just out of a sense of moral responsibility but also under international law." In a similar vein, Herbert Leuninger, a Catholic priest and head of the human rights group Pro Asyl, warned officials that their policies were a "flagrant violation" of the letter and spirit of the country's Aliens Act of 1965 and the Geneva Convention of 1951, which the Federal Republic had signed the same year it acceded to the UN Genocide Convention.[17]

At the same time that high-level officials were refusing to loosen entry requirements, others demanded that certain groups of Bosnians be given preferential treatment: former inmates from Serb detention centers, for example, and especially rape victims. Even Bavarian authorities, normally accused of "hard-heartedness" and "inhumanity" because of their strict refugee policies, agreed to welcome orphans, mothers with children, and wounded Bosnians during a special initiative launched in late May 1992. Determining "priority" lists like these went back to the mass exodus that had followed the failed Hungarian Revolution of 1956— an important turning point, when, for political reasons, West Germany became much more open to accepting refugees who were not ethnically German.[18]

FIG. 8.1. Bosnian refugees arrive at a train station in Unna, Germany, July 1992. "Come Together" was the slogan of a well-known cigarette advertisement campaign following German unification. IMAGO / Sepp Spiegl.

The public outcry over the visa requirement prompted additional moves and concessions. At a meeting of the *Länder* in July 1992, officials decided to admit 5,000 refugees from Bosnia—an "unparalleled humanitarian" act, they crowed. The first group arrived a week later aboard six special trains, reminiscent of the East Germans who had arrived from the West German embassy in Prague in the fall of 1989. Most were children, women, and the elderly, accompanied by dozens of doctors, midwives, nurses, and representatives from aid organizations. "Tears run down the wrinkled cheeks of an old woman," the *taz* movingly if melodramatically reported. "Even hardened journalists had to cry when the special train arrived."[19] Some 5,200 refugees arrived in all— to a "media circus," sniped *Neues Deutschland,* which lasted until the reporters had gotten enough "fodder." Phones rang off the hook at government offices, and the number of volunteers willing to take in refugees in places like Berlin and Bremen quickly exceeded the number of Bosnians delegated to those cities. "Even" authorities in the eastern German town of Hoyerswerda—infamous for its "xenophobic pogroms" against asylum seekers in 1991—wanted to take in refugees, the *Wirtschafts-woche* reported.[20]

That same month, the *taz* organized a campaign of its own, working together with the local Green Party in Berlin and two human rights associations. Aktion Fluchtweg (Escape Route) called on private individuals and families, church parishes, and other organizations to host Bosnians in need. The goal was to help the refugees *and* sound a "political signal" to pressure the government to abolish the visa requirement. The *Berliner Zeitung* and the *Bild-Zeitung* followed suit and organized similar programs, as did Minden, a medium-size town in North Rhine–Westphalia, the state that not only took in the largest number of Bosnians but also assumed the entire cost of their upkeep.[21]

Curious about personal motivation, the *taz* conducted a telephone survey with Berliners who had volunteered to take in refugees. Most, it seems, wanted to do something practical to help. At the same time, they hoped to "shame" German authorities and exert pressure on them to do even more. After all, one woman explained, average citizens had to come forward if the government was "too stupid" to act. But there were other motivations as well. One West Berliner said that he wanted to demonstrate that there was "another Germany," a nod to the more ignoble aspects of his country's past. Others hoped, in this way, to "take a stand" against the recent spate of xenophobic violence in Germany and make it clear that the Muslims were not "typical abusers" of the country's generous asylum policies. In fact, opined journalist Klaus Wolschner, the willingness of so many to help demonstrated that German "television viewers" could indeed differentiate between those suspected of "tapping" social security benefits and those who really "needed to be helped"—a distinction that demonstrated just how ingrained such prejudices were.[22]

The images of mass destruction and suffering broadcast nightly on German television—often from places that had been beloved vacation spots—clearly played an important role in shaping Germans' reactions. A source of "shock" and "anger," they reportedly moved hardened politicians like Helmut Kohl just as much as ordinary Germans, who were tired of feeling "powerless," of "just watching" from the sidelines. As one Berliner who had lived through World War II as a child explained, "I still feel that in my bones. One simply has to help."[23] For many, the images recalled once again the millions of Germans who had fled the East right after World War II. Others, like Social Democrat Herbert Schnoor, North Rhine–Westphalia's minister of the interior and a fierce advocate for the refugees, were reminded of the suffering of German Jews in the 1930s. He later explained that he had first read about Bergen-Belsen in a POW camp after the war, and that he had specifically wanted to accept a thousand Sinti and Roma from the region because of past Nazi crimes.[24]

There were other important initiatives as well. Martin Fischer, a composer from Vienna who had lived and worked in the Federal Republic for many years as a radio journalist, established Den Winter Überleben (Survive the Winter) in 1992. Dedicated to rescuing victims of ethnic cleansing, the organization found Bosnians places to stay with private individuals and families in Germany and Sweden. With just four assistants, including his wife, Fischer managed to rescue almost 7,000 Bosnians by the summer of 1995.[25] Their organization had greater success than an ill-fated rescue expedition launched by two members of the Saxon-Anhalt state parliament in late July 1992: Jürgen Angelbeck and Karsten Knolle of the CDU, West Germans who had both moved to the East after unification. In the wake of what they saw as empty promises by Foreign Minister Kinkel to rescue injured and orphaned children from the besieged Bosnian capital, the two politicians decided to take matters into their own hands and "set an example" for Germany and other Western nations. With the support of their state government, which promised to assume financial responsibility for any rescued children, the two men managed to "smuggle" sixty orphans out of Sarajevo on July 27. But because of a "misunderstanding," Serb snipers shot and killed two of the children at a roadblock. The tragic incident sparked widespread outrage and condemnation of the two politicians and their "Rambo manners." (Knolle had earlier been a West German paratrooper, in fact.) The actions of these "publicity-seeking risk-takers," fumed journalist Michael Sontheimer, had "frivolously called into question the . . . credibility of the entire aid industry."[26]

That was an exaggeration. Still, for all the largesse, some individuals did seem to have less noble motives for taking in refugees. Officials in the state of Hesse had been "downright swamped" by the "spontaneous wave of helpfulness." But at least a third of the proposals were "un-serious," a government spokesperson claimed—more or less "undis-guised" ploys for "cheap and willing" domestic servants. One Bavarian in search of a wife requested a widow; another, a "handsome young boy"; and one older woman, a "blond puppet" she could "dress up smartly." Childless couples, for their part, tried to circumvent normal adoption procedures by agreeing to take in only young children. In short, moti-vations ran the gamut from "stalwart selfishness" to "sheer altruism." A sense of religious and moral duty also played a role. "We're Christians, aren't we?" Pastor Adelheid John responded when asked why she had taken in refugees and not just donated money or goods. "Besides, I could no longer take these horrible images on television every night."[27]

Whatever the reasons, the sheer number of refugees made such ef-forts a mere drop in the bucket, and that was why applying for asylum became an increasingly common strategy. It was the only legal way, in fact, for most Bosnians to enter the Federal Republic. As a result, the total number of asylum applications jumped from roughly a quarter million in 1991 to 438,191 in 1992.[28] Every person who applied received a tempo-rary "right to remain" while their case was being adjudicated, along with a variety of welfare benefits: clothing, food, and lodging, all paid for by the federal government to the tune of 10 billion DM in 1992 alone. This was precisely why local officials and agencies counseled refugees to say the "magic word *asylum*": to lessen their own financial burden by passing the deutsch mark, so to speak, to state and federal officials. But this, in turn, produced an exponential increase in the number of applicants.[29]

The question of *who* exactly would assume the costs of their up-keep—the federal government, the *Länder,* or the local communes—quickly became a major source of discord. And the outlays were indeed considerable, especially at a time when, in the wake of unification, na-tional debt was soaring and there were already severe housing shortages. Spiraling costs and a huge spike in the number of applications would produce a veritable "crisis," many Germans feared, leading once again to complaints that the country's "super liberal" asylum policy (Klaus Kinkel's phrase) was being abused for purely venal reasons. But not all Germans were convinced that the "boat was full." Thomas Schmid of the *taz* suspected a devious strategy at work behind current practices.

German politicians, he surmised, were artificially producing asylum seekers and "'floods' of foreigners who 'inundate' Germany"—and they would cynically use this as a reason to abolish the right to asylum.[30]

The soaring number of applicants did indeed encourage those who had long been calling for an overhaul of Germany's asylum process to step up efforts to exclude those who "do not require our protection." One strategy involved a stricter reading of Art. 16 of the constitution, which meant that those fleeing civil wars were not eligible unless they could demonstrate they were being "persecuted politically." (This was why so many German officials insisted on calling the conflict a "civil war.") Advocates of reform finally achieved their goal in the summer of 1993— right in the midst of the Bosnian conflict—when restrictions making it more difficult to obtain asylum were added to the Basic Law. The most of important of the new regulations sped up the deportation process and refused asylum to persons who had previously been in a "safe" third country, such as Austria, effectively cutting off all land access to the Federal Republic (at least in theory).[31]

This outcome had been long sought by those who believed that there were already too many foreigners living in Germany. Such sentiments were not new, as the earlier response to refugees from Indochina made clear. In his first speech as chancellor in the fall of 1982, Helmut Kohl spoke in no uncertain terms against "unlimited and uncontrolled immigration." A decade later, public opinion surveys revealed that a majority of Germans considered immigration the main challenge faced by their country, and believed that dishonest asylum practices were so widespread only a new law could stop them.[32] The reform did indeed lead to a dramatic drop in the number of applicants, but it also provided those already living in the Federal Republic with a more secure legal status. Whatever the grumbling, most Germans agreed on the need to provide sanctuary to refugees from Bosnia and the Balkans, and the suggestion that officials did "more" to "stem and then turn back the tide . . . than they sought to provide them a safe haven" misses the mark.[33]

Just how many could feasibly be allowed into the country and absorbed nevertheless remained a major sticking point. Following the lead of the European Union (which absorbed the EC in November 1993), the German government argued that it was better for refugees to remain in the Balkans until hostilities subsided—for reasons again reminiscent of the earlier response to the influx of refugees from former Indochina. It would lessen their "deracination" and make it easier for them to return home later. Besides, the government argued, taking them in only "encouraged" the criminal actions of the Serbs—and thus unwittingly helped make ethnic cleansing a fait accompli. Martin Fischer, who brought thousands of Bosnians abroad to safety, shared this concern, and even the leftist *Frankfurter Rundschau* acknowledged it was a form of "blackmail," that accepting more refugees only made this "dirty business easier for the blackmailer. But what is the alternative?"[34]

One alternative, of course, was to intervene militarily to stop the slaughter—but that was not a realistic choice for the Federal Republic. Another was to increase humanitarian aid to the region, and Germans did indeed provide substantial support to Croatia so that Bosnian refugees could remain there, closer to home. To that end, the German government relied on a liaison office set up in the Croatian capital Zagreb to review requests and coordinate the distribution of humanitarian relief. By July 1992, Germany had donated some 150 million DM to the region.[35] That figure reached 276 million DM by October—"higher than the assistance from all non-EC members of the G24 together," Hartmut Koschyk of the Christian Social Union pointed out. It climbed to 445 million DM by the fall of 1993, and to more than 800 million DM by the close of 1994. These sums included German moneys administered by the European Community, and then the EU, as well as a series of "emergency expenditures" during the cold winter months or to assist civilians trapped in besieged cities and towns. German contributions amounted to roughly 30 percent of all EU goods and services in the region between 1993 and 1995, making it the largest donor. On top of this, the government spent approximately 3.6 billion DM annually to clothe, lodge, and provide medical assistance to all refugees from former Yugoslavia living in Germany.[36]

But the Federal Republic did more than expend vast sums on humanitarian aid. It also participated, for instance, in an international airlift that brought necessary supplies to Sarajevo. Between July 1992 and September 1995, German crews flew more than 1,200 flights and transported tens of thousands of tons of food and medicine to the besieged Bosnian capital. In March 1993 the cabinet also authorized the air force to participate in nighttime drops of goods to Muslim civilians holed up in eastern Bosnia. Serb deployment of antiaircraft systems made this extremely dangerous, and the Serb leader Radovan Karadžić made it clear he considered any aid to his enemies a "hostile action." Shooting down a German plane would have been a "special triumph," Werner Perger pointed out in *Die Zeit*. After all, a special focus of Serb propaganda was Germany's "old Prussian Great Power interests" in the region: "Hating Germans is considered bon ton among Serbs today."[37]

German soldiers themselves spoke out about the dangers, complaining that authorities had not been entirely open with them. "We are like targets in a shooting gallery," one officer complained. Another claimed that these were not "relief flights" but "combat missions." The first German soldier was seriously injured, in fact, while participating in the airlift to Sarajevo in February 1993. Truck convoys were more efficient and more cost-effective, a government spokesperson acknowledged, but they were equally dangerous because of snipers and the "shenanigans" of Bosnian Serbs, who attacked and sometimes murdered aid workers, stole goods, demanded bribes ("customs duties"), and otherwise impeded humanitarian assistance from reaching civilians. The "denial" of humanitarian aid was once again being used as a "weapon of war," just as it had a decade earlier following the ouster of the Khmer Rouge.[38]

Rudolf Neudeck got involved in these aid efforts, too, transporting hundreds of tons of medicine, food, and other supplies by ship and then returning to Germany with hundreds of refugees on board. Working together with the German Foreign Office, his organization set up a "wagon village" for refugees made up of dozens of old German train cars, located in a town close to the Croatian border, as well as a hospital in Sarajevo and a treatment center for paraplegics. Together with Bishop Franz Kamphaus of Limburg, an old school friend, Neudeck also managed to secure free medical care for dozens of badly injured Bosnians in church-run hospitals back in Germany. And, with his son Marcel and a medical doctor from the former GDR, he even risked his life running into burning buildings in the Bosnian capital to save elderly occupants.[39]

Relations between Neudeck and German officials had vastly improved since the early 1980s. Klaus Kinkel, he later wrote, always had a "sympathetic ear" for humanitarian organizations. In turn, officials now spoke in glowing terms about his efforts, as well as about those of the many other NGOs active in Bosnia: German branches of the Red Cross, Amnesty International, CARE, and Doctors Without Borders. Hundreds of initiatives across Germany raised money and sponsored various projects, from the construction of schools and lodging to building facilities for clean drinking water.[40]

Local youth organizations, peace activists, and women's groups were especially active in these relief efforts, procuring trucks and organizing "aid convoys" to Bosnia, or initiating donation drives to collect clothing, food, medicine, and other necessary supplies. Working together with local businesses, one group of youths in Berlin sent a truck filled with bicycles, tools, and assorted spare parts to Bosnia, where they planned to set up a bicycle repair and rental shop. Other initiatives to raise money included benefit concerts featuring prominent German performers, Christmas "galas," art sales, and even an auction in Berlin, in which one could bid on personal items donated by prominent German politicians and entertainers—including an outfit once worn by the internationally renowned pop singer Nena and the iconic red scarf worn by Mayor Walter Momper the night the Berlin Wall fell. Politicians across the political spectrum—from Christian Schwarz-Schilling of the CDU to Marieluise Beck of the Greens, Irmgard Schaetzer and Jürgen Schmieder of the Free Democrats to Freimut Duve and Karsten Voigt of the SPD—were equally proactive. "They have all shown," Foreign Minister Kinkel gushed, "that our country has a heart."[41]

Officials also heaped fulsome praise on the generosity of ordinary Germans, who, through "countless small personal initiatives" at the grass roots, demonstrated their "spontaneous solidarity" with the victims of the war—whether because of "personal ties" to the region, a "bad conscience" resulting from a sense of "powerlessness," a "humanitarian and Christian mindset," or "simply out of compassion" and a desire to "ease the suffering." Even Minister of the Interior Seiters had nothing but praise for this "unprecedented wave of humanity"—which was all the more admirable given the results of a recent nationwide survey that found about half of all Germans thought public appeals for donations were "too frequent."[42] Ordinary Berliners rummaged through their closets for clothing and toys, which they handed to Bosnians through a fence surrounding a refugee center in the Weißensee section of eastern Berlin. Many brought along fresh fruit as well, a symbolic choice with special significance for East Germans—much like the meaning "real" coffee still had for Germans who had lived through the last war. Both had been rare and thus highly desired commodities.[43]

There were less rosy reports as well. The "'humanitarian' cargo" on one plane to Sarajevo consisted mainly of condoms, and at a time when civilians there had not had any fresh produce for more than a year, the bulk of all German aid supposedly consisted of "spoiled flour, insect-infested beans, and verminous macaroni." A representative from the Evangelical Women's Aid Society in Brunswick acknowledged that the aid efforts were "well intended." But, she added, "the women in the [refugee] camps are crammed with discarded clothes from German wardrobes and stuffed full of spaghetti. They have no use for this. More important are fruit, vegetables, medication"—not "alms" and "rubbish." Reports like these prompted one commentator to dismiss such activities as "German self-gratification" intended to "ease one's conscience."[44] That was unduly cynical. After all, it was often those Germans who had little themselves who were most generous in their support—like the group of homeless people who, because they knew what it meant to "stand in the cold," distributed hot tea and coffee to Bosnians forced to wait in long lines in the winter to register with authorities. The man who headed a round-the-clock security detail at another refugee center in the western half of Berlin explained his own engagement in equally personal terms. As a former East German refugee to the West, he knew what it was like to live in a refugee camp—"namely, crappy."[45]

Concern for rape victims was especially motivational. The German government set up a special house in Zagreb where women were provided with medical and psychological treatment, and Chancellor Kohl and Foreign Minister Kinkel explicitly spoke out in favor of allowing into Germany all women who had been sexually abused.[46] The Berlin Senate similarly pledged to take in every rape victim who wished to come to the German capital, and in the spring of 1993, Bremen offered sanctuary to 150 women in need of immediate assistance. Women's groups in that Hanseatic city raised tens of thousands of deutsch marks for their upkeep, and a realtor even provided them with apartments free of charge. "We can afford to give up a part of our wealth," one declaration asserted. A group of women working at Bremen's hospitals and clinics was even instrumental in procuring a mobile dental laboratory, especially helpful for women whose teeth had been knocked out or otherwise damaged during the beatings and sexual violence they had endured.[47]

Other important grassroots initiatives were clearly inspired by Germany's own difficult history. Sixty-five-year-old Ingeborg Michael of Berlin, daughter of a Christian father and a Jewish mother, organized a series of demonstrations and donation drives. "I go crazy when I think of these women just sitting there, waiting to be raped and hoping for help," she explained. She, her mother, and her sister had spent much of World War II hiding in a village. Her mother later perished at Auschwitz, her sister committed suicide, and her other Jewish relatives all starved to death in the Warsaw Ghetto.[48] The idea of helping those who help themselves served as the inspiration for the Anna O. Institute, named for an Austrian-Jewish feminist who had founded a Jewish women's organization in 1904 and later fought against international trafficking of young girls. Established in the spring of 1993 in Berlin by the local Green Party and the Unabhängiger Frauenverband, an independent women's association, the institute offered a crash training course for volunteers from Bosnia who wished to provide "expert care" back home for traumatized women. Ingrid Lottenburger, who had founded the women's group Scheherazade in opposition to the recent Gulf War, helped get the project off the ground, citing her own experience as a nine-year-old living in Berlin in 1945. "Even though my mother and I were not raped, I can vividly remember the fear."[49]

Monika Hauser, a gynecologist in Cologne, launched the best known of these private initiatives. Born in 1959 to German-speaking parents in South Tirol, Hauser grew up in Switzerland but later did her medical training in Essen, where she worked closely with rape victims. Witnessing their "callous" treatment by the police and other medical personnel, she later explained, was what first made her aware of the urgent need for a more "sensitive," feminist approach. That indelible experience shaped her response to the mass rapes in Bosnia, which she first read about in *Stern* magazine in December 1992. Hauser was put off by the "sensational" approach taken by journalists like Alexandra Stiglmayer in *Stern*. She "had" to go there to help, she felt, in a way that made it about the women, not about producing a "terrific" news article. Besides "revictimizing" the victims, who felt "wrung out like a dish towel," such "sensationalist" reporting "retraumatized" German readers and viewers who had themselves suffered sexual abuse. When asked whether the response in Germany would have been as great if the reporting on mass rape had been more sober and less shocking, Hauser acknowledged that it was a difficult "balancing act." It was important to "move people" and "document" what happened, but in an "ethical way" that protected the "dignity" of the women.[50]

"Jolted" into action by the media reports, the thirty-three-year-old doctor traveled to Zagreb in December 1992 to offer her services to the women's health organizations she had expected to find there. She was "seized with such rage" when she discovered that there were none that she decided to set up something herself. On hearing that thousands of refugees were heading to Zenica, a small industrial city located deep inside Serb-controlled territory, Hauser traveled there just before the New Year. She returned to Zenica several months later—this time with twenty-five tons of supplies, thanks to millions in donations from various women's groups, to set up three therapy centers for rape victims.[51]

After the first center opened its doors in April 1993, Hauser put into practice the "standards" she had embraced since her training as a gynecologist in Essen: treatment that was "autonomous, feminist, politically independent" and decidedly "not nationalistic," which was why the center's teams were made up of women from all ethnic groups. Insisting on a nonpolitical approach that prioritized the interests of the women, and critical of how rapes were being "instrumentalized" for political reasons— to justify outside military intervention, for instance—Hauser made it clear to local authorities that she wanted to work "fully independently"— taking a strictly nonpartisan approach reminiscent of Rupert Neudeck and his concept of "radical humanism." There was another parallel to

FIG. 8.2. Monika Hauser (*second from right*) sits with her team in the office of Medica mondiale. The poster in the background reads, "War always involves violence against women." Cologne, 1999. Courtesy of Ursula Meissner.

Neudeck: Hauser's "engagement" had a great deal to do with her own experiences. She heard as a young girl that her "beloved" grandfather, a Nazi Party member who had fought on the Eastern Front, had raped and impregnated her grandmother because he wanted to marry her. The idea that "war and sexualized violence go together" was a lesson she learned early, and she began to read all she could about World War II.[52]

Hauser and Neudeck had something else in common as well. They were both extremely critical of traditional aid organizations. Even with all their "sophisticated logistics," Hauser complained, none provided assistance in active war zones. Her own work in Zenica, she stressed, was the first time traumatized women were assisted while a war was still being waged, and all the interviews her teams conducted were documented for later use at the UN's International Criminal Tribunal for the Former Yugoslavia (ICTY). Visiting journalists, like Erich Rathfelder, praised Hauser's "courage," her "almost inhuman capacity for work," and her "masterly, organizational achievements," despite all the bureaucratic obstacles and dangers she faced in Zenica, which was frequently shelled during her time there. *Tagesthemen*, Germany's most popular television news show, named her "woman of the year" in 1993 for her efforts, and Hauser's stay in Bosnia marked the beginning of a long personal commitment to humanitarian activities—just as Neudeck's experiences a decade earlier in Southeast Asia had affected him. She went on to establish Medica mondiale, a humanitarian organization that would later help rape victims in places like Kosovo and Afghanistan. With offices and staff on three continents, it continues to do so today.[53]

Pointing to public and private efforts like these, German officials boasted repeatedly about all that the Federal Republic had done to assist Bosnians—"more than all the other [countries] put together," Hans Stercken of the CDU, the head of the Bundestag's Foreign Affairs Committee, told colleagues. "That was not an expression of some German longing for this region"; rather, he cryptically added, it was done out of "gratitude toward history." German generosity was clearly a source of pride, even if Press Secretary Hanns Heinrich Schumacher of the Foreign Office appeared somewhat abashed: "I am ashamed to say it," he commented in a radio interview in mid-November 1992, "but it is true—we stand . . . at the forefront, distinctly ahead of all other European countries of a comparable size." Ashamed or not, it was Schumacher's own superior, Foreign Minister Kinkel, who most energetically called attention at home and abroad to Germany's humanitarian performance. Journalists chimed in as well, with Peter Scholl-Latour noting sardonically that Bosnians had received "more aid" from Germany than from the "entire 'Umma,'" that is, the global Muslim community.[54]

There was less effusive commentary as well, especially on the Left. Kinkel might have liked to portray the Federal Republic as the "champion of solidarity," *Neues Deutschland* characteristically carped, but it was all about "easing one's conscience." Journalist Christina Matte, who had been working at the former propaganda organ of the Socialist Unity Party since 1982, wanted to know "how many pediatricians and schoolbooks Germany sent—and how many weapons," in a world where millions of minors were dying as result of genocide. Others on the left were equally dismissive. Christian Semler published an essay in the *taz* titled "Humanity Public Relations Inc." and Michael Sontheimer—who, just a few years earlier, had criticized the Federal Republic for not providing aid to Cambodia—likewise complained that humanitarian assistance had "mutated into a media spectacle, a business, a political vehicle." Aid organizations were competing on the "mercy market," rushing to places that received the most media attention.[55]

The deaths of the two orphans killed during the botched rescue in Sarajevo had precipitated these sharp comments, typical criticism on the Left of postwar Germany's "mediated," capitalist society, but not entirely unfounded. Whatever the reasons, the faultfinders were also quick to point out that German generosity was less impressive when considered in proportion to overall population figures. According to calculations from July 1992, the Federal Republic had donated 45 cents per citizen (in US currency)—right behind the United States (46 cents), but far behind Norway ($9.53) and Sweden ($6.87). A year later, *Der Spiegel* reported that Switzerland, Sweden, Austria, and Hungary had taken in the most refugees from former Yugoslavia, proportional to their populations. In a piece provocatively titled "Level of the 1930s"—an allusion to the earlier plight of German Jews under the Nazis—the economic weekly *Wirtschaftswoche,* no leftist tabloid, questioned the widespread perception that Germany had borne the brunt of the Balkan refugee wave. There were 640 Yugoslavian refugees for every 100,000 inhabitants in Austria, 516 in Sweden, and 570 in "poor" Hungary—as opposed to "just" 271 in the "affluent Federal Republic."[56]

Still, there was no question that Germany had taken a leading role in providing humanitarian aid to the region, and government representatives not only defended their efforts but also demanded that other countries do more, especially when it came to accepting refugees. Calling for a "fair distribution of burdens," Chancellor Kohl complained that the "normal experience" in the EU was that "one silently looks to the Germans" whenever something costs money. If Europe "simply" left the region "to hang out to dry," the chancellor concluded, "we'll all bitterly pay the piper" in the end. Despite strenuous diplomatic efforts by Kohl and especially by Kinkel at various international conferences, EU representatives failed to adopt a more equitable distribution.[57]

Others were much less diplomatic in their condemnation of this "heavy blemish" on Europe as a whole. Konrad Weiß of the Greens called it "shameful" that the EU seemed to "really" be in agreement only when it came to "military actions." Freimut Duve of the SPD acknowledged his own "bitterness" on this score but cautioned his colleagues "not to enter into a contest . . . a sort of Helpfulness Olympics" with Germany's allies. "Stinginess" and fears about socioeconomic burdens were not the only reason Germany's neighbors showed so much "restraint" on this issue, diplomats suspected. It was also a form of "payback" for Foreign Minister Genscher's earlier pressure to recognize the separatist regions of former Yugoslavia. Because "the pan-German pursuit of influence" was supposedly a main cause of the conflict, they were "not unhappy" to see Germany "shoulder the greatest burden" and "suffer the consequences" of its earlier policies.[58]

The Federal Republic might have been, as one conservative British politician put it, "fully isolated" on the refugee issue, but its general willingness to accept refugees from the region enjoyed broad support across the political spectrum at home—at least initially and within limits. How long that would last was unclear. It was doubtful, the *Wirtschaftswoche* remarked pessimistically, that the "momentary cordiality" would continue once it became "clear" that many of those taken in would "remain for the long haul." In fact, as early as the summer of 1992, there were indications that the enthusiasm was already "subsiding," that the initial excitement was giving way to "disillusionment." That was even true on the part of those serving as hosts. Language difficulties, cultural and religious differences, and concerns about high costs and the length of stay all played a role. According to a survey of 1,300 families, domestic tensions tended to surface after about three months—though one Bavarian family kicked out a refugee couple after just one night because the husband smoked and the wife "coughed."[59]

Other hosts were upset because entire families had shown up, even though they had explicitly requested just mothers and children. The "macho" behavior of some Bosnian fathers was an additional source of tension, but the cultural "learning curve" went both ways. A young couple in Kassel took in two young Bosnian mothers who were supposedly "irritated," at first, by the fact that the German husband helped around the house. This clashed with their understanding of traditional gender roles, although one of the women nevertheless acknowledged, "half amused, half envious," that she would be glad to be a woman in Germany.[60]

Encounters like these came at a time when the Federal Republic had just grabbed international headlines because of a sensational string of xenophobic incidents right after unification. The "largest wave of helpfulness toward refugees to date," lamented journalist Ute Scheub, had followed the "greatest wave of violence to date." Frequently questioned about those domestic attacks when abroad, Foreign Minister Kinkel tried to emphasize other themes. The country's largesse toward the Bosnian refugees—its "humanity in action," as he put it—should also be a part of Germany's image, which was now "covered with shame" because of "excesses" by the extreme right. The conservative *Bild* chimed in as well: "The supposedly xenophobic German people willingly and heartily take in Bosnian children"—and would take in even more if accommodations were not "clogged with bogus asylum seekers."[61] Perhaps. But claims like these stood in stark contrast to local civic initiatives arising across Germany to halt the building of additional lodging for asylum seekers. Residents of the Iserbrook district in Hamburg, for example, criticized the planned construction of a container village for refugees. They had nothing against Bosnians or ethnic Germans from the former Soviet Union, they explained, but they *did* object to housing "colored" people there—"monkeys" who could not be "integrated," objected one "red-faced philistine" (the journalist's phrase) in front of running television cameras. "They turn everything to shit."[62]

Unbridled racism like this was not the only motivating factor—at least not directly. Xenophobic attacks in places like Rostock and Mölln made some landlords wary of taking in refugees because of concerns about violence and property damage. At a large town hall meeting in the Lichtenberg section of eastern Berlin, residents spoke out against setting up a new home for Bosnian refugees for fear of a Rostock-like "pogrom" in the neighborhood. That meeting came on the heels of an arson attack near the construction site, where a group of German youths had been overheard shouting "Sieg Heil."[63] Many refugees were understandably worried about their safety, especially those assigned to the eastern half of Germany—no surprise given the widespread impression that violent outbursts of xenophobia were more frequent there. For that reason, a large group that had been sent to Mecklenburg insisted on going instead to western Germany, and even threatened to go on a hunger strike if they were forced to "go back to the East, to the Nazis." They fled to a town just east of Hamburg, where, the local pastor explained to them, the situation was not any better. Right-wing extremists had received 14 percent of the vote in the last election, he said, which was why he was "ashamed" to be a German. "Schleswig-Holstein is not heaven, Mecklenburg not hell. The West is no paradise."[64]

Such fears and incidents notwithstanding, Bosnian refugees appear, on the whole, to have received a warm welcome in both halves of Germany. Most were treated with "tolerance und respect," SPD leader Rudolf Scharping claimed, and there were few complaints about their behavior— so long as they acted lawfully. Two years after the conflict had begun, Ulrich Irmer of the FDP publicly (if patronizingly) thanked those who had found sanctuary in the Federal Republic for having acted "peacefully here up to now."[65] Occasional reports of illicit activity were nevertheless frowned on: slipping illegally into Germany without proper paperwork; engaging in black market activity or weapons sales to help their brethren back home; using tricks (such as applying for "church asylum") to avoid repatriation. But as a rule, the refugees spoke in glowing terms about their positive experiences in the Federal Republic and most did not seem to have experienced overt instances of xenophobia. The head of the foreigners' registration office in Karlsruhe noted, by way of explanation, that the Bosnians were "very close culturally" to the Germans and easily assimilated because of their education, language abilities, and work ethic.[66]

Not everything was rosy, of course, and there were indeed concerning stories about physical assaults. A gymnasium housing Muslim refugees was attacked in the Saarland, and there was an arson attack against a Bosnian family in Lower Saxony. One young Bosnian showed a German reporter his missing teeth, explaining that "Nazis broke them. I was leaving school and they asked me if I were a foreigner." Skinheads and neo-Nazis were usually involved in such incidents, but that was not always the case—and it was not always clear that xenophobia or racism was the motivation. Some physical run-ins involved rival ethnic groups from former Yugoslavia, for instance.[67]

More common than violence were accounts of everyday forms of racism. A bank clerk told one young Bosnian woman that she could not open an account because the accounts were "constantly overdrawn" by foreigners who then "disappeared." Another young Muslim complained about being asked "every five minutes" why he had come to Germany and when he planned to return. An impatient older woman in Eisen-hüttenstadt, a steel town in former East Germany, had even told him to stop using a public telephone booth—still a rare commodity in the former GDR—because they were "only for Germans." Another confided to a journalist that he did not wish to remain in the Federal Republic because everyone regarded him as a "foreigner." His "dream" was to go to America or Australia.[68]

Some Bosnian refugees who wound up outside of Europe would have jumped at the opportunity to live in the Federal Republic. Those who were sent to Asia or the Middle East, for example, complained about culture shock—because of the food and heat, the language and customs, the religious practices—and many wished to return to Europe. "We don't want to go to Jordan or Pakistan, we want our children to learn English or German, not Arabic. . . . If we can't go back home right away, we want to remain in Europe at least. We are Europeans, after all!" This confirmed the general impression in Germany that most Bosnian Muslims—Bosniaks, a term first used after Austria-Hungary occupied the region in 1878, and increasingly embraced by the Muslims after 1991—were moderate in their beliefs, practices, and politics. Their orientation and outlook were Western, explained Claus Leggewie, a professor of political science in Giessen, and they saw themselves as "advanced Europeans." These Muslims, affirmed Die Welt, were "completely different-looking" from most refugees. "Their women wear skirts, the men shorts, many have blond hair and blue eyes." The young couple from Kassel who hosted two Bosnian mothers and their children were "relieved" that their guests did not seem "so foreign." The wife had expected them to wear "veils" and worried about offending them by having pork in the refrigerator, but, a visiting journalist noted, both women wore jeans and sweatshirts and even enjoyed a good smoke.[69]

The overwhelming majority of Bosnian Muslims were not "religious fanatics," as many Germans had feared. But as the conflict dragged on, there were signs in the region—troubling ones, from a German perspective—of growing interest in Islamic fundamentalism and political Islam: the wearing of headscarves by Muslim women, the observance of Ramadan, the signing of military orders with "Allahu Akbar, Allah is great," the hanging of the Prophet's green flag in besieged cities like Mostar. There was even a report that one rape victim had named her son Jihad (holy war) "so that he never forgets."[70]

Incipient Islamic fundamentalism, including its potential consequences for Germany, was a popular theme in articles and editorials by conservative firebrand Carl Gustaf Ströhm. Noting the allegedly high birthrates of Muslim women—their *"Geburtenfreudigkeit"*—he warned that time was "on the side of the minarets"—a typical trope about the supposed threat of ethnic and demographic "time bombs" for the white West. More to the point, Ströhm argued, one need not have a "special prophetic talent" to predict that "avengers and terrorists" would one day be recruited from the Bosnian Muslim refugee milieu: "Doubtful whether these people will, in their frustration and anger, then make distinctions between Serbs and other Christian Europeans." Ströhm's panicky comments must be seen in the context of his larger sympathies for the Bosniaks and his urgent calls for Western intervention on their behalf. Muslim youths might have been speaking more openly about "holy war," but their "radicalization" was "not surprising." They were being "driven in this direction," Ströhm maintained, by the Serbs and by Western inaction, and when the "bombs explode," he predicted, the West will finally realize what "fateful mistakes" it had made.[71]

Still, such conjecture confirmed prevailing anti-Muslim prejudices, which had received fresh wind following the Iranian revolution of 1979 and the subsequent rise of Islamic fundamentalism. The Serbs (and Croats) had themselves long expressed fears about the creation of an Islamic theocracy in Bosnia, and they frequently used this concern to justify their actions against the Muslims. A manifesto published in 1970 by Bosnian president Alija Izetbegović had fueled such concerns. In it, critics charged, the author had called for the imposition of Sharia law and the creation of an Islamic state. The German media nevertheless portrayed Izetbegović as tolerant, as a "voice of reason" who possessed a "good measure of Oriental equanimity" and "Oriental cunning." Even if meant favorably, backhanded compliments like these were not uncommon—and not unlike the racist comments made during the Cambodian genocide about the furtive "Asian smile."[72]

Concerns about increasing religious fundamentalism appeared in tandem with reports that the military tide of the conflict was turning— more specifically, that the Muslims and the Bosnian army were finally making strides against the Serbs and, after fighting broke out with their erstwhile allies in the spring of 1993, the Croats. This contrasted starkly with reports from the early phase of the conflict, when the consensus was that the Muslims were faring so poorly because their leaders had not prepared adequately for the looming military confrontation. By early 1993, scattered reports claimed that they now had access to more and better weapons, that their military organization was improving, and that they were recouping territory. Journalist Heiko Flottau predicted that the Muslims would "not resign themselves to their fate as patiently as the North American Indians" once had. Drawing on a different historical analogy, the popular newsmagazine *Stern* commented that the Muslims would no longer be "beasts for slaughter"—reminiscent of the language used to describe the supposedly passive response of European Jews to Nazi persecution.[73]

Reports that the Muslims were now seriously "on the march" began appearing in late 1993 and throughout 1994. At this point the German media increasingly gave the impression that all sides in the conflict were committing atrocities, that the "pendulum was swinging" in the other direction.[74] Seeking revenge for past brutalities and to make up for territory lost to ethnic cleansing, Muslims in paramilitary units like the Muslim Armed Forces, a radical outfit whose ranks included mercenaries from Islamic countries, were now purportedly committing a variety of "cruelties" themselves: using Serb civilians as human shields in towns like Srebrenica, massacring, "cleansing," and burning down the houses of Croats in places like Mostar. In Sarajevo, "fanaticized" Muslim "hard-liners" and "mafiosi" had created a "veritable pogrom atmosphere" against the Serb minority. The "victims of genocide," Carl Gustaf Ströhm shook his head, had now become "perpetrators" themselves.[75]

Most commentators in Germany nevertheless maintained that the Serbs were still committing the most—and most egregious—atrocities, and sympathy remained squarely on the side of the Muslims. That became abundantly clear in late February 1994, when, on orders from NATO, two US Air Force F-16s shot down four Serbian jet fighters near the city of Banja Luca after they had violated the no-fly zone. Foreign Minister Kinkel delivered a public statement several days after the incident, NATO's first combat mission ever. After acknowledging that a German radio mechanic had been aboard the AWACS plane that had detected the no-fly violation, Kinkel outlined the legality and justification for the historic NATO action. It was "bitter," he conceded, that "force, in the final analysis, can often only be stopped by counterforce," but that was the "reality" of the situation.[76]

Indeed, the UN and NATO had been threatening to use force for more than a year but had not taken any concrete measures up to that point—a continuing source of frustration in much of the mainstream German media. That situation finally changed on February 5, when an especially deadly attack was carried out on the marketplace in Sarajevo. The disturbing images of carnage that were broadcast around the globe by the cable news agency CNN elicited worldwide outrage—what became known as the "CNN effect." Chancellor Kohl expressed his personal "horror" about this "testimony to inhumanity," and the German government released a statement "utterly" condemning the "bloodbath" and underscoring its firm conviction that "targeted military measures . . . may no longer be ruled out." Secretary-General Manfred Wörner of NATO was dying of cancer at the time but reportedly "dragged himself" from the hospital to ensure passage of a motion demanding that the Serbs remove all heavy weapons and artillery from the hills surrounding the Bosnian capital. "Enough words have been exchanged," the former West German minister of defense declared. "It's time to act."[77]

The action came later that month when NATO launched the air attack near Banja Luca. This was a "declaration of war," the *Süddeutsche Zeitung* announced with great fanfare, but also an opportunity for the Atlantic alliance to demonstrate its newfound steadfastness in the face of Serb aggression. A second air strike followed six weeks later, on April 10–11, in response to a major Serb offensive against Goradze, one of six "safe havens" the UN had set up a year earlier to protect major Muslim enclaves.[78] Aerial interference in ground fighting was yet another first for NATO, and Kinkel again spoke out in support of the attack. It was "justified, necessary, and legal," he told the Bundestag, not least because of the danger posed to UN personnel. Even Karsten Voigt of the SPD, known for his vehement opposition to German participation in military missions like this one, acknowledged that the air strike had not only been "permissible according to international law" but also "politically and morally legitimate."[79] The tide had clearly started to shift, even on the part of those normally opposed to military measures. But by that point, the world's attention had shifted momentarily to a different armed conflict—a genocide taking place this time in the heart of Africa.

9

Germany Cannot Play the Role
of Global Gendarme

For Peter Schäfer, the genocide in Rwanda began with a loud bang. The thirty-three-year-old had been working in the former German colony for two years as an engineer with Deutsche Welle, the renowned international broadcasting service, when he heard a sudden "popping" sound on the evening of April 6, 1994. It was not, as he initially suspected, the typical machine gun fire one heard so often in the nearby capital city Kigali. A rocket had just brought down a private jet bringing Rwandan president Juvenal Habyarimana back home from Tanzania, where he had participated in peace talks to end the ongoing conflict in his country between Hutus and Tutsis. The crash killed everyone on board. *That* was when the actual shooting began.

A day later, a heavily armed group of Hutus appeared on the grounds of the radio station and shot two Tutsi women who tried to flee; they were among the dozens who had sought refuge there. News soon reached Schäfer that many of his Rwandan colleagues had been killed, including an entire family from his own crew. Farther south, Herman Unglaub, an automobile mechanic who had been working in Rwanda for the previous eight years as a project leader for a major German development agency, watched from afar as smoke rose above the nearby hills. "First the houses are set aflame," he reported, then "the people are chased away.

Whoever gets in the way is butchered. Then the plundering begins." Hutus were murdering Tutsis, "hacking" them to death with machetes. "It begins in one spot and then progresses from hill to hill"—the same "lovely green hills" that had once prompted Belgian colonizers to refer to Rwanda as "Africa's little Switzerland."[1]

Tensions between the country's two main ethnic groups had been rife since the colonial period of the late nineteenth century. They took a violent turn in the late 1950s and broke out periodically over the next three decades; violence resumed once again in October 1990, when 4,000 members of the Rwandan Patriotic Front (RPF) launched a large-scale invasion from Uganda. Despite the numerical and material superiority of the Rwandan army, the RPF—Tutsi refugees who had left the country en masse following independence and the creation of a Hutu-dominated republic in 1962—made significant territorial gains in the northern part of the country by 1993. That had led to diplomatic talks and eventually the signing of a peace accord in the Tanzanian city of Arusha that summer.[2]

Speculation began immediately about who was behind the assassination, with foreign observers, also in Germany, quickly pointing fingers at both sides. Fighting broke out in the capital, the Hutu-dominated Rwandan army set up barricades and closed the border to Zaire, and the first reports of massacres, atrocities, and other "horrific scenes" began to seep out. On April 12, Deutsche Welle reported that up to 20,000 Rwandans had already been killed by "marauding soldiers" and that corpses were "lying around everywhere," even in churches. The massacres "far surpass, in their savagery" and extent, one's "imaginative powers," commented Claus Jäger of the Christian Democratic Union. The *Frankfurter Allgemeine Zeitung* agreed: "The carnage in Rwanda," ran one headline, "is much worse than one can imagine from afar."[3]

The notion that what was taking place in Rwanda was unimaginable was an established trope, familiar from earlier responses to the genocide in Cambodia. If that were indeed the case, it was not for lack of trying on the part of German media, as journalists feverishly tried to convey the carnage.[4] In hospitals, churches, and refugee assembly points in Kigali and elsewhere, Hutu soldiers and civilians "literally hacked away at everyone. Everyone was equal before the slasher, be it the gravely ill or mothers in labor, old men or infants." The "slasher" was a reference to the *panga,* a machete used, in times of peace, to hack wood or cut Napier grass but now serving as an "instrument of death." On April 21, journalist Wolfgang Kunath graphically described the "traces of a mass murder" he had seen in a church in Kiziguro, a Catholic parish to the northeast of Kigali. "One cannot walk across the room without stepping on the Eucharist vestments of church officials, which lie on the floor with hundreds of communion wafers." He also came across pieces of a thick hosepipe used to "beat and whip" victims who had sought refuge in the church. "But the most harrowing traces of panic and mortal fear" were scattered items of clothing "soiled with human excrement." The thousands of dead from Kiziguro had simply been "thrown" into a giant hole in the ground, one of many mass graves that would be discovered over the coming months and years.[5]

Once the mass murder subsided that July and German journalists had the opportunity to speak with witnesses and survivors, more detailed reports of the atrocities began to appear. This was a qualitatively different type of killing, "a new dimension of criminality," many German observers declared, even if the gruesome accounts eerily echoed earlier reports about the Khmer Rouge. The more recent carnage in Bosnia came to mind as well, prompting *Der Spiegel* to run a story titled "Bosnia in Africa." One Hutu perpetrator, a village police officer, told a German correspondent that they had burned down hundreds of houses so the refugees could not return—"ethnic cleaning" *à l'africaine.* But there were echoes of more distant horrors as well. This was "all the fault of the Tutsis," the officer added. "We killed them because they are accomplices of the RPF. . . . The women and children as well. This is normal. The children of accomplices are accomplices. So we killed them. . . . *We had orders*"—a chilling phrase with obvious associations for German readers.[6]

Coming face-to-face with actual killers often elicited the same kind of surprise Germans had experienced in their encounters with Khmer Rouge perpetrators a decade and a half earlier: "And those are supposed to be the perpetrators?" Just like the Cambodians, the Rwandan *génocidaires* were clearly recognizable by their uniforms and superior nutrition—even the younger ones. *Spiegel* reporter Erich Wiedemann spoke with a group of youths who "made no secret" of their involvement because, he suspected, the government's "hate propaganda" had "narcoticized" them against any sense of guilt. One ten-year-old admitted that he and two friends had "hacked" to death a baby with a panga, but quickly added that it was a "very small baby. . . . 'They can't feel anything yet.'" Besides, he added, they had only done what the adults had told them to do.[7]

Not all the murderers were "this frank," journalist Thankmar von Münchhausen pointed out. When asked where their Tutsi neighbors were, others simply said they were "gone," a response often accompanied by "embarrassed laughing." If that did not bring to mind the fate of Jewish neighbors who had "disappeared" in the 1930s and 1940s, other recurrent media images of the carnage in Rwanda must have surely awoken memories of that dark period in Germany. The "treacly foul stench" and "sweet whiff of pestilence" emanating from the ubiquitous "piles" of decomposing cadavers were one olfactory reminder of a different past. But there were less familiar images as well, of bloated, mutilated bodies flowing along Rwanda's streams and rivers. "The brown water moves rapidly," one extremely graphic report began. "One of the dead has no head, the brain of a second can be seen through its open skull. . . . Underneath a woman drifting on her back [is] the corpse of her child." Tens of thousands of "mutilated, nibbled, spotted, decomposing victims" blocked Rwanda's waterways for months.[8]

Reports like these gave some sense of the magnitude of the murder spree. Like Phnom Penh, Kigali made a "deserted impression. . . . Where are all the people?" Günter Krabbe of the *FAZ* wanted to know. Estimates of the total number of murdered Rwandans began appearing soon after the mass atrocities began. Just two weeks into the genocide, his newspaper placed the figure at 100,000, supposedly making this the "bloodiest massacre" ever to have taken place in Africa. Those estimates climbed rapidly over the following weeks, reaching a half million by May in a country with 7.2 million inhabitants—approximately 15 percent of the population. The German Foreign Office confirmed that figure; by summer, journalists speculated, half of all Tutsis had been killed.[9]

The focus on magnitude and raw numbers prompted reflections about the desensitizing effect of amorphous statistics like these. Who "wished to measure" the degree of "unhappiness hidden behind such numbers?" Bartholomäus Grill asked rhetorically in *Die Zeit*. More to the point, Wolfgang Kunath wrote indignantly in the *Frankfurter Rundschau*, the "unbelievably high numbers rob the victims of their identity [and] individuality," making them "just an anonymous crowd." Poignant statements like these recalled contentious discussions about the number of Jews killed during the Holocaust, but they also prompted further reflections. "How does a society process this murderous nightmare?" Kunath wanted to know. "How should erstwhile neighbors, who suddenly became mortal enemies, face each other ever again? . . . Will Rwandan society repress what happened? Or come to terms with it? And how does that even proceed?"[10]

The UN took a first step that November when it established the International Criminal Tribunal for Rwanda (ICTR) to bring the perpetrators to justice and help the country deal with what had just transpired. "Nobody denies that mass murderers . . . should be held accountable," Günther Krabbe wrote in the *FAZ*. "But is that even feasible?" Estimating the number of perpetrators at 100,000, he wanted to know what kind of court could cope with such numbers. "How should they be punished? Where are there enough prisons?" Just as important, how would the hundreds of thousands of family members respond?[11] The overtones were again unmistakable. Similar issues had been at stake in Germany following World War II, and comments like these obliquely hinted once again at an unintended consequence of foreign genocides: They allowed Germans to address their own troubled past, indirectly, perhaps subconsciously, without necessarily drawing conscious conclusions—to engage in a form of *Vergangenheitsbewältigung* by proxy.

Death estimates would climb to a million by the fall of 1994. This included three-quarters of Rwanda's indigenous minority, the 30,000 Twa who made up 1 percent of the population before the mass killing began—the "forgotten victims" of the genocide. That loaded term quickly surfaced in the face of such mind-numbing numbers. But not everyone agreed that a genocide was taking place. "If the Hutus and Tutsis were not one people, if they did not speak one language, if they did not share one culture, if they did not live in one territory," Kunath ventured in the *Frankfurter Rundschau,* "one *could* speak of a genocide."[12] The implication was clear—that it was not genocide—and the UN Security Council initially agreed. But the European Union issued a declaration in mid-May that explicitly used the term *genocide,* and by the end of the month, German journalists, aid workers, and representatives of the major political parties did so as well, with some calling the Rwandan "killing fields" the "worst" instance of genocide since the Khmer Rouge. "In its ferocity and contempt for mankind," the Greens declared in late June, the Rwandan "civil war . . . long fulfills all the criteria of genocide."[13]

It was easier for the political opposition and the media to invoke the term than it was for the government, given the potential legal and political ramifications of the UN Genocide Convention. That may be why high-level government officials were at first circumspect about using it—and not just in Germany.[14] But during a speech Klaus Kinkel gave in Bonn in early June to celebrate the thirty-first anniversary of the Organization of African Unity, the foreign minister stated unambiguously that an "unimaginable genocide" was taking place. Chancellor Kohl used similar language at that time, and UN officials now did as well. Secretary-General Boutros Boutros-Ghali stated unequivocally in an interview with *Der Spiegel* that what was "unfolding" in Rwanda was not a "massacre—*it is genocide,*" and the influential newsmagazine agreed. The "orgy of violence" in Central Africa "counted among the greatest crimes of the century," it declared, alongside the massacre of the Armenians and the Holocaust. Nigerian novelist Wole Soyinka, the first sub-Saharan African to win the Nobel Prize in Literature, agreed in a *Spiegel* interview that what was taking place in Rwanda was "only comparable to the Nazi Holocaust"—a soundbite predictably chosen for the headline.[15]

In a speech to the German Society for Foreign Policy, a think tank in Bonn, Kinkel went even further, referring to Rwanda as a "human tragedy of an up-to-now *unknown* magnitude." He may have been specifically referring to the rapidity of the killing, an aspect of the murder spree that, many believed, did make it different from previous genocides.[16] Still, the idea that the killing in Rwanda was somehow "unprecedented," somehow worse than (or at least on par with) previous mass murders, was a notion familiar from the earlier slaughter in Cambodia. In a remarkable piece that appeared in the *Süddeutsche Zeitung* in early August, foreign correspondent Rudolph Chimelli directly addressed such comparisons. "Nothing in this century is so insipid and pointless as the search for superlatives of suffering," he wrote:

> The Khmer Rouge murdered more than a million countrymen to reeducate Cambodia. Deportation and hunger cost the lives of millions of Ukrainian peasants during agricultural collectivization. After Stalin's forced settlement of Central Asian nomads, there were suddenly a million fewer Kazakhs. Of the twelve million Germans expelled from the eastern territories after World War II, one to two million never arrived in the West. *And Hitler's crimes are well-known.*[17]

What "distinguished" the Rwandan "catastrophe" from others in the twentieth century, he continued, was "its suddenness, its pointlessness, its preventability . . . and its visibility." The almost incidental mention here of German crimes—personified in Hitler, just as Khmer Rouge crimes were personified in Pol Pot; the failure, in contrast to the other atrocities, to cite specific victims or numbers with regard to "Hitler's crimes," which are mentioned almost as an afterthought and in false chronological order, that is, *after* the expulsion of ethnic Germans from the East: all of this was curious, as was the implicit suggestion that the other genocides were somehow *not* "pointless" or "avoidable." Still, Chimelli was correct on one point. The "visibility" of this murder spree did indeed differentiate it from the other ones he mentions. This time German journalists and aid workers witnessed firsthand the massacres and their immediate aftermath, to a much greater extent than even in Bosnia.

Their searing reports once again led to a great deal of hand-wringing, voluble expressions of outrage, calls for humanitarian assistance, and even isolated demands for a military response. The world was not "largely indifferent," as some scholars claim. Equally incorrect is the notion that "Germany largely kept quiet about Rwanda for most of the duration of the genocide" and, in contrast to its "occasional outspokenness" about the genocide in Bosnia, did not make "public denunciations." Still, in the end, no one in Germany lifted a finger to stop the killing. In that respect, Germany was no different from anyone else in the international community.[18]

Calls to "do something" to stop the slaughter in Rwanda complemented cutting criticisms of international inaction and even "criminal" apathy. "We Europeans watched on and flew the coop," renowned humanitarian Rupert Neudeck carped in his memoirs, "as 800,000 Rwandans were murdered in cold blood." Six weeks into the genocide, Claus Jäger demanded to know why the German government and the United Nations were not doing more to stop the "gruesome bloodshed." In fact, Boutros Boutros-Ghali, the first African to serve as UN general secretary, had vigorously come out in favor of international intervention, which met with a cool reception, especially in other African nations and the United States.[19] In a *Spiegel* interview, the Egyptian diplomat angrily criticized the "scandalous failure" of the international community to act in Rwanda; after all, it was "obliged" to act in cases of genocide—a rare allusion to the UN Genocide Convention in the German media (and by a foreigner, no less). Why could the UN send tens of thousands of soldiers to Somalia and Bosnia, he wanted to know, but not even 5,000 to Rwanda? German critics had an explanation for the international community's failure to act. Africa did not represent a "military threat," it had no "economic significance" for the industrial world, and the West showed interest only when a "spectacular" event of tragic proportions took place there.[20]

The criticism was understandable but not entirely fair. Leaving aside the recent UN mission to Somalia, more than 2,500 Blue Berets had been deployed to Central Africa in the fall of 1993 as part of UNAMIR, the United Nations Assistance Mission in Rwanda. Its task was to uphold the Arusha Peace Accords. But those numbers quickly dwindled after the massacres got under way, beginning with Belgium's decision to pull out its troops after Hutu extremists executed ten Belgian soldiers. Would they have been removed, mused Africa correspondent Bettina Gaus in the *taz,* if "white [Africans] had been threatened instead?"[21]

Fewer than 500 UN Blue Berets remained in Rwanda by early May, a month after the killing spree had begun. But later that month, under increasing international pressure, the Security Council announced that the UN would send 5,500 soldiers to Rwanda to protect civilians and secure humanitarian aid—although that was more easily said than done. By mid-August, a month *after* the genocide had ended, only a fifth of the peacekeeping contingent had arrived. This lukewarm response underlined how little appetite there was for military measures—linked, no doubt, to the debacle in Somalia a year earlier during the infamous Battle of Mogadishu. That traumatic experience had made it clear, Constanze Stelzenmüller commented in *Die Zeit,* that "civil war infernos can hardly be extinguished by 'humanitarian interventions.'" And it was why so many countries were now unwilling to send their own soldiers.[22] That was certainly the position of the Federal Republic, where officials made it clear from the beginning that no Bundeswehr soldiers would be sent to Rwanda. There were some exceptions, though. Walter Zuber, minister of the interior of Rhineland-Palatinate, called for a "humanitarian mission" involving German forces, but *after* the war had ended. In the end, Bundeswehr assistance was limited to trucks and armored cars for UN personnel.[23]

On May 19, two days after the UN's decision to redeploy Blue Berets to the region, Minister of State Helmut Schäfer set forth the government's position, in response to a question by parliamentarian Gernot Erler of the Social Democrats. Erler wanted to know why it had been possible to send soldiers—including German ones—to Somalia but not to Rwanda, where the "violations against humanity" were "even worse." The UN had not requested any, Schäfer explained, and because of constitutional limitations, the Federal Republic would not participate in any sort of mission involving soldiers. That was why, he added, "everything we demand" that others do "will always provoke the response: And what are you doing?" The Federal Republic would not be taken seriously if it "constantly" acted as a "moral critic . . . without being in a position to participate itself militarily in such operations." This was familiar fare from the debates about Cambodia and Bosnia.[24]

An even lower threshold for intervention was apparently out of the question as well. On the same day Schäfer addressed the Bundestag, a journalist asked a government spokesman if the cabinet had discussed the possibility of sending combat medics to Rwanda, as it had recently done in Cambodia. There had not been "a single word" about that, Vogel tersely acknowledged. Another journalist followed up by pointedly asking whether there was a sense among government officials that developments in Rwanda did not directly affect German "interests," and, if so, if that had any influence on official policy. "To be honest," Vogel responded, "I can hardly imagine that.... Every civilized state naturally has an interest in providing assistance in such a situation. The question is whether aid can or may be provided. But it is not a question of insufficient or nonexistent interest."[25] The two men were clearly talking about different kinds of interest.

The issue of Germany's national interest did indeed spark a great deal of debate. In a Bundestag session that July devoted to possible German military action in Bosnia, it became clear that many of the same conservatives strongly in favor of some form of intervention in the Balkans opposed any German involvement whatsoever in Rwanda—even after the genocide had ended. "For us," declared Michael Glos of the Christian Social Union, the deployment of the Bundeswehr had to abide by "clear principles." The security of "our own citizens" and Germany's allies had "top priority." When it came to more distant "trouble spots," the Federal Republic could not, "as a regional power, play the role of global gendarme."[26]

Karl Lamers of the CDU struck a more ambivalent note. The events in Rwanda were "horrible," he acknowledged, which was why it was so important that "we very carefully consider whether we want to commit ourselves so definitively *not* to do such a thing." He nevertheless remained opposed to taking action "at the moment," given "how extraordinarily difficult" such an undertaking would be. "But we must also realize," he quickly added, that "our moral self-respect" was at stake here as well. Karsten Voigt of the SPD, an expert on security and defense issues, voiced similar reservations about a German military presence in Rwanda—as even Blue Helmets on a peacekeeping mission. The Federal Republic had had "exceptionally little experience" in such matters, and the country "easily" risked being branded a "neocolonial power" if it were to participate.[27]

That the Federal Republic should not intervene in Rwanda was a point on which politicians across the political spectrum agreed, then. Many were similarly adamant that the French in particular should not do so either, a chorus that included one surprising voice: Stefan Schwarz, the young CDU parliamentarian who had argued so vehemently in support of military action in Bosnia. Schwarz just as vigorously condemned France for embarking on a unilateral military "adventure" in Rwanda motivated solely, he believed, by French "national interests."[28]

The controversial French mission in Rwanda, dubbed Opération Turquoise, had been approved by the UN Security Council on June 22. Its ostensible goal was to protect civilians by setting up safe havens for refugees and other endangered civilians—not unlike the ones in Bosnia. French foreign minister Alain Juppé emphasized the humanitarian nature of the military operation and was the first foreign official to speak of a "duty to intervene" in Rwanda. He was also one of the first, along with his German counterpart Klaus Kinkel, to label the Hutu atrocities a genocide. Juppé invoked a "sense of honor and the most elementary moral considerations," but hardly anyone in Germany—or elsewhere, for that matter—believed in the "altruism" of France's mission. Other considerations were at play, critics suspected—above all, economic and geopolitical ones. Besides, German journalists pointed out, the French had gone into Rwanda "months after . . . the massacres had begun." They were "too late" to prevent the genocide, and there was "not much left to save" anyway, by then.[29]

That was not entirely true. The genocide continued even after the arrival of the French, who were "nursing back to health," Rupert Neudeck alleged, those responsible for the genocide. Many believed, in fact, that the French were there only to defend the Hutus from the RPF, whom French president François Mitterrand tellingly referred to as the "Black Khmer." Besides, sending soldiers at that point, with the Tutsi rebels on the verge of victory, was like "intervening in Berlin in April 1945 to stop the Allies from defeating Hitler." The reasons for such suspicions were understandable. France had long-established ties to the authoritarian Habyarimana regime, which it had propped up with massive amounts of military aid. That was one reason, journalists speculated, why the war in Rwanda attracted much less media attention in the Federal Republic than in France, where Kigali seemed to be "closer than Sarajevo."[30]

For all these reasons, German correspondents reported, there was a great deal of "surprise" when the French "actually" began to make good on their humanitarian promises and evacuate threatened Tutsis. And "when everyone else wavered," it was the French who finally "took the initiative"—perhaps because their recent policies in Rwanda had given them a "guilty conscience," some speculated. What the French were now doing in Rwanda, one journalist concluded, was the "very least they owed" the victims.[31] The underlying sentiment seemed to be that Germany's neighbors across the Rhine needed to confront and come to terms with their own recent history. After all, that was something the Germans had been doing themselves for some time.

That the Federal Republic would not intervene in any meaningful way to stop the bloodshed quickly became clear; instead it resorted once again to what it did best. It promised humanitarian aid. But despite heartrending media reports about a major refugee crisis sparked by the genocide, even that proved problematic and controversial in the case of Rwanda, an important recipient of West German aid since the 1960s.[32]

More than a million Rwandans had already been displaced since the start of the civil war in 1990. That number jumped to more than two million by the spring of 1994, as hundreds of thousands fled to neighboring countries to escape the violence. In just two days in mid-May, a quarter of a million people crossed a bridge to Tanzania. There, with 330,000 refugees perched on a mere 3.5 square kilometers, Tanzania's Camp Benaco—a "hell on earth"—quickly became the world's largest refugee camp. This "exodus of biblical proportions" continued through the summer, with estimates of up to 3.5 million refugees—roughly half the country's prewar population—living in the neighboring states of Tanzania, Zaire (today, the Democratic Republic of the Congo), and Burundi. "Never before had so many people fled their country in such a short period of time," *Der Spiegel* reported in late July.[33]

Living conditions in the dangerously overfilled refugee camps were abysmal: "Hunger, epidemics, poisoned wells, suffering like at the time of the Black Death or the Thirty Years' War." In mid-May, Bartholomäus Grill wrote in *Die Zeit* that "images and words" could not "express" what was happening in the camps, which reeked of decaying bodies and feces. "Mountains of fresh corpses line the streets"; children everywhere with "bloated bellies, spindly little legs, knees as large as billiard balls, skin withered like parchment"; babies who "suckle the remaining life out of their mothers' breasts." So much suffering took an emotional toll on those bearing witness, Grill added. It was "as if the entire misfortune of the world" were bearing down on them. There were not enough aid workers to assist those in need, and the UN was now calling this the "most difficult humanitarian crisis" in its history. To make matters worse, a cholera epidemic broke out in mid-July in a camp near the city of Goma in Zaire. Some 1.7 million refugees had sought refuge in this arid, volcanic region, making *this* now the world's largest refugee camp. Up to 3,000 Rwandans were supposedly dying there every day—"every day one Rwandan village less," as Grill powerfully put it. This "next stage of the apocalypse," Erich Wiedemann warned in *Der Spiegel,* would "complete" the genocide begun three months earlier.[34] It seemed to be a repeat of Cambodia—and also of the Holocaust, as media images obliquely suggested.

Harrowing reports like these understandably elicited great shock and outrage in the Federal Republic, giving rise to insistent demands for more humanitarian assistance. That May, Boutros-Ghali called on Germany to provide Transall transport aircraft for a planned airlift of humanitarian supplies to the region. The *Lübecker Nachrichten,* a local paper in northern Germany, came out strongly in favor of German participation, calling it a decision that should be "self-evident to all who live here in peace and security." Minister of Justice Sabine Leutheusser-Schnarrenberger of the Free Democratic Party was less forthcoming. It was necessary, she explained, to clarify whether this constituted the kind of "out-of-area" military engagement prohibited by the Basic Law. But not everyone agreed. Foreign Minister Kinkel had made it clear a month earlier that he foresaw no difficulties *if* security conditions permitted and the warring factions were willing to accept such deliveries. The Foreign Office subsequently released a statement declaring that the Transall aircraft would indeed be provided once those conditions were met. All the major political parties came out in support, except, predictably, the PDS—*and* one skeptical television moderator, who confronted Kinkel in late May: "Much more relevant than such [humanitarian] missions in Africa is: How can the Germans help in Bosnia?" Kinkel rejected this: "The world cannot and must not watch this, and neither can we."[35]

FIG. 9.1. French soldiers use bulldozers to bury Rwandans who died of cholera at a refugee camp in Zaire (now Democratic Republic of the Congo). This disturbing image, with its unmistakable echoes of the Holocaust, appeared in the *Süddeutsche Zeitung*. Goma, July 1994. © *SZ* Photo / Rainer Unkey / Bridgeman Images.

The Constitutional Court in Karlsruhe released a groundbreaking decision in mid-July, that such out-of-area missions were indeed permissible—with parliamentary approval. Later that month—*after* the genocide had ended—Germany finally sent two German Transalls and a Boeing 707 to take part in the airlift.[36] That "poetic word first used during the Berlin Blockade makes ones think of an uninterrupted chain of airplanes that bring salvation day and night, in rapid succession." But that was not "how one should imagine" this humanitarian effort, Rudolph Chimelli explained to readers of the *Süddeutsche Zeitung*. It was true that the German air force had successfully transported tens of thousands of tons of humanitarian goods to the region during the first week of the operation. But serious logistical challenges impeded deliveries to those most in need, which meant the mission was only supplying, at most, about a fifth of the necessary foodstuffs. Continuing shortages of other indispensable items, like medications and clean water, were what eventually led to the cholera epidemic—which, Rupert Neudeck later

FIG. 9.2. Foreign Minister Klaus Kinkel (*second from left*) and humanitarian Rupert Neudeck (*center*) visit a Rwandan orphanage. Ndera, July 1995. Bundesarchiv, Bild B 145 Bild-00108486 / photographer: Julia Fassbender.

commented, "almost caused greater excitement" and interest than the genocide itself. The money that suddenly started to pour in, he lamented, could have been used four months earlier to outfit another contingent of Blue Helmets—but instead, he said, one evacuated one's own countrymen and felt "happy to have quickly escaped the horrors" of the mass slaughter. His own organization collected 10 million DM in donations, which it used to set up a hospital in Gyseni, by then a "fully apocalyptic" city in western Rwanda.[37]

Whatever its failings and difficulties, the German government provided close to a quarter of a billion deutsch marks in assistance by the fall of 1994: 91.5 million DM to various NGOs active in the region, and the rest in aid packages sponsored by the European Union. This made it the second largest donor of foreign aid for Rwandans after the United States. (By comparison, Germany had contributed some 800 million DM in aid to former Yugoslavia at that point.[38]) Most of the money was spent on hygienic measures, including fresh-water facilities transported directly from Germany, important for reining in the cholera epidemic.

To facilitate the rebuilding of the country's infrastructure, German officials set up a bureau in the Goma-Bukavu region of Zaire. Similar to the one in Zagreb to help the Bosnians, its task was to coordinate German aid to the Rwandans.[39]

This outpouring of assistance was not surprising, given the burst of media attention. Dozens of aid organizations were active, including the Gesellschaft für Technische Zusammenarbeit (Society for Technical Cooperation), whose volunteers included private citizens like Herman Unglaub, the automobile mechanic who had described the unfolding drama to German journalists in early April. Under the direction of co-ordinator Rainer Bolz, its volunteers worked on various projects, from the construction of latrines to the installation of fresh drinking water facilities. Also active was the Rwanda Committee of Bad Kreuznach, a quaint spa town in Rhineland-Palatinate that had formed an official partnership with Rwanda a decade earlier—one of several dozen sister-city connections between the two countries. One of the committee's most dedicated volunteers was Konrad Mohr of the CDU, a former professor in Coblenz and state secretary in the Rhineland-Palatinate Ministry of Culture. Following his retirement in 1986, Mohr had traveled to Rwanda to construct schools and hospitals and work on other aid projects, efforts he continued following the genocide.[40]

The usual complaint that not enough was being done could still be heard, however. In a motion filed in early September, the SPD used withering language to criticize the government for providing "vastly insufficient" aid. Some 80,000 people in refugee camps on Rwanda's borders had died since mid-July from epidemics and hunger, and thousands could have been saved, the SPD indignantly claimed, if the Federal Republic and other industrial states had had support systems in place that could be activated on short notice. Such "calamities" were not isolated or "unforeseeable," the motion continued, and there had been "numerous warnings" beforehand, but those had been ignored. That was true. SPD politician Werner Schuster, a physician born and raised in East African Tanganyika, had traveled to Rwanda in the summer of 1993 and, on his return, called on Chancellor Kohl to help finance the deployment of 4,000 Blue Helmets, in hopes of averting catastrophe. To avoid similar disasters in the future, his party recommended the creation of an Environment and Catastrophe Aid Service or a German Auxiliary Corps. The CDU initially rejected the suggestion, but as the tragedy in Rwanda unfolded that summer, Kohl increasingly warmed to it—as an alternative to sending the Bundeswehr, as a form of "community service" (*Zivildienst*), and as a "catalyst for compassion, especially among young people."[41]

Germans' compassion for the Rwandans did seem more limited than it was for the Bosnians, if one uses aid amounts as a measure. There were, to be sure, a series of emergency appeals on behalf of the sorely afflicted Rwandans. These included a benefit performance of George Gershwin's *My One and Only* in Berlin, and a donation drive sponsored by the local media in Berlin that raised more than a million deutsch marks in just a few days in late July. But overall there appears to have been only a "rather modest . . . willingness to donate money." A survey from early August found that the main German aid organizations had received only 17 million DM in donations altogether—a paltry amount compared to what was flowing to Bosnia at the time. There were several reasons for this, suspected Lutz Worch, head of the German Central Institute for Social Issues in Berlin: Germany's strained economic situation in the wake of unification, for example, and the fact that the crisis was taking place during the holiday season. "The terrifying images," he added, "also trigger a sort of inner blockade"—a sign that Germans were becoming inured to so much suffering. But there may have been something else at play: blatant racism. "What do you want with those monkeys?" one German asked his doctor, who had volunteered to help Rwandan refugees in Zaire. "There's enough [to do] here."[42]

The lackluster response to the Rwandan refugee crisis expressed itself in other ways as well, most visibly in the adoption of "rigid" and "resolute" measures designed, critics suspected, to "keep out" unwanted Africans seeking entry to the Federal Republic. Authorities denied these allegations, but there was ample evidence. Visas were denied to the family of the former ambassador to Germany, for example, as well as to Rwandans who had worked closely with German aid organizations. This was "scandalous and shameful," boomed Herbert Schnoor, the interior minister of North Rhine–Westphalia who had done so much on behalf of Bosnian refugees. Representatives from a Christian Boy Scout organization in his state went even further, calling the "cynical" decision a "clear signal" to voters on the extreme right in an important election year.[43]

Federal authorities offered a variety of excuses, ranging from the bureaucratic and procedural—an agreement first had to be reached with the *Länder,* which had failed to reach one at a meeting in early May, when the genocide was in full swing—to the ludicrous: "Sufficient aid" was available in Rwanda's neighboring states, and anyway, it was best for the refugees to stay in the region to avoid "deracination," a common argument used about the Cambodians and Bosnians as well.[44] Besides, officials claimed, the refugees were not experiencing political persecution "in a narrow sense" of the term—whatever that meant. According to one internal memo, written in "frigid German legalese," exceptions could not be made for individuals who did not "suffer any more or less" than other Rwandan refugees—a stipulation that could be interpreted broadly. A mere 123 Rwandans applied for asylum from early April to late June, and only 3 had been successful as of late July; 71 had been rejected, and the other cases were still pending. Genocide was apparently insufficient "grounds for asylum," Dominic Johnson angrily concluded in the *taz.*[45]

Was something else at play here? The leftist politician Ulrich Briefs—an independent formerly of the SPD, the Greens, *and* the PDS—suspected "discriminatory racist motives. . . . One accepts white refugees from Yugoslavia, even if not especially gladly, but one obviously wants to keep out blacks, preferably entirely." Was the refusal to accept Rwandan refugees "a triumph," he wanted to know, for the "dull instincts of large segments of the German population," the same ones who had just carried out a "pogrom" in former East Germany? He was referring to an incident that had taken place a week earlier involving "hooligans" and "skinheads" who had attacked black Africans in the streets of Magdeburg. A public opinion poll conducted in late July found that 41 percent of all Germans were indeed opposed to taking in refugees from Rwanda. But almost half were in favor, and that percentage was even higher in the eastern half of unified Germany—a noteworthy statistic, given widespread claims that racism and xenophobia were much more pronounced there.[46]

It is difficult to say, in the end, how much of a role racism played in deciding whether to accept refugees from Africa. It is true that West

German officials had not felt especially "called upon" to welcome non-Europeans when there was a surge in refugees coming from Asia and Africa in the late 1960s, including the victims of the bloody war in Biafra. Instead, they called on other West European states to do their part—much as they would do later, during the conflict in Bosnia.[47] But one thing is certain. The German response to the Rwandan genocide laid bare subtle forms of prejudice, as well as more explicit expressions of condescension, toward black Africans. One detected this, for instance, in attempts to explain the seemingly unfathomable nature of what was happening in Rwanda. "Can one understand inhumanity?" journalist Wolfgang Kunath asked with clear exasperation after witnessing the aftermath of the church massacre in Kiziguro. "Perhaps, to a certain extent; people are sometimes inhuman." Nevertheless, what had occurred there remained simply "incomprehensible." And that, *Der Spiegel* suggested on several occasions, was precisely what made Africa a "lost" continent devoid of any "hope."[48]

Whether language and sentiments like these dulled a "sense of empathy" for the victims is debatable.[49] Still, Africa expert Peter Molt feared, curt remarks about "hopelessness" were why Western observers would once again attribute the Rwandan genocide to "irrational African tribal warfare" and see it as "a relapse into . . . barbarism." Some of the language adopted by the media certainly veered in that direction. An "entire *Volk*" had "mutated into brutes" using archaic instruments—"machetes, knives, spears, and arrows"—to murder in a "bestial manner." The Khmer Rouge had been depicted in similarly backward, animalistic ways, of course, but not the Serbs or Croats. In fact, the German media never referred to those fellow Europeans as "eloquent" or "well-spoken"— coded, or at least culturally insensitive terms freely used to describe prominent Africans like the new Rwandan prime minister or a leading figure in the RPF who happened to be a university professor. That sort of arrogance, condescension, and implied cultural superiority obscured the "manifold causes of this tragedy in the heart of Africa," concluded Molt, a political scientist and coordinator of the Rhineland-Palatinate / Rwanda Partnership Association.[50]

Jörg Zimmermann, a Presbyterian pastor who had lived in Rwanda since 1991, took up the theme as well:

> The world of children's books is a simple one: Proud [African] warriors, at the bidding of their chieftains, fight out age-old tribal feuds, whose causes remain ultimately unfathomable. They fight with spears and lances, wear clothing made of leaves and straw—and, ideally, their faces are fearsomely painted. The real world is different, but Rwanda is learning now that the racist clichés of the colonial period are still too present to allow for actual analysis abroad.[51]

That was a bit unfair, given the many nuanced analyses of the conflict appearing at the time in the more serious German press and in discussions among political elites. But the pastor's observations were not completely off the mark. Racist clichés, or at least condescending comments about "backward" Africans, were standard fare, sometimes blatant, sometimes more subtle. In late April, Minister of State Helmut Schäfer referred to a recent appeal Foreign Minister Kinkel had issued to both sides in Rwanda to halt the killing. As an "experienced foreign policy official," he superciliously explained, "allow me" to point out the difficulty of communicating such appeals to soldiers fighting in the "jungle" (*Busch*), a distinctly pejorative term. He dismissively commented as well on an appeal for assistance by the Organization of African Unity, which acknowledged it was unable to cope alone with the situation. That, Schäfer explained, was "the usual experience. Africa is not able to end conflicts on its own . . . using its own means."[52] This was a curiously tone-deaf comment, even leaving aside the complete disregard for Europe's own contribution to Africa's many troubles during the colonial period. After all, the Europeans were proving singularly inept themselves at dealing with the atrocities in Bosnia. And, as many German politicians would soon acknowledge, it was only American action in the Balkans that, in the end, allowed for a peaceful resolution of *Europe's* bloodiest conflict since World War II.

In a dispatch filed at the start of the genocide—provocatively titled "The Black Man Disgusts Europe"—journalist Bettina Gaus captured the unmistakable sense of Western superiority toward the Africans. There was still a widespread belief in the Old World that they had a "much different mentality," that an "individual life" had "no value" to them, that it was "easy to get over the death of one child if you have fifteen." Many Westerners considered death by "hunger or gun shots" to be a "cultural trait" in Africa, added her colleague Dominic Johnson. The genocide was a "volcanic eruption" of sorts—"as if murder were a state of nature in Rwanda, as if black Africans were wolves among wolves, as if peace, security, and human dignity were concepts applicable only to whites."[53] Prejudices like these found expression in other ways as well, especially in complaints that humanitarian assistance was being poured down the proverbial drain. Affluent states had an "important duty" to fight poverty by improving economic conditions, Hans-Joachim Fuchtel of the CDU declared in a speech that fall. "But how should that be accomplished," he wanted to know, when previous achievements were "destroyed by clan feuds"—like the current one in Rwanda. How should one explain to the German "taxpayer" that these countries needed assistance "when, at the same time, they have enough money to fund wars!"[54]

"Clan feuds" or "tribal feuds" were the most popular terms used to characterize the Rwandan genocide—supposedly the crescendo of a decades-long struggle for power following independence from Belgium in 1962. But several German journalists and experts vehemently rejected that facile explanation. "Were Hitler's mass extermination camps the setting for a German-Jewish tribal war?" Dominic Johnson asked rhetorically in the *taz*. Such "code words" from the colonial period failed to get at the real causes of the conflict, Bartholomäus Grill similarly objected in *Die Zeit*. They were just an "excuse" for looking on and refusing to act. Besides, he added, "tribal feuds" were not a scourge only in Africa: "Just look at Bosnia." Two years earlier, Hans Magnus Enzensberger, one of Germany's best known intellectuals, had similarly remarked to a group of Africans that "tribal wars" were not an "African specialty," as most Europeans believed. "When you hear about developments in Yugoslavia, are you not overcome with an element of schadenfreude?"[55]

Clichés about the ethnic origins of the genocide were "much too crude" for another reason: The conflict did not just pit Hutus against Tutsis. Leaving aside decades of intermarriage and other forms of "mixing" between the two groups, there were many Hutus who were themselves critical of the government and of "Hutu Power," the racist ideology that triggered the genocide. That was why such explanations "distort reality" and why the "description of a situation disguises itself as an explanation."[56]

More substantive analyses of the Rwandan genocide focused on three interconnected themes: political struggle, socioeconomic tensions, and the colonial heritage. The political conflict between the Hutus and Tutsis was, the argument went, a straightforward, decades-old struggle for political power and privilege that had flared up following the RPF invasion in the fall of 1990. Both sides now feared that they would lose out if the Arusha Peace Accords were enforced. But the struggle also had "modern" causes that went beyond mere political differences. In essence, this "bitterly poor" country had all the "classic characteristics" of an underdeveloped land: overpopulation, land erosion, scarce resources, and poor infrastructure, resulting in widespread hunger and acute land shortages—which, in turn, had produced intractable "social frictions" and "economic disadvantages."[57] Peter Molt explicitly drew the connection between these developments and the recent outbreak of violence—a result of "social envy, aggression, criminality, and a dwindling willingness to provide neighborly help and cooperation." In short, it was "social disintegration" that accounted for the "marginalized population's disposition toward unconditional friend-or-foe behavior and anarchic violence. Only those familiar with the bitter and hopeless situation of the poor in Rwanda can imagine how easily radical slogans and senseless violence can seduce them."[58] Observers in Germany and elsewhere had offered similar explanations for the bloodletting in Cambodia two decades earlier; they might have mentioned, too, how social and economic frictions during the Weimar Republic had helped pave the way for Hitler and the NSDAP.

Others went much further back in time, tracing the contours of the centuries-old relationship between the country's two main ethnic groups. After conquering what was now Rwanda and Burundi in the fifteenth century, German correspondents explained, the "tall" Tutsi "herder aristocracy" had acted like "feudal masters" over the "shorter" but numerically superior Hutu, a "peasant people." Real tensions between the two groups only really emerged in the late nineteenth century, the argument went, because of machinations by the colonial powers—first the Germans, then the Belgians. Contemporary Rwanda and Burundi had been part of German East Africa, the Wilhelmine empire's largest colony from 1885 to 1919. The Belgians took over the region as a mandate after World War I, when Germany was stripped of its colonies. "The largely peaceful symbiosis came to a sudden end," Constanze Stelzenmüller explained in *Die Zeit*, with the arrival of the Germans and, "above all, the Belgians," who adopted a strategy of divide and rule.[59]

The conflict—and, by extension, the genocide—was, in short, a "product of colonialism." Less than a week after Stelzenmüller's analysis appeared, Ulrich Briefs told his Bundestag colleagues that the Belgians (but not, apparently, the Germans) had "destroyed" the "long-time . . . symbiosis" between the Hutus and Tutsis through their "systematic playing-off of one *Volk* against the other." The "result" was the "brutal, reciprocal genocide." That pat explanation experienced pushback. Referring "solely to the past" was "too tacky," objected Pastor Zimmermann, and one could not simply attribute the conflict to ethnic tensions and colonial machinations.[60]

Colonial rule might have been at the root of the conflict, others pointed out, but it was "not an excuse" for the current slaughter—just as earlier American actions in Cambodia were no "excuse" for Khmer Rouge atrocities, they might have added. Bartholomäus Grill went a step further: "Slavery, colonialism, the unjust global free market, the dictates of the World Bank. All these factors, we hear in a *ceterum censeo* of shock and dismay, are mainly responsible for suffering and war in Africa today and for all eternity." There was "no doubt" the Germans and Belgians had "systematically stratified" Rwandan society. But colonialism "falls short as an explanatory model. . . . Is there really a causal link between the acts of violence committed by the German captain Hans Ramsay, who hoisted the imperial eagle in 1897," and the "current terror" in the region? Rejecting the "romanticized ideal" of "noble savages" as victims who had lived in paradisial harmony before the "evil Europeans" arrived, Grill drew on the work of Cameroonian journalist Axelle Kabou, who had written at length about "anticolonial myths" propagated by the "Third-World Movement."[61] The Africa correspondent for *Die Zeit* was clearly engaging in polemics, but the German media featured African voices that similarly emphasized the role of the Rwandans themselves. Théogéne Rudawingwa, general secretary of the RPF, argued in an interview with *Der Spiegel* that the country's own politicians bore "greater blame" than the Belgians. After all, they were the ones who had "only too gladly adopted colonial models." He pointed in particular to the country's passports, which documented "tribal membership"—and thus "abetted" the genocide.[62]

That example must have resonated with German readers. After all, the Nazis had used special markings in passports to help identify Jews, beginning in 1938.[63] But if it did not, other common words and phrases, already familiar from public debates about Cambodia and Bosnia, would have struck a chord. The Hutus were described as "barbaric war criminals" conducting a struggle over "living space." They carried out "pogroms" and were now slaughtering fellow Hutus, who were "ethnic traitors" for having supported reconciliation between the two groups. And there were even more direct references to the Third Reich and the plight of European Jewry in the 1930s and 1940s. The Tutsi were the "Jews of Central Africa"; they faced "extermination"; and the ones who had been in exile for decades "never abandoned hope of returning to their homeland, like the Zionists long ago." A suggestive image in *Der Spiegel* of fully clothed corpses arranged in a pile underscored the parallel in a somewhat more subtle manner. This, the caption read, attested to the "horrific need" to send "cremation ovens" to Africa.[64]

Nazi atrocities were once again the default historical analogy. But certain claims about Rwanda represented a departure from the usual set of tropes. The idea that "bloodthirsty bands . . . besotted with beer and blood" were killing and destroying in a "furious" fashion, as if in a "murderous frenzy" or "fog" (*Rausch*), suggested that there was something qualitatively different about what was taking place in Central Africa.[65] But this characterization, too, met with resistance. Allusions to "bloodlust" (*Blutrausch*), Bartholomäus Grill objected once again, were empty phrases used to explain everything and therefore nothing—from German neo-Nazis and Serb militias to the "landless sons" of Hutu peasants: "Rowdy machos simply embody the bad everywhere." An uneasy tension existed between this notion and other claims at the time about the "impressive," if surprising, "thoroughness" with which the Hutus had carried out a genocide—"planned well in advance" by "master-minds," no less, who were "not stupid butchers," Grill maintained, "but rather politically urbane and clever people with experience on the diplomatic parquet." The "bloodbath," journalist Ullrich Fichtner similarly concluded, was a product of "deliberate policies" by elites who had "superimposed racial ideology" on the country's actual conflicts. "The procedure is familiar: One must merely blame powerless minorities for politically manufactured problems—outraged majorities are then usually easy to find. Europe has experience here, too, but finds the goings-on in Rwanda completely incomprehensible."[66]

Such "procedures" were indeed familiar in Europe, not least in Germany, and the allusion to the country's own past would not have escaped many readers. In fact, such allusions may have even influenced how some Germans thought about the horrors of the Third Reich. Two years after the Rwandan genocide, during a heated podium discussion about *Hitler's Willing Executioners,* Daniel J. Goldhagen's controversial 1996 book about German perpetrators during the Holocaust, historian Hans Mommsen claimed that the members of the mobile units responsible for the killing of Eastern European Jews did "not know what they were doing" at the time because they had been in such a "*Rausch*" (frenzy).[67] That had been one of the most common terms used to describe the recent killing spree in the heart of Africa.

In his June 1994 speech to the Organization of African Unity, Foreign Minister Kinkel concluded by reminding his audience that Africa was, "by far," the most important recipient of German aid. In 1992, the continent had received almost 3.5 billion DM in assistance—more than 40 percent of the Federal Republic's total commitments. "Believe me, Africa and its people remain close to my heart!" Later that month, the foreign minister stated once again, this time at a press conference on Corfu, that the "tragedy" in Rwanda was a "genocide" and that Germany would naturally do what it could to help in the "humanitarian realm." But he hastened to add a disclaimer already familiar from discussions about Bosnia: "We cannot do other things because of constitutional reasons"—a clear allusion to military assistance. This was not surprising.

If outside intervention in Bosnia were "controversial" at the time, it seemed "futile" in an "impenetrable and confusing" country like Rwanda. But why did those individuals in Germany normally "keen" to intervene in foreign lands not bang the drum when it came to Rwanda, *Neues Deutschland* wanted to know.[68]

There were a number of reasons: Germany's "culture of restraint," perceived constitutional limitations, a preoccupation at the time with the Balkans, and a sense that Rwanda was not vital to the country's national "interest." Besides, in contrast to Bosnia, Central Africa was very far away, both geographically and culturally. Some form of intervention was not "unimaginable," as recent deployments to Cambodia and Somalia had made clear—though the recent military debacle in the Horn of Africa would have made even those willing to get involved in Rwanda think twice. Memories of Germany as a "perpetrator of gross human rights violations," its "special relationship" with its former colony, and the "human rights rhetoric of political elites" did not outweigh those "stark facts," political scientist Jutta Helm concludes.[69] Africa may have been near to Kinkel's heart, but, in the end, clearly not as "near" as Bosnia. Just how true that was would become even more obvious in the year to come.

10

Crossing the Rubicon

On April 6, 1994, Foreign Minister Klaus Kinkel gave a radio interview to mark the second anniversary of the European Union's recognition of Bosnia. It was, by chance, the very same day the Hutu genocide of the Tutsis began *and* the anniversary of the Luftwaffe's bombing of Belgrade in 1941. Kinkel did not address the day's developments in Central Africa, or the historical anniversary, but instead spent much of the interview emphasizing recent advances in former Yugoslavia. These included the creation a month earlier of a Muslim-Croat Federation that had put a (temporary) end to fighting between the two ethnic groups; the removal of Serb soldiers from the hills surrounding Sarajevo; and a truce between Croat and Serb forces in the Krajina region of Croatia, the site of sporadic violence since 1991. He acknowledged that there was still heavy fighting and there were even reports of ethnic cleansing in some areas, but there were positive signs, all in all. A week later, Kinkel reiterated his sanguine assessment of the situation in a formal report to the Bundestag. "Everything must now be done to maintain the positive momentum."[1]

Just days after Kinkel's radio interview, American fighters bombed a Bosnian Serb military outpost—a "first" in the history of NATO that had been carried out in response to a UN request to help protect Goražde, one of the so-called safe areas it had set up in June 1993. The Serbs responded aggressively to the attack, taking approximately 150

UN personnel as hostages on April 14, which ushered in an even more forceful Western response involving further sporadic air attacks by NATO forces. These, in turn, prompted further Serb aggression against international forces. The spiral of violence culminated in two major aerial strikes in late November 1994, which one Serb official, in a polemical if crafty historical comparison, likened to the Luftwaffe attack of April 6, 1941.

The NATO attacks did not bring an end to the fighting and killing, and the international community did not make much progress that year toward negotiating a peaceful resolution. The year 1995 started out more auspiciously. On New Year's Eve, former American president Jimmy Carter persuaded the warring factions to sign a temporary truce, and Radovan Karadžić assured his German interlocutors in an interview that appeared in *Der Spiegel* in May that a peace treaty would be signed that year. The Bosnian Serb leader was indeed correct, even if most of 1995 did not bode well for an end to hostilities. The New Year's truce brokered by Carter quickly fell apart, like dozens of earlier ones, and continuing tensions between Croats and Muslims underscored the fragility of their recently created federation. Serious NATO air attacks resumed in May, eliciting a rabid response from Karadžić, who ordered the kidnapping of more than 300 UN Blue Helmets and observers to be held as hostages following air strikes against the Bosnian Serb capital, Pale. This amounted to an "official declaration of war" against the international community, Matthias Rüb commented in the *Frankfurter Allgemeine Zeitung*. The Bosnian Serbs, he wrote, had finally "crossed the Rubicon."[2]

During the months leading up to this latest episode in the Bosnian drama, there had already been talk of withdrawing UN personnel from the region because of heightened danger. Planning for this contingency had begun in November 1994, and in mid-January, UN and NATO officials approached the German government about its possible participation. Secretary-General Boutros Boutros-Ghali also raised this issue during a visit to Bonn in January 1995 and tried to make the request more palatable by offering a carrot: the possibility of a permanent German seat on the Security Council. A spokesperson for the Ministry of Defense

announced that the government was prepared to send naval ships, reconnaissance aircraft, and transport planes. But officials also made it
clear once again that, because of Germany's "historical entanglement"
in the region, sending German soldiers into Bosnia was not possible.
They would only become "part of the problem," Minister of Defense
Volker Rühe contended, "not part of the solution."[3]

That was the context for the government's partial reversal a half year
later, in June 1995, when it decided to commit German military forces
more directly to the region. The turnaround came in response to a UN
Security Council vote earlier that month to create a so-called Rapid
Reaction Force (RRF), whose primary responsibility was to protect and
possibly extricate the remaining UN soldiers. France, the Netherlands, and Britain, the states with the largest military contingents in
Bosnia, had proposed the measure in reaction to the abduction of the
Blue Helmets, who had been placed in chains and used as human
shields, images of which were broadcast on Serb television. That created
a "completely different situation," Kinkel explained on June 26, and the
cabinet decided to provide substantial military support to the RRF.[4]

This marked the first time the Bundeswehr would take part in an
international peace mission organized by the UN and NATO. To help
with reconnaissance activities, the government agreed to deploy its Tornado Electronic Combat / Reconnaissance aircraft, which NATO had
explicitly requested. The planes were specially equipped to deal with the
type of precision, surface-to-air missiles recently acquired by the Serbs.
The main reason for Germany's participation, Chancellor Kohl explained,
was that their allies did not have the requisite planes.[5] The Luftwehr
would also supply air support to help transport supplies to UN soldiers
stationed outside Bosnia, and German army medics would staff a
Franco-German field hospital set up in the Croatian city of Split to provide first aid to wounded UN soldiers. The cabinet decided as well that the
Bundeswehr would help evacuate UN Protection Force (UNPROFOR)
soldiers and personnel, if it came to that. But, Kinkel and Minister of
Defense Rühe once again made clear, there would be no German
ground troops in Bosnia itself. No one in the international community
had requested any, and if they had, it was a request "we would have to
reject." This elicited a pointed question by one journalist, who wanted

to know the difference between a German soldier "on the ground" and one "in a fighter plane." Another journalist followed up with a different point: "Is not the historical decision and qualitative change this: That, for the first time on foreign soil—at that, soil that is historically fraught—foreign soldiers could die by German hands?"[6]

That very theme dominated a marathon, seven-hour debate in the Bundestag on June 30. Addressing a formal government motion to participate in the new UN mission, almost three-quarters of the speakers that day referred in some way to the weight of German history, the lessons Germans should draw from it, and the role that memories of the Third Reich and World War II should play in the vote. What was most striking, once again, was the *fungible* quality of that history, which the speakers used in vastly different ways to make their cases for diametrically opposed arguments about military entanglements abroad.[7]

Foreign Minister Kinkel opened what would be a raucous, often emotional session with a lengthy statement setting forth the government's position. He began by emphasizing the weighty historical significance of the mission as one in a series of "important political turning points" since 1949: from the creation of the Bundeswehr and the decision to join NATO in the 1950s, to the *Ostpolitik* of the late 1960s and 1970s. The Federal Republic, Kinkel solemnly acknowledged, was again entering "uncharted political territory." His main arguments echoed familiar ones made on numerous occasions by those in favor of German participation in humanitarian interventions: the Federal Republic needed to demonstrate solidarity with its allies, who had "unconditionally" stood at Germany's side since 1945; it had certain duties and responsibilities as a member of the international community that had only grown since unification in 1990; a failure to act would hurt its image and credibility abroad. "We have a political and moral duty to assist, also and precisely *in light of* our past. After all, it was the Allies who—using military force, by the way—freed us from the Nazi dictatorship."[8]

Opponents countered these arguments head on. Acts of "solidarity," argued Joschka Fischer of the Greens, depended on what was "doable" and "politically and morally responsible" in the context of a country's own interests and history. A "mere" fifty years after the end of World War II, he reasoned, Germany's partners would understand that "a burned child

FIG. 10.1. Green parliamentarian Joschka Fischer (*lower right*) gives a speech in the Bundestag opposing the deployment of the Bundeswehr to the Balkans. Foreign Minister Klaus Kinkel (*left*) and Chancellor Helmut Kohl (*center*) listen in the background. Bonn, June 30, 1995. IMAGO / Sepp Spiegl.

must avoid fire." The goal of German military deployment, first in Cambodia, then in Somalia, and now in Bosnia—a place where "history" was "still very much alive" and where the Wehrmacht had once "rampaged in the cruelest way"—was clear, he charged: to "abandon" the reigning precept of "self-restraint" that had guided German foreign policy since 1945. Fischer, who would soon change his tune, conceded that "brutal" acts of violence like mass murder, rape, and ethnic cleansing posed the "greatest challenge" for pacifists. But if the government were "honest," it would admit it had people in its ranks who wanted "much, much more."[9]

Kinkel's talk of forcing the Serbs "to their knees"—and Bundeswehr general inspector Klaus Naumann's use of the term *combat mission* in a television interview—only reinforced that impression, leading Social Democrats pointed out.[10] But it was Gregor Gysi of the Party of Democratic Socialism who offered the most pointed response to the foreign minister. The alliance had been of no concern when Germany had decided to take a "solitary path" without its partners, he claimed, a pointed reference to Bonn's push for rapid recognition of Croatia and Slovenia in 1991. More to the point, it was "simply maddening" that the "growing responsibility" of the Federal Republic was viewed "more and more in military-political" terms. It was no longer a question of a "European Germany but rather of a German Europe," he added, a provocative statement that produced "great turmoil" in the chamber. Marie Dobberthien of the SPD made similarly provocative statements about "creeping" militarization, alleging that the regions where a mission could take place were becoming "arbitrary" as well: "Yesterday Somalia, today rump Yugoslavia. And tomorrow?"—an arch allusion to "The Rotten Bones Are Trembling," an infamous Nazi fight song.[11]

The lessons of World War II were indeed self-evident to those who opposed the government's motion. "Down with weapons!" they demanded, "No more war!" Gerhard Zwerenz of the PDS—who had volunteered for the Wehrmacht at age seventeen, later deserted, and then wound up in Soviet captivity—drew on his personal experiences to explain why his own "lifelong, unforgettable culpability" made it "impossible" for him to raise his hand "for any sort of combat operation or war." Not everyone on the Left concurred. Former East German dissident Gerd Poppe of the Greens urged caution in Bosnia but argued that anyone who spoke out against German military participation in the Balkans by drawing an analogy with the Third Reich either failed to understand the reason for UN peacekeeping—"or was engaging in pure demagoguery." Marieluise Beck, also of the Greens, drew a much different lesson from the past as well. As a sixty-eighter, she pointed out, she belonged to a generation that had demanded their parents "finally . . . take responsibility" for their "entanglement" in the Third Reich. The history of the Nazi period had taught her that the only practical response to fascism was armed resistance. "Auschwitz was liberated by soldiers," after all. She agreed that war should "never again go forth from German soil," but she said it was the "inheritance of our fathers" that "obliges us to oppose violence when a *Volk* is once again being destroyed."[12]

Members of the ruling coalition were even more vehement in their support for the government motion. It was not a question of securing "greater power" for Germany or waging war for war's sake, but about "protecting human lives and making peace possible." One could not merely "lament" human rights abuses; one also had to work hard to make sure there were fewer victims. And the way to do that, argued Wolfgang Schäuble, leader of the Christian Democratic Union / Christian Social Union caucus in the Bundestag, was to vote for the government motion—as "difficult" as that might be. After all, "Nobody gladly deploys soldiers."[13]

Several members of the coalition invoked earlier statements by past SPD luminaries to bolster their case. Willy Brandt had once warned, declared Michael Glos of the CSU, that "in a world in which everyone is increasingly dependent on . . . everyone else, policies aimed at achieving peace cannot stop at one's own front door." The conservative parliamentarian might have also mentioned former SPD leader Carlo Schmid, who, in the mid-1960s, had remarked that the "time was past" when German soldiers could not participate in such missions. But while Glos praised Social Democrats of an earlier generation, he also condemned their party's positions on a series of related foreign-policy issues. Their current objection to sending Tornado reconnaissance planes into Bosnia—the one substantive point most SPD parliamentarians disagreed with in the government motion—stood in a long "historical tradition" of saying "no": to Western integration in the 1950s, to the creation of the Bundeswehr that same decade, to the NATO "double-track" decision of December 1979 (the brainchild, incidentally, of an SPD chancellor, Helmut Schmidt). The country's allies would interpret the SPD's most recent refusal, Glos harshly concluded, as "national selfishness" and "cowardly shirking." It was, in short, "cynical and inhuman."[14]

This provoked an angry and indignant reaction that quickly devolved into ad hominem attacks. "What kind of person are you," Günther Verheugen of the SPD challenged Glos, to brand doubts about a combat mission that might lead to the death of innocent civilians as "cynical and inhuman." He responded in kind to the references to past leftist luminaries by reminding the governing coalition of a quote he (mistakenly) attributed to Konrad Adenauer before the first West German chancellor had embraced remilitarization in the early 1950s: "Any hand that ever picks up a weapon again should rot away." Verheugen followed this up with a thinly veiled allusion to conservative military policies from the period before 1945: "It would be better for our country, for our reputation in the world . . . if you had more frequently asked your political predecessors whether it was correct to use military force." This attack set off a furious exchange of accusations and insults, with Theodor Waigel of the CSU objecting to this "personal and political effrontery." Waigel recalled the fate of conservatives who had been prepared to go to Nazi concentration camps because of their "convictions," and pointed out that his party had been "newly established" in 1945, "deliberately to learn from the mistakes of the past." Wolfgang Schäuble lashed out even more sharply, bellowing that his opponents on the Left were "born traitors. Seldom have I experienced anything rottener. *Pfui Teufel* [disgusting]!"[15] So much for the solemnity of the hour.

Despite the nasty histrionics, several broad points of agreement emerged: above all, that the government's motion represented a "historic caesura" in German foreign policy. For the first time since 1945, and since the Federal Constitutional Court's fateful decision from July 1994, Germany would "willingly" be sending armed soldiers into an active war zone and participating in "direct" combat missions.[16] Joschka Fischer, who had rejoined the Bundestag after the federal elections of 1994, emphasized just how difficult it was, "precisely for us Germans," to make such a weighty decision. Indeed, Green parliamentarian Winifried Nachtwei remarked, the "difference of opinion" about the deployment went straight through all the parties and their constituencies—and "also through many of us" individually. A recent survey had found, he claimed, that 48 percent of CDU/CSU voters opposed the mission; only 47 percent supported it. But in the end, every member of the CDU/CSU was among the 386 members of parliament who voted in favor of the government motion to participate in the mission; 258 voted against it (including all members of the PDS), and 11 abstained. A significant number of parliamentarians broke ranks with the rest of their party, with 45 members of the SPD (one-fifth) and 4 Greens (one-tenth) supporting the motion.[17] Whatever qualms they may have had at the time, those who signed off on the deployment would feel vindicated just two weeks later when news broke about a fresh round of Serb atrocities—this time in the small town of Srebrenica.

Germans following developments in Bosnia would likely have heard of Srebrenica even before the town became the site of the worst massacre to have taken place in Europe since the 1940s. In the spring of 1993,

Bosnian Serb forces laid siege to the strategically significant town in eastern Bosnia, creating a humanitarian crisis. On April 16 that year, the UN declared the town a demilitarized safe area under the protection of UN forces, which, after disarming local Muslim fighters, were now responsible for protecting the approximately 60,000 civilians there. UN officials on site made it clear that, if attacked, "we will hit back." Helmut Kohl and Klaus Kinkel released strong statements of their own in response to the "brutal" siege and bombardment, though the chancellor continued to maintain that a "comprehensive" military intervention would not solve the conflict.[18]

The fragile protection of Srebrenica was still an issue two years later when, in late June 1995, journalists filed the first reports of Serb plans to "storm" this and other Muslim enclaves in eastern Bosnia. That the town, nominally protected by some 400 Dutch Blue Helmets, would fall to the Bosnian Serbs became clear by the second week of July. American planes carried out a limited attack on July 11, but it came "shamefully" too late, German observers bitterly noted. The attack was "half-hearted" and "timid," and the town fell to Serb forces that afternoon. They were now in control of almost all of eastern Bosnia—their main territorial goal from the beginning.[19]

Condemnation of the Serbs—and of the international community— was swift. On July 13, foreign correspondent Wolfgang Koydl of the *Süddeutsche Zeitung* published one of the earliest and most damning denunciations, calling Srebrenica a major turning point in the conflict and the West's "last chance to salvage some credibility." He specifically censured the Europeans and Americans, who had "no desire to burn their fingers in the bubbling Balkan cauldron"—just like Otto von Bismarck, who had been more "worried in his day about the bones of a Pomeranian grenadier." (This was an allusion to a famous quip made by the Iron Chancellor during the Great Eastern Crisis of 1875–1878.) But the West *did* have an interest there—the "defense of Western values"—and its response to Srebrenica would determine the "kind of world we wish to live in." Koydl angrily concluded that if the West did not respond to the "horrors" of Srebrenica, "no one will ever again take it seriously." The price would have to be paid with the "blood" of French, American, and "also German soldiers, in the end."[20]

Srebrenica remained a hot topic in the media that summer and fall, especially following the first reports of atrocities, including the "violent separation" of men from their families and their subsequent deportation to internment camps, "in plain view" of the UN. Chancellor Kohl declared on July 17 that "barbarians" had committed "crimes against humanity" in Srebrenica, and two weeks later, journalist Walter Mayr published a lengthy report in *Der Spiegel* that seemed to confirm the allegations.[21] It was based on an interview with Mevludin Oric, who had witnessed an "unprecedented crime." The twenty-five-year-old father of two claimed to be one of 10,000 Muslim men who had fled Srebrenica on July 10 for sanctuary in a nearby forest. The next day he and his companions were caught in a Serb ambush, thrown on a truck, and sent to a school gymnasium with hundreds of other Bosnian prisoners. He was taken away with a cousin later that day and brought to a field: "Seconds later the first shots rang out. . . . He felt the blood of his cousin on his naked upper body. Oric remained recumbent, pretending to be dead. . . . Six hours later, as evening approaches, he becomes unconscious. He heard shots ring out till the very end." After awakening, he heard a voice say, "Enough. There is no one left." As backhoes "ripped the earth open" to dig mass graves, Oric decided to flee. Upon removing his blindfold, he saw corpses "piled up orderly, in two rows, each several hundred meters long." He also recognized graves in the moonlight, "a good three meters deep." Oric later met another survivor who told him that he had managed to partially remove his own blindfold and saw General Ratko Mladić, the Bosnian Serb general whose soldiers had taken Srebrenica, sitting in a red Ford observing the executions.

Reports and rumors about the atrocities continued to appear well into the fall. Tadeuz Mazowiecki—a former Polish prime minister who had recently resigned in protest as UN special rapporteur to the region—told Michael Thumann of *Die Zeit*, drawing on eyewitness reports, that "barbaric things" had clearly occurred. In mid-September, State Secretary Werner Hoyer confirmed that Bosnian Serb soldiers had indeed "committed significant violations against humanitarian international law," including the mass imprisonment and "arbitrary" shooting of youths and adult male civilians.[22]

A great deal of uncertainty nevertheless remained. The members of the Dutch battalion ("Dutchbat") stationed in Srebrenica claimed on their return home that there had been "no hint" of mass executions— much less of genocide, a term already being used by Dutch authorities.[23] What the Dutch had witnessed—and, more important, done—to help the civilians in Srebrenica quickly became a source of heated controversy. Despite initial claims that they had not seen any atrocities, it soon became apparent that many Dutchbat members had indeed witnessed horrible acts of violence against civilians—or at least their aftermath, including the use of tractors to bury bodies in mass graves. In late October, *Der Spiegel* reported comments by an anonymous Dutch soldier who described his "mute horror" as he watched the "victims and their executioners. . . . Everything was sorted. . . . Bags, passports, photos landed in a large pile." One of the Muslims gave money and a gold chain to a Serb soldier, who "spit in his face and hit him with the butt of his rifle. . . . The thought immediately came to me that this was Auschwitz." There were similar allusions to the Holocaust elsewhere in the German media, along with sharp criticism of Dutchbat—a theme in the Netherlands as well. "In an upsurge of self-recrimination," reported the *FAZ*, "commentators compared the behavior of the Dutchbat with the Dutch railroad workers who had supervised, in a consistently punctilious and reliable manner, the transport of Dutch Jews to the extermination camps."[24]

"What Took Place in Srebrenica?"—a lengthy investigative report that appeared in *Die Zeit* on November 3—summarized much of what was known up to that point. Colonel Thom Karremans, the commander of Dutchbat, had not allowed his soldiers to participate in the *Selektion* of the Muslims into four groups: the sick, the weak, women and children, and men who could perform military service. But they did witness the "selection of presumptive candidates for death. . . . Did Karremans's people turn from spectators into accomplices?" the report asked.[25] Other critics were less circumspect in their condemnation. Tilman Zülch's Society for Threatened Peoples made serious accusations against the "cowardly" Dutchbat at a press conference in early November. The charges were based on testimony from almost two dozen Muslim refugees, who claimed that the soldiers had, among other offenses, taken advantage of

FIG. 10.2. Exactly one year after the genocide, a young girl stands amid a sea of
question marks: 8,000 sheets of paper symbolizing the murdered men of Srebrenica.
Tilman Zülch's Society for Threatened Peoples organized this action as a reminder
of the massacre. Bonn, July 1996. dpa picture alliance / Alamy Stock Photo.

the "plight of young women by demanding sexual favors of them"—
some as young as fourteen, and sometimes for just a couple of cigarettes or a bar of chocolate. The impression quickly spread that the sins
of the Dutch had been ones of commission and not just omission. But
they were not the only sinners. There were also allegations that the
Bundeswehr and the Bundesnachrichtendienst (Federal Intelligence Service) had been informed "beforehand and much more precisely than

previously known" about the "imminent plans and intentions" of the Bosnian Serbs.[26]

Government representatives vigorously denied such accusations, and Helmut Kohl responded to criticism of the Dutch by rhetorically asking how he could criticize soldiers risking their lives there while "we Germans . . . cannot and do not wish to participate?" Those soldiers had earned "our respect," not criticism—especially by politicians or journalists who sit "at a desk . . . and write commentaries" and could not say how they would have acted themselves "if they had been in this situation." After echoing this popular refrain among those too young to have been implicated in Nazi crimes, the chancellor added: "I was fifteen at the end of the war in 1945 and . . . that is why I know very concretely what war means." Foreign Minister Kinkel demanded, for his part, that the actual perpetrators be called to account for their "dire crimes" in Srebrenica and elsewhere. This could not be "swept under the rug," he told the Bundestag that November—a declaration that drew rare applause from all political parties—and a "cloak of forgetfulness" could not be "spread on top all the dreadful things" that had taken place. Just as important, the horrific events in Srebrenica could not be allowed to "repeat themselves." These were noble words, of course, and ones often used in conjunction with the Holocaust. But what was the government doing in practical terms?[27]

German officials insisted they were engaging with the UN Security Council and the EU to ensure that the International Criminal Court would one day punish "the guilty."[28] But the official response to Srebrenica involved more than just noble-sounding platitudes and behind-the-scenes diplomatic efforts to bring the perpetrators to justice. As the details slowly emerged, Srebrenica became an important turning point in German foreign policy. "Enough is enough," Helmut Kohl thundered in mid-July, and Klaus Kinkel publicly called for the bombing of Pale, the Bosnian Serb capital, to show the Serbs "where the limits" lay. Genocide and ethnic cleansing "demand" a different response, agreed Walter Kolbow of the SPD: "Srebrenica dramatically testifies to this." The mainstream media came out in full support of military intervention, too, once reports of the atrocities in Srebrenica began appearing. Robert Leicht, an editor at *Die Zeit* who had strongly opposed such measures in the past, grudgingly agreed they were now necessary. And even Roderich Reifenrath, editor in chief of the *Frankfurter Rundschau,* decried the West's shameful "reluctance to make moral criteria the foremost measure of action." If it did nothing, charged another journalist at the leftist daily, genocide would lose its "reprehensibility."[29]

For all the talk of how Germany could not send soldiers to the region because of its brutal actions there during World War II, a public consensus now emerged that some sort of German military participation was necessary in NATO peacekeeping missions. The question, in other words, was no longer *whether* German soldiers would be deployed, but in what capacity, and at a press conference on July 26, authorities announced that up to 5,000 German soldiers would be "ready for action" by the end of the month—all volunteers and none to be stationed in Bosnia directly. By this time there had been a real shift in public opinion. A majority of the population, especially in the West, supported German participation in an international humanitarian mission, so long as it did not involve actual combat. But first a peace deal had to be reached.[30]

On the day of US president Bill Clinton's inauguration in January 1993, Klaus Kinkel told a radio interviewer that he did not expect "any decisive changes" in American policy toward the Balkans—another false prognosis, it turned out.[31] The new president decided to use force in the winter of 1994, marking a sharp departure from earlier US policy; indeed, the aerial attacks that February were a first for NATO since its creation more than four decades earlier. Under George H. W. Bush, Washington's reactions to the crisis in Bosnia, closely monitored in Bonn as well as in the German press, had remained restrained. American officials certainly talked tough and decried the bloodletting, but that administration had made it clear it would not send soldiers to the Balkans under any circumstances. The United States will not and cannot "play global policeman everywhere," declared *Der Spiegel,* summarizing Bush's position—especially during a presidential campaign. America's seeming lack of resolve under Bush drew strong criticism from veteran foreign correspondent Peter Scholl-Latour, who compared America's "reluctant acknowledgment" of the "appalling conditions in the Serb concentration camps" with the "lack of interest" Washington had shown in reports about the "Jewish Holocaust in Auschwitz and Treblinka."[32]

The new administration proved more open to the use of force, although, like its predecessor, it focused in the main on diplomacy. In the spring of 1995, Clinton, who had been in "close personal contact" with Chancellor Kohl about the peace process since becoming president, sent diplomat Richard Holbrooke to the region to exert pressure—"sundry threats," in the words of journalist Josef Joffe—on the warring factions to accept a peace plan. A portrait of the top American diplomat published in the *FAZ* informed readers that Holbrooke was a former investment banker who had served a short stint as American ambassador to the Federal Republic in 1994. The diplomat, the son of a Jewish mother originally from Hamburg, made no secret of his belief that Bosnia represented the "West's greatest collective failure since the 1930s."[33]

Holbrooke's assignment to the Balkans paid off. He quickly became the "motor and mentor" of negotiations that ultimately led to a peace settlement. But developments took a turn for the worse at first. Not long after the Srebrenica massacre, another Serb grenade attack in late August caused the death of more than thirty people in Sarajevo's main marketplace. Ten days earlier, three American diplomats carrying a new peace plan had died in an accident on a craggy road to Sarajevo.[34] But by late September, amid two weeks of intense NATO aerial attacks against Serb forces, Holbrooke announced that all sides had accepted, in principle, a new American plan to divide Bosnia into two federated states. This was a "triumph of American diplomacy," gushed Leo Wieland, Washington correspondent for the *FAZ*, and an "outstanding success" for the American president, who had long seemed "irresolute." Clinton's "double strategy of retribution and negotiation" had paid off, he said, thanks to Holbrooke's "energetic mediation." Kinkel, Kohl, and other German politicians were full of praise as well. In a press statement on October 5, the chancellor thanked Clinton and the American team for "their tenacious negotiating efforts."[35]

A truce was announced five days later, but a great deal of hard work remained. Starting on November 1, representatives from the warring factions met for three weeks with members of the so-called International Contact Group (ICG) at the Wright-Patterson Air Force Base near

Dayton, Ohio. The ICG, established in the spring of 1994, consisted of high-level diplomats from Britain, France, Russia, the United States, and, last but not least, the Federal Republic. German participation marked the end of the country's "diplomatic restraint" during the conflict, which had much to do with its unwillingness to deploy the Bundeswehr.[36] Germany's eight-member delegation was led by Wolfgang Ischinger, a future German ambassador to the United States whom Holbrooke later called a "true son of modern Germany: sensitive, urbane, and determined to see his country play a positive role in the world." Ischinger and his team remained in close contact with Bonn. They sent instructions for when to release statements to the press and kept officials back home apprised of developments via a steady stream of telephone calls and telegrams.[37] This occasionally led to direct interventions from afar. Foreign Minister Kinkel made targeted calls to the Balkan envoys when they were acting especially obstinate, and Chancellor Kohl personally intervened in the peace process just days before the conference concluded. Through Ischinger, he sent a pointed private message to the Bosnian president on November 18, pressuring Alija Izetbegović to sign off on the deal despite the "painful" concessions being demanded of the Muslim side.[38]

Clinton announced three days later that a formal deal had finally been reached. Much of it drew on earlier peace plans, but there was one crucial difference. This one had the firm backing of the United States, which agreed to deploy soldiers to the region as part of an international Implementation Force led by NATO. One of its main tasks would be to enforce a demarcation line between the Serb-dominated Republika Srpska, and the Federation of Bosnia and Herzegovina, which was mainly populated by Croats and Muslims. The two separate governing "entities" would make up a single sovereign state, whose territory was to be divided almost equally, based largely on where their soldiers stood at the time hostilities ceased.[39]

The Dayton Accords generated a fresh wave of analysis and criticism in the German media, which emphasized the decisive role of the Americans. The developments in Ohio had shown that "Europe still needs leadership, leadership from America," concluded Kurt Kister, Washington correspondent for the *Süddeutsche Zeitung*, even if that leadership had come much "too late." Others wondered aloud why the Americans had been able to achieve what the Europeans had attempted many times "in vain." Holbrooke and US secretary of state Warren Christopher were more persuasive "in the end," wrote Dieter Buhl in *Die Zeit*, thanks to an "aura" of "will, decisiveness, and power" that Europe sorely lacks. That was precisely why the "Old World" had been unable to prevent the "spilling of blood before its own front door."[40]

German officials were nevertheless quick to point out the important part their own diplomats had played. This was an important corrective to the narrative, they claimed, because Holbrooke had supposedly "fed" privileged American journalists with stories that downplayed the role of the other participants. Wolfgang Ischinger later revealed, for example, that his team had hammered out important aspects of the treaty especially dear to Germany's heart, including ones dealing with arms control and the refugee situation. He also pointed out that the Germans had been the "driving force" behind the very first success achieved in Dayton, namely, the signing on November 10 of a major agreement that strengthened the Muslim-Croat federation. German diplomats and politicians stressed, too, that the origins of the accords went back to the work of the ICG, where the Federal Republic played a prominent role. Its peace plan lay at the "core" of the final agreement, Kinkel maintained. "Yet, there is no doubt," the foreign minister also acknowledged, "America's political and military engagement and weight" were crucial for the final settlement.[41]

Far from endangering the peace process, as many in Germany had feared, the NATO air strikes, most German politicians and pundits now acknowledged, were what made the Bosnian Serbs finally agree to a peace settlement. There were other important factors as well, above all a rapid deterioration of the Serbs' military position, beginning the previous spring. Over the course of the summer, their control of Bosnian territory had dropped from more than 70 percent to just under half. But the real turning point, most agreed, was America's decision to get involved in a conflict it had considered a largely European affair.[42]

Several journalists—and politicians, like Joschka Fischer—leveled a good deal of criticism at the plan. Dayton was "grotesque"—a "bitter peace," a "lazy" one.[43] One feature drew the most censure: the Serbs were permitted to hold on to the territories they had conquered by force. This legitimized the practice of ethnic cleansing, critics charged, and divided a sovereign state previously recognized by the international community. Johann Georg Reißmüller of the *FAZ* condemned the West for asking the Muslims and Croats to sit at the same table with the "perpetrators" and accept the loss of territory taken by force. "Rewarding" the Serbs for having conducted a "war of aggression" was tantamount to "abandoning the principles" and "values" that had guided the actions of the "civilized world" against Hitler, Mussolini, and, most recently, Saddam Hussein. "The guilty shake hands," *Der Spiegel* chimed in, and the Europeans—the "losers who couldn't prevent mass murder"—"drink to their health."[44]

The Dayton conference ended on November 21, 1995, and exactly one week later, the German government filed a motion in the Bundestag that, if approved, would allow the country to deploy some 4,000 soldiers and up to 180 officers to the Balkans, making the Federal Republic an integral part of the international mission to enforce the peace. The German contingent was to be stationed in Croatia and "just temporarily deployed" to Bosnia to carry out nonlethal tasks limited to transportation and the evacuation of ill or injured individuals. Government spokespersons announced that the deployment would last for up to twelve months. The last soldiers finally left, in fact, in the fall of 2012, making it the Bundeswehr's longest foreign mission ever.[45]

The Bundestag conducted two lengthy debates dedicated to Germany's role in the peace settlement—one on November 30, another on December 6—and the same earlier themes about German participation were rehashed. The weight of German history played a central role, with the PDS and most Greens arguing that German soldiers had "no business" in the Balkans, "where their fathers, together with Croatian Ustaše fascists, had massacred hundreds of thousands of Serbs and Jews." Those who supported the government motion—who now included a considerable number of Greens and most members of the SPD—argued that that was the wrong historical lesson to draw. It was "a questionable proposition," Günther Verheugen of the SPD objected, that the proper response to an "earlier injustice" should now be a "failure to provide assistance." Karsten Voigt, the SPD's defense expert, agreed: "The goals of this peace mission are the antithesis of Hitler's war goals," and Germany was now helping to enforce "norms of peace and international law" that had been formulated after World War II *in response to* "Hitlerian barbarism." German participation, Voigt concluded, was "the *correct* answer to our history." Taking a similar tack, the FDP argued that this was a "unique chance" for the country to "use German soldiers" to make amends for past mistakes and "offer a glimmer of hope" to a country where there had "once been German soldiers who gave no hope."[46]

Genocide as a reason for German participation played a larger role in these debates than it had before, no doubt a result of the recent reports about Srebrenica. Minister of Defense Rühe put it succinctly during the first debate on November 30: A "no" to the peace mission would be "immoral" after the "events of the first half of this century," which included Auschwitz. Christian Schwarz-Schilling of the CDU was similarly adamant: "This genocide and cultural barbarism on European soil—who would have thought that such a thing was possible fifty years after the defeat of the murderous National Socialist dictatorship!" The former minister, who had resigned from Kohl's cabinet two years earlier to protest the government's lackluster policies toward Bosnia, reminded his colleagues of an inscription—a quote by Jimmy Carter—at the entrance to the Holocaust Museum, which had opened in Washington in the spring of 1993: "Out of our memory . . . of the Holocaust we must forge an unshakable oath with all civilized people that never again will the world stand silent, never again will the world . . . fail to act in time to prevent this terrible crime of genocide." At the "end of this century," Schwarz-Schilling admonished, "we have not kept this promise." His more confrontational CDU colleague Thomas Kossendey argued that those who opposed sending soldiers to Bosnia were acting in a "profoundly reprehensible way." He took special aim at those on the Left who had frequently attended "so-called peace demonstrations" in recent years wearing "stickers with the garbled [Bertolt] Brecht quote: 'Imagine there is a war and no one goes' . . . I say to you: If no one goes [to Bosnia], the genocide will continue."[47]

That theme resurfaced in the debate on December 6, with members of the governing coalition characteristically accusing those on the left of acting as if their position were somehow morally superior. "What is more moral?" Ulrich Irmer of the FDP wanted to know: "Helping and defending others, or oneself?" Friedbert Pflüger of the CDU similarly contended that denying aid to people "threatened by genocide" had "nothing to do with a higher morality." The tenor of the debates was clearly just as testy as it had been in late June, with especially nasty exchanges on December 6. Wolfgang Schäuble of the CDU sparked one altercation by drawing attention to a recent "counterdemonstration" in late October protesting the fortieth anniversary of the Bundeswehr's founding. What he found especially troublesome was that members of the Greens had participated at the rally, where soldiers were "reviled as murderers." Like the reference to Brecht, this was an allusion to a well-known quote by another famous leftist, journalist and World War I veteran Kurt Tucholsky. The reaction was predictably furious, with Joschka Fischer angrily warning Schäuble that he would "manage to make us reconsider!"—an implicit threat to reverse his own personal support for the government's motion, which had come in the wake of Srebrenica. "Some soldiers are and were murderers," Fischer continued. "But there were also soldiers who liberated the concentration camps: the soldiers of the Red Army in Auschwitz, just the same as the soldiers of the Western Allies in Bergen-Belsen, Dachau, and other places."[48]

The Bundestag accepted the government motion by a vote of 543 to 107. The Greens were evenly divided, 22 voting for and 22 against (5 abstained)—a deceptive outcome since most of the party's rank and file remained opposed to German participation. Fischer acknowledged that his party found itself in a "real conflict over core values"—between a sense of "duty to nonviolence," on the one hand, and, on the other, a feeling of "solidarity" with those suffering in Bosnia—and warned that the issue threatened to "rip apart" his party.[49] His comments portended the internecine battle over Kosovo later that decade, when, as the first Green foreign minister, Fischer would preside over the first German combat mission since 1945.

There was greater clarity in the other parties, with the CDU/CSU, FDP, and PDS voting along strict party lines. "I never met anyone in the PDS," Gregor Gysi later recalled, "who supported the deployment of the German military." By contrast, there was some dissension within

FIG. 10.3. A member of the Green Alternative Youth Movement holds up a poster during a speech by Joschka Fischer (*right*) at the Green Party conference in Bremen in December 1992. It was here that the future foreign minister called for a "genocide clause." The sign reads "Are soldiers still murderers?"—a reference to a famous quote by journalist Kurt Tucholsky. dpa picture alliance / Alamy Stock Photo.

the ranks of the SPD, though to a much lesser degree than among the Greens. Slightly more than one-fifth of the SPD's delegates voted against the motion—a clear reversal from its vote six months earlier on June 30.[50] Rudolf Scharping, head of the party's caucus in the Bundestag, acknowledged that the SPD had "reassessed" the matter. There was now "broad support" in its ranks for permitting the Bundeswehr to provide the sort of military "protection and enforcement" decided on at Dayton.

Anticipating accusations of flip-flopping, he quickly noted that almost all the parties in the Bundestag had "moved away from their previous positions," including the ruling coalition itself. The issue had caused a bitter struggle in the SPD and a shake-up in party leadership two weeks earlier. Still, on one issue most Social Democrats remained firm: they opposed the deployment of Tornado reconnaissance planes for combat missions. A majority of Germans did as well.[51]

As the peace talks were progressing in the fall of 1995, international authorities began to estimate the cost of rebuilding Bosnia. That December, the EU announced it would allocate $1 billion to reconstruction efforts; the Federal Republic would assume about 30 percent of the burden. Such a high amount set off alarm bells in Germany—not surprising, given the high costs of unification and the ongoing reconstruction of former East Germany. "First they destroy everything there, bash their heads in, now even burn down their houses," one constituent complained to Karl-Heinz Hornhues of the CDU, "and now we should pay" to help them rebuild. Hornhues, who had been serving since 1994 as the chair of the Bundestag's Foreign Affairs Committee, said he could understand such sentiments, which had also been expressed a year earlier about Rwanda. He nevertheless insisted that Germans must not forget that "fifty years ago, our country was also . . . in a bad way" and that those who had "liberated" the concentration camps subsequently offered their assistance to Germany.[52]

Helmut Kohl made similar points on more than one occasion. Providing assistance was "an obvious duty" of the German *Volk,* he declared, especially given Germany's own "splendid experience" receiving assistance after World War II. Distancing himself from earlier comments, he told reporters at a press conference in late November that it would not be "wise" to exclude certain groups (that is, Serbs) from assistance. The peace deal instead offered an opportunity to demonstrate to those in Belgrade and elsewhere who had "verbally attacked" the Germans—and the chancellor himself—that they had been mistaken and that the Germans were now "entirely different. The year is 1995, not 1914."[53]

Politicians on all sides of the aisle spoke in moving terms of Germany's obligation to help rebuild the region, reflecting a general sense that it was in everyone's interest—for both pragmatic and historical reasons. But, as Kohl and other officials emphasized again and again, the financial costs of reconstruction could not fall solely on the Federal Republic. Burden sharing needed to be "fairer and better," Minister of the Interior Rudolf Seiters declared, even if all eyes were once again focused on Germany.[54] There was a broad consensus, too, that Germany might also play a different role—one of a nonmonetary nature. It could serve as a model for teaching the warring factions in the Balkans how to put their past behind them and comport themselves more peacefully in the future. As Wolfgang Schäuble put it, right after exchanging a series of extremely sharp barbs in the December 6 debate: "We can help [them] learn to live with one another." Karsten Voigt of the SPD concurred. The refugees living in Germany could play an important role, he believed, by "conveying" to those living in places like Sarajevo and Mostar, Belgrade and Zagreb, the positive experiences they had had over the past three years "here in our democratic society."[55] Germans were clearly proud of the progress their country had made since World War II, and comments like these attested to a healthy dose of political and moral self-confidence—even if they smacked of the nineteenth-century nationalist adage, "The German spirit will heal the world."

The positive role that returning refugees could play aligned with growing demands, especially by members of the governing coalition, that they return home as quickly as possible to help with reconstruction efforts. A rapid return was, Richard Holbrooke later noted, the "one firm instruction" given to the German delegation in Dayton.[56] The Bosnians needed to take a page from Germany's own history, it was believed, and rebuild their country on their own, just as Germans had done a half century earlier. That was a flawed comparison, of course. Not many Jews had returned after 1945, and, for those who did, Germany was—in contrast to Bosnia—no longer a perilous place. As Christian Schwarz-Schilling pointed out, "war criminals and *génocidaires*" were still roaming freely about. Members of the political opposition agreed in principle on repatriation. Indeed, the international community had long insisted on a "right of return" for those driven from their homes, and it would be "immoral," they argued, to accept the results of ethnic cleansing. But even those who believed the Bosnians should return at some point warned against it taking place too hastily. It was also important, cautioned Christa Nickels of the Greens, not to make the refugees have "an even worse conscience than they already do, for very many . . . feel guilty that they have survived"—an empathetic point often made about Holocaust survivors.[57]

The immense costs of their upkeep were another important consideration. In fact, those very costs—especially the ones incurred by ordinary Germans who had sponsored individuals and families out of their own pocket—had led to a noticeable decrease in a "willingness to donate." Government support for humanitarian assistance was also ebbing, at least in relative terms. By the winter of 1995, the United States and Britain had surpassed the Federal Republic in aid to the Balkans. Official assistance nevertheless remained considerable, reaching slightly more than a billion deutsch marks by November 1995, a month before the official signing of the Dayton Accords.[58]

The government would go on to fund a variety of humanitarian projects after the peace plan went into effect. Klaus Kinkel, for example, assumed direct sponsorship of the university clinic in Sarajevo, which received 3.5 million DM to provide medical care. The foreign minister personally visited the Bosnian capital in mid-December to take part in a ceremony celebrating the connection of an electric power cable delivered by the giant engineering conglomerate Siemens, installed by German technicians and paid for by the German government. "Finally, there is hope for peace for the citizens of Sarajevo," the foreign minister exulted, "finally hope for light at the end of the tunnel! Finally, light again in all apartments—beginning today!"[59]

His words stand in sharp contrast to a moving scene Rupert Neudeck would later recall in his memoirs. During a visit to the war-torn capital in the winter of 1994, the renowned humanitarian had sat one evening in a Bosnian friend's apartment, reading—out of necessity by candlelight—a book about the Wehrmacht's occupation of Poland fifty years earlier. Waking to the sound of explosions early the next day, he looked out the window at all the destruction in the street below: "That was precisely how I imagined early mornings in the Warsaw Ghetto."[60]

Memories of Germany's past were indeed always present.

Conclusion

Acting after Auschwitz

At the official signing of the Dayton Peace Accords in Paris on December 14, 1995, Helmut Kohl was in a celebratory mood. He lauded the agreement as a "signal of hope" for millions of people. "Out of solidarity with the afflicted and with our partners," Germany was participating "for the first time to such an extent in an international peacekeeping force." This was, he added, something the "vast majority" of Germans supported. Two weeks earlier, the chancellor had similarly emphasized the solemnity of the moment in front of the Bundestag. The decision to participate in the international mission in former Yugoslavia marked a "caesura in the life of our *Volk*" that will "reach far into the future."[1]

The planned deployment—the largest in the history of the Bundeswehr up till that point—was the topic of a heated debate at a Protestant high school in Berlin just before Christmas. Journalist Bascha Mika of the newspaper *taz* opened the discussion by provocatively asking the students whether they would "gladly grab a weapon and join in." Only one came out strongly against any sort of German participation—"because of our history," Wolf explained (all names are pseudonyms). "I find it problematic, in general, that Germany has its own army and should now fight outside the Federal Republic. German soldiers have already been on the go enough as it is." It would be "more sensible," his classmate

Marko agreed, to provide civilian forms of assistance, like building schools and daycare centers.

The other students would have none of this. Only "pressure" works in such situations, maintained a young woman called Leonie, and even Wolf acknowledged that "we had been glad when the Allies liberated Germany." The others appealed to their country's history as well, but drew different lessons. The deployment was a "signal," Johannes explained, that Germans were "no longer willing to hide behind their history." One could not "forget" the past, he added, but one should not use it as a "cop-out"—especially when it came to stopping genocide, Friederike agreed. "One can't use German history as an excuse in such a situation." Besides, her classmate Katrin added, the Germans were different nowadays. "One thinks, of course, because of our history: My God, a German is picking up a weapon. But Germans in a UN unit aren't fighting to secure our national interests. . . . Germans always have a bad conscience. But I find it problematic that alarm bells go off" whenever anyone hears the word *German*. "Precisely," Eric agreed, it was used as a "curse word." Such notions were "obsolete" fifty years after the war, Leonie concurred. "Our generation has nothing more to do with the Nazis."

Several of the students nevertheless acknowledged a certain degree of hypocrisy on the part of the Federal Republic. "On the one hand," Zerbst pointed out, "it's always said we want peace everywhere in the world, but at the same time we are the second largest weapons supplier." That was true, Mundo agreed, Germans "earned a fortune" through the sale of arms and land mines. Still, he added, the whole world knew that Germany "no longer acted" as it had a half century earlier. Their classmate Eric had the final word: "After the first French atomic test on Mururoa" in the 1960s, "10,000 students took to the streets here in Berlin, only 500 after the second, and after the third, it only got three lines" in the local paper. "It'll be just like that with Bundeswehr deployments. But if we're lucky, maybe it won't happen so fast this time."[2]

Supporters of the controversial decision to participate in the international mission clearly saw this foreign-policy shift in a positive light. But Cassandras at home and abroad feared that a newly aggressive Germany was looming on the horizon and the hoary "German Question" would return with a vengeance.[3] Those concerns were largely unwarranted. Unified Germany remained committed to the same core principles that had guided the Federal Republic's foreign policy since its inception, though there were certainly some changes. Leading public figures called for—and the Federal Republic proved willing to assume—a more robust role on the world stage. Germany remained a reliable partner, on the whole, but it exhibited a noticeable increase in self-confidence and a greater willingness to assert its independence—especially now the Cold War was over, the threat of nuclear annihilation had receded, and unification had finally been achieved. This gave the country greater room to maneuver, which allowed it to be more self-assertive *and* more interventionist. Germany's role in the recognition of Croatia and Slovenia in the winter of 1991, its (unsuccessful) bid to gain a permanent seat on the UN Security Council, and its participation in international military deployments to Cambodia, Bosnia, and other countries were all prominent examples of this. But so, too, was the country's steadfast refusal later on to participate in the Iraq War of 2003 and the implementation of a no-fly zone over Libya in 2011.[4]

Those very refusals gave the lie to exaggerated fears in the early 1990s about slippery slopes, "creeping" remilitarization, and the rebirth of an aggressive, trigger-happy German *Großmacht*. But they also caused great anger and consternation in some Western capitals, putting Germans in the unenviable position of being damned if they did and damned if they didn't. That is to say, a too zealous willingness to use force was just as "suspect" as a desire to stay "aloof." Or, as Helmut Kohl memorably put it during the Gulf War: "First the Germans were accused of not taking off their combat boots and now they are accused of not putting them on."[5]

In short, continuity and change characterized German conduct in the realm of foreign affairs. The clearest shift was a new if unenthusiastic willingness to use military force to resolve violent conflicts and achieve humanitarian goals in foreign lands—though never unilaterally, only after much soul-searching, almost always under pressure from abroad, and without fail as part of an international peacekeeping or humanitarian mission. Since 1991, the Federal Republic has participated in dozens of these and deployed more than 100,000 soldiers abroad—from Southeast Asia to Southeast Europe, from Central Africa to the Middle East. The most important milestone was Germany's participation in March 1999 in the NATO-led Kosovo War, the first time German soldiers had engaged in actual combat since 1945. Germany's postwar era "ended" that month, one historian has claimed with dramatic flair. One thing is certain. Military missions beyond NATO territory would have been well-nigh "unthinkable" before the fall of the Berlin Wall. Increasingly bold, piecemeal deployments set "new precedents" and became gradually more acceptable. But because of old mindsets, they remained "far from routine."[6]

It was ironic but not altogether surprising that Joschka Fischer was serving as foreign minister when the first bombs fell in the early spring of 1999. After all, the former leftist radical and star of the traditionally pacifist Greens had already made it clear earlier that decade—when stories about Serb "concentration camps" in Bosnia first broke, then much more forcefully following the Srebrenica massacre—that he believed Germany and the world had a "moral obligation" to put a stop to genocide, even if it meant using force. His evocation of Auschwitz and the Holocaust to characterize Serb treatment of the Kosovo Albanians and justify armed intervention was nothing new. For Fischer, "Never again Auschwitz" trumped "Never again war"—a position that revived the internal debates of the early 1990s and this time nearly did tear his party apart.[7]

But if German leaders like Fischer considered a military response the appropriate answer to every major international challenge, as some critics charged, it was clearly one of Berlin's best-kept secrets. In fact, their reticence remained palpable, and whether and when interventions were justified—politically, strategically, or morally—continued to be a source of vigorous public debate. Humanitarian and emotional arguments played a major role in these heated discussions, but more pragmatic issues did as well: political and economic costs and benefits, military risks and feasibility, constitutional limitations, and, last but not least, public opinion. In 2015, more than two-thirds of all Germans still believed their country should "limit its military role in world affairs" because of its history, and this was true across party lines.[8] Restraint remained written in the DNA of German officials and the public.

Kosovo was in a league of its own, but the Rubicon had already been crossed earlier in the decade. The Cambodian mission of 1991–1993 marked the first major deployment of the Bundeswehr since the end of World War II, the largest German military contingent ever sent on a UN peacekeeping mission, and the Bundeswehr's largest out-of-area assignment up to that point. The deployment to Bosnia had marked an even greater break, involving active participation in noncombat military measures, a *novum* solemnly and sometimes angrily acknowledged by all leading politicians.[9] In a clear case of poetic justice, both missions involved countries that had recently experienced the scourge of genocide. But did that have any influence on the decision to participate or to come out in favor of German participation?

Petra Kelly of the Greens argued on the eve of unification that Germany needed to act to prevent the Khmer Rouge from returning to power, and she did so, in part, by drawing parallels between their atrocities and those of the Nazis. But there is no evidence that the Cambodian genocide was a direct motivation for the 1991 mission. No one in favor of sending the Bundeswehr to Southeast Asia openly invoked Germany's earlier crimes or described it as a way of "making amends" for past transgressions. That would have been too platitudinous perhaps, too facile, too trivial. Nazi atrocities were nevertheless on the minds of many, especially when it came to how the Federal Republic was viewed abroad—and that included, as we have seen, the soldiers who had volunteered for the Cambodian mission. Even when trying to do something beneficial for others, Germans were always painfully aware of their country's dark history.

The past weighed much more heavily in the fierce debates about appropriate responses to the carnage in neighboring Bosnia, and the question of genocide played a much greater role there as well—at least for a handful of prominent politicians across the political spectrum: Joschka Fischer of the Greens, Freimut Duve of the Social Democrats, Christian Schwarz-Schilling and Stefan Schwarz of the conservative Christian Democrats. High-level government officials like Chancellor Kohl and Foreign Minister Kinkel invoked the term early on—earlier than most other world leaders, in fact—but the genocide of the Jews was not a direct motivation for their decision to commit armed forces. In fact, the absence of any military response to the contemporaneous atrocities in Rwanda made it clear that the "crime of crimes" did not trigger any sort of automatic intervention or support for intervention.[10]

There were several reasons for the different responses. For one, remorse about the failure to act in Central Africa was a "shaming experience" that may have figured, consciously or not, in the decision to commit to Bosnia a year and a half later. More important, the Balkans were much closer geographically and culturally than Rwanda. Germany's historic ties to the Balkans were also different—and more fraught, at least in popular memory. Few Germans recalled that Rwanda had once been part of a German colony, and the general silence on that score was both remarkable and revealing. Germany's contentious role in the recognition of Croatia and Slovenia in 1991 played a part, too, if only out of a sense of responsibility for what later transpired in Bosnia.

The sizable Yugoslav diaspora in the Federal Republic, as well as economic and leisure ties to the Balkans, also explain the more muted reaction to the slaughter in Rwanda, where the speed of the killing made a rapid response extremely difficult. In short, Bosnia had "all the advantages Rwanda lacked," including a sense of outrage that "such horrors could occur again *in Europe*."[11] But there was an even stronger motivation for ending the conflict as soon as possible: the social and economic stress caused by the storm of refugees. In any event, the end of the Cold War made some form of intervention possible, simply by allowing for international actions and alliances that would have been unimaginable just a few years earlier. That was why the idea of intervening in Cambodia had not entered anyone's mind in the late 1970s, apart from that of a handful of idealists like US senator George McGovern. Cambodia was anyway "very far away," SPD politician Egon Bahr later explained, and "our possibilities to do anything were very slim."[12]

Is there some general statement to be made about the specific role genocide played in shaping German reactions to atrocities in foreign lands? Whether the massacres in Cambodia, Bosnia, and Rwanda actually constituted the "crime of crimes" never attracted much debate. The term was used freely in all three cases, also by top German officials in the early 1990s. There was some discussion among politicians and in the media about its applicability, especially in the case of Bosnia—but even greater discussion about the (in)appropriateness of drawing parallels to the Holocaust. In the end, the question of *why* such atrocities were taking place preoccupied Germans much more than the issue of *whether* they constituted genocide.

There was also very little discussion about the UN Genocide Convention and its significance for the Federal Republic. Only three public figures explicitly invoked the Convention: Joschka Fischer, Freimut Duve, and Tilman Zülch, founder of the Society for Threatened Peoples and a vigorous proponent of humanitarian intervention. The Convention is "near and dear to my heart," Zülch declared in late 1992 at the Bundestag hearing about mass rape in Bosnia. "We accepted this Convention at one point because of the crimes committed during the Third Reich, but we have never made use of it anywhere."[13] That was only half-true. During the accession debates of the early 1950s, there was little discussion of any connection between Nazi crimes and Raphael Lemkin's brainchild. The focus was almost solely on the potential benefits that might accrue one day to Germany. The obligations were a non-issue and would remain so for the next four decades—prompting German journalist Henryk M. Broder, the son of two Holocaust survivors, to dismissively remark, "We are world champions" of looking on and doing nothing about foreign massacres.[14]

The silences on that score might explain why German leaders invoked the term with such alacrity in the early 1990s, which demonstrated just how little awareness (or concern) there was for the "legal implications of its usage."[15] At the very least, they must have suspected it would have no real-world consequences when no major power was acting to prevent, much less stop, genocide. In fact, the international community's dilatory behavior was precisely what made it possible for the Federal Republic to remain on the sidelines as well. Had that not been the case, Kohl, Klaus Kinkel, and others would likely have thought twice about using the term. But the slow international response had another effect. It allowed the government to commit to humanitarian missions piecemeal, while slowly habituating Germans to their country's new international role.

Other possibilities appeared on the horizon as the old constellations and antagonisms of the Cold War receded. These included the first international efforts since the Nuremberg and Tokyo trials of the late 1940s to hold individuals accountable for their actions. In fact, the Federal Republic played a prominent role in bringing about the first indictment at the ICTY.[16] In February 1994, German police arrested Duško Tadić, a Bosnian Serb who had been living since the fall of 1993 in his brother's apartment in Munich. Like Nazi war criminals whom Holocaust survivors later recognized walking free on the streets, Tadić was spotted in the Bavarian capital city that October. Word spread among members of the exile community, and the sighting came to the attention of Monika Gras, a young journalist already familiar with Tadić and his heinous reputation for violence. He played a prominent role in a television documentary she had made in early 1993 about atrocities against Muslims in Kozarac, the village where he had lived before fleeing to Germany. Working together with Andree Kaiser, the photojournalist whose images had played such an important role in breaking the story about Serb "concentration camps," Gras rented an apartment across the street from where Tadić was living and "staked him out. . . . When he emerged, [Kaiser] got his photo; and the police got their culprit."

The arrest and its aftermath marked a number of firsts: the first time a suspect was arrested outside Yugoslavia for participating in "ethnic cleansing," and the first time that Germany exercised "universal jurisdiction" to file charges of genocide. (This legal principle permits states to claim jurisdiction regardless of where a crime supposedly took place or the alleged perpetrator's nationality.) This was a "step of uncharacteristic boldness on Germany's part," the New York Times reported. "With their Nazi past, Germans normally strive for the lowest possible profile in the moral realm. . . . Most Germans would rather forget the past, and even those on the left fear that Balkan war crimes trials could open the country to accusations that it is 'relativizing' its own incomparable guilt." In the end, Tadić did not go on trial in Germany—but for a different reason. Hoping to capitalize on what promised to be a high-profile case, prosecutors at The Hague requested that the Federal Republic surrender Tadić to their custody, which, after some legal wrangling, finally took place in April 1995. The ICTY's subsequent indictment did not include the charge of genocide, and the deputy prosecutor later commented that his team was "amazed that Germany had no specific evidence on that charge."

The two international criminal tribunals responsible for investigating the war crimes committed in former Yugoslavia and Rwanda—the first postwar trials to include the crime of genocide in their remit—would nevertheless go on to convict dozens of individuals for that crime (or for the lesser charge of "aiding and abetting" genocide). Just as important, the tribunals gave rise to new juridical concepts like the "responsibility to protect" and the doctrine of humanitarian intervention.[17] These developments confronted Germans with difficult choices that threw into disarray the old postwar consensus on foreign policy and the use of force. But none of this—not even calling genocide by its name—was a guarantee of concrete action, as Germany's federal president remarked during a major speech in early 2015. What value did the mantra "Never again" have, Joachim Gauck demanded to know, when genocides continued to occur in places like Cambodia and Bosnia, Rwanda and Darfur? Instead, Berlin, Paris, and Washington became more willing to acknowledge *some* past genocides for what they were: from that of the Herero and Nama in the former German colony of Southwest Africa, the "first German genocide" of the twentieth century, to that of the Armenians during World War I.[18]

The passive reaction to other genocides since Srebrenica—in Darfur, for example, or against the Rohingya in Myanmar—only confirmed the impression that the UN Genocide Convention was and remains a paper tiger. For Germany this was not a matter of inconsistency per se but rather an assessment of feasibility *and* of what was in the interest of Germany and other countries. The Federal Republic's seemingly erratic foreign policy nevertheless gave rise to accusations of unpredictability, and it perplexed political theorists who believe that states always act in terms of "rational" self-interest aimed at maximizing power and self-preservation. As we have seen, however, more "cognitive" factors also play a role: values and beliefs, culture, morals, and emotions—all of which are heavily shaped by historical experience and perceived lessons of the past. This was especially true for postwar Germany, where an especially intense "culture of remembrance" about the Third Reich had been cultivated in its western half since the 1960s, and about the Holocaust since the late 1970s. Foreign policy choices throw a country's values into "sharp relief," and decisions that may have seemed inconsistent or "irrational" were indeed made in accordance with a sense of Germany's own interests—*and* its history.[19]

That history loomed large, and its presence made itself felt in many ways, not least in the evocative imagery and jarring language used to describe foreign genocides and other atrocities. Stark references to gas, ovens, and burning human flesh, the use of terms like *concentration camp* and *extermination,* contained unmistakable echoes of the Third Reich and the Final Solution that resonated with German audiences. The parallels and "cross-referencing" were sometimes straightforward, more often suggestive or implicit.[20] They became more direct and more explicit over the course of the 1980s, as the public's preoccupation with the genocide of the Jews intensified. But to what end? Such appeals and allusions allowed officials and politicians, human rights activists and concerned citizens, journalists, pundits, and public intellectuals alike to convey their shock and horror in the most effective and damning way available to them: by associating ghastly developments abroad with what was by now commonly considered to have been *the* worst crime in the history of humanity. Motivations varied. Some hoped to appeal to emotion and a sense of guilt to compel the government and fellow citizens to act. For others, it was a form of *Vergangenheitsbewältigung* by proxy, a way to "come to terms" with their country's dark history in a roundabout manner, through the prism of other genocides.

Political motives were sometimes at play as well. Genocide could serve as a moral and political cudgel useful for scoring points against political adversaries. It gave conservatives—and self-critical leftists like Petra Kelly—a chance to "stick it" to the Left rhetorically at home. This was especially true in the case of Cambodia, where a self-styled leftist regime had committed unspeakable atrocities that provided a clear "example of communist criminality" at the very height of the Cold War.[21] The silence and skepticism about these atrocities—committed by revolutionaries whom the Left had vocally supported during the antiwar protests of the preceding decade—came back to haunt German progressives, and conservatives used this to their advantage. That may explain why two respected German historians known for their leftist sympathies indignantly claimed years later that "nobody" had known "anything" about what was happening in Cambodia at the time.[22] Whatever purpose such amnesia may have served after the fact, their protests were eerily reminiscent of postwar claims that "no one" had known about Nazi atrocities in the East.

Using the Third Reich in an instrumental way for political gain was a questionable pursuit, but it was certainly better than suppressing the past—which, in turn, was far preferable to *repeating* the past. Still, its inflationary invocation did run the risk of relativizing or somehow "trivializing" the Holocaust. The common use of superlatives to describe foreign atrocities as "unprecedented," as the "worst" ever committed— including, by implication, ones committed during the Third Reich— seemed to veer in that direction, wittingly or not. There were certainly concerns in Germany, especially on the Left, that frivolous comparisons to the genocide of the Jews and the use of loaded terms like *concentration camp* were reckless and dangerous—not unlike in the United States, where fierce debates arose about the use of that charged term to describe holding facilities for migrants on its southern border.[23] Discussions about semantics and the use of words freighted by their association with National Socialism highlight just how attuned Germans were to the importance of language and metaphor. But this was not an issue that pitted progressives against conservatives. For one, many on the Right also found such analogies troublesome. Just as important, even those who could not be accused of "downplaying" the Holocaust or German complicity drew such parallels—again, to express outrage or as a spur to action. One should be wary of taking "discursive analysis" too far. Analogies and associations with Nazism were often "just" rhetorical devices. But words and images influence perceptions, even if in ways difficult to measure precisely. In the end, *how* Germans talked about foreign genocides is important because it helps us understand *why* they responded as they did.

With few exceptions, then, there was no exculpatory undercurrent, at least on a conscious level. Still, in an ungenerous reading, such language connoted a certain degree of willful forgetfulness about the Third Reich—or, to be more precise, about the exact extent of Nazi crimes. But similar locutions in places like France, Britain, the United States, and elsewhere caution us not to read too much into such turns of phrase, even if the use of such language by Germans had a different quality.[24] For better or worse, it had even less significance in East Germany, where the response to the Cambodian genocide did not focus primarily on the genocide of the Jews. Instead, Khmer Rouge atrocities forced "true believers" to grapple with a different issue: how self-styled communists could have committed such heinous crimes against humanity. For all the differences in memory work in the two postwar German states, clear allusions to the

Final Solution by East German officials, journalists, and cultural figures in the context of the Cambodian genocide nevertheless revealed the extent to which the Holocaust had indeed become a theme there by the early 1980s. It was not by chance that, in the spring of 1990, the very first act of the GDR's first freely elected People's Chamber was a statement explicitly acknowledging German responsibility for Nazi crimes against the Jews.

Did revelations of "unimaginable" brutality in foreign lands—did looking at the Holocaust through the prism of other genocides—recast German perceptions of the Final Solution in some way? Khmer Rouge crimes certainly played a part in the historians' controversy of the mid-1980s, the spirited—and increasingly mean-spirited—debate that focused on questions about the Holocaust's origins and supposed singularity. But did the incontrovertible evidence about the magnitude of the Cambodian genocide and the realization that other peoples were also capable of such horrendous deeds place German crimes in a different light—just when the Final Solution had come to be considered the measure of all evil? A careful reading of Ernst Nolte's initial interventions does not offer much evidence for claims about relativization. But provocative claims by him and other conservatives—like historian and journalist Joachim Fest, whose contribution to the exchange was accompanied by a photograph of the skulls of Khmer Rouge victims, intended to drive home the point that genocide was a "widespread occurrence"—were certainly part and parcel of a defiant backlash fueled by growing resentment that the Holocaust was receiving "too much" attention.[25]

A series of similar controversies in the mid-1990s about the history, memory, and commemoration of the Third Reich offer compelling clues that the genocides in Bosnia and Rwanda may have had similar reverberations. The year 1995 was especially eventful—a "political memory marathon."[26] Germany's decision to participate in international military measures in Bosnia took place right on the heels of the fiftieth anniversary of the end of World War II. And it was precisely at this juncture that major controversies about the Nazi past erupted once again. The first surrounded a controversial exhibit that opened in Hamburg in the spring of 1995, dedicated to documenting atrocities committed by the Wehrmacht during World War II. A year later, just months after the Bundeswehr deployed to the Balkans, a German translation of *Hitler's*

Willing Executioners, Daniel J. Goldhagen's controversial study about the causes of the Holocaust, grabbed headlines in Germany and became the focus of another, equally passionate debate and media spectacle. All of this coincided with the beginning of a third controversy about plans for erecting a mammoth monument in the heart of the German capital dedicated to preserving the memory of the Final Solution.[27]

These debates made clear just how much popular interest and scholarly controversy the Third Reich and the Final Solution continued to attract after unification, despite competition from the many sordid stories about the infamous Stasi in the former German Democratic Republic. One can only speculate about the effects the Bosnian and Rwandan genocides may have had on German memory, but there are strong hints. Exposure through the media to Serb, Tutsi, and Khmer Rouge *génocidaires* "in the flesh" may account for the spike in interest since the 1990s in the motivation and agency of *German* perpetrators, who suddenly seemed more "ordinary."[28] One thinks, in this connection, of Hans Mommsen's emotional interjection during the Goldhagen debate, that members of the mobile killing units responsible for the mass murder of Eastern European Jews did not "know what they were doing" during their orgies of violence because they were in such a "frenzy," or *Rausch,* a term popularized two years earlier to describe the killing spree in Rwanda.

If there was a connection, it was likely subtle and subconscious. But not always. Take, for example, the nasty controversy surrounding the 1995 Wehrmacht exhibition—which, by coincidence, prominently featured German crimes in the Balkans during World War II. The contemporary conflict in Yugoslavia was "repeatedly addressed" at the large number of events organized in response to the exhibit, one of its organizers later pointed out. And, one of his colleagues added, there were many "attempts to extract an appropriate lesson from it," either in support of or against the deployment of the Bundeswehr to Bosnia and later Kosovo.[29]

But the revelations about Bosnia and Rwanda and the debates about appropriate responses might have had another effect. They seem to have set the stage for a pushback against Germany's "obsession" with the genocide of the Jews, against a "surfeit of memory"—or at least certain *types* of memory. That went hand in hand with a renewed focus in the

1990s on *German* suffering and perceived victimhood. Cases in point included novelist Martin Walser's controversial comments about the use of the Holocaust as a "moral bludgeon"; renewed efforts to build monuments and museums dedicated to the hardships suffered by German expellees in the 1940s; the sudden focus on mass rape by the Red Army at the close of World War II, long a taboo subject. Growing attention to and condemnation of the aerial bombing of German cities during World War II represented another symptom, especially given heated debates about the appropriateness of bombing Serb targets in Bosnia and later Kosovo. The most prominent examples were historian Jörg Friedrich's graphic descriptions of that aerial "holocaust"—his language—in a book that grabbed headlines in Germany and abroad; novelist W. G. Sebald's ruminations in a series of lectures about the supposed repression of that national trauma in postwar German literature; and Günter Grass's *Crabwalk,* a novel about "repressed" memories inspired by the sinking of the *Wilhelm Gustloff*—the ship that humanitarian Rupert Neudeck and his family had almost boarded during their flight from the East.[30] It is important to emphasize that these were not "conservatives"—far from it, in fact. Walser, Friedrich, Sebald, and Grass all had impeccable "progressive" credentials and had frequently addressed Nazi crimes against humanity in their writing and public statements.

How they and other Germans confronted the genocide of the Jews underwent a qualitative change starting in the late 1970s that involved increased use of the Final Solution for political purposes, including in foreign policy debates. This was especially true following unification, when Germany's violent past was used to draw vastly dissimilar conclusions and justify much different positions about armed intervention. The question of what those lessons were was an even greater source of vexed debate when it came to foreign genocide. Discussion quickly moved beyond the theoretical in response to the atrocities in the Balkans, where unified Germany faced its first and most significant foreign-policy challenge since unification: whether to participate in military efforts intended to stop genocide and other human rights abuses on foreign soil. Progressives and conservatives, advocates and opponents of "humanitarian interventions" alike, all invoked the Holocaust to different ends. Those who believed that German history obliged their country to exercise the utmost restraint met with an equally compelling argument, namely, that it was immoral for Germans *not* to act after Auschwitz. Those positions cut across political lines, transcending traditional Left / Right divisions and often making for curious bedfellows. No one took the matters lightly, the issues at stake were not black and white, and a great deal of personal ambivalence remained—all of which explains the consistently elevated quality of public debate, both in terms of content and emotional register.

At stake was nothing less than the Federal Republic's "proper" place in the international arena, and the Third Reich continued to serve as a challenge, a warning, and an exhortation—a *Mahnung*, the Germans would say—to act appropriately on the world stage. The years between 1995 and 1998 marked a "decisive turning point in the history of memory politics," one German-born historian has argued, and once military missions abroad became "almost routine" after Bosnia, memories of World War II no longer provided "useful moral and rhetorical ammunition" in his native country. That supposition is a stretch, as Joschka Fischer's renewed invocation of the Holocaust during the Kosovo crisis made clear. But what *is* true is that the burden of history no longer allowed for clear-cut choices or determined policy "in one direction or the other."[31] It is a paradox, but the "burden of history" sometimes outweighed the burden of history.

Wherever one came down on these issues, the difficult challenge of navigating the burdens and demands of a painful past remained a constant, which was why the country's history—during the Cold War and especially during the Third Reich—permeated public discussion. This was true to a much greater extent in the case of Bosnia than it had been during debates about Cambodia a decade earlier—no doubt a legacy of the spike in public and scholarly discussion about the Holocaust in the 1980s. German history was now on everybody's mind, and a solemn sense of responsibility toward that history was an encumbrance policymakers and pundits across the political spectrum took seriously.

In the end, the use of military force remained the exception, nonlethal responses—strong verbal condemnation of perpetrators and lofty demands for justice—the rule. Talk may be cheap, but not for the Federal Republic, where "checkbook diplomacy" remained the most important arrow in its foreign-policy quiver. Such largesse went far beyond official aid, however. Stories of foreign genocides and their aftermath prompted outpourings of private donations, as well as an array of grassroots humanitarian activities by ordinary citizens and celebrities, politicians and political parties, human rights groups and religious charities, media organizations and individual journalists. There was little ordinary Germans *could* do, apart from supporting and engaging in such endeavors.

Individual Germans were motivated by a mixture of personal and political reasons. Some by a sense of moral duty or an ethical obligation to act—as Christians, say, or as inhabitants of a country that had benefited from foreign aid after World War II and was now one of the wealthiest in the world. Others, by a commitment to "human rights," a buzzword that became popular just as news of the Cambodian genocide broke in the 1970s. Political considerations were also important, both at home and abroad. Humanitarian assistance, coupled with insistent demands that more be done to help those suffering elsewhere, offered Germans a chance to occupy the moral high ground against domestic political foes. At the same time, it accrued to the Federal Republic in the form of political capital, burnishing the image and increasing the credibility and "likability" of Germany and Germans abroad. Last but not least, it mitigated pangs of guilt for failing to prevent or stop genocide.

Remorse and a desire to make amends in some way for Nazi transgressions were also factors. Some explicitly acknowledged this sense of responsibility as an impetus for donating money, hosting refugees, or even traveling to troubled regions to help in person. This was *Vergangenheitsbewältigung* in practice *and* by proxy. But an equal if not more important historical stimulus was also at play, namely, the hardships Germans themselves had endured. Mass displacement, mass rape, and mass destruction in the 1940s were all within living memory, and an intimate familiarity with such suffering motivated Germans like Rupert Neudeck, Tilman Zülch, Herbert Czaja, and others to assist those damaged and displaced by mass atrocities. It is difficult to "measure" motivation with any precision, but the grief, pain, and trauma Germans had earlier inflicted on others—*and* experienced themselves—were clearly crucial influences.[32] And it was precisely here that the role of the media was so significant in a "mediated" society like the Federal Republic, where the dividing line between news reports and editorials was often porous.

More than anything else, though, the daily deluge of grisly and graphic news reports—especially in the cases of Bosnia and Rwanda, which dominated the nightly news for months on end in the first half of the

1990s—influenced perceptions and fundamentally shaped official and popular responses to foreign genocides by making inaction seem "downright immoral and heartless." It would be difficult to overstate the powerful effect of the pervasive allusions to Germans' own past crimes—and past suffering. Visual memories and the "shock of recognition" prompted by those spectacular images inspired empathy, emotional indignation, and an array of humanitarian activities by ordinary Germans who wanted their government to do more.[33] Often overshadowing pragmatic political considerations, the many grim reports from afar influenced the public statements and even the policy agendas of leading politicians—not least to burnish Germany's reputation in light of past crimes and recent xenophobic outrages following unification. It was not by chance that Joschka Fischer began his letter of July 1995 calling for a military response to Srebrenica with a quote penned two days earlier by journalist Michael Thumann in *Die Zeit:* "The Bosnian war is above all a struggle of armed criminals against an unarmed civilian population. The Serb occupation of Srebrenica featured once again the usual methods: selection and expulsion, the rounding up of men fit for military service, like cattle, and, if the testimony is true, their subsequent slaying."[34] There was no escaping the Third Reich, especially when it could skillfully be put to use as a political tool.

The Federal Republic has been hailed the "world champion" of memory, the "consummate country of contrition," a nod to its indefatigable efforts over the past half century to confront the darkest side of its history. Germans may indeed "lead the world in agonized self-examination," and their fixation on the mistakes of the past is indeed in a league of its own.[35] Some might say that that is as it should be, given the enormity of Nazi crimes. But, without collapsing distinctions, what country does not have good reason to confront the less sanguine aspects of its history?

The German experience offers other peoples and places with complicated pasts a "master class" in coming to terms with the more sinister facets of their own history. This is certainly true for the United States, where Americans continue to struggle with the difficult legacy of racism. Justified or not, fears during the Trump presidency that the United States might embark on the same path Germany did in the 1930s also make the postwar German case noteworthy.[36] The willingness of even conservative Germans to countenance their country's difficult past and draw lessons from it distinguishes them from many of their counterparts in the United States, who seem disinclined to confront, much less take responsibility for past transgressions. The contrast is nevertheless reassuring, because it reminds us that such efforts need not be politically exclusive or one-sided. Nor should remorse.

Germany is frequently praised for the way in which it has dealt with its past—a positive example of "memory work" from which others might profit. Anyone who has spent time there in recent years or encountered young Germans abroad will appreciate the soundness of such positive portrayals.[37] But they have also experienced pushback, with some claiming that the focus on the plight of the Jews has inured Germans to the suffering of other groups. And, the argument continues, in their effort to make amends for the Holocaust, German elites have unequivocally embraced Israel, supposedly to the detriment of other historically oppressed groups, like the Palestinians. Some have even suggested that the preoccupation with Nazi atrocities against the Jews has made Germans insensitive to issues of race and endemic, everyday racism in today's Germany.[38] If true, that would be the paradoxical downside of Germany's vaunted *Vergangenheitsbewältigung*.

How Germans spoke and wrote about the genocides in Cambodia, Bosnia, and Rwanda reinforce such arguments. After all, they frequently resorted to hoary cultural stereotypes and condescending, offensive, racist images about the cunning "Asian" smile, "backward" if "well spoken" Africans living "in the jungle," and "wild and cruel" Serbs. Even the East Germans cast racially tinged aspersions on the Khmer Rouge and the Chinese. The lack of inhibition with which such phrases flowed from the lips and pens of some politicians and journalists underscores how the open, honest, and otherwise admirable reckoning with the Holocaust may have unwittingly desensitized Germans. The conviction that they had left the rabid racism of their forebears far behind them may have paradoxically allowed for the unabashed expression of *different* forms of racism.[39]

It is easy to find signs of continuity and racism in the two postwar German states. The disturbing wave of xenophobic violence that came in the wake of unification in the early 1990s was the most prominent example. And there are more recent ones. The old debates and controversies about immigration that coincided with the refugee crises in Cambodia, Bosnia, and Rwanda have returned with a vengeance in recent years, as Germany faces new challenges stemming once again from a massive influx of foreign refugees: fears that Germany cannot absorb so many foreigners, for economic and cultural reasons, anger about alleged abuses of the country's generous social welfare policies, arguments that migration is not in the "best interests" of the refugees themselves. All these issues lay and continue to lie at the root of calls to curb immigration. They even led to the birth of a new xenophobic movement, Pegida (Patriotic Europeans against the Islamification of the Occident), and a highly successful far-right political party, Alternative for Germany.

All eyes are once again on Germany, but not just because of fears that fascism might once again rear its ugly head there. There is another side to the coin. Chancellor Angela Merkel calmly assured her compatriots in 2015 that they would "manage this," they would master the influx of refugees: one million in that year alone, from places like Afghanistan and Syria. In response to those who harshly criticized her, Merkel reminded her fellow citizens of their "humanitarian responsibility" and the basic principles on which their country had been founded—and since flourished. These included the "fundamental right" of asylum for politically persecuted individuals, as well as respect for the "human dignity of every person." That moral largesse *also* drew global attention to Germany.[40] But neither it nor the political backlash it caused should have been a surprise—at least not to those familiar with the story of what Germans have talked about *and done* in response to genocide and mass suffering in foreign lands.

The marked increase in xenophobia and resentment toward refugees makes the broad willingness to take in so many from the Balkans even more remarkable—even if the acceptance of Bosniaks as *Westernized* Muslims was in itself a subtle form of discrimination. It draws attention to two contradictory impulses in Germany since the 1970s: a rampant fear of overburdening the state and "over-foreignization" (*Überfremdung*), on the one hand, and, on the other, a widespread desire—even a compulsion, for some—to help the less fortunate. The genocides in Cambodia, Bosnia, and Rwanda brought those impulses to the fore. Whatever the shortcomings of German *Vergangenheitsbewältigung*, the many concrete actions Germans have taken to make amends in some way for past crimes powerfully bear out the undeniably beneficial character of German memory work. It is nevertheless more ambivalent than some suggest. That makes the German experience doubly important, because it draws our attention to something else, namely, pitfalls to avoid when confronting national skeletons in the closet. After decades of deafening silence about the Holocaust, the pendulum swung in the opposite direction in the Federal Republic. That was clearly a desirable development, but the almost obsessive public preoccupation since the late 1970s with the most horrific aspects of Germany's past also had a downside. It periodically produced disturbingly truculent backlashes.

A "hypertrophic virtue" can devolve into a harmful, debilitating, "hypertrophic vice," Charles Maier warned shortly after German unification, when a fixation on memory becomes "inauthentic and unhealthy." So what might a "healthy" and "successful" *Vergangenheitsbewältigung* look like? "Telling the history as thoroughly as possible without shirking," historian Hope Harrison has suggested, "demonstrating contrition" through some form of "restitution toward victims and their families, commemorative ceremonies, and memorials," explaining "why it is still relevant, and making sure young people are taught about it," and, last but not least, "drawing lessons from it"—also as a guide to concrete behavior in the future. Most of us would agree on the soundness of these principles, even if the supposed lessons to be gleaned from atrocities like the Holocaust are not as clear as one might suspect.[41]

Germans have abided by these precepts for decades, in fact, which is why their experience offers such valuable lessons for places like the United States, Britain, France, Italy, Japan, and elsewhere—not just as a model worth emulating but also as one that can be improved upon. The backlash against "too much memory" is in large part a defiant response to style and approach, to excessive moralizing and finger-pointing, to the instrumental use of memory to score political points and attack one's foes across the aisle. Finding a balance between "too little" and "too much" memory, striking a decorous tone that does not give rise to nasty recriminations and indignant rejoinders, learning from the Germans what to avoid doing—that is perhaps the most important lesson their admirable efforts to "come to terms" with the past can offer.

Epilogue

Three days after Russian bombs began falling on Ukraine in late February 2022, German chancellor Olaf Scholz dropped a proverbial bomb of his own. At a special session of the Bundestag on February 27, Angela Merkel's successor announced that the world was experiencing a *Zeitenwende*—a watershed moment, a historical turning point, an epochal shift. Scholz did not mince words. The "inhuman" Russian invasion was a "war of aggression . . . an opprobrious breach of international law . . . a disgrace!" This called for a decisive response, he said, which was why he was announcing a series of spectacular decisions. His government would set up a "special fund" involving a onetime investment of 100 billion euros to make the Bundeswehr "ultramodern" and provide it with "bold, new capabilities." Germany would also fulfill one of NATO's long-standing goals by annually investing at least 2 percent of its GDP in defense—a point American officials had been especially adamant about. That was "a great deal of money," Scholz conceded, but it was important to protect "our freedom and democracy."[1]

The chancellor, a member of the Social Democratic Party, also announced that the Federal Republic would send heavy weapons to Ukraine. Foreign Minister Annalena Baerbock of the Greens came out in full support of that decision, which, she averred, did not break any "taboos" or cross any "red lines." Not everyone agreed. In fact, the decision to send heavy weapons to Ukraine triggered a fierce debate in

Germany—precisely three decades after the start of hostilities in Bosnia. In a series of opinion pieces and open letters, dozens of prominent individuals, including renowned philosopher Jürgen Habermas and Alice Schwarzer, founder of the preeminent feminist journal *Emma,* came out strongly against sending weapons. That would only prolong the war, they said, and lead to more death and destruction—the same arguments used by those who had supported the UN weapons embargo on the Balkans thirty years earlier. It would drag Germany into the conflict as a participant, with "unforeseen consequences." A "political solution" was the appropriate response, they believed—even in the wake of allegations that Russian soldiers had already committed genocide in places like Bucha. In response to those who denounced such arguments as a "policy of fear," Habermas framed the debate as a generational divide. Those who had lived through the Cold War, he believed, had a different "mentality" and had taken another lesson from that conflict: a profound fear of World War III.[2]

The consensus at home and abroad was that Scholz's "radical" initiative represented a "foreign policy revolution," that the government had "discarded decades of foreign policy tradition." It was a "180-degree turn," maintained the Green foreign minister, who was even more gung ho about sending weapons to Ukraine than the chancellor. "Today Germany leaves behind its special, solitary restraint in foreign and security policy. . . . When our world is a different one, then our policies must also be different." Joschka Fischer could not have put it any better, but the Greens' founding generation, which had called for the dissolution of NATO in the 1980s, must have been shocked when the foreign minister added that NATO was the "guarantee for our security and freedom." Baerbock, born in 1980, belonged to a different generation— to "Generation '89," in the words of young SPD parliamentarian Nils Schmid. Vladimir Putin's war was especially "bitter" for his age cohort, Schmid explained. It marked the "end of hope for an entire generation not shaped by '68 and the rearmament debate" of the early 1980s.[3]

The government's response to Ukraine was not as groundbreaking as most believed. It was the logical outcome of developments that had begun in the 1990s in response to violence and genocide in the Balkans and elsewhere. The debate about "appropriate" responses to the Russian invasion rehashed familiar arguments from that period, not least concerning the appropriateness of supplying arms to war-torn regions.

Still, there were important differences. For one, there were few accusations or warnings this time about slippery slopes to militarization or a secret German desire to become a "great power." There were indeed allusions to the Nazis and World War II, to antisemitism and the Holocaust, to dreams of achieving *Großmacht* status once again. But these were now directed at Putin, whom German leaders branded a "war criminal" committing "barbarous" acts. At the same time, they vigorously condemned his "cynical" justification of the invasion, namely, that Russian soldiers were "denazifying" Ukraine and liberating it from Volodymyr Zelenskyy, a "drug addict" and "Nazi." This was especially "perfidious," Friedrich Merz of the Christian Democrats indignantly pointed out, given that the Ukrainian president came from a Jewish family. There were still Nazis, the message seemed to be, but they were not in Kyiv or Berlin but rather Moscow.[4]

During the three-and-a-half-hour special session of the Bundestag on February 27, only one politician spoke directly to the "heavy mortgage" of German history: Vice Chancellor Robert Habeck of the Greens. "Ukraine, Russia, Poland, Belarus: we hardly know which country we should apologize to first because of the German massacres, wars of aggression, and rampaging in these countries." That sense of guilt or remorse—along with German dependence on Russian oil, no doubt—explained why so many Germans were wary of criticizing Russia and the Russian people as a whole, and why they were quick to distinguish between the country's president and those who opposed him—the "other Russia," as they put it, a formulation reminiscent of an earlier distinction drawn between Hitler and the "other Germany."[5]

Alternative for Germany, the right-wing populist party founded in 2013, walked a fine line between condemning the invasion and expressing understanding for Russian motivation. The West had "antagonized" Moscow and committed a "historical failure" by extending NATO eastward and "denying" Russia's "status as a great power." More to the point, one of its parliamentarians asked, did the government really want to "send soldiers to war again against Russia?" At the same time, the party happily jumped on the rearmament bandwagon. One member called for

Germany's "largest armament offensive since World War II," and members of the CDU spoke in similar terms. The Federal Republic must "finally be ready" to "assert" its global interests, Merz maintained. "More armaments, more military technology," and more respect for German soldiers were all necessary, his conservative colleagues agreed. And because "nuclear deterrence" was effective, "we Germans need it, too."[6]

In the end, the absence of any real discussion about the weight of Germany's history was more of a rupture than the decision to send heavy weapons to Ukraine. There were, to be sure, brief allusions to the Third Reich reminiscent of earlier ones in the debates about Bosnia. One of the open letters to Chancellor Scholz obliquely referred to "our historical responsibility," and in a direct rejoinder, dozens of public intellectuals and cultural figures from across the political spectrum called the German response to the Russian invasion a "touchstone" for how "seriously" Germans embraced the sentiment of "'Never again.' German history demands every effort to prevent new wars of expulsion and annihilation—all the more in a country where the Wehrmacht and SS once rampaged with utmost brutality."[7]

Yet, in a bizarre twist, Nazi crimes now served as an admonition for others, for *Russia*. The "blood toll" paid by the USSR during World War II, one SPD official admonished, "compels us" to say to Putin, "Never again war!"[8] Those who embraced that sentiment tended to be those most critical of Scholz's decision to send weapons to Ukraine—not for moral reasons or because of Germany's fraught history, but for practical ones: fear of finding themselves in another world war that would end this time in nuclear annihilation. Scholz and the majority of Germans nevertheless tended toward the alternative, "Never again Auschwitz." And they did so in the broadest sense of that phrase. When mass atrocities were being committed somewhere in the world—especially so close to home— Germans could not look on silently, whatever the weight of the past.

The paucity of allusions to the Third Reich and the Holocaust as guides to *German* behavior—their mention merely an afterthought in open letters to the chancellor—was striking. Had Germany finally become a "normal" nation once again? Perhaps. But sending arms to Ukraine roiled Germany like no other place in the West, and that in itself showed just how much the country's conflicted past continued to count.

ABBREVIATIONS

NOTES

ARCHIVAL SOURCES AND INTERVIEWS

ACKNOWLEDGMENTS

INDEX

ABBREVIATIONS

AA	Auswärtiges Amt
ACDP	Archiv für Christlich-Demokratische Politik
AdL	Archiv des Liberalismus
AdsD	Archiv der sozialen Demokratie
AGG	Archiv Grünes Gedächtnis
APuZ	*Aus Politik und Zeitgeschichte*
BArch	Bundesarchiv
BPA	Presse- und Informationsamt der Bundesregierung
CEH	*Central European History*
DAS	*Deutsches Allgemeines Sonntagsblatt*
DB	Deutscher Bundestag
DB-P / SB	Deutscher Bundestag, Plenarprotokoll, Stenographischer Bericht
DLF	Deutschlandfunk
DOMiD	Dokumentationszentrum und Museum über die Migration in Deutschland
dpa	Deutsche Presse-Agentur
DRA	Deutsches Rundfunkarchiv
FAZ	*Frankfurter Allgemeine Zeitung*
fdk	*Freie Demokratische Korrespondenz*
FR	*Frankfurter Rundschau*
GA	*General-Anzeiger*

HR	Hessischer Rundfunk
MfAA	Ministerium für Auswärtige Angelegenheiten
ND	*Neues Deutschland*
NDR	Norddeutscher Rundfunk
NYT	*New York Times*
PA	Politisches Archiv
PdDB	Parlamentsarchiv des Deutschen Bundestags
PK	*Pressekonferenz*
PM	*Pressemitteilung*
PV	*Parteivorstand*
RM	*Rheinischer Merkur*
SWR	Südwestrundfunk
SZ	*Süddeutsche Zeitung*
taz	*Die Tageszeitung*
UZ	*Unsere Zeit*
VfZ	*Vierteljahrshefte für Zeitgeschichte*
VR	*Volksrepublik*
WDR	Westdeutscher Rundfunk

NOTES

PROLOGUE

1. AGG, Bestand Ludger Volmer 23, "Erklärung zum Fall von Srebrenica" (Christian Schwarz-Schilling, Freimut Duve, Marieluise Beck, Hildebrecht Braun), 7/14/95; "'Unvorstellbare Barbarei,'" *taz,* 11/17/95.

2. Joschka Fischer, "Die Katastrophe in Bosnien," *Blätter für deutsche und internationale Politik* 40, no. 9 (1995): 1141–1452. Also see Joschka Fischer, *Die rot-grünen Jahre: Deutsche Außenpolitik—vom Kosovo bis zum 11. September* (Cologne: Kiepenheuer & Witsch, 2007), 211–220.

3. See Margit V. Wunsch Gaarmann, *The War in Our Backyard: The Bosnia and Kosovo Wars through the Lens of the German Print Media* (Berlin: Neofelis, 2015), 151–155; Paul Hockenos, *Joschka Fischer and the Making of the Berlin Republic: An Alternative History of Postwar Germany* (Oxford: Oxford University Press, 2008), 243–249.

4. See David Rohde, *Endgame: The Betrayal and Fall of Srebrenica, Europe's Worst Massacre since World War II* (New York: Penguin, 2012); Matthias Fink, *Srebrenica: Chronologie eines Völkermords oder Was geschah mit Mirnes Osmanovic* (Hamburg: Hamburger Edition, 2015).

5. For "tactical reasons," Fischer later claimed, he did not specify whether he thought German troops should also participate in such interventions. See AGG, Landtagsfraktion 219, Joschka Fischer, "Auf der Flucht vor der Wirklichkeit?" 11/27/95; Fischer, *Die rot-grünen Jahre,* 219.

6. They also took a gratuitous swipe at the United States, which had "only come into existence" thanks to the "genocide of the North American Indians." See AGG, Bestand Frieder Otto Wolf 206, "Wohin führt die Forderung nach einer militärischen Interventionspflicht gegen Völkermord?" (Kerstin Müller, Claudia Roth, Jürgen Trittin, Ludger Volmer), 10/31/95.

7. Fischer, "Auf der Flucht?"

8. See the motions in AGG, Bestand Kristin Heyne 147; Bestand Frieder Otto Wolf 206, 209.

9. Ignatz Bubis et al., "Sind Militäreinsätze bei Völkermord gerechtfertigt?" *taz,* 12 / 1 / 95; Sibylle Tönnies, "Viel Pazifismus bleibt nicht übrig," *taz,* 12 / 5 / 95; "Wer weiß die richtige Antwort?" *taz,* 11 / 11 / 95; "Antifaschistische Harke," *taz,* 12 / 7 / 95. For reactions by the Green rank and file, see AGG, Bestand Kristin Heyne 147.

10. Quotes from Jürgen Gottschlich, "Die Grünen trauen," *taz,* 12 / 4 / 95; Hans Monath, "Papiersieger ohne Beute," *taz,* 12 / 4 / 95. Also see Fischer, *Die rot-grünen Jahre,* 213, 219.

11. On the political evolution of this former "street-fighting militant," see Paul Berman, *Power and the Idealists* (Brooklyn, NY: Soft Skull, 2005), 3–96 (quote on 29). Also see Hans-Peter Kriemann, *Hineingerutscht? Deutschland und der Kosovo-Krieg* (Göttingen: Vandenhoeck & Ruprecht, 2021).

INTRODUCTION

1. This may explain why the international focus has been on punishment after the fact, not intervention. See Karen E. Smith, *Genocide and the Europeans* (Cambridge: Cambridge University Press, 2010), 107. Also see Samuel Totten and Henry Theriault, *The United Nations Genocide Convention: An Introduction* (Toronto: University of Toronto Press, 2020); William A. Schabas, *Genocide in International Law: The Crime of Crimes,* 2nd ed. (Cambridge: Cambridge University Press, 2009), 400–592.

2. PA AA, B80 Bd. 202, Lie to Adenauer, 12 / 20 / 50; Vermerk (Kaufmann), 3 / 2 / 51.

3. Hermann Mosler, "Erich Kaufmann zum Gedächtnis," *Zeitschrift für ausländisches öffentliches Recht und Völkerrecht* 32 (1972): 235–238; PA AA, B80 Bd. 202, "Weltdiskussion um die deutschen Kriegsgefangenen," *Bulletin,* 11 / 22 / 53.

4. "Gegen 'Genocide,'" *Abendpost und Milwaukee Deutsche Zeitung,* 6 / 19 / 51; PA AA, B80 Bd. 202, Vermerk (Sauer), 9 / 29 / 51; Roemer to AA, 1 / 22 / 52. Also see Norbert Frei, *Adenauer's Germany and the Nazi Past,* trans. Joel Golb (New York: Columbia University Press, 2002).

5. See the documents in PA AA, B80 Bd. 202; William H. Landsberg, "Gruppenmord als internationales Verbrechen," *Außenpolitik* 4, no. 5 (1953): 310–321.

6. See the correspondence and newspaper clippings in PA AA, B80 Bd. 202.

7. See the correspondence in PA AA, B80 Bd. 202. On Lemkin's activities during this period, see Raphael Lemkin, *Totally Unofficial: The Autobiography of Raphael Lemkin,* ed. Donna-Lee Frieze (New Haven, CT: Yale University Press, 2013), 180–222; Douglas Irvin-Erickson, *Raphaël Lemkin and the Concept of Genocide* (Philadelphia: University of Pennsylvania Press, 2017), 197–229; John Cooper, *Raphael Lemkin and the Struggle for the Genocide Convention* (Houndmills: Palgrave Macmillan, 2008), 173–229, 260–271.

8. See the draft in PA AA, B80 Bd. 202. Emphasis added.

9. The other speakers also referred to German suffering, as well as to the "many premeditated mass exterminations" of the "last decades." See DB-P / SB, 10. Sitz., 2. Wahlperiode (1 / 21 / 54), 291–293.

10. PA AA, B80 Bd. 221, Protokoll, 5 / 3 / 54.

11. See Georg Stötzel, "Der Nazi-Komplex," in *Kontroverse Begriffe: Geschichte des öffentlichen Sprachgebrauchs in der Bundesrepublik Deutschland,* ed. Georg Stötzel and Martin Wengeler (Berlin: Walter de Gruyter, 1995), 356–359; Cornelia Schmitz-Berning, *Vokabular des Nationalsozialismus* (Berlin: Walter de Gruyter, 1998).

12. DB-P / SB, 37. Sitz., 2. Wahlperiode (7 / 8 / 54), 1764–1767; Christoph Moss, *Jakob Altmaier: Ein jüdischer Sozialdemokrat in Deutschland (1889–1963)* (Cologne: Böhlau, 2002).

13. PA AA, B80 Bd. 221; Hans E. Riesser, *Von Versailles zur UNO: Aus den Erinnerungen eines Diplomaten* (Bonn: Bouvier, 1962). For the full text of the law, see Bundesgesetzblatt, Teil II, Nr. 15 (8 / 12 / 54): 729–734.

14. PA AA, MfAA LS-A270, Protokoll, 12/6/54; Vorlage Nr. 658, 11/26/54; Jeffrey Herf, *Undeclared Wars with Israel: East Germany and the West German Far Left, 1967–1989* (Cambridge: Cambridge University Press, 2016), 432–434.

15. See Franz-Josef Meiers, *Zu neuen Ufern? Die deutsche Sicherheits- und Verteidigungspolitik in einer Welt des Wandels, 1990–2000* (Munich: Schöningh, 2006), esp. 262–315.

16. For arguments against the "privileging" of genocide as the so-called crime of crimes, see A. Dirk Moses, *The Problems of Genocide: Permanent Security and the Language of Transgression* (Cambridge: Cambridge University Press, 2021).

17. Bernd Faulenbach, "Die doppelte 'Vergangenheitsbewältigung,'" in *Die geteilte Vergangenheit: Zum Umgang mit Nationalsozialismus und Widerstand in beiden deutschen Staaten*, ed. Jürgen Danyel (Berlin: Akademie, 1995), 112.

18. Ian Buruma, *The Wages of Guilt: Memories of War in Germany and Japan* (New York: Farrar, Straus and Giroux, 1994), 203.

19. See Andrew I. Port, "Democracy and Dictatorship in the Cold War: The Two Germanies, 1949–1961," in *The Oxford Handbook of Modern German History*, ed. Helmut W. Smith (Oxford: Oxford University Press, 2011), 615.

20. Wulf Kansteiner, *In Pursuit of German Memory: History, Television, and Politics after Auschwitz* (Athens: Ohio University Press, 2006), 313; Robert G. Moeller, *War Stories: The Search for a Usable Past in the Federal Republic of Germany* (Berkeley: University of California Press, 2001), 174.

21. Overviews include Detlef Siegfried, *1968: Protest, Revolte, Gegenkultur* (Ditzingen: Reclam, 2018); Christina von Hodenberg, *Das andere Achtundsechzig: Gesellschaftsgeschichte einer Revolte* (Munich: C. H. Beck, 2018).

22. Jeffrey K. Olick, *The Sins of the Fathers: Germany, Memory, Method* (Chicago: University of Chicago Press, 2016), 99, 139, 145, 150, 208, 237–238, 311. On the trope of German victimhood, see Moeller, *War Stories*.

23. Konrad H. Jarausch, "Critical Memory and Civil Society: The Impact of the 1960s on German Debates about the Past," in *Coping with the Past: West German Debates on Nazism and Generational Conflict, 1955–1975*, ed. Philipp Gassert and Alan E. Steinweis (New York: Berghahn, 2006), 20–24.

24. Hans Kundnani, *Utopia or Auschwitz: Germany's 1968 Generation and the Holocaust* (New York: Columbia University Press, 2009), 15–18, 31, 121; Paul Berman, *Power and the Idealists* (Brooklyn, NY: Soft Skull, 2005), 40; Berthold Molden, "Vietnam, the New Left and the Holocaust: How the Cold War Changed Discourse on Genocide," in *Memory in a Global Age: Discourses, Practices and Trajectories*, ed. Aleida Assman and Sebastian Conrad (Houndmills: Palgrave Macmillan, 2010), 79–96.

25. Kundnani, *Utopia*, 11, 31; Molden, "Vietnam," 81, 92. Also see Alan S. Rosenbaum, ed., *Is the Holocaust Unique? Perspectives on Comparative Genocide* (Boulder, CO: Westview Press, 2009).

26. Olick, *Sins of the Fathers*, 99, 279, 291, 304–305. Also see Christian Wicke, *Helmut Kohl's Quest for Normality: His Representation of the German Nation and Himself* (New York: Berghahn, 2015), esp. 170–206; Kristina Meyer, *Die SPD und die NS-Vergangenheit, 1945–1990* (Göttingen: Wallstein, 2015), esp. 353–431.

27. For a different take that misleadingly valorizes East German treatment of the Holocaust, see Susan Neiman, *Learning from the Germans: Race and the Memory of Evil* (New York: Farrar, Straus and Giroux, 2019), 81–132.

28. Detlef Siegfried, "Zwischen Aufarbeitung und Schlußstrich," in *Dynamische Zeiten: Die 60er Jahre in den beiden deutschen Gesellschaften*, ed. Axel Schildt, Detlef Siegfried, and Karl Christian Lammers (Hamburg: Hans Christians, 2000), 77–113.

29. Christoph Classen, "Zum öffentlichen Umgang mit der NS-Vergangenheit in der DDR," in Schildt, Siegfried, and Lammers, *Dynamische Zeiten*, 189, 193; Katrin Hammerstein, *Gemeinsame Vergangenheit—getrennte Erinnerung? Der Nationalsozialismus in Gedächtnis-diskursen und Identitätskonstruktionen von Bundesrepublik Deutschland, DDR und Österreich* (Göttingen: Wallstein, 2018), 90, 151–152; Jürgen Danyel, "Die Opfer- und Ver-folgtenperspektive als Gründungskonsens? Zum Umgang mit der Widerstandstradition und der Schuldfrage in der DDR," in Danyel, *Vergangenheit*, 34.

30. Bill Niven, "Remembering Nazi Anti-Semitism in the GDR," in *Memorialisation in Germany since 1945*, ed. Niven and Chloe Paver (Houndmills: Palgrave Macmillan, 2010), 206, 211; Classen, "Zum öffentlichen Umgang," 173. Also see Andrew Beattie, "East Germany's Handling of the Holocaust," *H-Net Reviews* (May 2009), https://www.h-net.org/reviews /showpdf.php?id=24456.

31. Danyel, "Opfer- und Verfolgtenperspektive," 36; Classen, "Zum öffentlichen Umgang," 189–190.

32. Mary Fulbrook, "Die DDR und der Nationalsozialismus: Historische Erfahrung und kollektives Gedächtnis," in *Erfahrung, Erinnerung, Geschichtsschreibung* (Göttingen: Wall-stein, 2016), 28.

33. In turn, growing awareness of Nazi atrocities against the Jews may have emboldened East German dissidents in the 1980s and thus contributed to the collapse of the GDR re-gime. See Siegfried, "Zwischen Aufarbeitung und Schlußstrich," 112. On alleged links be-tween memory work and the strengthening of democratic values in postwar Germany, also see Jenny Wüstenberg, *Civil Society and Memory in Postwar Germany* (Cambridge: Cam-bridge University Press, 2017).

34. Charles S. Maier, "A Surfeit of Memory? Reflections on History, Melancholy and Denial," *History & Memory* 5, no. 2 (1993): 136.

35. There is a vast literature on the theoretical aspects of collective memory. Good places to start include Aleida Assmann, *Shadows of Trauma: Memory and the Politics of Postwar Identity*, trans. Sarah Clift (New York: Fordham University Press, 2016), 9–93; Jeffrey K. Olick, Vered Vinitzky-Seroussi, and Daniel Levy, eds., *The Collective Memory Reader* (Oxford: Oxford University Press, 2011); Jay Winter, "The Generation of Memory: Reflec-tions on the 'Memory Boom' in Contemporary Historical Studies," *GHI Bulletin* 27 (Fall 2000): 69–92.

36. Jeffrey Herf poses a useful counterquestion: "Why did German politicians after 1945 raise the issue of the Holocaust and other crimes of the Nazi era at all?" See Jeffrey Herf, *Divided Memory: The Nazi Past in the Two Germanys* (Cambridge, MA: Harvard Univer-sity Press, 1997), 2.

37. On the psychological effects of "coming to terms" with the past, see Alexander and Margarete Mitscherlich, *Die Unfähigkeit zu trauern: Grundlagen kollektiven Verhaltens* (Munich: Piper, 1967).

38. Buruma, *Wages of Guilt*, 27.

39. See Herf, *Undeclared Wars*; Anetta Kahane, "The Effects of a Taboo: Jews and Anti-semitism in the GDR," in *After Auschwitz: The Difficult Legacies of the GDR*, ed. Enrico Heitzer et al. (New York: Berghahn, 2021), 32–40; Amadeu Antonio Stiftung, ed., *"Das hat's bei uns nicht gegeben!" Antisemitismus in der DDR* (Berlin: Amadeu Antonio Stiftung, 2010).

40. See the declaration in Peter Reichel, *Vergangenheitsbewältigung in Deutschland: Die Auseinandersetzung mit der NS-Diktatur von 1945 bis heute* (Munich: C. H. Beck, 2001), 15–16. On xenophobia in the GDR, see Quinn Slobodian, ed., *Comrades of Color: East Ger-*

many and the Cold War World (New York: Berghahn, 2015); Jan C. Behrends, Thomas Lindenberger, and Patrice G. Poutrus, eds., *Fremd und Fremd-Sein in der DDR: Zu historischen Ursachen der Fremdenfeindlichkeit in Ostdeutschland* (Berlin: Metropol, 2003).

41. Presidential candidate Bill Clinton, speaking about Bosnia in 1992. See Peter Novick, *The Holocaust in American Life* (New York: Houghton Mifflin, 1999), 252. Also see David W. Blight, *Race and Reunion: The Civil War in American Memory* (Cambridge, MA: Belknap Press of Harvard University Press, 2001); David E. Stannard, *American Holocaust: The Conquest of the New World* (Oxford: Oxford University Press, 1992); Neiman, *Learning from the Germans.*

42. On the Japanese, see Buruma, *Wages of Guilt;* Thomas U. Berger, *War Guilt and World Politics after World War II* (New York: Cambridge University Press, 2012), 123–229. More generally, see Alfons Kenkmann and Hasko Zimmer, eds., *Nach Kriegen und Diktatur: Umgang mit Vergangenheit als internationales Problem—Bilanz und Perspektive für das 21. Jahrhundert* (Essen: Klartext, 2005); Katrin Hammerstein et al., *Aufarbeitung der Diktatur—Diktat der Aufarbeitung? Normierungsprozesse beim Umgang mit diktatorischer Vergangenheit* (Göttingen: Wallstein, 2009).

43. This traditional approach is taken in Olick, *Sins of the Fathers.* For a different approach that focuses on how "memory activists" working at the grass roots "transformed memorial culture" in Germany, see Wüstenberg, *Civil Society.*

44. See Hoffmann's foreword to Henry Rousso, *The Vichy Syndrome: History and Memory in France since 1944,* trans. Arthur Goldhammer (Cambridge, MA: Harvard University Press, 1991), vii, x.

45. For literary responses to Bosnia, for example, see Steffen Hendel, *Den Krieg erzählen: Positionen und Poetiken der Darstellung des Jugoslawienkrieges in der deutschen Literatur* (Osnabrück: V&R unipress, 2018), 91–191; Paul Michael Lützeler, *Bürgerkrieg Global: Menschenrechtsethos und deutschsprachiger Gegenwartsroman* (Munich: Wilhelm Fink, 2009), 69–145.

46. See Thomas Risse-Kappen, "Public Opinion, Domestic Structures and Foreign Policy in Liberal Democracies," *World Politics* 43, no. 4 (1991): 479–512; Daniel Hucker, *Public Opinion and Twentieth-Century Diplomacy: A Global Perspective* (London: Bloomsbury, 2020).

47. Richard Cobb, *Modern French History in Britain* (London: Oxford University Press, 1974), 14. Emphasis in original.

48. Quotes from Jay Winter, *War beyond Words: Languages of Remembrance from the Great War to the Present* (Cambridge: Cambridge University Press, 2017), 2; Margit V. Wunsch Gaarmann, *The War in Our Backyard: The Bosnia and Kosovo Wars through the Lens of the German Print Media* (Berlin: Neofelis, 2015), 75–79.

49. Quotes from Eric Langenbacher, "Still the Unmasterable Past? The Impact of History and Memory in the Federal Republic of Germany," *German Politics* 19, no. 1 (2010): 24; Thomas Berger, "The Power of Memory and Memories of Power: The Cultural Parameters of German Foreign Policy-Making since 1945," in *Memory and Power in Post-War Europe: Studies in the Presence of the Past,* ed. Jan-Werner Müller (Cambridge: Cambridge University Press, 2002), 89; Andrei S. Markovits and Simon Reich, *The German Predicament: Memory and Power in the New Europe* (Ithaca, NY: Cornell University Press, 1997), 9. Also see Birgit Schwelling, "Die Außenpolitik der Bundesrepublik und die deutsche Vergangenheit," in *Handbuch zur deutschen Außenpolitik,* ed. Siegmar Schmidt, Gunther Hellmann, and Reinhard Wolf (Wiesbaden: VS Verlag für Sozialwissenschaften, 2007), 101–111.

50. On the foreign policy of the GDR, see, e.g., Hermann Wentker, *Außenpolitik in engen Grenzen: Die DDR im internationalen System, 1949–1989* (Munich: Oldenbourg, 2007).

51. Markovits and Reich, *German Predicament*, 2; Rainer Baumann and Gunther Hellmann, "Germany and the Use of Military Force: 'Total War,' the 'Culture of Restraint' and the Quest for Normality," *German Politics* 10, no. 1 (2001): 61.

52. Quoted in Ulrich Krotz, *History and Foreign Policy in France and Germany* (Houndmills: Palgrave Macmillan, 2015), 131. More generally, see Hanns W. Maull, "Zivilmacht Bundesrepublik Deutschland: Vierzehn Thesen für eine neue deutsche Außenpolitik," *Europa Archiv* 43, no. 10 (1992): 269–278.

53. Markovits and Reich, *German Predicament*, 3, 8–13; Samantha Power, *"A Problem from Hell": America and the Age of Genocide* (New York: Perennial, 2003), 260.

54. See William Glenn Gray, "Germans from Venus? The Out-of-Area Problems in U.S.-German Relations," in *Safeguarding German-American Relations in the New Century*, ed. Hermann Kurthen et al. (Lanham, MD: Lexington, 2006), 67.

55. Power, *"Problem from Hell."* For a similar indictment of UN inaction, see Adam LeBor, *"Complicity with Evil": The United Nations in the Age of Modern Genocide* (New Haven, CT: Yale University Press, 2006). For a different approach, see Keith Pomakoy, *Helping Humanity: American Policy and Genocide Rescue* (Lanham, MD: Lexington, 2011); Stephen Wertheim, "A Solution from Hell: The United States and the Rise of Humanitarian Interventionism, 1991–2003," *Journal of Genocide Research* 12, no. 3–4 (2010): 149–172. Also see Peter Ronayne, *Never Again? The United States and the Prevention and Punishment of Genocide since the Holocaust* (Lanham, MD: Rowman & Littlefield, 2001).

56. See Ulf von Krause, *Die Bundeswehr als Instrument deutscher Außenpolitik* (Wiesbaden: Springer VS, 2013), 161; Baumann and Hellmann, "Use of Military Force," 68.

57. Overviews include Ben Kiernan, *Blood and Soil: A World History of Genocide and Extermination from Sparta to Darfur* (New Haven, CT: Yale University Press, 2007); Adam Jones, *Genocide: A Comprehensive Introduction*, 3rd ed. (New York: Routledge, 2017); Donald Bloxham and A. Dirk Moses, eds., *The Oxford Handbook of Genocide Studies* (Oxford: Oxford University Press, 2010); Eric D. Weitz, *A Century of Genocide: Utopias of Race and Nation* (Princeton, NJ: Princeton University Press, 2003); Philip Spencer, *Genocide since 1945* (London: Routledge, 2012); Boris Barth, *Genozid: Völkermord im 20. Jahrhundert—Geschichte, Theorien, Kontroversen* (Munich: C. H. Beck, 2006). On West German responses to other instances of mass murder, see Lasse Heerten, *The Biafran War and Postcolonial Humanitarianism: Spectacles of Suffering* (Cambridge: Cambridge University Press, 2017), 175–204, 218–235; Florian Hannig, "West German Sympathy for Biafra, 1967–1970: Actors, Perceptions, Motives," in *Postcolonial Conflict and the Question of Genocide: The Nigerian-Biafra War, 1967–1970*, ed. A. Dirk Moses and Laase Heerten (New York: Routledge, 2018), 217–238; A. Dirk Moses, "West Germans and the East Pakistan Secessionist War, 1971," paper presented at German Studies Association, Washington, DC, Sept. 2015.

58. See Samuel Moyn, *The Last Utopia: Human Rights in History* (Cambridge, MA: Belknap Press of Harvard University Press, 2010); Michael Cotey Morgan, "The Seventies and the Rebirth of Human Rights," in *The Shock of the Global: The 1970s in Perspective*, ed. Niall Ferguson (Cambridge, MA: Belknap Press of Harvard University Press, 2010), 237–250; Mark Philip Bradley, "The Origins of the 1970s Global Human Rights Imagination," in *The "Long 1970s": Human Rights, East-West Détente and Transnational Relations*, ed. Poul Villaume, Rasmus Mariager, and Helle Porsdam (London: Routledge, 2016), 15–32.

59. See Lora Wildenthal, *The Language of Human Rights in West Germany* (Philadelphia: University of Pennsylvania Press, 2013); Young-sun Hong, *Cold War Germany, the Third*

World, and the Global Humanitarian Regime (Cambridge: Cambridge University Press, 2015); Ned Richardson-Little, *The Human Rights Dictatorship: Socialism, Global Solidarity, and Revolution in East Germany* (Cambridge: Cambridge University Press, 2020). Also see Frank Bösch, Caroline Moine, and Stefanie Senger, *Internationale Solidarität: Globales Engagement in der Bundesrepublik und der DDR* (Göttingen: Wallstein, 2018).

60. Wildenthal, *Language of Human Rights*, 11, 173. Wildenthal refers to West Germans, but a similar case can be made for East Germans. See, e.g., Hong, *Cold War Germany*, 153; Slobodian, *Comrades of Color*. Also see Philipp Rock, *Macht, Märkte und Moral: Zur Rolle der Menschenrechte in der Außenpolitik der Bundesrepublik Deutschland in den sechziger und siebziger Jahren* (Frankfurt am Main: Peter Lang, 2009); Lily Gardner Feldman, "The Role of Non-State Actors in Germany's Foreign Policy of Reconciliation: Catalysts, Complements, Conduits, or Competitors?" in *Non-State Actors in International Relations: The Case of Germany*, ed. Anne-Marie Le Gloannec (Manchester: Manchester University Press), 15–45.

61. See Quinn Slobodian, *Foreign Front: Third World Politics in Sixties West Germany* (Durham, NC: Duke University Press, 2012).

62. Quote from Peter Gatrell, *The Unsettling of Europe: How Migration Reshaped a Continent* (New York: Basic, 2019), 10. More generally, see Ulrich Herbert, *Geschichte der Ausländerpolitik in Deutschland: Saisonarbeiter, Zwangsarbeiter, Gastarbeiter, Flüchtlinge* (Munich: C. H. Beck, 2008); Matthias Frese and Julia Paulus, eds., *Willkommenskulturen? Re-Aktionen auf Flucht und Vertreibung in der Aufnahmegesellscahft der Bundesrepublik* (Paderborn: Schöningh, 2020).

63. Gaarmann, *War*, 17–20; Yehuda Bauer, *Rethinking the Holocaust* (New Haven, CT: Yale University Press, 2001), xi.

64. See Hans Kundnani, "The Concept of 'Normality' in German Foreign Policy since Unification," *German Politics and Society* 102, no. 2 (2012): 38–58; Baumann and Hellmann, "Germany and the Use of Military Force," 61–82; Peter Katzenstein, ed., *Tamed Power: Germany in Europe* (Ithaca, NY: Cornell University Press, 1997); Dirk Verheyen, *The German Question: A Cultural, Historical, and Geopolitical Exploration,* 2nd ed. (Boulder, CO: Westview Press, 1999); Marcus Hawel, *Die normalisierte Nation: Vergangenheitsbewältigung und Außenpolitik in Deutschland* (Hannover: Offizin, 2007).

65. Smith, *Genocide*, 105; Jean H. Quataert, *Advocating Dignity: Human Rights Mobilizations in Global Politics* (Philadelphia: University of Pennsylvania Press, 2009), xi, 14. On the power and use of images, see Heide Fehrenbach and Davide Rodogno, eds., *Humanitarian Photography: A History* (Cambridge: Cambridge University Press, 2015); Peter Burke, *Eyewitnessing: The Uses of Images as Historical Evidence* (Ithaca, NY: Cornell University Press, 2001); Jennifer Evans, Paul Betts, and Stefan-Ludwig Hoffmann, eds., *The Ethics of Seeing: Photography and Twentieth-Century German History* (New York: Berghahn, 2018). Also see Matthew Hilton et al., "History and Humanitarianism: A Conversation," *Past & Present* 241, no. 1 (2018): e1–e38.

66. For a critical exploration of these issues, see Johannes Paulmann, "The Dilemmas of Humanitarian Aid: Historical Perspectives," in *Dilemmas of Humanitarian Aid in the Twentieth Century,* ed. Johannes Paulmann (Oxford: Oxford University Press, 2016), 1–31; Michael Barnett, *Empire of Humanity: A History of Humanitarianism* (Ithaca, NY: Cornell University Press, 2011); David Rieff, *A Bed for the Night: Humanitarianism in Crisis* (New York: Simon & Schuster, 2002); Bertrand Taithe and John Borton, "History, Memory and 'Lessons Learnt' for Humanitarian Practitioners," *European Review of History* 23, no. 1–2 (2016): 210–224. Specifically for Germany, see Florian Hannig, *Am Anfang war Biafra: Humanitäre Hilfe in den USA und der Bundesrepublik Deutschland* (Frankfurt am Main:

Campus, 2021); Nina Berman, *Impossible Missions? German Economic, Military, and Humanitarian Efforts in Africa* (Lincoln: University of Nebraska Press, 2004).

67. Classic statements include Konrad H. Jarausch, *After Hitler: Recivilizing Germans, 1945–1995*, trans. Brandon Hunziker (Oxford: Oxford University Press, 2006); Heinrich August Winkler, *Germany: The Long Road West*, vol. 2: *1933–1990*, trans. Alexander J. Sager (Oxford: Oxford University Press, 2007). For a critical rejoinder, see Frank Biess and Astrid M. Eckert, "Why Do We Need New Narratives for the History of the Federal Republic?" *CEH* 52, no. 1 (2019): 4–10.

1. POL POT IS LIKE HITLER

1. Stephan Weichert and Leif Kramp, *Die Vorkämpfer: Wie Journalisten über die Welt im Ausnahmezustand berichten* (Cologne: Halem, 2011), 235. For images from the footage, see *Cambodia 1975–2005, Journey through the Night: A Photo Exhibition of the Friedrich-Ebert-Stiftung* (Bonn: Friedrich-Ebert-Stiftung, 2006), 15, 21.

2. "1,4 Millionen 'Befreite' verloren Obdach und Habe," *Welt*, 5/9/75; "Traurige Heimkehr," *FAZ*, 9/10/75; "Mitarbeiter Sihanouks setzen sich nach Paris ab," *SZ*, 10/14/75.

3. "Blut getauscht," *Spiegel*, 5/12/75.

4. Archiv des WDR Hörfunks 6126244107, "Mittagsmagazin," 5/9/75.

5. "Zeitspiegel," *Zeit*, 5/15/75.

6. PA AA, MfAA G-A368, Bericht, 5/20/75; MfAA C6696, Dossier (April 1975).

7. "'Was wir machen, gab es noch nie,'" *Spiegel*, May 9, 1977; Ewa Tabeau and They Kheam, "Demographic Expert Report: Khmer Rouge Victims in Cambodia, April 1975–January 1979," 19, 41–50, www.eccc.gov.kh/sites/default/files/documents/courtdoc/E3_2413_EN .PDF. Also see Ben Kiernan, "The Cambodian Genocide: 1975–1979," in *Century of Genocide*, ed. Samuel Totten, William S. Parsons, and Israel W. Charny, 2nd ed. (New York: Routledge, 2004), 339–374. German-language overviews of Cambodian history include Daniel Bultmann, *Kambodscha unter den Khmer Rouge* (Paderborn: Schöning, 2017), 23–69; Bernd Stöver, *Geschichte Kambodschas: Von Angkor bis zur Gegenwart* (Munich: C. H. Beck, 2015).

8. David Hirschmann, "'Angka befiehlt es, mehr mußt du nicht wissen,'" *Stuttgarter Nachrichten*, 8/19/75. The *Washington Post* wrote as early as May 1975 of "genocide by natural selection." See Samantha Power, *"A Problem from Hell": America and the Age of Genocide* (New York: Perennial, 2003), 106.

9. See "Sihanouk," *FAZ*, 4/6/76; "Kommunisten in Pnom [*sic*] Penh rotten das Bürgertum aus," *Berliner Morgenpost*, 4/9/76; Günter Graffenberger, "Politik der Härte regiert Indochina," *Stuttgarter Zeitung*, 7/14/76; Carlos Widmann, "Ein Steinzeit-Sozialismus der Khmer Rouge," *SZ*, 4/20/76. There was a marked increase in West German media coverage, as well as coverage in France, Britain, and the United States, around the one-year anniversary. See Jamie Frederic Metzl, *Western Responses to Human Rights Abuses in Cambodia, 1975–80* (Basingstoke: Macmillan, 1996), 49–59.

10. See "Drei kleine Köche," *Spiegel*, 4/12/76; Gabriele Venzky, "Trauriges Kambodscha," *Zeit*, 4/23/76.

11. See "Ein Flüchtling berichtet über Kannibalismus in Kambodscha," *Welt*, 4/21/76; "Massaker in Kambodscha," *Welt*, 4/22/76; "Wie die Hühner abgeschlachtet," *Vorwärts*, 4/6/76. One West German television report later featured an interview with a Cambodian teacher who described in graphic detail similar acts of cannibalism. See NDR Fernseharchiv Hamburg, 1035548/6, "Weltspiegel: Erste Hilfe für die Verhungernden/Flüchtlingsstrom," 11/18/79.

12. "Fabrik der neuen Menschen," *Stuttgarter Zeitung*, 10 / 17 / 75.

13. Widmann, "Steinzeit-Sozialismus"; Hans Ulrich Luther, "Für ein paar Dollars erzählen sie alles," *FR*, 5 / 6 / 77; "Drei kleine Köche" (*Spiegel*).

14. Lutz Krusche, "Der Arzt von Pnom [*sic*] Penh über seine Greuel-Erzählungen," *FR*, 5 / 13 / 75; "Von Massaker-Märchen ist kein Wort wahr," *Unsere Zeit*, 5 / 13 / 75.

15. "Kambodschas Kommunisten brauchen den Prinzen," *SZ*, 8 / 22 / 75; "Kambodscha— ein Jahr danach," *Stuttgarter Zeitung*, 4 / 13 / 76; "Kommunisten" (*Berliner Morgenpost*).

16. PA AA, Zwischenarchiv 103.325.

17. See DB-P / SB, 73. Sitz., 8. Wahlperiode (2 / 17 / 78), 5803–5804; also see the official responses to these queries in DB Drucksache 8 / 2039, 7 / 31 / 78.

18. DB-P / SB, 86. Sitz., 8. Wahlperiode (4 / 20 / 78), 6839–6840; DB-P / SB, 106. Sitz., 8. Wahlperiode (9 / 27 / 78), 8386–8387.

19. Some even included the clippings. See PA AA, Zwischenarchiv 107.619.

20. PA AA, Zwischenarchiv 103.325, 105.097.

21. DB-P / SB, 63. Sitz., 8. Wahlperiode (12 / 15 / 77), 4901.

22. See the correspondence in PA AA, Zwischenarchiv 105.097. Also see Tim Szatkowski, "Von Sihanouk bis Pol Pot. Diplomatie und Menschenrechte in den Beziehungen der Bundesrepublik zu Kambodscha (1967–1979)," *VfZ* 1 (2013): 5–6.

23. See the correspondence, memoranda, and telegrams in PA AA, Zwischenarchiv, 105.097, 107.619, 107.622. Also see Khem Sou, "'Du hast mein Gewehr beleidigt,'" *Spiegel*, 2 / 20 / 78 and 2 / 27 / 78.

24. See Horst Möller, Klaus Hildebrand, and Gregor Schöllgen, eds., *Akten zur Auswärtigen Politik der Bundesrepublik Deutschland 1978* (Munich: Oldenbourg, 2009), 2:1472, 1527, 1549; PA AA, Zwischenarchiv 107.619, Vermerk, 9 / 12 / 78.

25. Samuel Moyn, *The Last Utopia: Human Rights in History* (Cambridge, MA: Belknap Press of Harvard University Press, 2010), 4.

26. PA AA, Zwischenarchiv 105.097. On the consequences in Eastern Europe, see Michael Cotey Morgan, *The Final Act: The Helsinki Accords and the Transformation of the Cold War* (Princeton, NJ: Princeton University Press, 2018), 214–234.

27. John Barron and Anthony Paul, *Murder of a Gentle Land: The Untold Story of a Communist Genocide in Cambodia* (New York: Reader's Digest Press, 1977); *Das Massaker* (Seewis: Stephanus Edition, 1979).

28. Sou, "'Gewehr.'"

29. "Wer Buntes trägt, wird hingerichtet," *Bild am Sonntag*, 12 / 4 / 77; "Wer liebt, der wird umgebracht," *Kölnische Rundschau*, 8 / 7 / 78; "Wer im Reisfeld flirtet, stirbt," *Welt*, 8 / 31 / 78; "Sofort hinaus," *Spiegel*, 3 / 7 / 77.

30. Quotes from "Licht aus," *Spiegel*, 1 / 30 / 78; Sou, "'Gewehr'" (2 / 20 / 78); Christian Roll, "Was aus dem Prinzen wurde, weiß niemand," *Kölner Stadt-Anzeiger*, 1 / 4 / 77; "Drei kleine Köche" (*Spiegel*). All of this was essentially accurate. See Ben Kiernan, *The Pol Pot Regime*, 3rd ed. (New Haven, CT: Yale University Press, 2008). On the Great Leap, see Frank Dikötter, *Mao's Great Famine: The History of China's Most Devastating Catastrophe, 1958–1962* (New York: Walker, 2010).

31. One of the most infamous denials at the time flowed from the pen of American linguist and leftist political activist Noam Chomsky, who summarily dismissed the refugee reports in a lengthy *Nation* essay titled "Distortions at Fourth Hand." See "Positive Äußerung über Kambodscha," *FAZ*, 12 / 30 / 77; Noam Chomsky and Edward S. Herman, "Distortions at Fourth Hand," *Nation* (6 / 25 / 77): 789–794. On the skepticism of Swedish intellectuals,

see Peter Fröberg Idling, *Pol Pots Lächeln*, trans. Andrea Fredriksson-Zederbauer (Zurich: Unionsverlag, 2015).

32. NDR Fernseharchiv Hamburg, 1032875 / 5, "Weltspiegel," 6 / 19 / 77.

33. Carlos Widmann, "Eine spielerische Art des Tötens," *SZ*, 4 / 5 / 78.

34. Widmann, "Spielerische Art." Emphasis added.

35. These figures were based on reports that appeared in the American press. See "Blutige Herrschaft in Kambodscha," *Kölnische Rundschau*, 4 / 13 / 76; "Flüchtlinge sahen Berge von Leichen," *Welt*, 1 / 24 / 77.

36. "Berichte über Greueltaten in Kambodscha," *Kölnische Rundschau*, 1 / 24 / 78. For claims about genocide and atrocities against the Vietnamese, see "Völkermord," *FAZ*, 1 / 25 / 77; "In Kambodscha wird buchstäblich Genozid am eigenen Volk betrieben," *Spiegel*, 3 / 7 / 77; "'Verschütte nicht den Tee deines Herrn!'" *Spiegel*, 2 / 13 / 78.

37. "'Was wir machen'" (*Spiegel*); PA AA, Zwischenarchiv 107.622, Antrittsbesuch, 10 / 27 / 78.

38. For an overview of diplomatic relations and German-German rivalry, see the undated comment (*Vermerk*) in PA AA, Zwischenarchiv 103.325; Szatkowski, "Sihanouk bis Pol Pot," 6–15.

39. PA AA, Zwischenarchiv 107.619, Genscher to Vogel, 12 / 14 / 78.

40. See the reports in PA AA, Zwischenarchiv 103.325, 105.097, 105.098, 107.619, 107.622, 121.124; Robert Loeffel, "*Sippenhaft,* Terror and Fear in Nazi Germany: Examining One Facet of Terror in the Aftermath of the Plot of 20 July 1944," *CEH* 16, no. 1 (2007): 51–69.

41. See PA AA, Zwischenarchiv 103.325, Bericht, 4 / 27 / 76; "Beziehungen zu Kambodscha," 9 / 9 / 76; PA AA, Zwischenarchiv 107.622, Fernschreiben, 7 / 7 / 78; Szatkowski, "Sihanouk bis Pol Pot," 17–18, 20–21.

42. PA AA, MfAA C6671, Note Nr. 58 / 75, 423 / 75; PA AA, MfAA C6672, Vermerk, 7 / 7 / 75. Also see Christian Oesterheld, "East German Socialism and the Khmer Rouge Revolution: Insights from the GDR's Diplomatic Archive," in *Proceedings of the 10th International Academic Conference of the International Institute of Social and Economic Sciences* (Vienna, June 2014), 561–566; Szatkowski, "Sihanouk bis Pol Pot," 8–9.

43. See the reports in PA AA, MfAA C6525, C6671, C6672, C6689, C6691, C6696, C6705, C6706; BArch I / 4 / 3510 (174. Sitz. des Präsidiums des Ministerrates), Anlage 1 (2 / 19 / 76). Also see Andrew Mertha, *Brothers in Arms: Chinese Aid to the Khmer Rouge, 1975–1979* (Ithaca, NY: Cornell University Press, 2014).

44. PA AA, MfAA C6691, "Information zur Entwicklung in Kampuchea," n.d.

45. See the report from March 1976 in PA AA C6691; also see BArch DY / 30 / J IV / 2 / 2J / 7590, Information Nr. 49 / 1977, 4 / 27 / 77.

46. See PA AA, MfAA G-A368, Bericht, 5 / 20 / 75; PA AA, MfAA C6691, "Innen- und außenpolitische Maßnahmen," 4 / 17 / 75; PA AA, MfAA C6692, "Information über die Entwicklung der KPK," n.d. Officials did not use the term *genocide,* but a report by the GDR embassy in Laos did report the "widespread execution of opponents." See Oesterheld, "Insights," 569.

47. PA AA, MfAA C6689, "Demokratisches Kampuchea," 9 / 15 / 78.

48. Quotes from "3. Frage," *Junge Welt*, 7 / 6 / 78; Manfred Zander, "Antwort auf Lesefragen," *Volksstimme* (Magdeburg), 7 / 19 / 78.

49. See PA AA, MfAA C6705, Informationsmappe; PA AA, MfAA C6706, "Zur gegenwärtigen Lage," n.d.; "Zur Lage in der VR Kampuchea," 1 / 18 / 79. Also see the reports in PA AA, MfAA C6525, C6679, G-A368; BArch I / 4 / 3510 (174. Sitz. des Präsidiums des Minister-

rates), Anlage 1, 2/19/76; Renate Wünsche and Diethelm Weidemann, *Vietnam, Laos und Kampuchea: Zur nationalen und sozialen Befreiung der Völker Indochinas* (Berlin [East]: Verlag der Wissenschaften, 1977), 337–344.

50. Carlos Widmann used almost all these catchphrases in articles in the *Süddeutsche Zeitung*; see Widmann, "Prinz Sihanouk als Anwalt der Chinesen," *SZ*, 9/5/75; "Sihanouk entsagte seinem weltlichen Amt" (4/7/76); and "Steinzeit-Sozialismus" (4/20/76).

51. Olivia Wendt, "Schmuggeln am Fluß," *Deutsche Zeitung*, 11/7/75. Also see Oskar Weggel, "Zwei Jahre 'Demokratisches Kampuchea,'" *APuZ* B26/77 (July 1977): 3–20.

52. Christel Pilz, "Die Revolution der Analphabeten," *FAZ*, 9/2/78; "Licht aus" (*Spiegel*).

53. Widmann, "Steinzeit-Sozialismus."

54. Quotes from Peter Grubbe, "Reich der Toten," *Stern*, 1/17/80; Ariane Barth, "'Wir werden alle getötet,'" *Spiegel*, 3/24/80; Oskar Weggel, "Der Krieg der Flöhe," *Vorwärts*, 7/12/79; Michael Sontheimer, *Kambodscha, Land der sanften Mörder* (Reinbek bei Hamburg: Rowohlt, 1990), 65–66.

55. "'Ich bin noch nicht besiegt,'" *Spiegel*, 10/29/79.

56. Christel Pilz, "Das Regime der Roten Khmer läßt sich von Prinz Sihanouk loben," *FAZ*, 10/12/78; Peter Scholl-Latour, "Le sourire khmer," in *Der Tod im Reisfeld: Dreißig Jahre Krieg in Indochina* (Stuttgart: Deutsche Verlags-Anstalt, 1980), 93–100 (quote on 95). On German clichés about the "exotic" Orient, see Wolfgang Kubin, ed., *Mein Bild in Deinem Auge: Exotismus und Moderne: Deutschland–China im 20. Jahrhundert* (Darmstadt: Wissenschaftliche Buchgesellschaft, 1995).

57. See, for example, Adelbert Weinstein, "Kambodscha: Straflager für ein Volk," *FAZ*, 4/15/77. The study of despotic "Asiatic modes of production" and "hydraulic civilizations" was a tradition within Marxism; see Karl August Wittfogel, *Oriental Despotism: A Comparative Study of Total Power* (New Haven, CT: Yale University Press, 1957). On the "racialized coding of communism as 'Asiatic,'" see Young-Sun Hong, *Cold War Germany, the Third World, and the Global Humanitarian Regime* (New York: Cambridge University Press, 2015), 24; Sontheimer, *Kambodscha*, 53–54.

58. Egon Bahr, in discussion with the author, Berlin, Dec. 2007. Quotes from Roll, "Was aus dem Prinzen wurde"; Alexander Pappenberg, "Mit Amuletten kämpfen sie gegen Hanoi und böse Geister," *Welt*, 1/16/80; Friedrich Herzog, "Menschen auf der Flucht," *Frankfurter Neue Presse*, 10/23/79; Sontheimer, *Kambodscha*, 36, 233–234.

59. Hong, *Cold War Germany*, 104.

60. "Pankraz und das Morden in Kambodscha," *Welt*, 3/7/77.

61. "Pankraz" (*Welt*). On the background of the Khmer Rouge leadership, see Ben Kiernan, *Blood and Soil: A World History of Genocide and Extermination from Sparta to Darfur* (New Haven, CT: Yale University Press, 2007), 540–545.

62. Quotes from NDR Fernseharchiv Hamburg, 22511277/2, "Wochenspiegel," 1/1/78; Sontheimer, *Kambodscha*, 59.

63. Archiv des WDR Hörfunks 6127046102, Klaus Mehnert, "Gedanken zur Zeit," 3/9/78.

64. Mehnert, "Gedanken zur Zeit"; Klaus Mehnert, *Ein Deutscher in der Welt: Erinnerungen 1906–1981* (Stuttgart: Deutsche Verlags-Anstalt, 1981), 403.

2. ASIA'S AUSCHWITZ

1. ACDP, Nachlass Wohlrabe, I-700-062/2, Bieberstein to Wohlrabe, 9/20/76. Also see Tim Szatkowski, "Von Sihanouk bis Pol Pot: Diplomatie und Menschenrechte in den Beziehungen der Bundesrepublik zu Kambodscha (1967–1979)," *VfZ* 1 (2013): 12–14, 19.

2. Overt comparisons to the Nazis and the Final Solution came earlier in France, Britain, and the United States. See Jamie Frederic Metzl, *Western Responses to Human Rights Abuses in Cambodia, 1975–80* (Basingstoke: Macmillan, 1996); 11, 24, 46–48, 58, 61, 79, 80, 83–85, 107–108, 113–114, 149; Samantha Power, *"A Problem from Hell": America and the Age of Genocide* (New York: Perennial, 2003), 102–103, 128–129. For one of the earliest claims about a "new holocaust," see John Barron and Anthony Paul, *Murder of a Gentle Land: The Untold Story of a Communist Genocide in Cambodia* (New York: Reader's Digest Press, 1977).

3. See Evan Gottesman, *Cambodia after the Khmer Rouge: Inside the Politics of Nation Building* (New Haven, CT: Yale University Press, 2003).

4. On the impact of the miniseries, see Frank Bösch, *Zeitenwende 1979: Als die Welt von heute begann* (Munich: C. H. Beck, 2019), 363–395; Erin McGlothlin, "January 1979: West German Broadcast of *Holocaust* Draws Critical Fire and Record Audiences," in *A New History of German Cinema*, ed. Jennifer M. Kapczynski and Michael D. Richardson (Rochester, NY: Camden House, 2012), 470–475. More generally, see Judith Keilbach, *Geschichtsbilder und Zeitzeugen: Zur Darstellung des Nationalsozialismus im bundesdeutschen Fernsehen* (Münster: LIT, 2008); Judith Keilbach, Béla Rásky, and Jana Starek, eds., *Völkermord zur Primetime: Der Holocaust im Fernsehen* (Vienna: New Academic Press, 2019).

5. Quote from McGlothlin, "January 1979," 470.

6. Gernot Müller-Serton, "Das Volk der Khmer," *FR*, 12 / 7 / 79; Horst Möller, Klaus Hildebrand, and Gregor Schöllgen, eds., *Akten zur Auswärtigen Politik der Bundesrepublik Deutschland 1979* (Munich: Oldenbourg, 2010), 1:888.

7. See the editorial, "Hausmitteilung," and Ariane Barth, "'Wir werden alle getötet, wir müssen fliehen,'" *Spiegel*, 3 / 16 / 80; part two appeared on Mar. 23.

8. Ariane Barth, in discussion with the author, Landrecht, Germany, Mar. 2007.

9. Barth, discussion. The Khao I-Dang camp was the "only official gateway for overseas resettlement"; see Bertrand Taithe, "The Cradle of the New Humanitarian System? International Work and European Volunteers at the Cambodian Border Camps, 1979–1993," *Contemporary European History* 25, no. 2 (2016): 341.

10. Ariane Barth and Tiziano Terzani, *Holocaust in Kambodscha* (Reinbek bei Hamburg: Rowohlt, 1982).

11. Christel Pilz, "Holocaust im Land der Khmer," *Weltwoche*, 5 / 2 / 79; Olivia Wendt, "Das gebrochene Volk," *Deutsche Zeitung*, 5 / 4 / 79.

12. "Asiens Auschwitz," *Spiegel*, 10 / 22 / 79; Jürgen Kramer, "Kambodscha mit einer gewaltlosen Armee retten," *Stuttgarter Zeitung*, 11 / 2 / 79; Jochen A. Bär and Jana Tereick, eds., *Von "Szene" bis "postfaktisch": Die "Wörter des Jahres" der Gesellschaft für deutsche Sprache, 1977 bis 2016* (Hildesheim: Georg Olms, 2017), 174–176.

13. SWR Historisches Archiv 2824, *"Report:* Friedensmarsch Kambodscha," 2 / 19 / 80.

14. Quotes from "Nun dankt Heng Samrin," *FAZ*, 11 / 7 / 79; Friedhelm Kemna, "Tiger und Krokodile," *Welt*, 10 / 23 / 79; *"Report:* Friedensmarsch Kambodscha" (Kaufmann).

15. All quotes are from *"Report:* Friedensmarsch Kambodscha."

16. "Zwischenruf," *Welt*, 4 / 26 / 76; Josef Riedl, letter to the editor, *Spiegel*, 11 / 19 / 79; Matthias Walden, "Tal des Todes," *Welt am Sonntag*, 10 / 21 / 79. Emphasis in original.

17. "Das große Schweigen," *National Zeitung*, 8 / 18 / 78.

18. A slew of articles comparing the Khmer Rouge to Hitler and Auschwitz appeared in the American press in April and May 1978, just after *Holocaust* aired. See Power, *"Problem from Hell,"* 129.

19. Karl-Heinz Janßen, "Erst Völkermord, dann Hungersnot," *Zeit*, 9 / 28 / 79; NDR Fernseharchiv, 1032875 / 5, "Weltspiegel," 6 / 19 / 77.

20. This was not just true in Germany. See Donald W. Beachler, "Arguing about Cambodia: Genocide and Political Interest," *Holocaust and Genocide Studies* 23, no. 2 (2009): 214–238.

21. Wolfgang Röhl, "Mord bleibt Mord oder: Linke Mythen leben länger," *das da*, March 1978. On similar responses by the Left in America and elsewhere in Europe, see Power, *"Problem from Hell,"* 112–115; Metzl, *Western Responses*, 90.

22. Michael Sontheimer, in discussion with the author, Berlin, Mar. 2007. Also see Sontheimer, *Kambodscha, Land der sanften Mörder: Ein Bericht aus Indochina* (Reinbek bei Hamburg: Rowohlt, 1990), 13.

23. Klaus von Dohnanyi, in discussion with the author, Hamburg, Germany, Mar. 2007.

24. AA PA Ref. 340, Zwischenarchiv 107622, letter, 12/15/78.

25. Power, *"Problem from Hell,"* 136–140.

26. Jürgen Elsässer, "War Pol Pot ein Kommunist?" *Jungle World*, 8/14/97.

27. Christian Semler, in discussion with the author, Berlin, Aug. 2010; E. Steinhauer and J. Horlemann, "Kampuchea 1979: Befreiung oder Aggression?" in *Kampuchea 1979: Befreiung oder Aggression?* (Cologne: Rote Fahne, 1979), 24–37. Schmierer's *Grußbotschaft* (Greeting) was published in *Kommunistische Volkszeitung*, 4/21/80. This would come back to haunt Schmierer, who joined the German diplomatic corps in 1999 at the invitation of Foreign Minister Joschka Fischer. See Jürgen Schreiber, "Fischers Django," *Tagesspiegel*, 4/1/2001.

28. Archiv des Westdeutschen Rundfunks 3042087, "Kambodscha," 3/13/79; Friedhelm Kelmna, "Kambodscha—einem Volk droht die Vernichtung" and Jan Myrdal, "Ein Pol-Pot-Sprecher: Ja, wir betteln," *Welt*, 11/13/79. On Wulff and Myrdal, see Young-sun Hong, *Cold War Germany, the Third World, and the Global Humanitarian Regime* (Cambridge: Cambridge University Press, 2015), 83, 109; Peter Fröberg Idling, *Pol Pots Lächeln: Eine Reise durch das Kambodscha der Roten Khmer*, trans. Andrea Fredriksson-Zederbauer (Zurich: Unionsverlag, 2015).

29. Olaf Ihlau, "Wo der Erbfeind ein Erlöser ist," *SZ*, 2/21/81. The second and third parts appeared on Feb. 24 and 27.

30. See Georg Stötzel, "Der Nazi-Komplex," in *Kontroverse Begriffe: Geschichte des öffentlichen Sprachgebrauchs in der Bundesrepublik Deutschland*, ed. Georg Stötzel and Martin Wengeler (Berlin: Walter de Gruyter, 1995), 365.

31. Quotes from Olaf Ihlau, "Zaghafte Rückkehr des Lächelns," *SZ*, 2/19/82; Erhard Haubold, "Statthalter Hanois in Kambodscha?" *FAZ*, 6/5/81; Fritz Sitte, "Nach dem Völkermord," *Frankfurter Neue Presse*, 6/25/82; "Vorhof der Hölle," *Zeitmagazin*, 12/14/84; Wolfgang von Erffa, "Mönche werden wieder umworben," *Welt*, 8/4/89.

32. On Nazi appropriation of words like *fanatic*, see Victor Klemperer, *LTI: Notizbuch eines Philologen* (Leipzig: Reklam, 1998), 70–75; Stötzel, "Nazi-Komplex," 355–382.

33. Stötzel, "Nazi-Komplex," 366, 379. Also see Gordon Craig, *The Germans* (New York: Penguin, 1982), 322–332.

34. See "Blut getauscht," *Spiegel*, 5/5/75; "Sofort hinaus," *Spiegel*, 3/7/77; NDR Fernseharchiv Hamburg, 5306/08, "Tagesthemen," 2/4/80.

35. "Flüchtlinge sahen Berge von Leichen," *Welt*, 1/24/77; "Das unbeschreibliche Elend in Kambodscha," *FAZ*, 1/25/80; Claus Happel, "Die Khmer verhungern," *RM*, 9/28/79. On the "trigger" function of Holocaust imagery, see Sebastian Schönemann, *Symbolbilder des Holocausts: Fotografien der Vernichtung im sozialen Gedächtnis* (Frankfurt am Main: Campus, 2019).

36. Quotes from "Prinz Sihanouk: Morde—ich habe sie nicht gesehen," *Hamburger Abendblatt*, 1/9/79; Amporn Tantuvanich, "Hat das Regime Pol Pots mehr als eine Million Menschen 'liquidiert'?" *Münchner Merkur*, 1/9/79; "Kambodscha ist ein Land ausgemergelter,

wandelnder Skelette," *FR,* 10 / 17 / 79; Verena Stern, "'Der Revolution geht es gut,'" *Deutsches Allgemeines Sonntagsblatt,* 11 / 13 / 77; Günther Graffenberger, "Politik der Härte regiert Indochina," *Stuttgarter Zeitung,* 7 / 14 / 76; Adelbert Weinstein, "Kambodscha: Straflager für ein Volk," *FAZ,* 4 / 15 / 77; "Amokläufer," *FAZ,* 11 / 18 / 77. Also see Power, *"Problem from Hell,"* 128–130.

37. Sontheimer, discussion; Sontheimer, *Kambodscha,* 11.

38. "Massenmord in Kambodscha," *Quick,* 11 / 22 / 79; "Möllemann: Die für den Massenmord in Kambodscha Verantwortlichen zur Rechenschaft ziehen," *fdk-Tagesdienst,* 10 / 17 / 79. Möllemann later became a controversial figure, accused of financial improprieties and antisemitism. See Christoph Greiner, *Jürgen W. Möllemann, 1945–2003: Ein politisches Leben* (Stuttgart: Ibidem, 2010), 7–27. For Stalin comparisons, see "Götzendienst," *Stuttgarter Zeitung,* 8 / 6 / 78.

39. "Pankraz und das Morden in Kambodscha," *Welt,* 3 / 7 / 77; Christel Pilz, "Töpfe und Pfannen werden Symbole der Freiheit," *FAZ,* 4 / 14 / 79.

40. This is meant metaphorically. Ranke-Heinemann was the eldest daughter of Gustav Heinemann, a former president of the Federal Republic with impeccable "antifascist" credentials. See Uta Ranke-Heinemann, "Jetzt waschen wir mit Asche," *Spiegel,* 1 / 14 / 80.

41. On the East German media, see Gunther Holzweißig, *Die schärfste Waffe der Partei: Eine Mediengeschichte der DDR* (Cologne: Böhlau, 2002); Stefan Zahlmann, ed., *Wie im Westen, nur anders: Medien in der DDR* (Berlin: Panama, 2010).

42. Quotes from Klaus-Dieter Pflaum, "Über Phnom Penh weht die Flagge der Befreiungsfront," *ND,* 1 / 10 / 79; "Der Sieg des kampucheanisches Volkes," *ND,* 1 / 10 / 79; "Ein historischer Sieg für Kampucheas Volk," *Neue Zeit,* 1 / 11 / 79; "Hinterhältige Wohltaten," *ND,* 11 / 6 / 79; DRA Potsdam, BC 12306 / 007851, *Objektiv,* 8 / 2 / 79. Emphasis added.

43. Klaus-Dieter Pflaum, "Das freie Kampuchea in diesen Tagen," *ND,* 1 / 27–28 / 79. For another East German journalist's impressions at the time, see Horst Hirt, *Wiedergeburt eines Volkes: Kampuchea im ersten Jahr nach seiner Befreiung* (Berlin: Solidaritätskomitee der DDR, 1980).

44. DRA Potsdam, BC 12306 / 007851, *Objektiv,* 8 / 30 / 79; B C18881 / 007835, *Objektiv,* 3 / 20 / 80.

45. For Leo's biography, see Maxim Leo, *Haltet euer Herz bereit: Eine ostdeutsche Familiengeschichte* (Munich: Karl Blessing, 2009).

46. Gerhard Leo, "Kampucheas Weg ins neue Leben," *ND,* 2 / 17–18 / 79.

47. DRA Potsdam, D 01319101, "Erlebnisse in Kampuchea," 6 / 19 / 80; Leo, "Kampucheas Weg."

48. Leo, "Kampucheas Weg"; Leo, "Die Henker sagen aus," *ND,* 3 / 31 / 79.

49. Klaus-Dieter Pflaum, in discussion with the author, Berlin, Dec. 2007.

50. Wsewolod Rybakow, "Die verheerende Kraft des Dogmas," *Probleme des Friedens und des Sozialismus* (Aug. 1980): 1115–1127.

51. Quotes from Manfred Zander, "Antwort auf Leserfragen," *Volksstimme* (Magdeburg), 7 / 19 / 78; Pflaum, "Historischer Sieg"; Wiesław Gornicki, "'Ihre Exzellenzen' waschen sich die Hände," *NZ,* May 1980; W. Toptschjan, "'Revolutionäres Experiment' mit brutalem Gesicht," *NZ,* 11 / 9 / 78; Rybakow, "Verheerende Kraft."

52. Wolfgang Colden, "Feindliche Brüder," *UZ,* 1 / 11 / 79; Harald Meinke, "Sihanouks 'kleine Schwester'—eine Prinzessin im Zentralkomitee," *UZ,*1 / 4 / 80; Rybakow, "Verheerende Kraft."

53. See Howard J. De Nike, John Quigley, and Kenneth J. Robinson, eds., *Genocide in Cambodia: Documents from the Trial of Pol Pot and Ieng Sary* (Philadelphia: University of

Pennsylvania Press, 2000); Craig Etcheson, *Extraordinary Justice: Law, Politics, and the Khmer Rouge Tribunal* (New York: Columbia University Press, 2019), 25–31.

54. BArch Berlin, DP/3/2228, Bericht, 8/29/79; DY/30/11551, Information Nr. 20/79, 2/6/79. Also see Klaus Bästlein, "The GDR's Judgment against Hans Globke," in *After Auschwitz: The Difficult Legacies of the GDR*, ed. Enrico Heitzer et al. (New York: Berghahn, 2021), 74–87.

55. BArch Berlin, DP/3/2228, Bericht, 8/29/79.

56. His objections were largely in vain. The Khmer Rouge were found guilty of "mass killings" that, "in some respects," were "more barbarous than those used by the Hitlerite fascists." See Metzl, *Western Responses*, 141, emphasis in original. For a revealing interview with Foth that suggests how present Germany's own genocidal past was in his argumentation, see Howard J. De Nike, "East Germany's Legal Advisor to the 1979 Tribunal in Cambodia," *Searching for the Truth* (2008): 39–43.

57. See Franzika Kuschel, *Schwarzhörer, Schwarzseher und heimliche Leser: Die DDR und die Westmedien* (Göttingen: Wallstein, 2016).

58. *Kampuchea—Death and Resurrection* (1980; H&S Filme, Berlin); *Die Angkar* (1981; H&S Filme, Berlin); *Exercises* (1981; H&S Filme, Berlin); Robert Michel and Wolfgang von Polentz, eds., *Der Dschungelkrieg: Ein Film von Walter Heynowski, Gerhard Scheumann, Peter Hellmich* (Berlin: VEB DEFA-Studio für Dokumentarfilme, 1983). Also see Hannes Riemann, *Eine Herausforderung an jeden Kommunisten: Die Khmer Rouge, der III. Indochinakrieg und Kambodscha im Fokus von Dokumentarfilmen des DDR-Dokumentarfilmstudios H&S (1979–1983)* (Erfurt: Thüringisch-Kambodschanische Gesellschaft, 2011).

59. Rüdiger Steinmetz and Tilo Prase, *Dokumentarfilm zwischen Beweis und Pamphlet: Heynowski & Scheumann und Gruppe Katins* (Leipzig: Leipziger Universitätsverlag, 2002), 15–16, 32, 47–72, 101–125. Also see Corinna Schier, Claudia Böttcher, and Judith Kretzschmar, *Walter Heynowski und Gerhard Scheumann—Dokumentarfilmer im Klassenkampf: Eine kommentierte Filmographie* (Leipzig: Leipziger Universitätsverlag, 2002).

60. Walter Heynowski, in discussion with the author, Berlin, Nov. 2010.

61. See Paul Williams, "Witnessing Genocide: Vigilance and Remembrance at Tuol Sleng and Choeung Ek," *Holocaust and Genocide Studies* 18, no. 2 (2004): 248.

62. *Kampuchea—Death and Resurrection.*

63. Heynowski, discussion. Also see Walter Heynowski, *Der Film meines Lebens: Zerschossene Jugend* (Berlin: Das Neue Berlin, 2007).

64. GDR officials often pointed to prominent East German Jews to show how "progressive" their country was. See Detlef Siegfried, "Zwischen Aufarbeitung und Schlußstrich," in *Dynamische Zeiten: Die 60er Jahre in den beiden deutschen Gesellschaften*, ed. Axel Schildt, Detlef Siegfried, and Karl Christian Lammers (Hamburg: Hans Christians, 2000), 88–90; also see the biographical entries for Heynowski and Norden in Jochen Cerny, ed., *DDR: Wer war wer: Ein biografisches Lexikon*, 2nd ed. (Berlin: Ch. Links, 1992), 192, 335; Steinmetz and Prase, *Dokumentarfilm*, 17–18.

65. Heynowski, discussion.

66. Heynowski, discussion.

67. See Mechtild Leutner, ed., *Bundesrepublik Deutschland und China 1949 bis 1995* (Berlin: Akademie, 1995), 178; Marcel Bode, *Die DDR und die Volksrepublik China in den Jahren 1978 bis 1990* (Potsdam: WeltTrends, 2013), 32–48; Zhong Chen, "Beyond Moscow: East German–Chinese Relations during the Cold War," CWIHP e-Dossier No. 57, https://5g .wilsoncenter.org/publication/beyond-moscow-east-german-chinese-relations-during-the -cold-war.

68. Both had earlier worked in television.

69. Steinmetz and Prase, *Dokumentarfilm*, 112, 156–157.

70. On Scheumann's fall from grace, see Steinmetz and Prase, *Dokumentarfilm*, 101–121; Andrew I. Port, "Courting China, Condemning China: East and West German Cold War Diplomacy in the Shadow of the Cambodian Genocide," *German History* 33, no. 4 (2015): 600–607.

71. Michel and Polentz, *Dschungelkrieg*, iii, 67, 69, 99, 127, 161, 163.

72. Michel and Polentz, *Dschungelkrieg*, 47–51.

3. WHY DON'T WE ACT?

1. Dr. Angela Warnecke, in discussion with the author, Hamburg, Mar. 2007. On Germans and overseas medical work, see Young-sun Hong, *Cold War Germany, the Third World, and the Global Humanitarian Regime* (Cambridge: Cambridge University Press, 2015), 84, 92–93, 215.

2. Gernot Müller-Serton, "Das Volk der Khmer ist von den eigenen Machthabern seelisch zerstört worden," *FR*, 12/7/79; Rupert Neudeck, "Wenn von Leben noch die Rede sein kann," *Vorwärts*, 11/15/79; Erich Follath, "Kambodscha: Und die Welt läßt sie sterben," *Stern*, 9/20/79; Friedhelm Kemna, "Kambodscha—einem Volk droht die Vernichtung," *Welt*, 11/13/79; A. Papenberg, "'Wie müssen auf Knien bitten,'" *Welt*, 11/2/79. On Biafran imagery, see Lasse Heerten, *The Biafran War and Postcolonial Humanitarianism: Spectacles of Suffering* (Cambridge: Cambridge University Press, 2017), 140–174.

3. AdsD, SPD-PV Internationale Abteilung 11086.

4. Joachim Schilling, "Pol Pots Partisanen geben noch nicht auf," *Rheinpfalz*, 7/10/79. On charges of genocidal equivalency, see Claus-Dietrich Möhrke, "Kambodscha stirbt," *Rheinische Post*, 10/24/79. For similar claims in the United States, see Jamie Frederic Metzl, *Western Responses to Human Rights Abuses in Cambodia, 1975–80* (Basingstoke: Macmillan, 1996), 144–149, 168. For a sober assessment, see Sophie Quinn-Judge, "Fraternal Aid, Self-Defence, or Self-Interest? Vietnam's Intervention in Cambodia, 1978–1989," in *Humanitarian Intervention: A History*, ed. Brendan Simms and D. J. B. Trim (Cambridge: Cambridge University Press, 2011), 343–362.

5. Jutta von Freyberg, "Vietnamhetze oder die mißbrauchte Hilfe," *UZ*, 12/27/79. On leftist disillusionment, see Patrick Merziger, "The 'Radical Humanism' of 'Cap Anamur'/'German Emergency Doctors' in the 1980s," *European Review of History* 23, no. 1–2 (2016): 174–175; Paul Berman, *Power and the Idealists* (Brooklyn, NY: Soft Skull, 2005), 58–64.

6. Erhard Haubold, "'Die neue Regierung muß überall bei Null anfangen,'" *FAZ*, 12/7/79; Erhard Haubold, in discussion with the author, Berlin, June 2008. Also see Evan Gottesman, *Cambodia after the Khmer Rouge* (New Haven, CT: Yale University Press, 2002), 81–88; Michael Barnett, *Empire of Humanity: A History of Humanitarianism* (Ithaca, NY: Cornell University Press, 2011), 149–155. For an overview of these issues, see Norbert Götz, Georgina Brewis, and Stefan Werther, *Humanitarianism in the Modern World: The Moral Economy of Famine Relief* (Cambridge: Cambridge University Press, 2020).

7. Uta Ranke-Heinemann, "'Jetzt waschen wir mit Asche,'" *Spiegel*, 1/14/80.

8. Uta Ranke-Heinemann, email to author, 12/21/06.

9. DRA Potsdam, DOK 1338-101, Telefoninterview, 12/20/79.

10. PdDB, 3104/292, Kurzprotokoll, 1/16/80.

11. NDR Fernseharchiv Hamburg, 40280/6, "Tagesthemen," 2/4/80.

12. Horst Möller, Klaus Hildebrand, and Gregor Schöllgen, eds., *Akten zur Auswärtigen Politik der Bundesrepublik Deutschland 1979* (Munich: Oldenbourg, 2010), 2:1539; Rupert Neudeck, "In den Lagern Indochinas: Ein Volk stirbt," *Westfälische Rundschau,* 12/15/79.

13. Friedhelm Kemna, "Tiger und Krokodile," *Welt,* 10/23/79; "Die Kambodschaner nicht im Stich lassen," *SZ,* 10/12/79.

14. Dietrich Strasser, "Am Ende des Weges," *Weltwoche,* 10/24/79.

15. See, for example, "Carstens: Mehr Hilfe für Kambodscha," *Berliner Morgenpost,* 10/27/79.

16. Eghard Mörbitz, "Im Gespräch," *FR,* 10/3/79; "Möllemann: UNO-Truppen gegen Massenmord," *Bild,* 11/12/79; "Möllemann: Die für den Massenmord in Kambodscha Verantwortlichen zur Rechenschaft ziehen," *fdk-Tagesdienst,* 10/17/79.

17. "Carstens: Mehr Hilfe" (*Berliner Morgenpost*). For aid figures, see DB Drucksache 8/3414, Unterrichtung, 11/20/79; DB-P/SB, 181. Sitz., 8. Wahlperiode (10/18/79), 14178–14179 (10/19/79), 14287; PdDB, BT 3104/291, Kurzprotokolle, 9/12/79, 11/14/79; PdDB, BT 1768/280, Kurzprotokoll (Anlage 2), 2/27/80; PA AA, Zwischenarchiv 121.059, "Leistungen der Bundesregierung," 12/18/79. On foreign aid figures, see Metzl, *Western Responses,* 162–177; Frank Bösch, *Zeitenwende 1979* (Munich: C. H. Beck, 2019), 194, 207.

18. The CDU's Vietnam Aid Bureau donated more than 300,000 DM that November. See PdDB, 3104/292, Kurzprotokoll 2/13/80; "'Freie Khmer' verbünden sich mit Pol Pot," *SZ,* 11/2/79; ACDP VIII-006-131/2.

19. See the correspondence in ACDP VIII-006-131/2.

20. Berthold Freiherr von Pfetten-Arnbach, in discussion with the author, Iffeldorf, Germany, Mar. 2007. Pfetten-Arnbach was a high-level German diplomat stationed in Indonesia at the time.

21. AdsD, SPD-PV 11535, "Programm," 8/29/79; PA AA, Zwischenarchiv 105.097, Fragestunde, 5/11–12/77; also see the reports and correspondence in PA AA, Zwischenarchiv 103.325; PdDB, 3104/291, "Aufnahme von Flüchtlingen," 2/6/79.

22. See AdsD, SPD-PV 11535, Dohnanyi to Kleipsties, 11/25/77; PdDB, 3104/291, "Aufnahme von Flüchtlingen," 6/12/79; Kurzprotokolle, 2/7/79, 5/30/79, 6/21/79.

23. PdDB, 3104/291 and 3104/292, Kurzprotokolle, 9/12/79, 11/14/79, 4/16/80; AdsD, SPD-Parteivorstand 10949, Aufzeichnung, 11/15/79.

24. Müller-Serton, "Das Volk der Khmer"; Josef Joffe, "Eine Flucht ohne Ende," *Zeit,* 7/13/79; Möller, Hildebrand, and Schöllgen, *Akten,* 1:933.

25. Jürgen Dauth, "Lautloser Schrei in die Welt," *General-Anzeiger,* 11/24/79.

26. Strasser, "Am Ende des Weges"; "Asiens Auschwitz," *Spiegel,* 10/22/79; Wilhelm Christbaum, "Das Blutgeld der Flüchtlinge," *Münchner Merkur,* 6/20/79; Walter Michler, "Sa Kaeo: Vorstufe der Hölle," *Saarbrücker Zeitung,* 2/2/80. Also see Primo Levi, *Ist das ein Mensch?,* trans. Heinz Riedt (Munich: Carl Hanser, 1958).

27. Heinz-Arndt Brüggemann, "Wo die Menschlichkeit in der Sackgasse steckt," *Westdeutsche Allgemeine,* 8/29/79; "Am Kreuz für eine Handvoll Reis . . . ," *Welt am Sonntag,* 7/29/79; "'Nehmen Sie nur die Besten,'" *Spiegel,* 11/5/79; "Ein Volk, zu schwach zu weinen," *Spiegel,* 10/29/79.

28. PA AA, Zwischenarchiv 112.897, "Vermerk," 10/22/79; AdL, A44-33, "Leitlinien," n.d.; Möller, Hildebrand, and Schöllgen, *Akten zur Auswärtigen Politik,* 1:934–935. On Genscher, see Hans-Dieter Heumann, *Hans-Dietrich Genscher: Die Biographie* (Paderborn: Schöningh, 2012), 16–26.

29. *fdk-Tagesdienst*, 7 / 20 / 79.

30. AdL, A38-551, Korte to Mischnik, 6 / 20 / 79.

31. See Hans-Ludwig Abmeier, "Herbert Helmut Czaja," in *Baden-Württembergische Biographien*, ed. Fred L. Sepainter (Stuttgart: Kohlhammer, 2007), 4:41–44.

32. See ACDP Nachlaß Herbert Czaja I-291-017 / 1, Czaja to Hüssler, 7 / 9 / 79; PdDB, 3104 / 290, Kurzprotokoll, 5 / 4 / 77. Also see Astrid Luise Mannes, "Herbert Czajas Tätigkeit im Deutschen Bundestag," in *Herbert Czaja: Anwalt für Menschenrechte*, ed. Christine Maria Czaja (Bonn: Kulturstiftung der Deutschen Vertriebenen, 2003), 126–129; Johannes Stollhof, *Zwischen Biafra und Bonn: Hungerkatastrophen und Konsumkritik im deutschen Katholizismus, 1958–1979* (Paderborn: Schöningh, 2019), 101–221.

33. Ernst Albrecht, *Erinnerungen, Erkenntnisse, Entscheidungen* (Göttingen: Barton'-sche Verlagsbuchhandlung, 1999), 55–58; "Erlösende Tat," *Spiegel*, 12 / 3 / 78.

34. Niederschrift des Parteitagsprotokolls des 27. Bundesparteitags der CDU, 3 / 25–27 / 79.

35. Albrecht, *Erinnerungen*, 55–58.

36. Landsberg-Velen was president of the German branch of the Malteser International, a Catholic aid organization. See ACDP VIII-001-1059 / 1, Fraktionsprotokoll, 12 / 10 / 79; PdDB, 3104 / 281, Stenographisches Protokoll, 11 / 7 / 79; "Bundesregierung erhöht Kambodscha-Hilfe," *GA*, 10 / 25 / 79; "Kambodschanische Flüchtlinge nicht nach Europa verpflanzen," *FAZ*, 2 / 22 / 80. For similar arguments elsewhere, see Mollie Gerver, "Helping Refugees Where They Are," *Ethics & International Affairs* 35, no. 4 (2021): 563–580.

37. Möller, Hildebrand, and Schöllgen, *Akten zur Auswärtigen Politik*, 2:1539; AdsD, SPD-Parteivorstand 11086, "Pressegespräch," 11 / 9 / 79; SPD-Parteivorstand 11524, Informationen, 5 / 16 / 79; Protokoll, 6 / 12 / 79.

38. Marie-Helene Lammers, "Volkswanderung aus größter Not," *Bayernkurier*, 1 / 26 / 80. Emphasis added.

39. Patrice G. Poutrus, *Umkämpftes Asyl: Vom Nachkriegsdeutschland bis in die Gegenwart* (Berlin: Ch. Links, 2019), 87.

40. PdDB, 3104 / 291, Kurzprotokoll, 2 / 7 / 79; 3104 / 280, Protokoll, 6 / 20 / 79; AdsD, SPD-Parteivorstand 12056, Dohnanyi to Kleipsties, 11 / 25 / 77; Aufzeichnung, 11 / 15 / 79. On the costs, see ACDP VIII-006-131 / 2, Protokoll, 15.11.1979. By the winter of 1978 the United States had accepted 164,000 Cambodian refugees and France 43,000. See Bösch, *Zeitenwende*, 187, 192. Also see Quan Tue Tran, "Responding to and Resettling the Vietnamese Boat People: Perspectives from the United States and West Germany," in *Refugee Crises, 1945–2000: Political and Societal Responses in International Comparison*, ed. Jan C. Jansen and Simone Lässig (Cambridge: Cambridge University Press, 2020), 181–208.

41. See Bösch, *Zeitenwende*, 190, 221–222.

42. Poutrus, *Umkämpftes Asyl*, 39, 74.

43. See Klaus J. Bade, "Zur Karriere und Funktion abschätziger Begriffe in der deutschen Asylpolitik," *APuZ* 25 (2015): 3–8; Martin Wengeler, "Multikulturelle Gesellschaft oder Ausländer raus? Der sprachliche Umgang mit der Einwanderung seit 1945," in *Kontroverse Begriffe: Geschichte des öffentlichen Sprachgebrauchs in der Bundesrepublik Deutschland*, ed. Georg Stötzel and Martin Wengeler (Berlin: Walter de Gruyter, 1995), 735–739; Daniel Kersting and Marcus Leuoth, eds., *Der Begriff des Flüchtlings: Rechtliche, moralische und politische Kontroversen* (Berlin: J. B. Metzler, 2020).

44. Karen Schönwälder, "Migration, Refugees and Ethnic Plurality as Issues of Public and Political Debates in (West) Germany," in *Citizenship, Nationality and Migration in Europe*, ed. David Cesarani and Mary Fulbrook (London: Routledge, 1996), 162, 166–167.

45. See Wengeler, "Multikulturelle Gesellschaft," 745–746; Peter Gatrell, *The Unsettling of Europe* (New York: Basic, 2019), 292; Elisabeth Noelle-Neumann and Renate Köcher, eds.,

Allensbacher Jahrbuch der Demoskopie, 1984–1992, vol. 9 (Munich: Sauer, 1993), 525. For a different take, see Christopher A. Molnar, "'Greetings from the Apocalypse': Race, Migration, and Fear after German Reunification," *CEH* 54, no. 3 (2021): 491–515. Also see Matthias Frese and Julia Paulus, eds., *Willkommenskulturen? Re-Aktionen auf Flucht und Vertreibung in der Aufnahmegesellschaft der Bundesrepublik* (Paderborn: Schöningh, 2020); Andreas Kossert, *Kalte Heimat: Die Geschichte der deutschen Vertriebenen nach 1945* (Munich: Siedler, 2009).

46. ACDP VIII-001-1060/1, Fraktionsprotokoll, 3/4/80. Emphasis added.

47. Gunter Hofmann, "Der Strom ins Land der Wunder," *Neue Bonner Depesche*, April 1980.

48. Stefan G. Heydeck, "Waisen voll Vorfreude," *Berliner Morgenpost*, 8/28/79.

49. Rupert Neudeck, *Die Menschenretter von Cap Anamur* (Munich: Heyne, 2002), 32.

50. Neudeck, "In den Lagern Indochinas."

51. Neudeck, "In den Lagern Indochinas."

52. Neudeck, *Menschenretter,* 9–59 (quote on 13); Neudeck, in discussion with the author, Troisdorf, Mar. 2007.

53. Neudeck, *Menschenretter,* 27–30 (quote on 29); Neudeck, discussion. Also see Tim Allen and David Styan, "A Right to Interfere? Bernard Kouchner and the New Humanitarianism," *Journal of International Development* 12 (2000): 825–842.

54. Neudeck, *Menschenretter,* 10–11; Neudeck, discussion.

55. Neudeck, *Menschenretter,* 40; ACDP, Nachlass Jürgen Wohlrabe, I-700-062/21, "Bericht," July 1979; Bösch, *Zeitenwende,* 203–206, 210–211, 214–215; Merziger, "'Radical Humanism,'" 175.

56. Neudeck, discussion.

57. Neudeck, discussion. Also see Merziger, "'Radical Humanism,'" 176–177.

58. Neudeck, "Wenn von Leben"; Neudeck, "In den Lagern Indochinas"; "Kinder essen nur noch Asche und Erde," *FAZ,* 11/30/79; Peter Schilder, "Fünf Wochen Kampf gegen Tod und Not," *GA,* 1/8/80. Also see PdDB, 3104/291, Kurzprotokoll, 12/12/79; Bösch, *Zeitenwende,* 214–215; Merziger, "'Radical Humanism,'" 175; Patrick Merziger, "Mediation of Disasters and Humanitarian Aid in the Federal Republic of Germany," in *Humanitarianism & Media: 1900 to the Present,* ed. Johannes Paulmann (New York: Berghahn, 2019), 247–249.

59. Bösch, *Zeitenwende,* 211, 209; Merziger, "Mediation," 250, 254.

60. Neudeck, discussion; Neudeck, *Menschenretter,* 38, 255. On the difficulties and "culture shock" the volunteers experienced, see Bertrand Taithe, "The Cradle of the New Humanitarian System? International Work and European Volunteers at the Cambodian Border Camps, 1979–1993," *Contemporary European History* 25, no. 2 (2016): 345; Merziger, "'Radical Humanism,'" 181.

61. Neudeck, *Menschenretter,* 42; PdDB, 3104/291, Kurzprotokoll, 10/17/79; Gernot Müller-Serten, "Rote und weiße Khmer halten Verhungernde fest," *Stuttgarter Zeitung,* 11/30/79. Also see Bösch, *Zeitenwende,* 216–219; Merzinger, "'Radical Humanism,'" 175; Taithe, "Cradle," 338.

62. ACDP VIII-006-131/2, Protokoll, 11/15/79; PdDB, 3104/292, Kurzprotokoll, 2/13/80, and Bargatzky to Möllemann, 2/26/80; PdDB, 3104/291, Kurzprotokoll, 12/12/79. The clash played out in the pages of *Der Spiegel.* See "Hochgradig albern," *Spiegel,* 3/10/80; "Nur ein Teil," *Spiegel,* 3/24/80. Also see Jürgen Schilling, "Sind wir fremdenfeindlich, provinziell, vermufft oder gar rassistisch?" *Zeit,* 11/21/80; Michael Vössing, "Competition over Aid? The German Red Cross, the Committee Cap Anamur, and the Rescue of the Boat People in South-East Asia, 1979–1982," in *Dilemmas of Humanitarian Aid in the Twentieth Century,* ed. Johannes Paulmann (Oxford: Oxford University Press, 2016), 347–368.

63. Rupert Neudeck, *Humanitäre Radikalität* (Troisdorf: Komitee Cap Anamur, 1988).

64. Neudeck, discussion.

65. Uta Ranke-Heinemann, email to author, 12/21/2006.

66. PdDB, 3104/291, Kurzprotokoll, 11/14/79; "Überfluggenehmigung verurteilt," *FAZ*, 12/1/79; Peter Sabinski, "Im Waisenhaus sang ein Kind ein Lied vom Tod des Vaters," *Westdeutsche Allgemeine*, 1/25/80. On similar complaints about "dark tourism," see Taithe, "Cradle," 357.

67. PA AA, MfAA C6718, Vermerk, 11/15/79.

68. Peter Scholl-Latour, *Der Tod im Reisfeld: Dreißig Jahre Krieg in Indochina* (Stuttgart: Deutsche Verlags-Anstalt, 1980).

69. Scholl-Latour, *Tod*, 283–295, 307–313; "Es geht um das Überleben," *Saarbrücker Zeitung*, 8/3/79; "Dîner mit vier Gängen und Whisky im Urwald," *RM*, 3/14/80; "Palästinenserproblem auch im Fernen Osten?" *Allgemeine Zeitung* (Mainz), 3/19/80; "Der Stellvertreter-Krieg in Kambodscha," *Bunte*, 3/27/80.

70. Ranke-Heinemann, "Asche"; DRA Potsdam, DOK 1338-101, "Telefoninterview," 12/20/79; Michael Sontheimer, *Kambodscha, Land der sanften Mörder* (Reinbek bei Hamburg: Rowohlt, 1990), 107.

71. The following is based on Rolf Dach, in discussion with the author, Berlin, Mar. 2007.

72. See Andrew I. Port, *Conflict and Stability in the German Democratic Republic* (New York: Cambridge University Press, 2007), 265–269.

73. On March 18, Honecker and Samrin signed a formal Treaty of Friendship and Cooperation during a state visit by Samrin to the GDR. See PA AA, MfAA DC/20/21692, DY/30/11413; "Gemeinsame Erklärung," *ND*, 3/22/80. On various forms of public and private aid, see PA AA, MfAA C6671, Protokoll, 8/2/79; PA AA, MfAA C6696; PA AA, MfAA DC/20-I/4/4499; "Regierungsabkommen mit der VR Kampuchea unterzeichnet," *ND*, 1/3/80; Christian Oesterheld, "East German Socialism and the Khmer Rouge Revolution: Insights from the GDR's Diplomatic Archive," paper presented at International Institute of Social and Economic Sciences, Vienna (2016), 567; Gottesman, *Cambodia*, 113, 146.

74. See the Oct. 1980 report in PA AA, MfAA DC/20-I/4/4723. Such tensions were not unusual; see Hong, *Cold War Germany*.

75. Sontheimer, *Kambodscha*, 157–159; Michael Sontheimer, in discussion with the author, Berlin, Mar. 2007.

76. Klaus-Dieter and Hannelore Pflaum, in discussion with the author, Berlin, Dec. 2007. For more on this approach, see Hubertus Büschel, *Hilfe zur Selbsthilfe: Deutsche Entwicklungsarbeit in Afrika, 1960–1975* (Frankfurt am Main: Campus, 2014).

77. On West Germans blaming aid recipients for failures to make progress, see Hong, *Cold War Germany*; Martin Wengeler, "Von der Hilfe für unterentwickelte Gebiete über den Neokolonialismus bis zur Entwicklungszusammenarbeit," in Stötzel and Wengeler, *Kontroverse Begriffe*, 693–694. On exports to the GDR, see Gottesman, *Cambodia*, 121, 153–154.

78. Sontheimer, *Kambodscha*, 162; Dach, discussion.

79. See the documents in PA AA, MfAA DC/20/4876, DY34/12207. There were exceptions. In the summer of 1980, Erich Mielke, the head of the Stasi, received word the Cambodians wanted to send a delegation to the GDR to learn how to build up their own state security service, along with twenty teenage orphans who would receive "long-term training" as spies. The East Germans rejected the request, for unspecified reasons. See PA AA, MfAA DO/1/11574. On aid levels, see Oesterheld, "Insights," 567.

80. Haubold, discussion.

81. Sontheimer, *Kambodscha*, 163–164.

4. NO ONE CAN SAY THEY DIDN'T KNOW

1. See Jamie Frederic Metzl, *Western Responses to Human Rights Abuses in Cambodia, 1975–80* (Basingstoke: Macmillan, 1996), 150–155, 178–180; Tim Szatkowski, "Von Sihanouk bis Pol Pot: Diplomatie und Menschenrechte in den Beziehungen der Bundesrepublik zu Kambodscha (1967–1979)," *VfZ* 1 (2013): 24–30; Suellen Ratliff, "UN Representation Disputes: A Case Study of Cambodia," *California Law Review* 87, no. 5 (1999): 1250–1259.

2. See the correspondence in PA AA, Zwischenarchiv 121.058, 121.059.

3. Gabriele Venzky, "Ein Volk zum Sterben verurteilt," *Zeit*, 10/12/79; Karl-Heinz Janßen, "Erst Völkermord, dann Hungersnot," *Zeit*, 9/28/79; "Hochbezahlte Prahlerei," *Spiegel*, 11/19/79; "Heuchler," *Unsere Zeit*, 10/27/79. Also see Rüdiger von Wechmar, *Akteur in der Loge: Weltläufige Erinnerungen* (Berlin: Siedler, 2000), 298–336. For similar criticism in the US and France, see Metzl, *Western Responses*, 178–179.

4. "Wahrer der Menschenrechte," *Spiegel*, 4/21/80; "Rechtmäßiger Einmarsch," *Spiegel*, 4/27/80.

5. See the correspondence in PA AA, Zwischenarchiv 121.058, 121.059; Horst Möller, Klaus Hildebrand, and Gregor Schöllgen, eds., *Akten zur Auswärtigen Politik der Bundesrepublik Deutschland 1979* (Munich: Oldenbourg, 2010), 1:227.

6. Peter Scholl-Latour, "Palästinenserproblem auch im Fernen Osten?" *Allgemeine Zeitung* (Mainz), 3/19/80; *FAZ*, 9/24/79.

7. See *SZ*, 9/24/79; "Ein Volk, zu schwach zum Weinen," *Spiegel*, 10/29/79; Janßen, "Völkermord."

8. Helmut Schmidt, in discussion with the author, Hamburg, Mar. 2007. Also see Kristina Spohr, *Global Chancellor: Helmut Schmidt and the Reshaping of the International Order* (Oxford: Oxford University Press, 2016).

9. Klaus von Dohnanyi, in discussion with the author, Hamburg, Mar. 2007. Also see Heinrich August Winkler, "Das Beste vom Westen," *Zeit*, 6/20/2013; Szatkowski, "Von Sihanouk bis Pol Pot," 33; Matthias Schulz and Thomas A. Schwartz, eds., *The Strained Alliance: U.S.-European Relations from Nixon to Carter* (Cambridge: Cambridge University Press, 2010), 279–352.

10. The final vote was 71–35, with 34 abstentions. See PA AA, Zwischenarchiv 121.058; Szatkowski, "Von Sihanouk bis Pol Pot," 25–29.

11. PA AA, Zwischenarchiv 121.058, Drahterlaß, 9/21/79.

12. See PA AA, Zwischenarchiv 128.034, "Gesprächselemente," 2/22/80; Möller, Hildebrand, and Schöllgen, *Akten*, 2:1316. Also see Mohammed Haflah Piei and Noor Aini Khalifa, "Die Wirtschaftsbeziehungen zwischen Europa und den ASEAN-Staaten," in *Europa und Asien-Pazifik*, ed. Hanns W. Maul et al. (Munich: de Gruyter, 1999), 93–102.

13. Möller, Hildebrand, and Schöllgen, *Akten*, 2:1538, 1597; Mechtild Leutner, ed., *Bundesrepublik Deutschland und China, 1949 bis 1995* (Berlin: de Gruyter, 1995), 139–146, 177–181, 209–216, 353–354.

14. PdDB, 3104/281, Stenographisches Protokoll, 11/7/79; Ernst-Jörg von Studnitz, in discussion with the author, Königswinter, Mar. 2007.

15. The same held true for Washington. See Samantha Power, *"A Problem from Hell": America and the Age of Genocide* (New York: Perennial, 2003), 142, 147. Quotes from Peter Grubbe, "Reich der Toten," *Stern*, 1/17/80; Möller, Hildebrand, and Schöllgen, *Akten*, 2:1310n10.

16. See the reports in PA AA, MfAA C4291; PA AA, MfAA C6711, Fischer to Honecker, 12/18/78; PA AA, MfAA C5543, Gespräch Honeckers mit Samrin, n.d. For the Waldheim quote, see Metzl, *Western Responses,* 162. On Florin, see Jeffrey Herf, *Undeclared Wars with Israel: East Germany and the West German Left, 1967–1989* (New York: Cambridge University Press, 2016).

17. PA AA, MfAA C6718, "BRD—Kampuchea," 1/24/79.

18. PA AA, Zwischenarchiv 128.034, letter, 6/18/80.

19. "'Pol-Pot-Regime ächten,'" *FR,* 7/5/80. Diplomat Hans-Dieter Siemes, who later served as ambassador to Thailand, claimed that Hans-Alfred Steger, head of the Foreign Office's Southeast Asia department at the time, opposed recognition of the Khmer Rouge. In a tense telephone conversation, Steger refused to comment on this, but wanted to know why an American was investigating German responses to Cambodia given what the United States had done in Vietnam and Cambodia. Hans-Dieter Siemes and Hans-Alfred Steger, in discussions with the author, Mar. 2007. Before the ouster of the Khmer Rouge, Steger was a lone voice in the Foreign Office calling for a tougher stance on human rights violations in Cambodia; see Szatkowski, "Von Sihanouk bis Pol Pot," 21.

20. See PA AA, Zwischenarchiv 128.034; on the 1980 vote, see Metzl, *Western Responses,* 156–180.

21. "Fehler gemacht," *Spiegel,* 10/20/80; Studnitz, discussion.

22. Studnitz, discussion.

23. For Kohl's statements, see DB-P/SB, 4. Sitz., 10. Wahlperiode (5/4/83), 72; DB-P/SB, 4. Sitz., 11. Wahlperiode (3/18/87), 71. For Hupka's queries, see, for example, DB-P/SB, 47. Sitz., 10. Wahlperiode (1/19/84), 3438.

24. Herbert Hupka, *Unruhiges Gewissen: Ein deutscher Lebenslauf: Erinnerungen* (Munich: Langen Müller, 1994).

25. Horst Szeponik, "Das Lächeln von Phnom Penh," *Wochenpost,* 1/31/86; Horst Szeponik, *Ho Chi Minh: Ein Leben für Vietnam* (Berlin: Neues Leben, 1981).

26. For the most recent study, see Gerrit Dworok, *"Historikerstreit" und Nationswerdung: Ursprünge und Deutung eines bundesrepublikanischen Konflikts* (Cologne: Böhlau, 2015). Also see Ernst Nolte, "Vergangenheit, die nicht vergehen will: Eine Rede, die geschrieben, aber nicht mehr gehalten werden konnte," *FAZ,* 6/6/86.

27. Ernst Nolte, "Between Historical Legend and Revisionism? The Third Reich in the Perspective of 1980," in *Forever in the Shadow of Hitler? Original Documents of the Historikerstreit,* trans. James Knowlton and Truett Cates (Atlantic Highlands, NJ: Humanities Press, 1993), 1–15.

28. The reference to "'Asiatic' deeds" played to the Western idea that totalitarianism was "nothing other than traditional Oriental despotism plus modern police technology." See Ernst Nolte, "The Past That Will Not Pass," in *Forever in the Shadow,* 21–22; Nolte, "Historical Legend," 5; John Kuo Wei Tchen and Dylan Yeats, eds., *Yellow Peril! An Archive of Anti-Asian Fear* (London: Verso, 2014), 294.

29. The Cambodian genocide played "no role whatsoever," he later claimed, but did "confirm my theses." Ernst Nolte, in discussion with the author, Berlin, June 2008.

30. Kusserow, a Social Democrat who was born in Berlin in 1939 and worked many years for the Arab Service of *Deutsche Welle,* did add this: "We Germans must always remember that Hitler embodied the most horrible and most consequential combination of insane mission and claim to power." See Mourad Kusserow, "Furcht vor Rückkehr der 'Roten Khmer,'" *Tagesspiegel,* 8/24/89.

31. Quote from Wulf Kansteiner, *In Pursuit of German Memory: History, Television, and Politics after Auschwitz* (Athens: Ohio University Press, 2006), 250. Also see Nicolas Berg, *The Holocaust and the West German Historians: Historical Interpretation and Autobiographical Memory,* trans. Joel Golb (Madison: University of Wisconsin Press, 2015); Hans-Christian Jasch and Stephan Lehnstaedt, eds., *Verfolgen und Aufklären: Die erste Generation der Holocaustforschung* (Berlin: Metropol, 2019).

32. See Jeffrey K. Olick, *The Sins of the Fathers: Germany, Memory, Method* (Chicago: University of Chicago Press, 2016), 358–366.

33. Kansteiner, *In Pursuit,* 248–263 (quotes on 251–253, 260).

34. See Evan Gottesman, *Cambodia after the Khmer Rouge* (New Haven, CT: Yale University Press, 2002).

35. Quotes from Emil Bölte, "Ein Lob für die Chinesen," *GA,* 8/3/89; Erhard Haubold, "Prinz Sihanouk noch einmal Präsident," *FAZ,* 6/23/82; Wolfgang von Erffa, "Mönche werden wieder umworben," *Welt,* 8/4/89; Erhard Haubold, "Seine königliche Hoheit auf diplomatischer Werbereise," *FAZ,* 7/1/82; "DDR unterstützt Forderung der Volksrepublik Kampuchea," *ND,* 10/27/82; Christel Pilz, "Die Roten Khmer sind hoffähig," *RM,* 1/22/82; Christel Pilz, "Rote Khmer sagen Hanoi: 'Wir sind unschlagbar,'" *Welt,* 5/4/82; Lothar Rühl, "Am Völkermord der Roten Khmer scheitert die Kambodscha-Konferenz," *Welt,* 9/6/89.

36. See, for example, Matthias Naß, "Vormarsch der Roten Khmer," *Zeit,* 7/20/90.

37. Saskia Richter, *Die Aktivistin: Das Leben der Petra Kelly* (Munich: Deutsche Verlags-Anstalt, 2010), 287; Sara Parkin, *The Life and Death of Petra Kelly* (London: Pandora, 1994), 204.

38. See the biographies by Parkin, *Life* (quotes on 146–147); Richter, *Aktivistin.* Also see Stephen Milder, "Thinking Globally, Acting (Trans-)Locally: Petra Kelly and the Transnational Roots of West German Green Politics," *CEH* 43, no. 2 (2010): 301–326.

39. See the correspondence in AGG, A-Kelly 1436 and 2272; Frieder Wolf-Borchert, in discussion with the author, Cologne, Feb. 2007. On Wolf, see Richter, *Aktivistin,* 144, 165.

40. AGG, A-Kelly 1436, Kelly to Genscher, 1/6/89. Emphasis in original.

41. DB Drucksache 11/3962, Antwort auf die Kleine Anfrage, 2/8/89.

42. AGG, A-Kelly 2151, Sontheimer to Kelly, 3/19/89; Michael Sontheimer, "'Ich bin kein Mensch, ich bin ein Tier,'" *Zeit,* 12/23/88.

43. See AGG, A-Kelly 1437, Pressemitteilung, 9/4/89.

44. AGG, A-Kelly 1437, Pressemitteilungen, 10/20/89, 11/11/89; Richter, *Aktivistin,* 126–127, 310; Parkin, *Life,* 149.

45. AGG, A-Kelly 1437, Pressemitteilung, 11/11/89.

46. DB Drucksache 11/6095, Antwort auf die Kleine Anfrage, 12/13/89.

47. DB Drucksache 11/6251, Antrag, 1/17/90.

48. For quotations in this paragraph and the next, see AGG, A-Kelly 1438, Pressekonferenz, 1/23/90. Emphasis in original.

49. For the transcript of the discussion, as quoted in the following paragraphs, see DB-P/SB, 191. Sitz., 11. Wahlperiode (1/25/90), 14705–14710.

50. AGG, A-Kelly 1437 and 1438.

51. See the correspondence in AGG, A-Kelly 1439.

52. For the transcript of the second discussion, quoted in the following paragraphs, see DB-P/SB, 202. Sitz., 11. Wahlperiode (3/15/90), 15754–15759.

53. For Duve's biography, see Wolfgang Weirauch, "Mein Leben begann mit einer Lüge: Interview mit Freimut Duve," *Flensburger Hefte* 88 (2005): 66–95.

54. Years later, Hamm-Brücher claimed that the federal government had had little interest in Cambodia at the time of the genocide and that the Foreign Office, where she served as state secretary from 1976 to 1982, had been only "marginally" concerned. Hildegard Hamm-Brücher, telephone discussion with the author, Jan. 2007.

55. *Moralapostel* was a common invective conservatives hurled at Kelly and other leftists; see Richter, *Aktivistin*, 286. On confronting China on human rights issues, see Katrin Kinzelbach, *The EU's Human Rights Dialogue with China: Quiet Diplomacy and Its Limits* (London: Routledge, 2015).

56. DB Drucksache 11/7474, Beschlußempfehlung und Bericht, 6/21/90; DB-P/SB, 218. Sitz., 11. Wahlperiode (6/22/90), 17304, 17357–17358.

5. EVEN ANGELS LIVE PERILOUSLY

1. Claus Larass, "Der Tod eines Soldaten," *Bild*, 10/15/93. Emphasis in original.

2. Peter Dienemann, "Rätsel um den Mord an Arndt," *Welt*, 11/11/93.

3. Peter Dienemann, "Tödlicher Ausflug," *Focus*, 10/18/93; "Nach dem Mord in Phnom Penh," *FAZ*, 10/16/93.

4. Peer Meinert, "'Trotzdem: Es hat sich gelohnt,'" *Leipziger Volkszeitung*, 10/19/93. Also see Béatrice Pouligny, *Peace Operations from Below: UN Missions and Local People* (Bloomfield, CT: Kumarian, 2006); Stefanie Eisenhuth, "Leben mit der 'Schutzmacht': Die amerikanische Militärpräsenz in West-Berlin," *Deutschland Archiv*, 12/1/17, www.bpb .de/260613.

5. "Toter Soldat," *Bild*, 10/15/93; Rüdiger Moniac, "Abschied von Feldwebel Arndt," *Welt*, 10/23/93.

6. See Evan Gottesman, *Cambodia after the Khmer Rouge* (New Haven, CT: Yale University Press, 2002), 301–315; Benny Widyono, "United Nations Transitional Authority in Cambodia (UNTAC)," in *The Oxford Handbook of United Nations Peacekeeping Operations*, ed. Joachim Koops et al. (Oxford: Oxford University Press, 2015), 363–370; Petra Hazdra, *Die UNO-Friedensoperation in Kambodscha: Vorgeschichte, Konzept, Verlauf und kritische Evaluierung des internationalen Engagements* (Frankfurt am Main: Peter Lang, 1997).

7. Peter K. Fraps, "Unter dem Blauen Barett," in *Von Kambodscha bis Kosovo: Auslandseinsätze der Bundeswehr seit Ende des Kalten Krieges*, ed. Peter Goebel (Frankfurt am Main: Report, 2000), 73, 75–76, 85; dpa-Meldung, "Bundeswehr schickt weitere Sanitätssoldaten nach Kambodscha," 2/17/92; "Deutschland schickt Sanitäter nach Kambodscha," *FAZ*, 4/9/92; "Rühe verabschiedet deutsche Blauhelme," *SZ*, 5/12/92.

8. See dpa-Meldung, "Bonn schickt Sanitätssoldaten und BSG-Beamte nach Kambodscha," 4/8/92; Bundesministerium des Innern, Ansprache (Lintner), 8/12/93.

9. See Bundesminister der Verteidigung Informations- und Pressestab, Mitteilung, 4/29/92; Stephan-Andreas Casdorff, "Soldaten, die Geschichte schreiben sollen," *SZ*, 6/1/92; "300 Menschen in Kambodscha von Deutschen operiert," *FAZ*, 9/28/93; Fraps, "Unter dem Blauen Barett," 73.

10. "Bonn schickt Sanitätssoldaten" (dpa-Meldung); Casdorff, "Soldaten." On public support (or the lack thereof), see Elisabeth Noelle-Neumann and Renate Köcher, eds., *Allensbacher Jahrbuch der Demoskopie, 1984–1992* (Munich: Sauer, 1993), 567. More generally, see Patrick Merziger, "Out of Area: Humanitäre Hilfe der Bundeswehr im Ausland (1959–1991)," *Zeithistorische Forschungen* 15, no. 1 (2018): 40–67.

11. Casdorff, "Soldaten"; Michael J. Inacker, "Statt Soldaten zu besuchen, speisten die Diplomaten im klimatisierten Restaurant," *Welt am Sonntag*, 6/7/92; "Rühe verabschiedet"

(*SZ*); Fraps, "Unter dem Blauen Barett," 80. "Thrill-seeking society" was likely a reference to a popular, recently published book: Gerhard Schulze, *Die Erlebnisgesellschaft: Kultursoziologie der Gegenwart* (Frankfurt am Main: Campus, 1992).

12. Helga Betram, "Haus der Engel," *DAS*, 12/25/92; Peter Dienemann, "Ein Kambodschaner kehrt zurück," *Welt*, 1/4/92; Claudia Decker, "'Ich hoffte nur, daß der Flug endlos weitergeht,'" *Tagesspiegel*, 3/26/93.

13. Betram, "Haus der Engel."

14. Betram, "Haus der Engel"; "Rühe verabschiedet" (*SZ*).

15. Martin Winter, "Die Kinder wühlen im Müll der Soldaten," *FR*, 6/1/92; Matthias Naß, "Praktikum am Mekong," *Zeit*, 8/28/92; Peter Bardehle, "Fernab von Bonner Eiertänzen," *DAS*, 10/2/92.

16. Fraps, "Unter dem Blauen Barett," 84–85; Naß, "Praktikum am Mekong."

17. "Sanitäter enttäuscht," *Spiegel*, 5/11/92; "Mehr Geld für die deutschen Blauhelme," *Welt*, 7/25/92; Casdorff, "Soldaten"; Rüdiger Moniac, "Leichtere Uniform—und dazu ein Orden?" *Welt*, 6/1/92; Winter, "Kinder wühlen."

18. See "Möglichst unauffällig," *Spiegel*, 6/1/92; Casdorff, "Soldaten"; Naß, "Praktikum am Mekong."

19. Naß, "Praktikum am Mekong."

20. "Möglichst unauffällig" (*Spiegel*). For context, see Gregor Schöllgen, *Angst vor der Macht: Die Deutschen und ihre Aussenpolitik* (Berlin: Ullstein, 1993).

21. Naß, "Praktikum am Mekong"; Moniac, "Leichtere Uniform."

22. Quotes from "Möglichst unauffällig" (*Spiegel*); Naß, "Praktikum am Mekong"; "Premiere in Kambodscha," *Stern*, 6/6/92; Arne Lorenz, "Sonderrolle auf Uno-Kosten," *RM*, 8/7/92. On the costs of the mission, see DB Drucksache 12/6055, reponses to Schriftliche Fragen #26–27, 10/29/93; DB Drucksache 12/7737, Bericht, 5/30/94; Fraps, "Unter dem Blauen Barett," 75.

23. For criticism of the costs, see Mainhardt Graf Nayhauß, "Germans to the Front—ganz schön teuer," *Bild*, 6/2/92.

24. The relevant constitutional passages were Art. 24, which governed collective security arrangements; Art. 25, which affirmed the primacy of international law; and Art. 87a, which dealt with the strength and duties of the armed forces.

25. Quotes from "Bonn schickt Sanitätssoldaten" (dpa-Meldung); "Verschlimmbesserung," *FAZ*, 6/2/92; also see Thomas W. Maulucci, "Die Regierung Schmidt und die Frage der Out-of-Area-Einsätze der Bundeswehr, 1974–1982," in *Deutschland und die USA in der Internationalen Geschichte des 20. Jahrhunderts: Festschrift für Detlef Junker*, ed. Manfred Berg and Philipp Gassert (Stuttgart: Franz Steiner, 2004), 521–541; William Glenn Gray, "Germans from Venus? The Out-of-Area Problems in U.S.-German Relations," in *Safeguarding German-American Relations in the New Century*, ed. Hermann Kurthen, Antonio V. Menéndez-Alarcón, and Stefan Immerfall (Lanham, MD: Lexington, 2006), 61–75.

26. See SPD-Bundestagsfraktion, "Kolbow: UNO-Blauhelmeinsätze nur nach Grundgesetzänderung," 6/4/92; "Besorgnis über Bundeswehr-Einsatz," *FAZ*, 3/19/92; "In der Grauzone," *SZ*, 4/11/92; A. Wasserman, "'Bundeswehr darf nicht für die UNO kämpfen,'" *Hamburger Morgenpost*, 6/6/92; DB-P/SB, 99. Sitz., 12. Wahlperiode (6/25/92), 8383; Franz Schmedt, "Hoyer: Dringend Grundgesetz ändern," *Neue Osnabrücker Zeitung*, 5/23/92. On the evolution of SPD/FDP policies on this issue, see Kerry Longhurst, *Germany and the Use of Force* (Manchester: Manchester University Press, 2004), 62. For an overview of this debate, see Ronald D. Asmus, *Germany's Contribution to Peacekeeping: Issues and Outlook* (Santa Monica, CA: RAND, 1995).

27. For public statements by the major parties, see *Neue Zeit,* 4 / 2 / 92; also see Karin Johnston, "German Public Opinion and the Crisis in Bosnia," in *International Public Opinion and the Bosnia Crisis,* ed. Richard Sobel and Eric Shiraev (Lanham, MD: Lexington, 2003), 270–271.

28. See DB Drucksache 12 / 2711, "Antwort der Bundesregierung," 6 / 1 / 92; Presseservice der SPD, Mitteilung, 5 / 8 / 92. The SPD was divided over the issue, and that became even clearer during the war in Bosnia. See Marie-Janine Calic, "German Perspectives," in *International Perspectives on the Yugoslav Conflict,* ed. Alex Danchev and Thomas Halverson (London: Palgrave Macmillan, 1996), 64–65.

29. "Von Oliv zu Blau," *FR,* 5 / 5 / 92; Günther Nolting, "'Eine unmißverständliche Klarstellung ist geboten,'" *Neue Zeit,* 4 / 2 / 92.

30. Bernd Wilz, "'Verweigerungshaltung schadet dem Ansehen Deutschlands,'" *Neue Zeit,* 4 / 2 / 92; "Wir dürfen nicht zurückzucken, wenn es ernst wird," *Dresdner Morgenpost,* 6 / 13 / 92; "Rühe: In Kambodscha Signal für UNO-Einsätze," *SZ,* 6 / 1 / 92; DB-P / SB, 120. Sitz., 12. Wahlperiode (11 / 12 / 92), 10194.

31. Otto Graf Lambsdorff, "Bei UNO-Militäraktionen die Bundeswehr einsetzen," *Passauer Neue Presse,* 6 / 26 / 92; "'Nicht zucken, wenn es ernst wird,'" *Stern,* 5 / 21 / 92; DB-P / SB, 101. Sitz., 12. Wahlperiode (7 / 22 / 92), 8639. On complaints about paying instead of playing, see Andrew I. Port, "'To Deploy or Not to Deploy': The Erratic Evolution of German Foreign Policy since Unification," in *United Germany: Debating Processes and Prospects,* ed. Konrad H. Jarausch (New York: Berghahn, 2013), 267–277.

32. See DB Drucksache 12 / 4755, "Entschließungsantrag," 4 / 20 / 93.

33. DB-P / SB, 98. Sitz., 12. Wahlperiode (6 / 24 / 92), 8156.

34. "SZ-Interview mit dem Verteidigungsminister: Rühe will deutsche Blauhelme," *SZ,* 5 / 8 / 92; Martin Wengeler, "Vom Wehrbeitrag bis zu Friedensmissionen," in *Kontroverse Begriffe: Geschichte des öffentlichen Sprachgebrauchs in der Bundesrepublik Deutschland,* ed. Georg Stötzel and Martin Wengeler (Berlin: Walter de Gruyter, 1995), 158. For an overview of these issues and on public opinion, see Johnston, "German Public Opinion," 255–259, 261–263, 269–270, 272; Elisabeth Noelle-Neumann and Renate Köcher, eds., *Allensbacher Jahrbuch der Demoskopie, 1993–1997* (Munich: Sauer, 1997), 1085.

35. This was part of a statement that appeared in major German newspapers on April 8, 1992. Also see "Rühes weiche Linie," *FAZ,* 5 / 12 / 92; "Rühe: Auch deutsche Soldaten könnten sterben," *Bild am Sonntag,* 6 / 21 / 92.

36. Hans-Helmut Kohl, "Die Lernschleifen," *FR,* 6 / 16 / 93; Winter, "Kinder wühlen."

37. "Rühe: In Kambodscha Signal" (*SZ*); Winter, "Kinder wühlen"; Michael Spreng et al., "Rühe: Auch deutsche Soldaten könnten sterben," *Bild am Sonntag,* 6 / 21 / 92; DB-P / SB, 101. Sitz., 12. Wahlperiode (7 / 22 / 92), 8639; "Wird SPD-Klage erweitert," *FR,* 9 / 1 / 92.

38. "Deutscher UN-Soldat erschossen," *Bild,* 10 / 15 / 93; Christian Stang, "Tod eines Helfers," *Freie Presse* (Chemnitz), 10 / 20 / 93; "Tragischer Tod," *FR,* 10 / 15 / 93; Meinert, "'Trotzdem.'" Also see "Wolfgang Lerke zum 3. Oktober," in *Kambodschanische Allgemeine Zeitung,* 10 / 1 / 13.

39. Moniac, "Abschied"; Stefan Dietrich, "Den Sinn im Leben suchen," *FAZ,* 10 / 23 / 93.

40. See Astrid Wirtz, "CDU-Politiker Pinger fürchtet Fehlschlag," *Kölner Stadt-Anzeiger,* 9 / 3 / 92.

41. Bundesministerium des Innern, Ansprache (Linter), 8 / 12 / 93.

42. "Bonn entsendet wieder Botschafter nach Kambodscha," *FAZ,* 12 / 30 / 93.

43. John Lewis Gaddis, *The Cold War: A New History* (New York: Penguin, 2005), 266. Emphasis in original.

44. See Karen E. Smith, *Genocide and the Europeans* (Cambridge: Cambridge University Press, 2010), 88–99; Jamie Frederic Metzl, *Western Responses to Human Rights Abuses in Cambodia, 1975–80* (Basingstoke: Macmillan, 1996); Samantha Power, *"A Problem from Hell": America and the Age of Genocide* (New York: Perennial, 2003), 87–154.

45. Power, *"Problem from Hell,"* 90, 113.

46. See the documents in PA AA, Zwischenarchiv 105.097; Power, *"Problem from Hell,"* 109, 120.

47. DB-P / SB, 73. Sitz., 8. Wahlperiode (2 / 17 / 78), 5803–5804.

48. See, e.g., Michael März, *Linker Protest nach dem Deutschen Herbst: Eine Geschichte des linken Spektrums im Schatten des "starken Staates," 1977–1979* (Bielefeld: Transcript, 2012).

49. On the reasons for European inaction, see Smith, *Genocide*, 91–92, 171.

50. In the 1960s, a popular set of ideas known as "convergence theory" posited that modern industrial societies like East and West Germany were facing similar challenges and, as a result, becoming more and more alike. For an overview of this critical response to "totalitarian theory," see Gabriele Metzler, *Konzeptionen politischen Handelns von Adenauer bis Brandt: Politische Planung in der pluralistischen Gesellschaft* (Paderborn: Schöningh, 2005), 225–231.

6. IT IS GENOCIDE AND MUST BE DESIGNATED AS SUCH

1. Marie-Janine Calic, *Krieg und Frieden in Bosnien-Hercegovina* (Frankfurt am Main: Suhrkamp, 2012), 53. More generally, see Marie-Janine Calic, *A History of Yugoslavia,* trans. Dona Geyer (West Lafayette, IN: Purdue University Press, 2019); John R. Lampe, *Yugoslavia as History: Twice There Was a Country,* 2nd ed. (Cambridge: Cambridge University Press, 2003); Holm Sundhaussen, *Jugoslawien und seine Nachfolgestaaten, 1943–2011* (Vienna: Böhlau, 2012).

2. Michael Thumann, in discussion with the author, Berlin, Dec. 2021. For an overview, see Josip Glaurdić, *The Hour of Europe: Western Powers and the Breakup of Yugoslavia* (New Haven, CT: Yale University Press, 2011).

3. "In Bosnien-Hercegovina droht Krieg. Serben gegen Volksabstimmung," *FAZ*, 1 / 26 / 92; Harry Schleicher, "Prüfstein für Frieden," *FR*, 1 / 27 / 92; Walter Mayr, "In den Köpfen ist Krieg," *Spiegel*, 1 / 20 / 92; Peter Sartorius, "Ein Canyon im Visier des Todes," *SZ*, 2 / 7 / 92.

4. Carl Gustaf Ströhm, "Verloren, geschossen," *Welt*, 3 / 3 / 92; Roland Hofwiler, "Straßenblockaden gegen die Unabhängigkeit," *taz*, 3 / 3 / 92; Viktor Meier, "Nach blutigen Auseinandersetzungen," *FAZ*, 3 / 4 / 92.

5. "Moslem-Milizen in Stellung," *Welt*, 3 / 5 / 92; "Bosnische Tragödie," *FR*, 4 / 7 / 92. Also see Karin Johnston, "German Public Opinion and the Crisis in Bosnia," in *International Public Opinion and the Bosnia Crisis,* ed. Richard Sobel and Eric Shiraev (Lanham, MD: Lexington, 2003), 260.

6. BPA-Bulletin 040-92, Erklärung zu Jugoslawien, 4 / 9 / 92.

7. Viktor Meier, "Mehrere hundert Tote," *FAZ*, 4 / 6 / 92; Carl Gustaf Ströhm, "Von den Höhen Sarajevo im Visier," *Welt*, 4 / 10 / 92.

8. Ute Scheub and Bascha Mika, "'Die Drina ist voll von Blut und Leichen,'" *taz*, 6 / 6 / 92. Also see Edina Becirevic, *Genocide on the Drina River* (New Haven, CT: Yale University Press, 2014), 86–95, 124–131.

9. Helga Hirsch, "Siegesparade der Überlegenen," *Zeit*, 12 / 11 / 92.

10. Matthias Drobinski, "Verbrechen, die niemand sühnt," *Zeit*, 9 / 25 / 92. Also see Lora Wildenthal, "Imagining Threatened Peoples: The Society for Threatened Peoples (*Gesellschaft*

für bedrohte Völker) in 1970s West Germany," in *Imagining Human Rights*, ed. Susanne Kaul and David Kim (Berlin: de Gruyter, 2015), 101–118.

11. BPA AA-PM DLF, Interview, 9/17/92; "Unter Schlacke und Geröll begraben," *Spiegel*, 10/30/95.

12. Christel Vollmer, "'Helft uns! Schickt endlich Soldaten!'" *Bild am Sonntag*, 7/12/92.

13. "Hilfe für Hinterbliebene," *FR*, 9/7/92. Also see Simone Richter, *Journalisten zwischen den Fronten: Kriegsberichterstattung am Beispiel Jugoslawien* (Opladen: Westdeutscher Verlag, 1999), 127–131.

14. DB-P/SB, 128. Sitz., 12. Wahlperiode (12/10/92), 11109.

15. Stefan Schwarz, in discussion with the author, Bonn, Apr. 2022. See the speech at https://www.youtube.com/watch?v=qU9ulTMzFPg&t=44s.

16. Private archive of Stefan Schwarz (Bonn), fax, 1/8/93; Schwarz, discussion. Also see "Folgen einer Rede," *FAZ*, 12/11/92.

17. Schwarz, discussion.

18. Schwarz, discussion.

19. DB-P/SB, 151. Sitz., 12. Wahlperiode (4/21/93), 12971. For a critical take on Schwarz, see Boris Gröndahl, "Ein Lichtblick gegen die Politikverdrossenheit: Stefan Schwarz, der kirchentagskompatibel Stahlhelmer," in *Serbien muß sterbien: Wahrheit und Lüge im jugoslawischen Bürgerkrieg*, ed. Klaus Bittermann (Berlin: Edition Tiamat, 1994), 173–177.

20. BPA-Bulletin 132-92, "Weltweite Zusammenarbeit," 12/8/92.

21. "'Der dümmste aller Kriege,'" *Spiegel*, 7/6/92. Also see Peter Sartorius, "Leiden unter feuerspeienden Bergen," *SZ*, 7/24/92.

22. "'Ich war Söldner, bezahlt von den Serben,'" *GA*, 9/24/92.

23. "Unterhalten Serben Vernichtungslager?" *Welt*, 8/6/92; Roy Gutman, *A Witness to Genocide* (New York: Macmillan, 1993), esp. 36–63, published in Germany as *Augenzeuge des Völkermords: Reportagen aus Bosnien*, trans. Siegfried Kohlhammer (Göttingen: Steidl, 1994). For other quotes, see Viktor Meier, "Eine militärische Intervention scheint unvermeidbar," *FAZ*, 6/29/92; "Bilder des Grauens," *FAZ*, 8/8/92; Tilman Zülch, "Genozid in Bosnien," in *"Ethnische Säuberung"—Völkermord für "Großserbien,"* ed. Zülch (Hamburg: Luchterhand, 1993), 65; Schwarz, discussion.

24. Thomas Schmid, "Rettungsanker für wenige Auserwählte," *taz*, 8/10/92. For claims that these reports were "one-sided" and based on "hearsay," see Thomas Fleiner, "Minderheiten und Nationalismus: Die Mitschuld der Medien im Jugoslawienkrieg," in Bittermann, *Serbien muß sterbien*, 61.

25. See Roland Hofwiler, "Kein Bleiberecht für Lageropfer," *taz*, 10/10/92; Renate Flottau, "'Dort kam keiner lebend heraus,'" *Spiegel*, 10/12/92.

26. "'Sie verhungern wie Vieh,'" *Spiegel*, 8/10/92; "Unterhalten Serben Vernichtungslager?" (*Welt*). Also see Gutman, *Witness*, xi.

27. See BPA AA-PM DLF, "Interview," 9/17/92; BPA-PK 92-123, Pressekonferenz Nr. 123/92, 11/12/92; "'Du bist blind geworden vor Macht,'" *Spiegel*, 6/8/92. On ethnic cleansing, see Norman N. Naimark, *Fires of Hatred: Ethnic Cleansing in Twentieth-Century Europe* (Cambridge, MA: Harvard University Press, 2001); Philipp Ther, *Die dunkle Seite der Nationalstaaten: "Ethnische Säuberungen" im modernen Europa* (Göttingen: Vandenhoeck & Ruprecht, 2011); Norman Cigar, *Genocide in Bosnia: The Policy of "Ethnic Cleansing"* (College Station: Texas A&M Press, 1995); Paul Mojzes, *Balkan Genocides: Holocaust and Ethnic Cleansing in the Twentieth Century* (Lanham, MD: Rowman & Littlefield, 2011); Andrew Bell-Fialkoff, *Ethnic Cleansing* (London: Macmillan, 1996); Marie-Janine Calic, "Ethnic

Cleansing and War Crimes, 1991–1995," in *Confronting the Yugoslav Controversies: A Scholars' Initiative,* ed. Charles Ingrao and Thomas A. Emmert (West Lafayette, IN: Purdue University Press, 2013), 115–153. On German support for the creation of an international tribunal, see Richard Holbrooke, *To End a War* (New York: Random House, 1998), 190.

28. Walter Mayr, "Frontstadt für die Ewigkeit," *Spiegel,* 2/7/93.

29. BPA AA-PM, Eingangserklärung, 8/26/92.

30. Gerd Prokot, "Faustpfänder," *ND,* 6/12/93; Bittermann, *Serbien muß sterbien.*

31. Michael Thumann, "Der faule Frieden der Kriegsparteien," *Zeit,* 10/16/92; Johannes Vollmer, "'Die noch lebten, erschoß Dragan,'" *taz,* 9/28/92. On the Handke controversy, see Thomas Deichmann, *Noch einmal für Jugoslawien: Peter Handke* (Frankfurt/Main: Suhrkamp, 1999); Kurt Gritsch, *Peter Handke und "Gerechtigkeit für Serbien"* (Innsbruck: StudienVerlag, 2009). Also see Volker Berghahn, Gregory Flynn, and Paul Michale Lützeler, "Germany and Europe: Finding an International Role," in *After Unity: Reconfiguring German Identities,* ed. Konrad H. Jarausch (Providence, RI: Berghahn, 1997), 188–197.

32. DB-P/SB, 128. Sitz., 12. Wahlperiode (12/10/92), 11107.

33. Alexandra Stiglmayer, in discussion with the author, Brussels, Dec. 2021; Alexandra Stiglmayer, "Der Krieg der Männer gegen die Frauen," *DAS,* 10/30/92. Also see Alexandra Stiglmayer, ed., *Mass Rape: The War against Women in Bosnia-Herzegovina,* trans. Marion Faber (Lincoln: University of Nebraska Press, 1994); Caroline Kennedy-Pipe and Penny Stanley, "Rape in War: Lessons of the Balkans Conflicts in the 1990s," *International Journal of Human Rights* 4, no. 3–4 (2007): 67–84.

34. Alexandra Stiglmayer, "Krieg gegen die Frauen," *Stern,* 11/26/92. For a critical response to her reports, see Martin Lettmayer, "Da wurde einfach geglaubt, ohne nachzufragen," in Bittermann, *Serbien muß Sterbien,* 37–49 (quote on 48).

35. See Cheryl Benard and Edit Schlaffer, "'Kleiner als ein Stück Dreck,'" *Spiegel,* 12/7/92; "Der Krieg gegen die Frauen von Bosnien," *taz,* 12/11/92.

36. Stiglmayer's report in the *Münchner Abendzeitung* appeared on Nov. 4. For transcripts of the *Mona Lisa* episode and the Bundestag hearing, see Maria von Welser, *Am Ende wünschst du dir nur noch den Tod: Die Massenvergewaltigungen im Krieg auf dem Balkan* (Munich: Knaur, 1993), 7, 65–145. The following section also draws on Maria von Welser, in discussion with the author, Hamburg, Dec. 2021.

37. Welser, *Am Ende,* 66–67, 76, 89.

38. Welser, discussion.

39. "Asyl für vergewaltigte Frauen gefordert," *taz,* 12/3/92.

40. Edgar Sebastian Hasse, "Mit menschlicher Nähe gegen das blanke Entsetzen," *DAS,* 12/18/92.

41. Welser, *Am Ende,* 118. On the "global television age," see Frank Bösch, *Mass Media and Historical Change: Germany in International Perspective, 1400 to the Present,* trans. Freya Buechter (New York: Berghahn, 2015), 155–166.

42. Welser, *Am Ende,* 167–171; Erica Fischer, "Geld allein ist für Hilfe zu wenig," *taz,* 12/17/92; Karin Flothmann, "Frauenkongreß in Zagreb umstritten" and "Wenn es Schwestern zu gut meinen," *taz,* 1/25/93; Karin Flothmann, "'Internationale Frauen-Solidarität,'" *taz,* 1/29/93; Lea Rosh, "Nun erst recht nach Zagreb," *taz,* 1/28/93.

43. A year later, the UN adopted a Declaration on the Elimination of Violence against Women, the first of its kind to explicitly address the topic and set forth guidelines for an international response. See Zülch, "Vorwort," in *"Ethnische Säuberung,"* 11; Rupert Neudeck, *Die Menschenretter von Cap Anamur* (Munich: Heyne, 2002), 296; Fischer, "Geld allein"; Eva Quistorp, in discussion with the author, Berlin, Apr. 2022. The European Parliament's

statement is reprinted in Eva Quistorp, ed., *Die bosnische Tragödie: Gewalt, Vertreibung, Völkermord* (Berlin: Traum und Raum, 1993). More generally, see Kelly Dawn Askin, *War Crimes against Women: Prosecution in International War Crimes Trials* (The Hague: M. Nijhoff, 1997), esp. 261–375.

44. BPA AA-PM, Pressekonferenz (Kinkel), 8/26/92. For similar statements by Kohl and Kinkel, see BPA-PK 92-086, Pressekonferenz Nr. 86/92, 8/10/92; BPA-Bulletin 101-92, "UNO Rede" (Kinkel), 9/25/92. In 2007, the International Court of Justice at The Hague determined that ethnic cleansing was not tantamount to genocide. See Hans-Peter Kriemann, *Hineingerutscht? Deutschland und der Kosovo-Krieg* (Göttingen: Vandenhoeck & Ruprecht, 2021), 121–122.

45. Kohl and Hans-Dietrich Genscher had earlier used the term to describe Iraqi treatment of the Kurds. See Karen E. Smith, *Genocide and the Europeans* (Cambridge: Cambridge University Press), 106, 116.

46. Samantha Power, *"A Problem from Hell": America and the Age of Genocide* (New York: Perennial, 2003), 289.

47. Freimut Duve, "Es ist Völkermord und muß auch so bezeichnet werden," *taz*, 7/13/92.

48. Duve, "Es ist Völkermord." Also see Freimut Duve, "Es ist Völkermord," *taz*, 3/11/93; "Es war Völkermord: Von Anfang an," *taz*, 12/24/94.

49. DB-P/SB, 113. Sitz., 12. Wahlperiode (10/15/92), 9635. For an equally impassioned case claiming "planned genocide," see Zülch, "Genozid," 67–69.

50. Freimut Duve, in discussion with the author, Hamburg, Mar. 2007.

51. DB Drucksache 12/4048, Antwort, 12/29/92; Drucksache 12/3071, Entschließungsantrag, 7/22/92; Carl Gustaf Ströhm, "'Serben vergewaltigen auf obersten Befehl,'" *Welt*, 10/1/92.

52. Joachim Geiger, "Die Täter stellen sich als Opfer dar," *DAS*, 3/5/93; Alexandra Stiglmayer, "The Rapes in Bosnia-Herzegovina," in Stiglmayer, *Mass Rape*, 151.

53. Quotes from Josef Joffe, "Balkan-Krieg, Teil Zwei," *SZ*, 4/22/92; Bascha Mika, "'Es ist ein extremer Männerkrieg,'" *taz*, 8/6/92; Ömer Erzeren, "Was wollt ihr Europäer eigentlich?" *taz*, 8/15/92; Ludger Volmer, "Weltinnenpolitik als Utopie, Pazifismus als Aufgabe," *taz*, 11/5/92; Pierre Simonitsch, "Schwierige Wahl zwischen Übeln," *FR*, 1/7/93; Josef Joffe, "Hilfe zur Selbsthilfe," *SZ*, 1/12/93; Herbert Kremp, "Kreide geschluckt," *Welt*, 1/21/93; Christoph Rabe, "Professionelle Kälte," *Handelsblatt*, 7/12/93; Viktor Meier, "Zusammengedrängt in Mittelbosnien," *FAZ*, 9/24/93; Pierre Simonitsch, "Gorazde, der Fall, die Not und die Demütigung," *FR*, 4/19/94; Till Briegleb, "Nachträgliche Legitimation eines Völkermordes," *taz*, 11/6/95; Freimut Duve, "Noch heißt 'Friede' Tod und Vertreibung für die Bosnier," *taz*, 12/24/94; "Weiter schlachten," *Spiegel*, 11/22/93.

54. "'Sie verhungern wie Vieh'" (*Spiegel*); "Unterhalten Serben Vernichtungslager?" (*Welt*); Walter Mayr, "'Ihr Stolz ist hart wie Stein,'" *Spiegel*, 11/16/92; Flottau, "'Dort kam keiner lebend heraus.'"

55. Herta Müller, "Die Tage werden weitergehen," *taz*, 9/8/92; "Sarajewo wieder unter heftigem Beschuß," *FR*, 7/9/92.

56. Helmut Lippelt and Claudia Roth, "Nie wieder Faschismus—nie wieder Krieg!," *taz*, 8/20/92; Jürgen Maier, "In Bosnien hilft Pazifismus nicht weiter," *taz*, 11/8/92; Volmer, "Weltinnenpolitik."

57. Peter Scholl-Latour, "Samariter in der Falle," *RM*, 10/30/92. Also see "'Du bist blind'" (*Spiegel*); "'Wo sind wir denn noch Menschen?'" *Spiegel*, 7/6/92; Walter Mayr, "'Das hier ist altes Ustascha-Land,'" *Spiegel*, 7/27/92. On Serb SS insignia, see "'Wir hacken ihnen die Hand ab,'" *Spiegel*, 10/5/92.

58. On the locution of Serb leaders, see Zülch, "Vorwort," 10; Christian Schwarz-Schilling, *Der verspielte Frieden in Bosnien: Europas Versagen auf dem Balkan* (Freiburg: Herder, 2020), 177. Green politician Eva Quistorp was also shocked by the "pitch" (*Tonlage*) of the statements by Serb leaders. Quistorp, discussion.

59. "Serben-Führer verhöhnt die Gefangenen," *Bild am Sonntag*, 8/9/92; Art Spiegelman, "Massenmord und Debatte?" *taz*, 11/27/92.

60. Cited in Thankmar von Münchhausen, "Den Kreis des Eisens," *FAZ*, 6/29/92.

61. BPA-Bulletin 101-92, UNO Rede (Kinkel), 9/25/92; Matthias Drobinski, "Verbrechen, die niemand sühnt," *Zeit*, 9/25/92; Erich Rathfelder, "Mit Schokolade kann man schlecht kämpfen," *taz*, 12/5/92. For the Goebbels quote, see "Stenographic Report of a Portion of the Interministerial Meeting at the Reich Aviation Ministry," *German History in Documents and Images*, German Historical Institute, https://ghdi.ghi-dc.org/docpage.cfm?docpage_id=2388. Few were as quick to draw direct Holocaust parallels as the head of the Society for Threatened Peoples; see Zülch, "Vorwort," 9–12; Zülch, "Genozid," 66, 70, 94–95.

62. Cheryl Benard and Edit Schlaffer, "Augenzeugen des Wahnsinns," *Spiegel*, 1/4/93.

63. Renate Flottau, "'Am Hals die Handgranate,'" *Spiegel*, 2/15/93.

64. Quote from Lothar Rühl, "Die Folterlager," *Welt*, 8/6/92.

65. DB-P/SB, 151. Sitz., 12. Wahlperiode (4/21/93), 12944.

66. DB-P/SB, 151. Sitz., 12. Wahlperiode (4/21/93), 12945.

67. DB-P/SB, 151. Sitz., 12. Wahlperiode (4/21/93), 12969–12971.

68. Duve, "Es ist Völkermord"; Peter Glotz, "Der Mannbarkeits-Test," *Spiegel*, 3/7/93; Peter Glotz, "Der Wahrheit eine Waffe," *Zeit*, 9/10/93. On Karadžić's "Goebbels-like language," see Johannes Vollmer, "'Schande über dieses Europa,'" in Zülch, *"Ethnische Säuberung,"* 35–36.

69. Freimut Duve, "Was heißt Völkermord," *SZ*, 5/25/94; Susanne Paas, "Entsetzen über die Verdrängungsleistung," *taz*, 3/8/93; also see Marieluise Beck, "Bosnien, nah bei Bremen," *taz*, 2/9/93.

70. Erich Rathfelder, "Ein neues Trauma der Geschichte," *taz*, 8/8/92. Also see Erich Rathfelder, *Sarajevo und danach: Sechs Jahre Reporter im ehemaligen Jugoslawien* (Munich: C. H. Beck, 1998).

71. Erich Rathfelder, in discussion with the author, Split (Croatia), Dec. 2021; Rathfelder, email to author, 12/30/2021. Also see Simone Richter, *Journalisten zwischen den Fronten: Kriegsberichterstattung am Beispiel Jugoslawien* (Opladen: Westdeutscher Verlag, 1999), 122–125, 250–264.

72. See CC Malzahn, "'Bitte keinen neuen Glaubenskrieg bei den Grünen!'" *taz*, 8/21/92; Bosiljka Schedlich, "Ein Stein darauf," *taz*, 1/30/95. Cohn-Bendit, a prominent leader of the student movement in Paris in 1968, was the son of German Jews who had fled to France in the 1930s. He came out in favor of outside military intervention in Bosnia long before Fischer did. See Daniel Cohn-Bendit, "Versager aller Länder, verteidigt Euch!" *taz*, 6/24/93; Daniel Cohn-Bendit, "Was haben wir getan!" *taz*, 4/20/94; Daniel Cohn-Bendit, "Bequemes und Unerträgliches," *taz*, 12/4/94; Joschka Fischer, *Die rot-grünen Jahre: Deutsche Außenpolitik—vom Kosovo bis zum 11. September* (Cologne: Kiepenheuer & Witsch, 2007), 211–212; Paul Berman, *Power and the Idealists* (Brooklyn, NY: Soft Skull, 2005), 14–16.

73. Hanns Heinrich Schumacher, the Foreign Office press secretary, similarly stated in a radio interview that he did "not wish to use" the term *KZ* so only spoke of "camps." See Susanne Paas, "'Und wenn die Muslime Juden wären?'" *taz*, 4/24/93; "Nicht wegschauen,'" *taz*, 7/21/93; "'Serbische Lager sind keine KZs,'" *taz*, 8/13/92; BPA AA-PM WDR, Interview, 11/12/92. Also see "Die Wiederkehr des Holocausts," in Cheryl Benard and Edit Schlaffer,

Vor unseren Augen: Der Krieg in Bosnien . . . und die Welt schaut weg (Munich: Wilhelm Heyne, 1993), 133–200. Many Jewish survivors in the United States called for outside intervention; see Power, *"Problem from Hell,"* 277.

74. Eberhard Brecht of the SPD referred to Sarajevo as "the largest concentration camp of all time." See DB-P / SB, 196. Sitz., 12. Wahlperiode (12 / 2 / 93), 17047; Carl Gustaf Ströhm, "Das KZ Sarajevo," *Welt*, 11 / 11 / 92. Also see Robert Leicht, "Sterben für Sarajevo: Contra," *Zeit*, 8 / 14 / 92.

75. Semler, "Kriegsflüchtlinge." For similar criticisms, see Klaus Bittermann, "Der Intellektuelle als Kriegshetzer," in Bittermann, *Serbien muß sterbien*, 198.

76. Egon Bahr, in discussion with the author, Berlin, Dec. 2007.

77. Berman, *Power and the Idealists*, 39. For direct references to the Holocaust elsewhere, see Power, *"Problem from Hell,"* 269–271, 276–277, 279, 282, 326 (quotes on 277, 279); Smith, *Genocide*, 111–214, 118, 125; David Owen, *Balkan Odyssey* (New York: Harcourt Brace, 1995), 15, 19.

78. Calic, "Ethnic Cleansing," 115.

79. See Georg Stötzel, "Der Nazi-Komplex," in *Kontroverse Begriffe*, ed. Georg Stötzel and Martin Wengeler (Berlin: Walter de Gruyter, 1995), 367–379.

80. Carl Gustaf Ströhm, "Endlich die Anerkennung," *Welt*, 8 / 8 / 92; "Bilder des Grauens," *FAZ*, 8 / 8 / 92.

81. See Peter Sartorius, "Ein Bypass ins Herz des verwundeten Landes," *SZ*, 7 / 18 / 92; Carl Gustaf Ströhm, "Dubrovnik: Von der 'Perle der Adria' zur Frontstadt," *Welt*, 12 / 22 / 92; Carl Gustaf Ströhm, "'Wer sich nicht taufen lassen will, muß sterben,'" *RM*, 8 / 13 / 93; Carl Gustaf Ströhm, "Das wohlfeile Mitleid," *Welt*, 12 / 2 / 92. Emphasis added.

82. See Anonyma, *Eine Frau in Berlin: Tagebuch-Aufzeichnungen vom 20. April bis 22. Juni 1945* (Frankfurt am Main: Eichborn, 2003); Miriam Gebhard, *Als die Soldaten kamen: Die Vergewaltigung deutscher Frauen am Ende des Zweiten Weltkriegs* (Munich: Deutsche Verlags-Anstalt, 2015).

83. See Ströhm, "Wohlfeile Mitleid."

84. Paas, "Entsetzen"; Birgit Ziegenhagen, "'Eine kaputte Tasse nimmt niemand mehr,'" *taz*, 8 / 6 / 92; Petra Schnitt, "'Menschenrechte sind Frauenrechte': Gespräch mit Helke Sander," *Stern*, 11 / 26 / 92; DB-P / SB, 128. Sitz., 12. Wahlperiode (12 / 10 / 92), 11110; Benard and Schlaffer, "'Kleiner.'"

85. See Günter Bannas, "500 Kriegsverbrecher namentlich bekannt," *FAZ*, 12 / 12 / 92.

86. Schnitt, "'Menschenrechte sind Frauenrechte.'"

87. Erich Wiedemann, "'Kein Teufel kann so schwarz sein,'" *Spiegel*, 5 / 25 / 92.

88. Margit V. Wunsch Gaarman, *The War in Our Backyard: The Bosnia and Kosovo Wars through the Lens of the German Print Media* (Berlin: Neofelis, 2015), 51; also see Calic, *Krieg und Frieden*, 9, 142–147.

89. Quotes from Roland Hofwiler, "Bosnien als neuer Krisenherd," *taz*, 1 / 11 / 92; Sartorius, "Canyon"; Wolfgang Koydl, "Fünf statt eins," *SZ*, 3 / 3 / 92; Christian Semler, "Die Fallstricke einer 'kantonalen Lösung,'" *taz*, 3 / 3 / 92; Power, *"Problem from Hell,"* 306.

90. Quotes from "'Du bist blind'" (*Spiegel*); Claus Leggewie, "Wir alle sind bosnische Muslime," *taz*, 8 / 10 / 92; Thomas Schmid, "Sarajevo im Fadenkreuz von Heckenschützen," *taz*, 7 / 20 / 92; Carl E. Buchhalla, "Profil: Radovan Karadžić," *SZ*, 6 / 22 / 92.

91. See Ivo Standeker and Ervin Hladnik, "Ivo Andic stürzte von der Brücke in die Drina," *taz*, 2 / 29 / 92; Sartorius, "Leiden"; Carl Gustaf Ströhm, "Ende in Sarajevo," *RM*, 3 / 6 / 92. For an in-depth analysis of Yugoslavia's recent history, see "'Der dümmste aller Kriege'" (Part 3), *Spiegel*, 7 / 20 / 92.

92. Klaus Kinkel, "Das Eis ist gebrochen," *Mainzer Allgemeine Zeitung*, 6/6/92; BPA, AA-PM, Rede (Kinkel), 6/19/92; Roman Arens, "Der Alptraum von Sarajewo," *FR*, 5/7/92.

93. See "'Der dümmste aller Kriege'" (*Spiegel*); Mayr, "In den Köpfen"; "Geister der Vergangenheit," *Spiegel*, 4/20/92; Gregor Gysi, email to author, 12/22/21.

94. See "'Der dümmste aller Kriege'" (Part 2), *Spiegel*, 7/7/92; Johann Georg Reißmüller, "Warum Bosnien leiden muß," *FAZ*, 5/29/92; Johann Georg Reißmüller, "Einst waren sie die Ersten im Land," *FAZ*, 8/19/92; Peter Nitsche, "Der jugoslawischen Tragödie dritter Akt," *Flensburger Tageblatt*, 5/21/92; Hirsch, "Siegesparade." Also see Wunsch Gaarman, *War*, 49, 59.

95. Quotes from Leggewie, "Wir alle"; Ströhm, "Endlich." The Bosnian government's failure to build up its military on the eve of war strongly suggests there were no plans to commit genocide against the Serbs. See Calic, "Ethnic Cleansing," 124. Also see George Lepre, *Himmler's Bosnia Division: The Waffen-SS Handschar Division, 1943–1945* (Atglen, PA: Schiffer, 1997).

7. OUR REVULSION AGAINST MILITARY FORCE IS UNDERSTANDABLE

1. DB-P/SB, 101. Sitz., 12. Wahlperiode (7/22/92), 8655; DB Drucksache 12/3073, Entschließungsantrag, 7/22/92.

2. BPA-PK 92-078a, Pressekonferenz Nr. 78 a/92, 7/23/92.

3. For the position of other Europeans and the Americans, see Karen Smith, *Genocide and the Europeans* (Cambridge: Cambridge University Press), 105–141; Brendan Simms, *Unfinest Hour: Britain and the Destruction of Bosnia* (London: Allen Lane, 2001); Samantha Power, *"A Problem from Hell": America and the Age of Genocide* (New York: Perennial, 2003), 247–327.

4. "Prüfungen—Ankündigungen—Drohungen," *FAZ*, 8/4/93. On early speculation in Germany about the possible use of military force, see BPA AA-PM, Rede (Kinkel), 7/2/92. For an overview of early international efforts, see Steven L. Burg and Paul S. Shoup, *The War in Bosnia-Herzegovina: Ethnic Conflict and International Intervention* (Armonk, NY: M. E. Sharpe, 1999), 189–316.

5. For a similar point, as well as an overview of the domestic debate, see Hans-Peter Kriemann, *Hineingerutscht? Deutschland und der Kosovo-Krieg* (Göttingen: Vandenhoeck & Ruprecht, 2021), 120–121, 139–154.

6. Pierre Simonitsch, "Der bosnische Knoten," *DAS*, 7/17/92; Pierre Simonitsch, "Schwierige Wahl zwischen Übeln," *FR*, 1/7/93; Peter Meyer-Ranke, "Sarajevo—eine Schande für die Welt," *Bild*, 6/9/92; Kurt Breme, "Schluß mit dem Palaver," *Bild am Sonntag*, 8/9/92.

7. DB-P/SB, 101. Sitz., 12. Wahlperiode (7/22/92), 8637; Jürgen Maier, "In Bosnien hilft Pazifismus nicht weiter," *taz*, 9/8/92. Emphasis added.

8. Klaus Hartung, "Wer will denn Bosnien retten?" *Zeit*, 8/21/92.

9. BPA-Bulletin 013-93, Rede (Kohl), 2/10/93; Helga Hirsch, "Die Opfer brauchen Schutz," *Zeit*, 1/22/93.

10. DB-P/SB, 151. Sitz., 12. Wahlperiode (4/21/93), 12944, 12954.

11. See the transcript of Kinkel's radio interview in BPA AA-PM, Interview, 4/10/93; other quotes from Helmut Lippelt and Claudia Roth, "Nie wieder Faschismus—nie wieder Krieg!" *taz*, 8/20/92; DB-P/SB, 101. Sitz., 12. Wahlperiode (7/22/92), 8614. On dangers

faced by aid workers, see Abby Stoddard, *Necessary Risks: Professional Humanitarianism and Violence against Aid Workers* (New York: Palgrave Macmillan, 2020).

12. Freimut Duve, in discussion with the author, Hamburg, Mar. 2007. Also see "Aufmarsch der Alliierten," *Stern*, 5/6/93; DB-P/SB, 176. Sitz., 12. Wahlperiode (9/23/93), 15278; "Militärschlag gegen Serbien," *Bild*, 8/11/92; Katrin Schreiter, "Revisiting Morale under the Bombs: The Gender of Affect in Darmstadt, 1942-1945," *CEH* 50, no. 3 (2017): 347–374.

13. Hartung, "Wer will denn Bosnien retten?"

14. DB Drucksache 12/5374, Unterrichtung, 7/6/93.

15. Theo Sommer, "Bomben gegen Gewissensbisse," *Zeit*, 8/13/93.

16. Hartung, "Wer will denn Bosnien retten?"

17. DB-P/SB, 101. Sitz., 12. Wahlperiode (7/22/92), 8627–8628, emphasis added; Carl Gustaf Ströhm, "Balkanische Legenden," *Welt*, 12/19/94.

18. BPA AA-PM DLF, Mitteilung 1019/93, 2/2/93.

19. Quotes from Michael Thumann, "Der faule Frieden der Kriegsparteien," *Zeit*, 10/16/92; Thomas Schmid, "Sarajevo im Fadenkreuz von Heckenschützen," *taz*, 7/20/92; DB-P/SB, 128. Sitz., 12. Wahlperiode (12/10/92), 11118–11119.

20. BPA-PK 93-067b, Pressekonferenz, 6/22/93; BPA-PK 92-078a, Pressekonferenz, 7/23/92; BPA-PK 92-086, Pressekonferenz, 8/10/92; BPA-PK 93-010a, Pressekonferenz, 1/26/93. Also see Christian Schwarz-Schilling, *Der verspielte Frieden in Bosnien: Europas Versagen auf dem Balkan* (Freiburg: Herder, 2020); Simms, *Unfinest Hour*.

21. Schwarz-Schilling had a lower-level American counterpart: George Kenney, the head of the Yugoslavia Desk at the State Department, who resigned in August 1992 to protest Washington's failure to "stop the genocide." See DB Drucksache 12/4080, Schriftliche Frage #7 (Jäger), 12/20/92; DB-P/SB, 196. Sitz., 12. Wahlperiode (12/2/93), 17052; DB-P/SB, 151. Sitz., 12. Wahlperiode (4/21/93), 12959; DB-P/SB, 155. Sitz., 12. Wahlperiode (4/29/93), 13236–13237; Schwarz-Schilling, *Frieden*, 51–55, 452–457; Power, *"Problem from Hell,"* 286.

22. Schwarz-Schilling, *Frieden*, 38, 403; William S. Walker, *German and Bosnian Voices in a Time of Crisis* (Indianapolis, IN: Dog Ear, 2010), 19–22.

23. Schwarz-Schilling, *Frieden*, 66, 234.

24. Carl Gustaf Ströhm, "Das Elend von Jajce," *Welt*, 11/2/92; Herbert Kremp, "Kreide geschluckt," *Welt*, 1/21/93. On Kremp's experiences as senior correspondent in Asia, see Herbert Kremp, *Die Bambusbrücke: Mein asiatisches Tagebuch* (Berlin: Ullstein, 1980).

25. Josef Joffe, "Hilfe zur Selbsthilfe," *SZ*, 1/12/93. Gerster is quoted in Johannes Vollmer, "'Schande über dieses Europa': Das Versagen des Westens," in *"Ethnische Säuberung"— Völkermord für "Großserbien,"* ed. Tilman Zülch (Hamburg: Luchterhand, 1993), 34. For similar debates in the United States, see Power, *"Problem from Hell,"* 261–262, 267–269, 282–287, 296–297.

26. See, for example, Wolf Biermann, "Kriegshetze Friedenshetze," *Zeit*, 2/1/91.

27. DB-P/SB, 101. Sitz., 12. Wahlperiode (7/22/92), 8638–8639, 8644. Emphasis added. These points had been made prior to the Balkans crisis; see Hans Kundnani, "The Concept of 'Normality' in German Foreign Policy since Unification," *German Politics and Society* 102, no. 2 (2012): 44.

28. DB-P/SB, 101. Sitz., 12. Wahlperiode (7/22/92), 8629, 8643. On Gansel, see Marie-Janine Calic, "German Perspectives," in *International Perspectives on the Yugoslav Conflict*, ed. Alex Danchev and Thomas Halverson (London: Palgrave Macmillan, 1996), 59; Walker, *German and Bosnian Voices*, 1–5.

29. DB-P/SB, 128. Sitz., 12. Wahlperiode (12/10/92), 11083, 11124.

30. Christoph Bertram, "Sterben für Sarajevo?" *Zeit*, 8/14/92.

31. Maier, "In Bosnien"; Lippelt and Roth, "Nie wieder Faschismus." Emphasis added.

32. The Greens were divided between so-called *fundis* (fundamentalists), who took a more unyielding position on issues like pacifism, and the *realos* (realists), who were took a more "pragmatic" approach. See the interview in CC Malzahn, "'Bitte keinen neuen Glaubenskrieg bei den Grünen!'" *taz*, 8 / 21 / 92; Paul Hockenos, *Joschka Fischer and the Making of the Berlin Republic: An Alternative History of Postwar Germany* (Oxford: Oxford University Press, 2008), 199–209, 232–236. Also see Kriemann, *Hineingerutscht?*, 119.

33. Former SPD mayor of Bremen Hans Koschnik, whose parents had been imprisoned in Nazi concentration camps, tried to accomplish just that as the city's EU administrator from July 1994 to April 1996. See DB-P / SB, 176. Sitz., 12. Wahlperiode (9 / 23 / 93), 15232; DB-P / SB, 219. Sitz., 12. Wahlperiode (4 / 14 / 94), 18924; BPA AA-PM, Rede (Kinkel), 7 / 23 / 94; Hans Koschnik, "Mostar: Der schmale Grat der Hoffnung," in *Entseeltes Land: Über Bosnien, Kulturzerstörung und unsere Zukunft* (Freiburg: Herder, 1995), 5–13.

34. BPA AA-PM DLF, Mitteilung, 8 / 10 / 92.

35. DB-P / SB, 101. Sitz., 12. Wahlperiode (7 / 22 / 92), 8645; DB-P / SB, 151. Sitz., 12. Wahlperiode (4 / 21 / 93), 12962; BPA-PK 92-136a, Pressekonferenz, 12 / 17 / 92.

36. DB-P / SB, 101. Sitz., 12. Wahlperiode (7 / 22 / 92), 8625, 8645, 8650; DB-P / SB, 151. Sitz., 12. Wahlperiode (4 / 21 / 93), 12928, 12939, 12947–12948. On the *Sonderweg* debate, see David Blackbourn and Geoff Eley, *The Peculiarities of German History: Bourgeois Society and Politics in Nineteenth-Century Germany* (Oxford: Oxford University Press, 1984), 1–35.

37. See DB-P / SB, 101. Sitz., 12. Wahlperiode (7 / 22 / 92), 8629, 8642. Also see Martin Wengeler, "Vom Wehrbeitrag bis zu Friedensmissionen: Zur Geschichte der sprachlichen Legitimierung und Bekämpfung von Rüstung und Militär," in *Kontroverse Begriffe*, ed. Georg Stötzel and Martin Wengeler (Berlin: Walter de Gruyter, 1995), 157.

38. DB-P / SB, 151. Sitz., 12. Wahlperiode (4 / 21 / 93), 12968–12970.

39. BPA AA-PM, Rede (Kinkel), 7 / 2 / 92; DB-P / SB, 151. Sitz., 12. Wahlperiode (4 / 21 / 93), 12928, 12934; DB-P / SB, 128. Sitz., 12. Wahlperiode (12 / 10 / 92), 11084; DB-P / SB, 101. Sitz., 12. Wahlperiode (7 / 22 / 92), 8638, 8642.

40. For UN Resolution 757, see United Nations Digital Library, https://digitallibrary .un.org/record/142881?ln=en.

41. BPA AA-PM, Interview, 5 / 29 / 92; Malzahn, "'Glaubenskrieg'"; Paul Berman, *Power and the Idealists* (Brooklyn, NY: Soft Skull, 2005), 1–3.

42. BPA AA-PM, Interview, 5 / 29 / 92.

43. See Ulf von Krause, *Die Bundeswehr als Instrument deutscher Außenpolitik* (Wiesbaden: Springer VS, 2013), 191.

44. "'Der dümmste aller Kriege,'" *Spiegel*, 7 / 6 / 92; DB Drucksache 12 / 5374, Unterrichtung, 7 / 6 / 93; BPA-PK, DokNr. 92-083, Pressekonferenz, 8 / 3 / 92.

45. BPA-PK, DokNr. 92-071d, Pressekonferenz, 7 / 10 / 92; BPA-PK, 92-074, Pressekonferenz, 7 / 13 / 92; BPA-PK, 92-078a, Pressekonferenz, 7 / 23 / 92; BPA-Bulletin, 126–192, Kommunique, 11 / 26 / 92. Also see Frank Ropers, "Embargo-Überwachung in der Adria," in *Von Kambodscha bis Kosovo: Auslandseinsätze der Bundeswehr seit Ende des Kalten Krieges*, ed. Peter Goebel (Frankfurt am Main: Report, 2000), 101–119.

46. DB Drucksache 12 / 3072, Entschließungsantrag, 7 / 22 / 92; DB Drucksache 12 / 3057, Entschließungsantrag, 7 / 21 / 92; Carl Gustaf Ströhm, "Die Sprache verschlagen," *Welt*, 7 / 16 / 92.

47. DB-P / SB, 101. Sitz., 12. Wahlperiode (7 / 22 / 92), 8609, 8612. Also see DB Drucksache 12 / 3073, Entschließungsantrag, 7 / 22 / 92.

48. DB-P / SB, 101. Sitz., 12. Wahlperiode (7 / 22 / 92), 8617, 8646, 8648.

49. DB-P / SB, 151. Sitz., 12. Wahlperiode (4 / 21 / 93), 12927.

50. DB-P / SB, 151. Sitz., 12. Wahlperiode (4 / 21 / 93), 12927; BPA AA-PM DLF, Mitteilung, 8 / 10 / 92; BPA AA-PM, Information, 8 / 13 / 92; BPA-Bulletin 013-93, Rede (Kohl), 2 / 6 / 93 (dated 2 / 10 / 93). On the so-called Kohl doctrine, see Krause, *Bundeswehr als Instrument*, 199–200.

51. Josef Joffe, "Ein Flugverbot ist kein Kriegsverbot," *SZ*, 12 / 22 / 92.

52. BPA-Bulletin, 141-92, Kommunique, 12 / 29 / 92. Also see Walter Jertz, "Einsatz der Luftwaffe über Bosnien," in Goebel, *Kambodscha bis Kosovo*, 136–153.

53. DB Drucksache 12 / 4711, Kleine Anfrage, 4 / 5 / 93; Drucksache 12 / 4710, Antrag, 4 / 6 / 93.

54. BPA-Bulletin 029-93, Beschluß, 4 / 2 / 93; Erklärung der FDP-Minister and Erwiderung auf Organklage, 4 / 7 / 93; BPA-PK 93-038b, Pressekonferenz, 4 / 8 / 93. Also see the court's official press release about the decision: Pressemitteilung Nr. 29 / 1994 (7 /12 / 94), www.bundesverfassungsgericht.de/SharedDocs/Pressemitteilungen/DE/1994/bvg94-029 .html.

55. In fact, he had threatened to quit the government if German soldiers participated aboard the AWACS before the court released its decision. See BPA-PK 93-038b, Pressekonferenz, 4 / 8 / 93; Schwarz-Schilling, *Frieden*, 84–91; Michael Thumann, "Sanktionen," *Zeit*, 4 / 23 / 92. Also see Karin Johnston, "German Public Opinion and the Crisis in Bosnia," in *International Public Opinion and the Bosnia Crisis*, ed. Richard Sobel and Eric Shiraev (Lanham, MD: Lexington, 2003), 272–274.

56. DB-P / SB, 151. Sitz., 12. Wahlperiode (4 / 21 / 93), 12928–12929, 12939.

57. DB-P / SB, 151. Sitz., 12. Wahlperiode (4 / 21 / 93), 12958, 12969–12970, 12954, 12956.

58. There were eight abstentions: three by SPD members (including Freimut Duve), five by members of the FDP. See DB-P / SB, 151. Sitz., 12. Wahlperiode (4 / 21 / 93), 12974–12976.

8. HUMANITY IN ACTION

1. BPA AA-PM DLF, Interview, 6 / 29 / 92; Roland Hofwiler, "Ein beschämendes europäisches Schauspiel," *taz*, 5 / 23 / 92; DB-P / SB, 219. Sitz., 12. Wahlperiode (4 / 14 / 94), 18910.

2. DB Drucksache 12 / 3838, Kleine Anfrage, 5 / 26 / 92; Alois Deubler, "Jetzt flüchten die Menschen," *FAZ*, 4 / 24 / 92. For accurate estimates, see Marie-Janine Calic, "Ethnic Cleansing and War Crimes, 1991–1995," in *Confronting the Yugoslav Controversies: A Scholars' Initiative*, ed. Charles Ingrao and Thomas A. Emmert (West Lafayette, IN: Purdue University Press, 2013), 115, 139.

3. "Leere Worte," *Spiegel*, 3 / 22 / 93; Dietrich Willier, "Ein schmaler Pfad im Vorhof der Hölle," *Tagesspiegel*, 1 / 24 / 93; Walter Mayr, "'Ihr Stolz ist hart wie Stein,'" *Spiegel*, 11 / 16 / 92; BPA-Bulletin 087-92, Appel, 7 / 29 / 92 (dated 8 / 4 / 92); BPA-Bulletin 017-93, Erklärung, 2 / 25 / 93. More generally, see Christopher A. Molnar, *Memory, Politics, and Yugoslav Migrations to Postwar Germany* (Bloomington: Indiana University Press, 2019).

4. Molnar, *Memory*, 175; Lauren Stokes, "The Permanent Refugee Crisis in the Federal Republic of Germany, 1949–," *CEH* 52, no. 1 (2019): 41; Peter Gatrell, *The Unsettling of Europe: How Migration Reshaped a Continent* (New York: Basic, 2019), 301.

5. BPA-PK 92-047, Pressekonferenz, 5 / 6 / 92; "PDS: Bonns Verhalten zu Flüchtlingen 'kaltschnäuzig,'" *ND*, 5 / 22 / 92; "'Die Grenzen öffnen!'" *taz*, 5 / 23 / 92; "Stau an Wohlstandsgrenzen," *ND*, 7 / 20 / 92; "Hilfe für Bosnier," *taz*, 7 / 22 / 92; letter to the editor, *ND*, 7 / 21 / 92; Lili Schlumberger-Dogu, "Ignoranz, Abwarten, Gleichgültigkeit," *taz*, 7 / 22 / 92; Susanne Paas, "Bosnische Frauen nach Bremen geholt," *taz*, 4 / 26 / 93.

6. BPA-PK 92-047, Pressekonferenz, 5 / 6 / 92; BPA-PK 92-053, Pressekonferenz, 5 / 20 / 92; Thomas Schmid, "Bosnier bleiben draußen vor der deutschen Tür," *taz*, 5 / 13 / 92.

7. "Bonn soll Visapflicht aufheben," *ND*, 7 / 24 / 92; "Nur dümmliche Propaganda?" *ND*, 8 / 1 / 95; Heide Platen, "Es gibt keinen Knopf zum Abschalten," *taz*, 8 / 10 / 95; "Kaputtes Leben," *Spiegel*, 7 / 24 / 95. Also see Molnar, *Memory*, 168.

8. BPA-PK 92-053a, Pressekonferenz, 5 / 22 / 92.

9. Jochen Kummer, "'Wenn alles ausgeschöpft ist, sagen wir: In Gottes Namen, nennen Sie das Zauberwort Asyl,'" *Welt am Sonntag*, 5 / 24 / 92.

10. BPA-PK 92-053, Pressekonferenz, 5 / 20 / 92; BPA-PK 92-053a, Pressekonferenz, 5 / 22 / 92.

11. Ute Scheub, "Es geht auch anders," *taz*, 9 / 12 / 92; Frank Wehner, "Doppelfront," *ND*, 1 / 18 / 93. On the costs incurred by private citizens, see Molnar, *Memory*, 162, 164–165.

12. "'Schreckgespenst für Europa,'" *Spiegel*, 7 / 27 / 92; Ole Schulz, "Hürdenlauf bis zum Gastgeber in Deutschland," *taz*, 7 / 31 / 95; Klaus Müller, "Familie Slobodan will 'auf alle Fälle' zurück," *ND*, 7 / 31 / 95. For similar examples, see William S. Walker, *German and Bosnian Voices in a Time of Crisis: Bosnian Refugees in Germany, 1992–2002* (Indianapolis, IN: Dog Ear, 2010).

13. "'Wo sind wir denn noch Menschen?'" *Spiegel*, 7 / 6 / 92; Erich Rathfelder, "Wo endet Europa?" *taz*, 5 / 5 / 92; "Jusos drohen mit Trennung von der SPD," *ND*, 5 / 25 / 92; Thomas Schmid, "Bund weist Balkan-Flüchtlinge ab," *taz*, 5 / 21 / 92; Karin Flothmann, "Ein Beispiel deutscher Gründlichkeit," *taz*, 3 / 20 / 93; "Gemischte Gefühle," *Spiegel*, 7 / 19 / 93.

14. There was another side to this. As one UNHCR staffer explained, officials were simply overwhelmed by the large influx of people—and some even handed out "emergency" visas. See DB Drucksache 12 / 3155, Antwort, 8 / 12 / 92; Bernd Siegler, "Endstation Salzburg—fünf Wochen Wartezeit," *taz*, 5 / 23 / 92; Walker, *German and Bosnian Voices*, 4.

15. Kuno Kruse, Stefan Scheytt, and Michael Schwelien, "Krieg ist kein Asylgrund," *Zeit*, 7 / 10 / 92.

16. BPA-PK 92-053a, Pressekonferenz, 5 / 22 / 92; BPA-Bulletin 102-92, "Verlängerung der Abschiebestopps," 9 / 26 / 92. For the positions of the SPD, Greens, and PDS, respectively, see DB Drucksache 12 / 2939, Antrag, 6 / 25 / 92; DB Drucksache 12 / 2832, Entschließungsantrag, 6 / 16 / 92; DB Drucksache 12 / 2630, Antrag, 5 / 21 / 92. For that of the governing parties, see DB Drucksache 12 / 3073, Entschließungsantrag, 10 / 7 / 92. Also see the joint motion of the CDU, FDP, and SPD in DB Drucksache 12 / 5714, Antrag, 9 / 21 / 93.

17. "Teufel öffnet Tore für Bosnier," *ND*, 12 / 15 / 92; DB Drucksache 12 / 2630, Antrag, 5 / 21 / 92 (for the *FAZ* quote); Herbert Leuninger, "Hammelsprung an der Grenze," *taz*, 5 / 23 / 92. On Leuninger, also see Walker, *German and Bosnian Voices*, 38–41.

18. BPA-PK 92-123, Pressekonferenz, 11 / 12 / 92; Kummer, "'Zauberwort'"; Tissy Bruns, "Bonn sortiert Flüchtlinge aus," *taz*, 5 / 23 / 92. For a list of privileged groups, see BPA-PK 92-053a, Pressekonferenz, 5 / 22 / 92; also see Patrice G. Poutrus, *Umkämpftes Asyl: Vom Nachkriegsdeutschland bis in die Gegenwart* (Berlin: Ch. Links Verlag, 2019), 41–47.

19. T. Brund and W. Jakobs, "5.000 Flüchtlinge dürfen einreisen," *taz*, 7 / 22 / 92; Klaus-Peter Klingelschmitt, "Per Sonderzug in Sicherheit," *taz*, 7 / 27 / 92.

20. Karin Nolt, "'Bis der Krieg zu Ende ist, dann wollen wir heim," *ND*, 7 / 29 / 92; Annette Ruess, Harald Schumacher, and Ursula Weidenfeld, "Niveau der Dreißiger," *Wirtschaftswoche*, 7 / 31 / 92; "Am Wochenende kommen die Flüchtlinge," *taz*, 7 / 24 / 92. A new government initiative in early August that year brought an additional 5,069 refugees to Germany. See "Bosnische Kämpfer wollen Waffen vom Westen," *Welt*, 8 / 11 / 92.

21. Ute Scheub and Dorothee Winden, "'Aktion Fluchtweg,'" *taz*, 7 / 22 / 92; Gabi Mischkowski, "Alle wollen helfen—aber wie?" *taz*, 12 / 7 / 92; Dirk Asendorpf, "Flüchtlinge in

Bremer Gästezimmer," *taz*, 7 / 23 / 92; Kathrin Gerlof, "Schamlos," *ND*, 7 / 23 / 92; Peter Kirschey, "Nur mit Kleidern auf dem leib auf der Flucht," *ND*, 7 / 23 / 92; "Der Letzte macht das Licht aus," *taz*, 8 / 11 / 92; Erica Fischer, "Geld allein ist für die Hilfe zu wenig," *taz*, 12 / 17 / 92.

22. Ute Scheub, "Endlich!" *taz*, 7 / 24 / 92; Ute Scheub, "'Ich wollte die Quote erhöhen,'" *taz*, 7 / 30 / 92; Ute Scheub, "Bonn sperrt Tür nicht zu," *taz*, 7 / 28 / 92; Klaus Wolschner, "Undankbare Welt!" *taz*, 8 / 3 / 92.

23. "Salto in Bonn," *Spiegel*, 5 / 25 / 92; Bettina Markmeyer, "Die Probe aufs Zusammenleben," *taz*, 7 / 30 / 92; Vera Gasserow, "Eine Welle läuft ins Leere," *Zeit*, 7 / 31 / 92; C. Emundts and H. Thomsen, "Pritzels Flüchtlinge gehen an den Kühlschrank," *taz*, 8 / 1 / 92; "Aus Partykeller wird Asyl für Flüchtlinge," *ND*, 3 / 26 / 93; Heide Platen, "Bosnisches Gebäck und wenig Hoffnung," *taz*, 2 / 22 / 95.

24. "'Schreckgespenst für Europa'" (*Spiegel*); Walker, *German and Bosnian Voices*, 50–53.

25. Rüdiger Rossig, "Hilfe für Bosnier ist möglich," *taz*, 4 / 5 / 94; Thomas Schmid, "Der Fluchthelfer von Zagreb," *taz*, 12 / 21 / 94; Schulz, "Hürdenlauf."

26. "Stau an Wohlstandsgrenzen" (*ND*); "Sonderstatus für bosnische Flüchtlinge," *taz*, 7 / 20 / 92; Dorothee Winden, "Die Tür geht einen Spalt weit auf," *taz*, 7 / 21 / 92; Eberhard Löblich, "Aus dem Waisenhaus evakuiert," *taz*, 8 / 1 / 92; Eberhard Löblich, "Kinder starben bei Evakuierung," *taz*, 8 / 2 / 92; "Dubiose Bosnien-Aktion fand ihren Abschluß," *ND*, 8 / 5 / 92; "Bestechungsverdacht hat sich verdichtet," *ND*, 8 / 12 / 92; Michael Sontheimer, "Auf dem Markt der Barmherzigkeit," *taz*, 8 / 5 / 92.

27. See Heide Platen, "Safa—zur Erntezeit in einem fremden Land," *taz*, 7 / 31 / 92; Hans Monath, "'Sie aufzunehmen, ist Christenaufgabe'" (interview with Heiner Geißler), *taz*, 7 / 31 / 95; Rüdiger Rossig, "'Jetzt habe ich keine Angst mehr,'" *taz*, 4 / 26 / 93. On motivations, also see Molnar, *Memory*, 164, 176.

28. More than a quarter came from the territories that made up former Yugoslavia; of these, approximately 5 percent were from Bosnia. See BPA-Bulletin 005-94, Asylbewerberzahlen (1993), 1 / 1 / 93 [*sic*]; BPA-Bulletin 005-93, Asylbewerberzahlen (1992), 1 / 15 / 93.

29. "Aktion Ungehorsam," *Spiegel*, 8 / 30 / 93; Kummer, "'Zauberwort Asyl.'"

30. DB-P / SB, 117. Sitz., 12. Wahlperiode (11 / 5 / 92), 9967; Schmid, "Bosnier bleiben draußen." On the costs, see, for example, Anita Kugler, "Wachschutzmänner als Sozialarbeiter," *taz*, 11 / 24 / 92; "Flüchtlinge in US-Unterkünften," *taz*, 12 / 21 / 92.

31. As a result, Germany saw a huge increase in the illegal smuggling of refugees from places like the Czech Republic. On the position of those demanding asylum reform, see BPA-Bulletin 075-92, Asylbewerberzahlen (1992), 7 / 7 / 92; BPA-PK 92-053a, Pressekonferenz, 5 / 22 / 92.

32. Karen Schönwälder, "Migration, Refugees and Ethnic Plurality as Issues of Public and Political Debates in (West) Germany," in *Citizenship, Nationality and Migration in Europe*, ed. David Cesarani and Mary Fulbrook (London: Routledge, 1996), 160; for Kohl's comments, see "Helmut Kohls Regierungserklärung, 13. Oktober 1982," www.1000doku mente.de/pdf/dok_0144_koh_de.pdf.

33. Molnar, *Memory*, 161; Christopher A. Molnar, "'Greetings from the Apocalypse': Race, Migration, and Fear after German Reunification," *CEH* 54, no. 3 (2021): 491–515. See the statistics in BPA-Bulletin 005-93, Asylbewerbezahlen (1992), 1 / 15 / 93; BPA-Bulletin 005-94, Asylbewerbezahlen (1993), 1 / 1 / 93 [*sic*]; BPA-Bulletin 95-000, Jahresübersicht 1994, 1 / 27 / 95; BPA-Bulletin 96002, Asylbewerberzahlen (1995), 1 / 11 / 96. On the reform, see Poutrus, *Umkämpftes Asyl*, 179–185.

34. Kummer, "'Zauberwort Asyl'"; Schmid, "Fluchthelfer von Zagreb"; "Bankrott der Reichen," *FR*, 7 / 31 / 92. The EU was formally established in November 1993.

35. BPA-PK 92-053, Pressekonferenz, 5/20/92; BPA-PK 92-077, Pressekonferenz, 7/20/92.

36. BPA-PK 92-114, Pressekonferenz, 10/21/92; DB-P/SB, 176. Sitz., 12. Wahlperiode (9/23/93), 15224; DB Drucksache 13/59, response to Schriftliche Frage #1, 12/2/94; DB-P/SB, 117. Sitz., 12. Wahlperiode (11/5/92), 18910. For an overview of total donations, see Martin Klingst, "Wettlauf um die Winterhilfe," *Zeit*, 12/25/92; BPA-Materialien, Spezial Nr. 4396, 11/28/95.

37. Kinkel and Rühe announced the decision on supply flights after a trip to Washington. See Werner A. Perger, "Plisch und Plum Zwo," *Zeit*, 7/10/92; DB-P/SB, 165. Sitz., 12. Wahlperiode (6/23/93), 14200. Also see Roger Evers, "Transportflieger in humanitärem Auftrag," in *Von Kambodscha bis Kosovo: Auslandseinsätze der Bundeswehr seit Ende des Kalten Krieges*, ed. Peter Goebel (Frankfurt am Main: Report, 2000), 86–100; Hans-Werner Ahrens, *Die Luftbrücke nach Sarajevo, 1992–1996* (Freiburg: Rombach, 2012).

38. That was why the UN Security Council passed a resolution on August 13, 1992, that offered military protection to aid convoys. Quotes from DB Drucksache 12/4020, response to Schriftliche Frage #2, 12/18/92; BPA-Bulletin, 017-93, Erklärung, 2/25/93; BPA-Bulletin 118-94, Tagung (Europäischer Rat), 12/19/94; Perger, "Plisch"; "Der verkannte Kriegseinsatz," *Spiegel*, 4/5/93. Also see Ahrens, *Luftbrücke*, 149.

39. Rupert Neudeck, *Die Menschenretter von Cap Anamur* (Munich: Heyne, 2002), 283, 287, 290–291, 300–301; Thomas Schmid, "Rettungsanker für wenige Auserwählte," *taz*, 8/10/92; Roman Arens, "Wenn zwei sich streiten," *FR*, 7/27/93; Roman Arens, "Die Stadt zählt wie im Chor die Tage ohne Tote," *FR*, 3/14/94; BPA-PK 92-114, Pressekonferenz, 10/21/92.

40. Neudeck, *Menschenretter*, 303. For a list of the main NGOs involved, sample projects, and local groups, see Erich Rathfelder, "Wachsendes Vertrauen in die deutsche Balkan-Politik," *taz*, 7/1/95; Molnar, *Memory*, 162, 165–166.

41. "Fahrräder für Bosnien," *taz*, 5/22/93; Miriam Hoffmeyer, "Mompers roter Schal an Koofmich versteigert," *taz*, 8/31/92; DB-P/SB, 74. Sitz., 13. Wahlperiode (11/30/95), 6428.

42. DB-P/SB, 196. Sitz., 12. Wahlperiode (12/2/93), 17045; Roman Arens, "Zu wenig für den Frieden," *FR*, 11/16/92; BPA-Bulletin 087-92, Rede (Seiters), 8/4/92. Also see Elisabeth Noelle-Neumann and Renate Köcher, eds., *Allensbacher Jahrbuch der Demoskopie, 1984–1992* (Munich: Sauer, 1993), 208, 256.

43. Bettina Markmeyer, "Die Probe aufs Zusammenleben" *taz*, 7/30/92; Jenny Niederstadt, "Bosnier freuen sich über hilfsbereite Berliner," *ND*, 7/31/92; Ute Scheub, "Kirchengemeinden retten Flüchtlinge," *taz*, July 31, 1992. For other examples of relief efforts by ordinary Germans, see Walker, *German and Bosnian Voices*, 11–17.

44. Edgar Sebastian Hasse, "Mit menschlicher Nähe gegen das blanke Entsetzen," *DAS*, 12/18/92; Corinna Raupach, "Weg von den Almosen für die Kriegsgebiete," *taz*, 4/30/93; Kai von Arpen, "Deutsche Befriedigung," *taz*, 7/28/92.

45. East Germans who fled the GDR in the spring and summer of 1989 found temporary lodging in refugee camps located in Hungary. See "Heißer Tee für Asylbewerber," *ND*, 11/5/92; Kugler, "Wachschutzmänner als Sozialarbeiter." For the refugees' reception elsewhere, see Barbara Franz, "The Plight of the First Post–Cold War Refugees: The Reception and Settlement of Bosnians in Austria and the United States," in *Refugee Crises, 1945–2000: Political and Societal Responses in International Comparison*, ed. Jan C. Jansen and Simone Lässig (Cambridge: Cambridge University Press, 2020), 235–259.

46. DB-P/SB, 128. Sitz., 12. Wahlperiode (12/10/92), 11119; DB Drucksache 13/841, responses to Schriftliche Fragen #1–4, 3/17/95. Also see the joint motion submitted by the

CDU / CSU, FDP, and SPD urging "priority admission" for rape victims, in DB Drucksache 12 / 3958, Entschließungsantrag, 12 / 9 / 92.

47. The nurses eventually persuaded the Ministry of Defense to donate a mobile lab from the remaining stock of the defunct East Germany army. See Paas, "Bosnische Frauen"; "Gegen die ausgeschlagenen Zähne, *taz,* 5 / 4 / 93.

48. The "small, witty" feminist had first become active in politics in the early 1980s, when she helped establish Frauen für den Frieden (Women for Peace) and Mütter gegen Gewalt (Mothers against Violence), two prominent women's groups in the West German peace movement. See "Der Herzensträgheit keine Chance," *taz,* 3 / 8 / 93.

49. See Karin Flothmann, "Crash-Kurse gegen sexuelle Gewalt," *taz,* 5 / 4 / 93; "'Wir wollen Erfahrungen bündeln,'" *taz,* 5 / 4 / 93. For similar organizations, see DB Drucksache 13 / 841, response to Schriftliche Fragen #1 and 3, 3 / 17 / 95.

50. This section is based on Monika Hauser, in discussion with the author, Cologne, Jan. 2022; Almut Nitzsche, "Monika Hauser," FemBio, www.fembio.org/biographie.php/frau /biographie/monika-hauser/; Erica Fischer, "Hilfe für vergewaltigte und gefolterte Frauen in Bosnien," *taz,* 2/18/93; Ingrid Müller-Münch, "Zuflucht im Backsteinhaus," *FR,* 11/8/93; "Unerreichbares wurde möglich," *ND,* 5/28/94; "4000 bosnischen Frauen geholfen," *ND,* 6/10/94; also see Mischkowski, "Alle wollen helfen."

51. Hauser, discussion; Maria von Welser, in discussion with the author, Hamburg, Dec. 2021.

52. Hauser, discussion.

53. Erich Rathfelder, "Ein Haus für die Opfer," *taz,* 4/15/93; "Das Medica-Projekt kennen alle," *taz,* 1/5/95. Also see https://medicamondiale.org/en/about-us/who-we-are.

54. DB-P / SB, 176. Sitz., 12. Wahlperiode (9 / 23 / 93), 15230; BPA AA-PM WDR, Interview, 11 / 12 / 92; BPA-Bulletin 101-92, Rede (Kinkel), 9 / 23 / 92; Peter Scholl-Latour, "Samariter in der Falle," *RM,* 10 / 30 / 92. For an official German estimate of aid provided by the major industrial nations, see BPA-Materiellen 92-000, "Deutsche Humanitäre Hilfe für die Opfer des Konflikts im ehemaligen Jugoslawien," 11 / 3 / 92.

55. Frank Wehner, "Champion der Solidarität," *ND,* Feb. 27, 1993; Christina Matte, "Alle Jahre wieder," *ND,* 12/22/93; Christian Semler, "Humanity Public Relations Inc.," *taz,* 8/17/93; Sontheimer, "Barmherzigkeit"; Kurt Stenger, "Der Großteil geht an die Marktführer erst," *ND,* 12 / 2 / 93. For an overview of these issues, see Johannes Paulmann, "Humanitarianism and Media: Introduction to an Entangled History," in *Humanitarianism & Media: 1900 to the Present,* ed. Paulmann (New York: Berghahn, 2019), 1–38.

56. Andreas Zumach, "Kritik an die falsche Adresse," *taz,* 7/30/92; "Flucht vor dem Bürgerkrieg," *Spiegel,* 6/28/93; Ruess, Schumacher, and Weidenfeld, "Niveau der Dreißiger." Also see Molnar, *Memory,* 174.

57. BPA-PK 93-067b, Pressekonferenz, 6 / 22 / 93; BPA-PK 92-078a, Pressekonferenz, 7/23/92; BPA-Materialien 92-000, "Aufname von Flüchtlingen," 9/3/92; DB-P/SB, 76. Sitz., 13. Wahlperiode (12 / 6 / 95), 6634. For Kinkel's efforts, see DB-P / SB, 101. Sitz., 12. Wahlperiode (7/22/92), 8610–8611; BPA-PK 92-123, Pressekonferenz, 11/12/92; DB-P/SB, 188. Sitz., 12. Wahlperiode (11 / 10 / 93), 1620.

58. DB-P / SB, 196. Sitz., 12. Wahlperiode (12 / 2 / 93), 17047; DB-P / SB, 101. Sitz., 12. Wahlperiode (7 / 22 / 92), 8610–8611, 8613, 8647; DB-P/SB, 117. Sitz., 12. Wahlperiode (11 / 5 / 92), 9962–9963; Pierre Simonitsch, "Im Herzen Europas droht ein Palästinenser-Problem," *FR,* 7 / 29 / 92; Dieter Schröder, "Rache für Sarajewo," *SZ,* 11/12/92.

59. Andreas Zumach, "Geld statt Aufnahme für die Flüchtlinge," *taz,* 7/30/92; Ruess, Schumacher, and Weidenfeld, "Niveau der Dreißiger"; Platen, "Bosnisches Gebäck"; "'Alles blödes Geschrei,'" *Spiegel,* 8/3/92.

60. Barbara John, a civil servant responsible for "integrating" foreigners in Berlin, published a brochure to increase understanding for the history and traditions of Bosnian Muslims. See Platen, "Bosnisches Gebäck"; Iris Mainka, "'Wer soll helfen, wenn nicht wir?'" *Zeit*, 4/23/93; "Flüchtlinge aus Bosnien in Berlin," *ND*, 8/15/92. On Barbara John's activities, also see Walker, *German and Bosnian Voices*, 78–82.

61. Scheub, "Es geht auch anders"; DB-P/SB, 117. Sitz., 12. Wahlperiode (11/5/92), 9967; Molnar, *Memory*, 165.

62. Sannah Koch, "Alltäglicher Rassismus," *taz*, 9/21/92; "'Am besten nach Sibirien,'" *Spiegel*, 5/24/93.

63. "Brandanschlag vor geplantem Wohnheim," *taz*, 11/9/92; Isabelle Yeginer, "Kein Haus für Flüchtlinge," *taz*, 10/24/92.

64. "Geflohene werden nun gewaltsam zurückgeholt," *ND*, 8/5/92. In the end, the group did return to the East. See Kai von Appen, "'Dann gehen wir nach Hamburg,'" *taz*, 8/6/92; "Bosnier mußten zurück," *taz*, 8/7/92; "Schwerin: Flüchtlinge aus Bosnien zog es in Alt-BRD," *ND*, 7/29/92.

65. DB-P/SB, 76. Sitz., 13. Wahlperiode (12/6/95), 6635; DB-P/SB, 219. Sitz., 12. Wahlperiode (4/14/94), 18916.

66. Walker, *German and Bosnian Voices*, 102–104. On illicit activities and church asylum, see Matthias Rüb, "Vor dem dritten Kriegswinter," *FAZ*, 12/3/94; DB-P/SB, 74. Sitz., 13. Wahlperiode (11/30/95), 6463. Also see Emily Greble, *Muslims and the Making of Modern Europe* (Oxford: Oxford University Press, 2021).

67. "Saarland: Polizei schützt Asylunterkunft," *ND*, 7/14/92; Hans Monath, "Bundesaußenminister mit Gedächtnislücke?" *taz*, 7/22/95; Kathi Seefeld, "Die Bilder kamen mit über die Brücke," *taz*, 4/18/95. For violence among ethnic groups, see, for example, Christian Arns, "Granate explodierte in Flüchtlings-Wohnheim," *taz*, 7/23/93.

68. Markus Grabitz, "Konto verweigert," *taz*, 6/3/93; Christina Matte, "Hass nahmen sie mit," *ND*, 6/13/92; Vera Gaserow, "Die Zeit ist gegen sie," *Zeit*, 12/2/94.

69. Anwar Mansuri, "Bosnier in Pakistan: 'Gäste, nicht Flüchtlinge,'" *Welt*, 8/5/93; Bernhard Imhasly, "Ungeliebter Fluchtort," *taz*, 4/6/94; Erich Rathfelder, "'Wir sind doch Europäer!'" *taz*, 7/13/93; Claus Leggewie, "Wir alle sind bosnische Muslime," *taz*, 8/10/92; Mainka, "'Wer soll helfen?'" Also see Molnar, *Memory*, 174; Patrick Rahir, "Bosnische Moslems halten es mehr mit Europa als mit dem Islam," *ND*, 9/2/92.

70. Birgit Ziegenhagen, "'Eine kaputte Tasse nimmt man nicht,'" *taz*, 8/6/92.

71. Carl Gustaf Ströhm, "Der bosnische Topf," *Welt*, 2/27/92; "Endlich die Anerkennung," *Welt*, 8/8/92; "Der Haß der Bosnier," *Welt*, 9/1/92; "Waffen von den Glaubensgenossen," *RM*, 9/18/92. For similar warnings in the United States, see Samantha Power, *"A Problem from Hell": America and the Age of Genocide* (New York: Perennial, 2003), 303.

72. Michael Schmitz, "Manchen schnitten sie die Kehle durch," *Zeit*, 4/24/92; "'Du bist blind geworden vor Macht,'" *Spiegel*, 6/8/92; Carl Gustaf Ströhm, "Angst vor der Flagge des Propheten," *RM*, 11/6/92; Carl E. Buchalla, "Im Profil: Alija Izetbegovic," *SZ*, 2/3/92; Walter Mayr, "In den Köpfen ist Krieg," *Spiegel*, 1/20/92. On West German reactions to the Iranian revolution, see Frank Bösch, *Zeitenwende 1979* (Munich: C. H. Beck, 2019), 18–60.

73. Heiko Flottau, "Bosniens Muslime als Indianer Europas," *SZ*, 5/29/93; Gabriel Grüner, "'Moslems sind Schweinehunde,'" *Stern*, 6/24/93. On improved Muslim preparedness, see, for example, "Wie Hitler," *Spiegel*, 1/18/93.

74. Michael Thumann, "'Wir haben alles versucht,'" *Zeit*, 12/3/93; Helga Hirsch, "Das Pendel schlägt zurück," *Zeit*, 8/13/93. Also see Calic, "Ethnic Cleansing," 127–128.

75. Carl Gustaf Ströhm, "Das bosnische Dreieck," *Welt,* 7/8/93. Also see Hirsch, "Das Pendel schlägt zurück"; Dietrich Willier, "'Unser Präsident ist gefährlich naiv,'" *Zeit,* 2/25/94. More generally on Muslim atrocities, see Calic, "Ethnic Cleansing," 128.

76. BPA AA-PM, Rede (Kinkel), 3/3/94.

77. BPA-Bulletin 013-94, "Bundesregierung verurteilt Überfall," 2/8/94; Christian Schwarz-Schilling, *Der verspielte Frieden in Bosnien: Europas Versagen auf dem Balkan* (Freiburg: Herder, 2020), 65. Also see Henrike Viehrig, "Öffentlichkeit und Auslandseinsätze nach dem CNN-Effekt," in *Außenpolitik im Medienzeitalter: Vom späten 19. Jahrhundert bis zur Gegenwart,* ed. Frank Bösch and Peter Hoeres (Göttingen: Wallstein, 2013), 319–340.

78. The safe havens had been established through an initiative by the foreign ministers of the United States, Russia, Britain, France, and Spain. The other five safe areas were Bihac, Sarajevo, Srebrenica, Tuzla, and Zepa. See Charles Ingrao, "Safe Areas," in Ingrao and Emmert, *Confronting the Yugoslav Controversies,* 203–231.

79. DB-P/SB, 219. Sitz., 12. Wahlperiode (4/14/94), 18908, 18918, 18921.

9. GERMANY CANNOT PLAY THE ROLE OF GLOBAL GENDARME

1. Peter Schäfer, "Die Belgier sind da," *Spiegel,* 5/17/94; Bettina Gaus, "'Die Dörfer brennen vollständig,'" *taz,* 4/12/94; "Kontinent ohne Hoffnung," *Spiegel,* 4/17/94.

2. Overviews include Linda Melvern, *Conspiracy to Murder: The Rwanda Genocide* (London: Verso, 2004); Gérard Prunier, *The Rwanda Crisis: History of a Genocide* (New York: Columbia University Press, 1995).

3. "Brennendes Afrika," *Welt,* 4/12/94; DB-P/SB, 228. Sitz., 12. Wahlperiode (19/5/94), 19766; Günter Krabbe, "Das Gemetzel in Ruanda," *FAZ,* 5/2/94.

4. For questionable claims that coverage in the German press was "rather thin," see Karen E. Smith, *Genocide and the Europeans* (Cambridge: Cambridge University Press, 2010), 152; Jutta Helm, "Rwanda and the Politics of Memory," *German Politics and Society* 23, no. 4 (2005): 11.

5. Wolfgang Kunath, "Das Bild einer Frau," *FR,* 5/21/94.

6. Quotes from Dominic Johnson, "Perfider Spruch von der Neutralität," *taz,* 11/26/94; "Bosnien in Afrika," *Spiegel,* 4/10/94; Thankmar von Münchhausen, "Grinsend begrüßen Mörder vom Stamm der Hutu die französischen Soldaten," *FAZ,* 7/2/94. Emphasis added. Also see the interviews in Jean Hatzfeld, *Machete Season: The Killers in Rwanda Speak,* trans. Linda Coverdale (New York: Picador, 2003).

7. Wiedemann, who had three decades of experience in Africa, later acknowledged this as the "worst" thing he had ever seen there. See Wolfgang Kunath, "Und das sollen die Täter sein?" *FR,* 5/6/94; Erich Wiedemann, "Wird der Genozid von der Cholera vollendet?" and "Hausmitteilung," *Spiegel,* 7/24/94.

8. Münchhausen, "Grinsend begrüßen Mörder"; Rupert Neudeck, *Die Menschenretter von Cap Anamur* (Munich: Heyne, 2002), 250; Günter Krabbe, "Der Kagera-Fluß spült die Leichen," *FAZ,* 5/31/94.

9. Krabbe, "Gemetzel"; Günter Krabbe, "Was soll man tun mit 100 000 Mördern in Ruanda?" *FAZ,* 11/7/94; "Ruandas Bürgerkriegsparteien wollen sich in Arusha treffen," *FAZ,* 5/23/94; Constanze Stelzenmüller, "Aus der Hölle in die Not," *Zeit,* 5/20/94.

10. Bartholomäus Grill, "Warten auf die Zeit der Rache," *Zeit,* 8/5/94; Kunath, "Bild einer Frau"; Wolfgang Kunath, "Verwesungsgeruch hängt über der Hügelstadt," *FR,* 6/6/94.

11. Krabbe, "100 000 Mörder." On the ICTR, see UN, International Residual Mechanism for Tribunals, https://unictr.irmct.org/.

12. Dominic Johnson, "Ruandas Pygmäen—vergessene Opfer," *taz*, 8 / 26 / 94; Kunath, "Täter." Emphasis added.

13. The Security Council refused to designate the massacre as *genocide* in early May but used the term in a resolution adopted one month later. See Smith, *Genocide*, 156–162, 169; Dominic Johnson, "Auf den 'killing fields' von Ruanda," *taz*, 5 / 31 / 94; "Schmähliches Versagen," *Spiegel*, 6 / 5 / 94; DB Drucksache 12 / 8154, Entschließungsantrag, 6 / 28 / 94.

14. Smith, *Genocide*, 154–157, 163–164.

15. BPA-Bulletin 055-94, Rede (Kinkel), 6 / 1 / 94; BPA-PK 94-064a, Pressekonferenz, 6 / 25 / 94; "'Das ist Völkermord,'" *Spiegel*, 6 / 5 / 94; "Völkermord in Ruanda," *taz*, 7 / 2 / 94; "Vergleichbar mit dem Holocaust," *Spiegel*, 8 / 14 / 94. For other international figures who used the term *genocide*, see Smith, *Genocide*, 156.

16. BPA-Bulletin 076-94, Rede, 8 / 24 / 94.

17. Rudolph Chimelli, "Herrschen über einen großen Friedhof," *SZ*, 8 / 2 / 94. Emphasis added.

18. Smith, *Genocide*, 142, 164. More generally, see Linda Melvern, *A People Betrayed: The Role of the West in Rwanda's Genocide* (London: Zed, 2000); Michael Barnett, *Eyewitness to a Genocide: The United Nations and Rwanda* (Ithaca, NY: Cornell University Press, 2002); Samantha Power, *"A Problem from Hell": America and the Age of Genocide* (New York: Perennial, 2003), 329–389.

19. Neudeck, *Menschenretter*, 259; DB-P / SB, 228. Sitz., 12. Wahlperiode (5 / 19 / 94), 19765–19767; "USA und UNO für Ruanda-Intervention," *taz*, 5 / 4 / 94.

20. "Das ist Völkermord" (*Spiegel*); Bettina Gaus, "Europas Ekel vorm schwarzen Mann," *taz*, 4 / 25 / 94. On media silence about the UN Convention, see Helm, "Rwanda," 11.

21. "Bonn prüfte GSG-9-Einsatz," *Spiegel*, 4 / 17 / 94; Bettina Gaus, "Vom Völkermord berichten," 4 / 29 / 94. Also see Bruce D. Jones, "Rwanda," in *United Nations Interventionism, 1991–2004*, ed. Mats Berdal and Spyros Economides (Cambridge: Cambridge University Press, 2009), 139–167.

22. Constanze Stelzenmüller, "Falsche Feuerwehr," *Zeit*, 7 / 1 / 94; Smith, *Genocide*, 170–171. On media speculation about a "Somalia complex," see Helm, "Rwanda," 12.

23. "Frankreich marschiert in Ruanda ein," *taz*, 6 / 24 / 94; "Zentral in Kigali beschossen," *taz*, 5 / 20 / 94; Dominic Johnson, "Die Hilfsbereitschaft für Ruanda wächst," *taz*, 7 / 30 / 94.

24. DB-P / SB, 228. Sitz., 12. Wahlperiode (5 / 19 / 94), 19765–19767. On the German deployment to Somalia, see Holger Kammerhoff, "Unterm Blauhelm am Horn von Afrika," in *Von Kambodscha bis Kosovo: Auslandseinsätze der Bundeswehr seit Ende des Kalten Krieges*, ed. Peter Goebel (Frankfurt am Main: Report, 2000), 120–135.

25. BPA-PK 94-049, Pressekonferenz, 5 / 19 / 94.

26. DB-P / SB, 240. Sitz., 12. Wahlperiode (7 / 22 / 94), 21177.

27. DB-P / SB, 240. Sitz., 12. Wahlperiode (7 / 22 / 94), 21192, 21202.

28. DB-P / SB, 240. Sitz., 12. Wahlperiode (7 / 22 / 94), 21208. Minister of Defense Rühe "scathingly" rejected French calls for joint action. See Helm, "Rwanda," 12.

29. Smith, *Genocide*, 157, 166–167; Freddy Gsteiger, "Notfalls allein," *Zeit*, 6 / 24 / 94; "Gendarm in Afrika," *Spiegel*, 6 / 26 / 94; Dominic Johnson, "Was treiben die Franzosen im Osten Zaires," *taz*, 6 / 22 / 94; "Einmarsch in Ruanda: Das durchdachte Fiasko," *taz*, 6 / 24 / 94. Also see Daniela Kroslak, *The French Betrayal of Rwanda* (Bloomington: Indiana University Press, 2007).

30. Rupert Neudeck, "Sans gêne, ohne Scham," *taz*, 7 / 7 / 94; Gsteiger, "Notfalls allein"; Dominic Johnson, "Die Eingreiftruppe greift nicht mehr," *taz*, 7 / 30 / 94; Stelzenmüller,

"Falsche Feuerwehr"; Willi Germund, "Koloniale Zier und Hoffnung auf Profit," *taz*, 12 / 30 / 94; "Durchbruch für Ruandas RPF-Guerilla," *taz*, 5 / 24 / 94; DB-P / SB, 240. Sitz., 12. Wahlperiode (7 / 22 / 94), 21177. On pushback in Germany against Mitterrand's claims about a "double genocide," a typical attempt to posit "moral equivalencies" in order to excuse inaction, see Smith, *Genocide*, 156, 162, 167–168.

31. Peter Dausend, "Auftakt der 'Operation Türkis,'" *Welt*, 6 / 23 / 94; Grill, "Rache."

32. On earlier aid, see Helm, "Rwanda," 7.

33. Stelzenmüller, "Aus der Hölle"; Hans-Werner Loose, "Geruch des Todes im Geisterdorf," *Welt*, 6 / 21 / 94; "Hölle auf Erden," *Spiegel*, 7 / 24 / 94.

34. Rudolph Chimelli, "Stumm geht die Welt zugrunde," *SZ*, 7 / 27 / 94; Bartholomäus Grill, "Warten auf die Zeit der Rache," *Zeit*, 8 / 5 / 94; Wiedemann, "Cholera"; Michael Birnbaum, "Exodus aus dem Schlachthaus," *SZ*, 5 / 10 / 94; Heike Schmidt, "Information statt Propaganda," *FR*, 10 / 10 / 94; Brunold, "'Welt.'"

35. Krabbe, "Kagera-Fluß"; BPA-PK 94-049, Pressekonferenz, 5 / 19 / 94; Helm, "Rwanda," 16. The *Lübecker Nachrichten* is cited in *Neues Deutschland*, 7 / 18 / 94. There were disagreements here between the Foreign Office and the Ministry of Defense. See Smith, *Genocide*, 171.

36. "Flucht in die 'Hölle auf Erden,'" *taz*, 7 / 18 / 94; BPA-PK 94-074, Pressekonferenz, 7 / 27 / 94.

37. Chimelli, "Stumm"; Wiedemann, "Wird der Genozid?"; Neudeck, *Menschenretter*, 250, 256–259.

38. DB Drucksache 13 / 59, response to Schriftliche Frage #1, 11 / 28 / 94.

39. Deutsche Welle helped rebuild Rwandan radio facilities. See Dominic Johnson, "Hilfe für Ruanda," *taz*, 9 / 20 / 94; BPA-PK 94-083, Pressekonferenz (8 / 17 / 94); PK 94-075, Pressekonferenz, 7 / 29 / 94; Helm, "Rwanda," 15–16, 18. More generally, see Hubertus Büschel, *Hilfe zur Selbsthilfe: Deutsche Entwicklungsarbeit in Afrika, 1960–1975* (Frankfurt am Main: Campus, 2014); Nina Berman, *Impossible Missions? German Economic, Military, and Humanitarian Efforts in Africa* (Lincoln: University of Nebraska Press, 2004).

40. DB Drucksache 12 / 8248, Antwort, 7 / 7 / 94; BPA-PK 94-073, Pressekonferenz, 7 / 25 / 94; BPA-PK 94-083, Pressekonferenz, 8 / 17 / 94; DB Drucksache 12 / 7737, Bericht, 5 / 30 / 94; Konrad Mohr, "Land der tausend Hügel, Land der tausend Schrecken," *FAZ*, 10 / 10 / 94. On the city partnership, see Rhineland-Palatinate / Rwanda Partnership Association, www.rlp-ruanda.de/en/partner/partner-detailseite/partner/ruanda-komitee-bad-kreuz nach/. For German aid to Rwanda and assistance from the Rhineland-Palatinate after the killing stopped, see DB Drucksache 12 / 7737, Bericht, 5 / 30 / 94; Helm, "Rwanda," 7.

41. Bartholomäus Grill, "Vor dem Abgrund," *Zeit*, 9 / 16 / 94; DB Drucksache 12 / 8447, Vorlage, 9 / 6 / 94; Dieter Buhl, "Geballte Kraft für schnelle Hilfe," *Zeit*, 8 / 5 / 94. On Schuster's visit, also see Helm, "Rwanda," 14.

42. "Künstler helfen Flüchtlingen," *ND*, 7 / 27 / 94; Johnson, "Hilfsbereitschaft"; Sven Christian, "'Jede Stunde kostet Menschenleben,'" *taz*, 7 / 27 / 94; "Welttreffen für Ruanda in Genf," *taz*, 8 / 3 / 94; Thorsten Schmitz, "Die Alpträume kamen erst in Berlin," 10 / 14 / 94.

43. Gaus, "Ekel"; "Flüchtlinge aus Ruanda müssen draußen bleiben," *taz*, 5 / 16 / 94; Walter Jakobs, "Bonn verweigert Visa," *taz*, 5 / 18 / 94; "'Im Einzelfall wahrscheinlich tödlich,'" *Spiegel*, 5 / 22 / 94.

44. BPA-PK 94-073, Pressekonferenz, 7 / 25 / 94; "Flüchtlinge aus Ruanda" (*taz*).

45. "Ruanda-Flüchtlinge bleiben," *ND*, 7 / 29 / 94; "'Im Einzelfall'" (*Spiegel*); Dominic Johnson, "An der deutschen Grenze endet die Hilfe für Ruanda," *taz*, 7 / 28 / 94; Dominic Johnson, "Abschiebung, jetzt noch nicht," *taz*, 7 / 29 / 94.

46. DB-P / SB, 230. Sitz., 2. Wahlperiode (5 / 26 / 94), 20080; "Ruanda-Flüchtlinge willkommen," *Spiegel*, 7 / 31 / 94.

47. Patrice G. Poutrus, *Umkämpftes Asyl: Vom Nachkriegsdeutschland bis in die Gegenwart* (Berlin: Ch. Links, 2019), 59.

48. Kunath, "Bild einer Frau"; "Kontinent ohne Hoffnung" (*Spiegel*).

49. Helm, "Rwanda," 11.

50. Peter Molt, "Ein Produkt der Kolonialherrschaft," *FR*, 6 / 20 / 94; other quotes from Birnbaum, "Exodus"; Gaus, "Mißtrauen"; Dominic Johnson, "Menschen, so weit das Auge reicht," *taz*, 5 / 2 / 94; Wolfgang Kunath, "Ruanda—die politische Erstarrung eines Landes," *FR*, 3 / 14 / 94; Constanze Stelzenmüller, "Ziegen im Foyer," *Zeit*, 8 / 12 / 94.

51. Quoted in Ullrich Fichtner, "Im Schatten der Weltpolitik gedieh Ruandas Haß," *FR*, 5 / 14 / 94.

52. DB-P / SB, 225. Sitz., 12. Wahlperiode (4 / 28 / 94), 19424; DB-P / SB, 228. Sitz., 12. Wahlperiode (5 / 19 / 94), 19767.

53. See Gaus, "Ekel"; Dominic Johnson, "Interventionslüftchen," *taz*, 5 / 13 / 94.

54. Or as Minister for Economic Cooperation and Development Carl-Dieter Spranger of the CSU warned, the recent events there had made it clear that "development assistance should not degenerate into a repair shop for catastrophes"—a fear that East German officials earlier had about Cambodia. See DB Drucksache 12 / 8551, Unterrichtung, 9 / 29 / 94; DB-P / SB, 9. Sitz., 13. Wahlperiode (12 / 15 / 94), 428.

55. Johnson, "Perfider Spruch"; Bartholomäus Grill, "Jeder gegen jeden," *Zeit*, 4 / 15 / 94; Bartholomäus Grill, "Ein Stammeskrieg? Niemals!" *taz*, 5 / 24 / 94; Hans Magnus Enzensberger, "Bosnien, Uganda: Eine afrikanische Ansichtskarte," *taz*, 9 / 5 / 92.

56. Bettina Gaus, "Blutbad unter Zivislisten in Ruanda," *taz*, 4 / 11 / 94; Gaus, "Ekel."

57. Kunath, "Erstarrung"; Wolfgang Kunath, "Spielball internationaler Mildtätigkeit," *FR*, 3 / 22 / 94; Günter Krabbe, "In Ruanda ist der Kampf zwischen Hutu und Tutsi wieder entbrannt," *FAZ*, 4 / 9 / 94; Chimelli, "Stumm."

58. Molt, "Produkt."

59. "Bosnien in Afrika" (*Spiegel*); Stelzenmüller, "Aus der Hölle." More generally, see Helmut Strizek, *Geschenkte Kolonien: Ruanda und Burundi unter deutscher Herrschaft* (Berlin: Ch. Links, 2006); Mahmood Mamdani, *When Victims Become Killers: Colonialism, Nativism, and the Genocide in Rwanda* (Princeton, NJ: Princeton University Press, 2001); Philip Gourevitch, *We Wish to Inform You That Tomorrow We Will Be Killed with Our Families: Stories from Rwanda* (New York: Picador, 1998).

60. Molt, "Produkt"; DB-P / SB. 230. Sitz., 12. Wahlperiode (5 / 26 / 94), 20080; Jörg Zimmermann, "Hutu gegen Tutsi—jeder gegen jeden?" *FR*, 4 / 25 / 94.

61. Dominic Johnson, "Ruanda ist keine Naturkatastrophe!" *taz*, 4 / 13 / 94; Grill, "Stammeskrieg?" On Ramsay, see Strizek, *Geschenkte Kolonien*, 73–76.

62. See "'Wir werden das Morden beenden,'" *Spiegel*, 5 / 29 / 94; "Über Leben und Tod," *Spiegel*, 7 / 10 / 94.

63. See Saul Friedländer, *Nazi Germany and the Jews: The Years of Persecution, 1933–1939* (New York: HarperCollins, 1997), 254–255.

64. DB Drucksache 13 / 28, Unterrichtung, 11 / 22 / 94; Günter Krabbe, "Versöhnung von oben?" *FAZ*, 5 / 4 / 94; Krabbe, "100 000 Mörder"; "'Wir werden das Morden beenden'" (*Spiegel*); "Hieb im Nacken," *Spiegel*, 9 / 11 / 94; "Zu Hause sterben," *Spiegel*, 7 / 31 / 94.

65. "Millionen im Exil" (*Spiegel*); Kunath, "Bild einer Frau"; Krabbe, "Gemetzel"; Kunath, "Kagera-Fluß spült"; Molt, "Produkt"; Stelzenmüller, "Ziegen."

66. Fichtner, "Im Schatten." For the other quotes, see Grill, "Stammeskrieg?"; Hartmut Dießenbacher, "Söhne ohne Land," *Spiegel,* 5/22/94; Dunja Melčić, "Die Rhetorik des 'Bürgerkriegs,'" *taz,* 5/16/94; Gaus, "Mißtrauen."

67. Andrew I. Port, "Holocaust Scholarship and Politics in the Public Sphere: Reexamining the Causes, Consequences, and Controversy of the *Historikerstreit* and the Goldhagen Debate: A Forum with Gerrit Dworok, Richard J. Evans, Mary Fulbrook, Wendy Lower, A. Dirk Moses, Jeffrey K. Olick, and Timothy D. Snyder," *CEH* 50, no. 3 (2017): 378.

68. BPA-Bulletin 055-94, Rede (Kinkel), 6/1/94; BPA-PK 94-064a, Pressekonferenz, 6/25/94; Grill, "Jeder gegen jeden"; "Neue Runde des Balkanschielens," *ND,* 4/25/94.

69. Helm, "Rwanda," 1–2, 18–19, 23.

10. CROSSING THE RUBICON

1. BPA AA-PM HR, Interview, 4/6/94.

2. "Die Deutschen rauswerfen," *Spiegel,* 5/22/95; Matthias Rüb, "Den Serben unter Karadzic und Martic bleibt nur die Flucht nach vorn," *FAZ,* 6/1/95.

3. BPA-PK 95007, Pressekonferenz, 1/16/95; BPA-PK 95016, Pressekonferenz, 2/7/95; Marie-Janine Calic, "German Perspectives," in *International Perspectives on the Yugoslav Conflict,* ed. Alex Danchev and Thomas Halverson (London: Palgrave Macmillan, 1996), 59. Also see the government responses to the Party of Democratic Socialism in DB Drucksache 13/607 (2/16/95) and 13/1175 (4/24/95).

4. BPA-PK 95063b, Pressekonferenz, 6/26/95; Neve Gordon and Nicola Perugini, *Human Shields: A History of People in the Line of Fire* (Berkeley: University of California Press, 2020), 117–128.

5. A desire to "remind" Germany of its "duties" might have also played a role, the *FAZ* speculated, "despite its heavy historical burden" in the region. See Matthias Rüb, "Die Serben haben die Lufthoheit, weil Milosevic zu ihnen steht," *FAZ,* 12/29/94.

6. BPA-PK 95063b, Pressekonferenz, 6/26/95.

7. DB-P/SB, 48. Sitz., 13. Wahlperiode (6/30/95), 3955–4039. The Social Democrats, Alliance 90/The Greens, and the Party of Democratic Socialism all filed countermotions: DB Drucksache 13/1802 (6/26/95); 13/1808 (6/28/95); 13/1828 (6/28/95); 13/1835 (6/28/95).

8. DB-P/SB, 48. Sitz., 13. Wahlperiode (6/30/95), 3955–3958. Emphasis added.

9. DB-P/SB, 48. Sitz., 13. Wahlperiode (6/30/95), 3971–3975. German Catholics faced a similar dilemma. See Andrea Claaßen, *Gewaltfreiheit und ihre Grenzen: Die friedensethische Debatte in Pax Christi vor dem Hintergrund des Bosnienkriegs* (Baden-Baden: Nomos, 2019).

10. DB-P/SB, 48. Sitz., 13. Wahlperiode (6/30/95), 3960, 4012; DB-P/SB, 76. Sitz., 13. Wahlperiode (12/6/95), 6635–6636.

11. DB-P/SB, 48. Sitz., 13. Wahlperiode (6/30/95), 3978–3979, 4034, 4035.

12. DB-P/SB, 48. Sitz., 13. Wahlperiode (6/30/95), 3988, 3996–3997, 4004, 4016, 4031.

13. DB-P/SB, 48. Sitz., 13. Wahlperiode (6/30/95), 3970, 3978, 3998.

14. DB-P/SB, 48. Sitz., 13. Wahlperiode (6/30/95), 3984–3985, 3987. On Schmid, see William Glenn Gray, "Germans from Venus? The Out-of-Area Problems in U.S.-German Relations," in *Safeguarding German-American Relations in the New Century,* ed. Hermann Kurthen et al. (Lanham, MD: Lexington, 2006), 66.

15. DB-P/SB, 48. Sitz., 13. Wahlperiode (6/30/95), 3987–3988, 4006–4009. The quotation about "rotting hands" was actually from Franz Josef Strauß. See Bernt Engelmann, *Das neue Schwarzbuch: Franz Josef Strauß* (Cologne: Kiepenheuer & Witsch, 1980), 46.

16. DB-P / SB, 48. Sitz., 13. Wahlperiode (6 / 30 / 95), 3978, 3988, 4011, 4031, 4034.

17. DB-P / SB, 48. Sitz., 13. Wahlperiode (6 / 30 / 95), 3978, 3991, 4017–4019.

18. BPA-Bulletin 031-93, Erklärung, 4 / 19 / 93; DB-P / SB, 151. Sitz., 12. Wahlperiode (4 / 21 / 93), 12927; Jens Schneider, "Serben und Kroaten bedrängen die Muslime," *SZ*, 4 / 24 / 93.

19. Quotes from "Bosnien: Schwarze Schwäne," *Spiegel*, 6 / 19 / 95; "Wenn Srebrenica fällt," *SZ*, 7 / 11 / 95; Matthias Rüb, "Sieg über Srebrenica, Nato und die Vereinten Nationen," *FAZ*, 7 / 12 / 95; Jens Schneider, "Die letzte Machtprobe vor dem Abmarsch," *SZ*, 7 / 12 / 95; Ulrich Lüke, "Der Anfang vom Ende," *GA*, 7 / 12 / 95; Johann Georg Reißmüller, "Um Srebrenica," *FAZ*, 7 / 12 / 95; Roman Arens, "Srebrenica: Ende der Lüge," *FR*, 7 / 13 / 95. Also see David Rohde, *Endgame: The Betrayal and Fall of Srebrenica, Europe's Worst Massacre since World War II* (New York: Penguin, 2012); Matthias Fink, *Srebrenica: Chronologie eines Völkermords oder Was geschah mit Mirnes Osmanovic* (Hamburg: Hamburger Edition, 2015).

20. Wolfgang Koydl, "Srebrenica und der Preis der Würde," *SZ*, 7 / 13 / 95. On the media coverage of Srebrenica, also see Margit V. Wunsch Gaarmann, *The War in Our Backyard: The Bosnia and Kosovo Wars through the Lens of the German Print Media* (Berlin: Neofelis, 2015), 83–119.

21. BPA-PK 95071a, Pressekonferenz, 7 / 19 / 95; "Bosnien: Reservat für die Moslems," *Spiegel*, 7 / 17 / 95; Walter Mayr, "Es ist keiner mehr übrig," *Spiegel*, 7 / 31 / 95.

22. Michael Thumann, "Tadeusz Mazowiecki über die vertriebenen Bosnier," *Zeit*, 8 / 4 / 95; DB Drucksache 13 / 2408, response to Schriftliche Frage #1, 9 / 22 / 95.

23. Ernst Levy, "Niederländischer Offizier würdigt Leistungen der Serben," *FAZ*, 7 / 26 / 95; "Kluft zwischen Politikern und Militärs," *SZ*, 7 / 26 / 95.

24. Bernhard Küppers, "Der Fall der bosnischen Enklave Srebrenica," *SZ*, 7 / 13 / 95; Erich Wiedemann, "Bosnien: Die Schande von Srebrenica," *Spiegel*, 10 / 30 / 95; Dirk Schümer, "Das richtige Gefühl für den Umgang mit Massakern," *FAZ*, 9 / 23 / 95. For other Holocaust comparisons at the time, see Gaarman, *War*, 104, 117.

25. Thomas Kleine-Brockhoff and Michael Schwelien, "Was geschah in Srebrenica?" *Zeit*, 11 / 3 / 95.

26. "Neue Vorwürfe gegen UN-Truppe," *FR*, 11 / 4 / 95; "Blauhelme beschuldigt," *FAZ*, 11 / 4 / 95; DB Drucksache 13 / 3025, Schriftliche Frage #61, 11 / 17 / 95. On sensational reports about sexual abuse by UN peacekeepers, see Sanam Naraghi Anderlini, "UN Peacekeepers' Sexual Assault Problem," *Foreign Affairs*, 6 / 9 / 2017.

27. BPA-PK, Pressekonferenz, 7 / 19 / 95; DB-P / SB, 74. Sitz., 13. Wahlperiode (11 / 30 / 95), 6428; BPA-PK, DB-P / SB, 63. Sitz., 13. Wahlperiode (10 / 25 / 95), 5350; DB Drucksache 13 / 3025, response to Schriftliche Frage #61, 11 / 17 / 95.

28. On the government's activities, see DB Drucksache, 13 / 2877, Antwort auf die Kleine Anfrage, 11 / 7 / 95.

29. Quotes from Jens Schneider, "Das sind keine leeren Drohungen," *SZ*, 7 / 15 / 95; BPA AA-PM, Mitteilung, 10 / 25 / 95; DB-P / SB, 74. Sitz., 13. Wahlperiode (11 / 30 / 95), 6460; Robert Leicht, "Das Konzept der Schutzzonen auf dem Balkan ist gescheitert," *Zeit*, 7 / 14 / 95; Roderich Reifenrath, "Die Logik des Krieges," *FR*, 7 / 15 / 95; Gaarman, *War*, 108.

30. BPA-PK 95074, Pressekonferenz, 7 / 26 / 95; 95097, Pressekonferenz, 9 / 25 / 95; 95103, Pressekonferenz, 10 / 11 / 95; 95108, Pressekonferenz, 10 / 24 / 95. Also see Karin Johnston, "German Public Opinion and the Crisis in Bosnia," in *International Public Opinion and the Bosnia Crisis*, ed. Richard Sobel and Eric Shiraev (Lanham, MD: Lexington, 2003), 249–250, 266–269; Elisabeth Noelle-Neumann and Renate Köcher, eds., *Allensbacher Jahrbuch der Demoskopie, 1993–1997* (Munich: Sauer, 1997), 1,147. For earlier attitudes, see Ronald D. Asmus, *Germany in Transition: National Self-Confidence and International Reticence* (Santa Monica, CA: RAND, 1992), 34–40.

31. BPA AA-PM DLF, Interview, 1/20/93.

32. "'Der dümmste aller Kriege,'" *Spiegel*, 7/6/92; Peter Scholl-Latour, "Die Schüsse hallen bis Teheran," *RM*, 8/14/92. On the American response in Washington, see Samantha Power, *"A Problem from Hell": America and the Age of Genocide* (New York: Perennial, 2003), 247–327.

33. Klaus-Dieter Frankenberger, "Am Berg Igman," *FAZ*, 8/22/95; Josef Joffe, "Die kurze Lunte im langen Krieg," *SZ*, March 8, 1995. Holbrooke was no stranger to the subject of genocide. In 1977 he had presented to Congress the executive branch's "first serious" public statement on Cambodia under the Khmer Rouge. See Jamie Frederic Metzl, *Western Responses to Human Rights Abuses in Cambodia, 1975–80* (Basingstoke: Macmillan, 1996), 84.

34. Martin Winter, "Demonstrative Zuversicht und keine Zeit zu trauern," *FR*, 8/21/95; "Bilder von Leid und Hilflosigkeit," *FR*, 8/29/95.

35. BPA-PM 339/95, Pressemitteilung, 10/5/95; Leo Wieland, "Perry: Zwei bis drei Nato-Divisionen als Friedenstruppen nach Bosnien," *FAZ*, 9/16/95; Leo Wieland, "Clintons Doppelstrategie: Vergeltung und Verhandlungen," *FAZ*, 8/31/95.

36. See Hans-Peter Kriemann, *Hineingerutscht? Deutschland und der Kosovo-Krieg* (Göttingen: Vandenhoeck & Ruprecht, 2021), 139, 163. Also see Christoph Schwegmann, *Die Jugoslawien-Kontaktgruppe in den Internationalen Beziehungen* (Baden-Baden: Nomos, 2003).

37. Richard Holbrooke, *To End a War* (New York: Random House, 1998), 244; Gaarman, *War*, 124.

38. Wolfgang Ischinger, "21 Tage Dayton," in *Deutsche Aussenpolitik 1995: Auf dem Weg zu einer Friedensregelung für Bosnien und Herzegowina: 53 Telegramme aus Dayton: Eine Dokumentation*, ed. Auswärtiges Amt (Bonn: Auswärtiges Amt, Referat Öffentlichkeitsarbeit, 1998), 29–35 (quotes on 30–32), 124–126.

39. On Dayton, see Steven L. Burg and Paul S. Shoup, *The War in Bosnia-Herzegovina: Ethnic Conflict and International Intervention* (Armonk, NY: M. E. Sharpe, 1999), 317–387.

40. Kurt Kister, "Triumph und Pflicht einer Supermacht," *SZ*, 11/23/95; Dieter Buhl, "Lange hat Bill Clinton gezögert," *Zeit*, 11/24/95. Also see Gaarmann, *War*, 121–155.

41. There was little mention in the media of the German delegation's role. One exception was Mainhardt Graf Nayhauß, who wrote in the *Bild-Zeitung* that Ischinger and his colleagues had written half of the final agreement. See Ischinger, "21 Tage Dayton," 32–34; DB-P/SB, 74. Sitz., 13. Wahlperiode (11/30/95), 6426; Gaarmann, *War*, 136.

42. See, e.g., "Härte zeigt Wirkung," *FAZ*, 9/2/95; "Überraschung für Karadzic," *FR*, 5/26/95.

43. See "Ein bitterer Friede," *Spiegel*, 11/27/95; Roman Arens, "Ein fauler Friede," *FR*, 11/23/95; Ewald Stein, "Bosnien-Abkommen mit Fragezeichen Paradox," *Handelsblatt*, 11/23/95; Johann Georg Reißmüller, "Ungerecht und unsicher," *FAZ*, 11/22/95; DB-P/SB, 76. Sitz., 13. Wahlperiode (12/6/95), 6657–6658.

44. The consensus was that the Muslims were the big losers in the deal. See Johann Georg Reißmüller, "Frieden braucht 'Gerechtigkeit,'" *FAZ*, 10/7/95; Johann Georg Reißmüller, "Desorientiert," *FAZ*, 10/17/95; "Ein bitterer Friede" (*Spiegel*); Rolf Paasch, "Wie ein Nußknacker zwischen den Gewinnern," *FR*, 11/23/95; Gaarman, *War*, 139.

45. DB Drucksache 13/3122, Antrag, 11/28/95.

46. DB-P/SB, 74. Sitz., 13. Wahlperiode (11/30/95), 6434, 6440, 6443, 6449; DB-P/SB, 76. Sitz., 13. Wahlperiode (12/6/95), 6697. Emphasis added. These debates are also discussed in *Hineingerutscht?*, 165–168.

47. DB-P/SB, 74. Sitz., 13. Wahlperiode (11/30/95), 6447, 6450–6453, 6466.

48. DB-P / SB, 76. Sitz., 13. Wahlperiode (12 / 6 / 95), 6640–6641, 6645, 6657, 6662–6663. On Fischer's reversal, see the Prologue.

49. DB-P / SB, 76. Sitz., 13. Wahlperiode (12 / 6 / 95), 6656; Stephanie Bauer, "Die Haltung von Bündnis 90 / Die Grünen zu militärischen Interventionen," master's thesis, Johannes-Gutenberg-Universität Mainz, 2000, 73–74.

50. Gregor Gysi, email to author, 12 / 22 / 2021. For the vote tallies, see DB-P / SB, 76. Sitz., 13. Wahlperiode (12 / 6 / 95), 6673–6675.

51. DB-P / SB, 76. Sitz., 13. Wahlperiode (12 / 6 / 95), 6634–6636; DB Drucksache 13 / 3135, Entschließungsantrag, 11 / 29 / 95; Johnston, "German Public Opinion," 266. On the positions of the major newspapers, see Gaarman, *War*, 147–148.

52. Christoph Rabe, "Der Wiederaufbau Bosniens kostet Milliarden," *Handelsblatt*, 10 / 9 / 95; Alois Berger, "Eine halbe Milliarde Dollar für Bosnien," *taz*, 12 / 22 / 95; DB-P / SB, 74. Sitz., 13. Wahlperiode (11 / 30 / 92), 6429, 6459.

53. DB-P / SB, 76. Sitz., 13. Wahlperiode (12 / 6 / 95), 6632–6634; BPA-PK95119a, Pressekonferenz, 11 / 24 / 92. For Kohl's earlier position, see BPA-PK 95089, Pressekonferenz, 9 / 4 / 92.

54. DB-P / SB, 74. Sitz., 13. Wahlperiode (11 / 30 / 95), 6437; DB-P / SB, 76. Sitz., 13. Wahlperiode (12 / 6 / 95), 6634; Werner Gumpel, "Viel Geld muß aus dem Ausland kommen," *RM*, 11 / 10 / 95.

55. DB-P / SB, 76. Sitz., 13. Wahlperiode (12 / 6 / 95), 6641, 6658; DB-P / SB, 74. Sitz., 13. Wahlperiode (11 / 30 / 95), 6448.

56. Holbrooke, *To End a War*, 275.

57. DB-P / SB, 74. Sitz., 13. Wahlperiode (11 / 30 / 95), 6448, 6452, 6462. For the positions of various politicians on returns, also see Christopher A. Molnar, *Memory, Politics, and Yugoslav Migrations to Postwar Germany* (Bloomington: Indiana University Press, 2019), 170–171. Also see Atina Grossman, "From Victims to 'Homeless Foreigners': Jewish Survivors in Postwar Germany," in *After the Nazi Racial State: Difference and Democracy in Germany and Europe*, ed. Rita Chin et al. (Ann Arbor: University of Michigan Press, 2009), 55–79.

58. Quote from Helmut Herles, "Die Vertreiber ächten," *GA*, 7 / 17 / 95. On aid levels, see DB-P / SB, 74. Sitz., 13. Wahlperiode (11 / 30 / 95), 6428; BPA-Materialien, BPA Spezial Nr. 4396, 11 / 28 / 95. On decreasing aid levels, see DB-P / SB, 39. Sitz., 13. Wahlperiode (5 / 19 / 92), 6459; DB Drucksache 13 / 643, response to Schriftliche Frage #3, 2 / 24 / 95; 13 / 1015, Antrag, 3 / 30 / 95; 13 / 1881, Beschlußempfehlung und Bericht, 6 / 29 / 95. Also see Molnar, *Memory*, 166–167, 175.

59. Kinkel added that he was "happy and grateful that it was possible to plug into the grid before Christmas"—a rather tone-deaf comment, given the city's sizable Muslim population. See BPA AA-PM, Mitteilung, 12 / 19 / 95. On subsequent assistance, see Peter Goebel, "Beteiligung der Bundeswehr am Wiederaufbau in Bosnien-Herzegowina," in *Von Kambodscha bis Kosovo: Auslandseinsätze der Bundeswehr seit Ende des Kalten Krieges*, ed. Peter Goebel (Frankfurt am Main: Report, 2000), 316–327.

60. Rupert Neudeck, *Die Menschenretter von Cap Anamur* (Munich: Heyne, 2002), 297.

CONCLUSION

1. BPA-PM 453 / 95, Rede (Kohl), 12 / 14 / 95; DB-P / SB, 76. Sitz., 13. Wahlperiode (12 / 6 / 95), 6632. On Germany's role in the Implementation Force, see Friedrich W. Riechman, "Von Kroatien in die 'Box,'" in *Von Kambodscha bis Kosovo: Auslandseinsätze der Bundeswehr seit Ende des Kalten Krieges*, ed. Peter Goebel (Frankfurt am Main: Report, 2000), 154–165;

Hans-Peter Kriemann, *Hineingerutscht? Deutschland und der Kosovo-Krieg* (Göttingen: Vandenhoeck & Ruprecht, 2021), 164–175. More generally, see Spyros Economides and Paul Taylor, "Former Yugoslavia," in *United Nations Interventionism, 1991–2004,* ed. Mats Berdal and Spyros Economides (Cambridge: Cambridge University Press, 2009), 65–107. On public attitudes, see Karin Johnston, "German Public Opinion and the Crisis in Bosnia," in *International Public Opinion and the Bosnia Crisis,* ed. Richard Sobel and Eric Shiraev (Lanham, MD: Lexington, 2003), 269.

2. Bascha Mika, "'Pech gehabt! Wir sind in der NATO," *taz,* 12 / 22 / 95. On the growth of German weapons exports, see William Glenn Gray, "Waffen aus Deutschland? Bundestag, Rüstungshilfe und Waffenexport 1961 bis 1975," *VfZ* 64, no. 2 (2016): 327–364.

3. On the Cassandras, see Kerry Longhurst, *Germany and the Use of Force* (Manchester: Manchester University Press, 2004), 6–8; John Mearsheimer, "Back to the Future: Instability in Europe after the Cold War," *International Affairs* 15, no. 1 (1990): 5–56; Wolfram Wette, "Deutschland übt 'out of area': Eine Kritik der Neuen Normalität mit militärischer Prägung," in *Österreichisches Jahrbuch für internationale Sicherheitspolitik* (1997): 112–116. For a more sanguine take, see Peter Katzenstein, ed., *Tamed Power: Germany in Europe* (Ithaca, NY: Cornell University Press, 1997); John S. Duffield, *World Power Forsaken: Political Culture, International Institutions, and German Security Policy after Unification* (Stanford, CA: Stanford University Press, 1998).

4. Overviews include Stephan Bierling, *Vormacht wider Willen: Deutsche Außenpolitik von der Wiedervereinigung bis zur Gegenwart* (Munich: C. H. Beck, 2014); Hanns W. Maull, ed., *Germany's Uncertain Power: Foreign Policy of the Berlin Republic* (Houndmills: Palgrave Macmillan, 2006); Christiane Lemke and Helga A. Welsh, *Germany Today: Politics and Policies in a Changing World* (Lanham, MD: Rowman & Littlefield, 2018), 189–208; Edgar Wolfrum, *Der Aufsteiger: Eine Geschichte Deutschlands von 1990 bis heute* (Stuttgart: Klett-Cotta, 2020), 57–77; Douglas Webber, "Introduction: German European and Foreign Policy before and after Unification," *German Politics* 10, no. 1 (2001): 1–18. Also see Gunther Hellmann, "Das neue Selbstbewusstsein deutscher Außenpolitik und die veränderten Standards der Angemessenheit," in *Deutsche Außenpolitik,* 2nd ed. (Wiesbaden: VS Verlag für Sozialwissenschaften, 2011), 735–757; Herfried Münkler, "Militärintervention in aller Welt," *FAZ,* 10 / 9 / 2006.

5. Andrei S. Markovits and Simon Reich, *The German Predicament: Memory and Power in the New Europe* (Ithaca, NY: Cornell University Press, 1997), 7; Johnston, "German Public Opinion," 259. Reflecting years later on his party's position, Gregor Gysi, the former head of the PDS, still believed that "we were right to be concerned about this. . . . German soldiers stay almost forever once they are deployed somewhere. . . . Besides that, there has been a gigantic increase in military build-up." Since 1995, in fact, the Federal Republic has decreased expenditures on defense as a percentage of the GDP, though its military expenditures remain among the highest in the world. Germany also decided to reduce the size of the Bundeswehr to well below the cap agreed to in the unification treaty and suspend conscription. See Lemke and Welsh, *Germany Today,* 198–199; Gregor Gysi, email to author, 12 /22 / 2021.

6. Lemke and Welsh, *Germany Today,* 190, 197, 208; Wolfrum, *Aufsteiger,* 64. For an overview of all missions since 1990, see Peter Goebel, "Von der Betroffenheit zur Selbstverständlichkeit," in Goebel, *Kambodscha bis Kosovo,* 11–20; also see "Auslandseinsätze der Bundeswehr: Interaktive Weltkarte," Bundeszentrale für politische Bildung, www.bpb.de /politik/grundfragen/deutsche-verteidigungspolitik/243585/weltkarte-auslandseinsaetze.

7. At a major party conference in 1999, one critic threw a symbolic bag of "blood" (red paint) at Fischer. See Paul Hockenos, *Joschka Fischer and the Making of the Berlin Republic: An Alternative History of Postwar Germany* (Oxford: Oxford University Press, 2008), 272.

8. Only a quarter of all Germans believed their country should "play a more active military role in helping to maintain peace and stability in the world." See Lemke and Welsh, *Germany Today,* 199.

9. See Kriemann, *Hineingerutscht?,* 154–163.

10. See Jutta Helm, "Rwanda and the Politics of Memory," *German Politics and Society* 23, no. 4 (2005): 11–12.

11. Karen E. Smith, *Genocide and the Europeans* (Cambridge: Cambridge University Press, 2010), 178; Helm, "Rwanda," 21; Samantha Power, *"A Problem from Hell": America and the Age of Genocide* (New York: Perennial, 2003), 277. Emphasis in original.

12. Power, *"Problem from Hell,"* 132–136, 144; Egon Bahr, in discussion with the author, Berlin, Dec. 2007.

13. Maria von Welser, *Am Ende wünschst du dir nur noch den Tod: Die Massenvergewaltigungen im Krieg auf dem Balkan* (Munich: Knaur, 1993), 130.

14. Henryk M. Broder, "Wir sind Weltmeister im Massaker-Zuschauen," *Welt,* 10 / 11 / 2014.

15. Margit V. Wunsch Gaarmann, *The War in Our Backyard: The Bosnia and Kosovo Wars through the Lens of the German Print Media* (Berlin: Neofelis, 2015), 117; for the American perspective, see Power, *"Problem from Hell,"* 321.

16. The following section draws on Michael P. Scharf, *Balkan Justice: The Story Behind the First International War Crimes Trial Since Nuremberg* (Durham, NC: Carolina Academic Press), 93–101. Quotes from Roy Gutman, email to author, 10 / 14 / 22; Melinda Crane-Engel, "Germany vs. Genocide," *NYT,* 10 / 30 / 94. For Monika Gras's film "Kozarac: Eine Stadt in Bosnien," see https://www.youtube.com/watch?v=PYs8yXNaXzs.

17. See Nicholas J. Wheeler, *Saving Strangers: Humanitarian Intervention in International Society* (Oxford: Oxford University Press, 2000); Gareth Evans, *The Responsibility to Protect: Ending Mass Atrocity Crimes Once and for All* (Washington, DC: Brookings Institution, 2008); Conor Foley, *The Thin Blue Line: How Humanitarianism Went to War* (London: Verso, 2008); Thomas G. Weiss, *Humanitarian Intervention: Ideas in Action,* 3rd ed. (Cambridge: Polity Press, 2016); D. J. B. Trim and Brendan Simms, "Towards a History of Humanitarian Intervention," in *Humanitarian Intervention: A History,* ed. Brendan Simms and D. J. B. Trim (Cambridge: Cambridge University Press, 2011), 1–24. For a succinct overview, also see Michael Humphrey, "International Intervention, Justice and National Reconciliation: The Role of the ICTY and ICTR in Bosnia and Rwanda," *Journal of Human Rights* 2, no. 4 (2003): 495–505.

18. "Der erste deutsche Völkermord," *Spiegel,* 6 / 6 / 2016. For Gauck's speech, see https://www.bundespraesident.de/SharedDocs/Reden/DE/Joachim-Gauck/Reden/2015 /01/150127-Bundestag-Gedenken.html. This is cited in Bill Niven, "Forgetting Remembering: Fake Taboos in German Memory Culture," unpublished manuscript, 2022. Niven also mentions "numerous exhibitions" in Germany about other genocides, including ones that took place during the colonial period; several have drawn "implicit links to the Holocaust." Also see Eldad Ben Aharon, "Recognition of the Armenian Genocide after Its Centenary: A Comparative Analysis of Changing Parliamentary Positions," *Israel Journal of Foreign Affairs* 13, no. 3 (2019): 339–352.

19. Markovits and Reich, *German Predicament,* 3, 8–13; Lemke and Welsh, *Germany Today,* 194–195; Wolfrum, *Aufsteiger,* 77; Andrew I. Port, "'To Deploy or Not to Deploy?' The Erratic Evolution of German Foreign Policy since Unification," in *United Germany: Debating Processes and Prospects,* ed. Konrad H. Jarausch (New York: Berghahn, 2013), 267–277; William Glenn Gray, "Foreign Relations: Where Germans Sell," *CEH* 51, no. 1 (2018): 106.

20. On "cross-referencing" and "interactions" among collective memories, see Michael Rothberg, *Multidirectional Memory: Remembering the Holocaust in the Age of Decolonization* (Stanford, CA: Stanford University Press, 2009).

21. Omer Bartov, "Seeking the Roots of Modern Genocide: On the Macro- and Micro-history of Mass Murder," in *The Specter of Genocide: Mass Murder in Historical Perspective*, ed. Robert Gellately and Ben Kiernan (New York: Cambridge University Press, 2003), 81–82.

22. The remarks followed a talk I presented at the American Academy in Berlin in June 2008.

23. Sheryl Gay Stolberg, "Ocasio-Cortez Calls Migrant Detention Centers 'Concentration Camps,' Eliciting Backlash," *NYT*, 6/18/2019.

24. See Power, *"Problem from Hell"*; Brendan Simms, *Unfinest Hour: Britain and the Destruction of Bosnia* (London: Allen Lane, 2001); Eleanor Davey, "French Responses to the Bosnian Crisis: Humanitarianism, Genocide, and Memory," unpublished honor's thesis, University of Melbourne, 2006; Eleanor Davey, *Idealism beyond Borders: The French Revolutionary Left and the Rise of Humanitarianism, 1954–1988* (Cambridge: Cambridge University Press, 2015), 144–178.

25. Charles S. Maier, *The Unmasterable Past: History, Holocaust, and German National Identity* (Cambridge, MA: Harvard University Press, 1988), 30.

26. Wulf Kansteiner, *In Pursuit of German Memory: History, Television, and Politics after Auschwitz* (Athens: Ohio University Press, 2006), 280.

27. Kansteiner, *Pursuit*, 270–315.

28. What is certain is that contemporary instances of state-sponsored mass murder have led to growing scholarly interest in "comparative genocide." See Frank Bajohr, "Holocaustforschung—Entwicklungslinien in Deutschland seit 1945," and Christopher Browning, "Die Entwicklung der Holocaust-Forschung: Eine amerikanische Perspektive," in *Aufarbeitung des Nationalsozialismus: Ein Kompendium*, ed. Magnus Brechtken (Göttingen: Wallstein, 2021), 136–142, 161–170; Dan Michman, "Characteristics of Holocaust Historiography and Their Contexts since 1990: Emphases, Perceptions, Developments, Debates," in *A Companion to the Holocaust*, ed. Simone Gigliotti and Hilary Earl (Hoboken, NJ: Wiley, 2020), 209–232.

29. Quotes from Walter Manoschek, email to author, 10/20/2021; Jan Philipp Reemtsma, "Am Abgrund der Erinnerung," *Zeit*, 5/27/99. Also see Christian Hartmann, Johannes Hürter, and Ulrike Jureit, eds., *Verbrechen der Wehrmacht: Bilanz einer Debatte* (Munich: C. H. Beck, 2005).

30. Jörg Friedrich, *The Fire: The Bombing of Germany, 1940–1945*, trans. Allison Brown (New York: Columbia University Press, 2006); W. G. Sebald, *On the Natural History of Destruction*, trans. Anthea Bell (New York: Modern Library, 2004); Günther Grass, *Crabwalk*, trans. Krishna Winston (Orlando, FL: Harcourt, 2002). For Walser's speech, see Martin Walser, "Experiences while Composing a Sunday Speech," *German History in Documents and Images*, https://germanhistorydocs.ghi-dc.org/pdf/eng/Chapter5_doc10 -English.pdf. Also see Stephan Scholz, Maren Röger, and Bill Niven, eds., *Die Erinnerung an Flucht und Vertreibung: Ein Handbuch der Medien und Praktiken* (Paderborn: Schöningh, 2015).

31. See Kansteiner, *Pursuit*, 290; Wolfrum, *Aufsteiger*, 77.

32. Also see Felix A. Jiménez Botta, "Politics of Memory in the West German Campaigns against the Chilean and Argentinian Regimes, 1973–1990," *Zeithistorische Forschungen* 17, no. 1 (2020): 65.

33. Patrick Merziger, "Mediation of Disasters and Humanitarian Aid in the Federal Republic of Germany," in *Humanitarianism & Media: 1900 to the Present*, ed. Johannes Paulmann (New York: Berghahn, 2019), 254; Power, *"Problem from Hell,"* 277–278. Also see Simone Richter, *Journalisten zwischen den Fronten: Kriegsberichterstattung am Beispiel Jugoslawien* (Opladen: Westdeutscher Verlag, 1999), 185–187. For critical reflections on the role and power of the media, see Bettina Gaus, *Frontberichte: Die Macht der Medien in Zeiten des Krieges* (Frankfurt am Main: Campus, 2004); Mira Beham, *Kriegstrommeln: Medien, Krieg und Politik* (Munich: DTV, 1996), esp. 218–230; as well as the essays in Frank Bösch and Peter Hoeres, eds., *Außenpolitik im Medienzeitalter: Vom späten 19. Jahrhundert bis zur Gegenwart* (Göttingen: Wallstein, 2013) and (with caution) Klaus Bittermann, ed., *Serbien muß sterbien: Wahrheit und Lüge im jugoslawischen Bürgerkrieg* (Berlin: Edition Tiamat, 1994).

34. Michael Thumann, "Volles Risiko," *Zeit*, 7 / 28 / 95. Fischer later told Thumann his own letter had already been drafted when he read the *Zeit* article, but he decided to use the formulation because he found it so "moving" and "incisive." Michael Thumann, in discussion with the author, Berlin, Dec. 2021. Also see Kriemann, *Hineingerutscht?*, 119–120.

35. Klaus Hartung, "Wer will denn Bosnien retten?" *Zeit*, 8 / 21 / 92; Brian Ladd, *The Ghosts of Berlin: Confronting German History in the Urban Landscape* (Chicago: University of Chicago Press, 1997), 39. Also see Alon Confino, *Germany as a Culture of Remembrance: Promises and Limits of Writing History* (Chapel Hill: University of North Carolina Press, 2006), esp. part 2.

36. See, for example, Timothy Snyder, *On Tyranny: Twenty Lessons from the Twentieth Century* (New York: Crown, 2017).

37. For Germany as a model for Americans, see Susan Neiman, *Learning from the Germans: Race and the Memory of Evil* (New York: Farrar, Straus and Giroux, 2019).

38. See the contributions to the "Catechism Debate," *New Fascism Syllabus*, http://newfascismsyllabus.com/wp-content/uploads/2021/08/The-Catechism-Debate.pdf; Rita Chin, "Thinking Difference in Postwar Germany: Some Epistemological Obstacles around 'Race,'" in *Migration, Memory, and Diversity: Germany from 1945 to the Present*, ed. Cornelia Wilhelm (New York: Berghahn, 2018), 206–229; Rita Chin et al., *After the Nazi Racial State: Difference and Democracy in Germany and Europe* (Ann Arbor: University of Michigan Press, 2009). Also see Rothberg, *Multidirectional Memory*, 10.

39. See Charmaine Chua, Julia Himmrich, and Asad Rahim, "'Something's Missing in Germany': An Exploration of Discriminatory Terminology in German Discourse," *Humanity in Action* (Jan. 2008), https://humanityinaction.org/knowledge_detail/some things-missing-in-germany-an-exploration-of-discriminatory-terminology-in-german -discourse/.

40. See Merkel's speech at "Sommerpressekonferenz von Bundeskanzlerin Merkel," 8/31/15, https://www.bundesregierung.de/bregde/aktuelles/pressekonferenzen/sommerpresse konferenz-von-bundeskanzlerin-merkel-848300. Also see Joachim C. Häberlen, *Citizens and Refugees: Stories from Afghanistan and Syria to Germany* (Abingdon: Routledge, 2023).

41. Charles S. Maier, "A Surfeit of Memory? Reflections on History, Melancholy and Denial," *History & Memory* 5, no. 2 (1993): 140–141; Hope M. Harrison, *After the Berlin Wall: Memory and the Making of the New Germany, 1989 to the Present* (New York: Cambridge University Press, 2019), 19–20; Peter Novick, *The Holocaust in American Life* (New York: Houghton Mifflin, 1999), 239–262.

EPILOGUE

1. DB-P / SB, 19. Sitz., 20. Wahlperiode (2 / 27 / 2022), 1350–1354. Good overviews include Tobias Bunde, "Lessons (to Be) Learned? Germany's *Zeitenwende* and European Security after the Russian Invasion of Ukraine," *Contemporary Security Policy* 43, no. 3 (2022): 516–530; Stephan Kieninger, "The World as It Is: Germany's New Foreign Policy and Russia's War in Ukraine," *H-Diplo*, Essay 413, 3 / 3 / 2022, https://hdiplo.org/to/E413.

2. See Jürgen Habermas, "Krieg und Empörung," *SZ*, 4 / 29 / 2022; "Offener Brief an Bundeskanzler Scholz," Change.org, https://www.change.org/p/offener-brief-an-bundes kanzler-scholz; "Offener Brief fordert von Scholz Stopp der Waffenlieferungen an die Ukraine," *Berliner Zeitung*, 4 / 22 / 2022, https://www.berliner-zeitung.de/politik-gesellschaft /offener-brief-fordert-von-scholz-stopp-der-waffenlieferungen-an-die-ukraine-li.223704. Also see Erika Solomon, "Calls to Give Heavy Weapons to Ukraine Divide Germany's Government," *NYT*, 4 / 20 / 2022.

3. DB-P / SB, 19. Sitz., 20. Wahlperiode (2 / 27 / 2022), 1359, 1383.

4. DB-P / SB, 19. Sitz., 20. Wahlperiode (2 / 27 / 2022), 1355, 1365, 1371.

5. DB-P / SB, 19. Sitz., 20. Wahlperiode (2 / 27 / 2022), 1366, 1368.

6. DB-P / SB, 19. Sitz., 20. Wahlperiode (2 / 27 / 2022), 1357, 1361, 1367, 1370, 1378–1379.

7. See "Offener Brief an Bundeskanzler Scholz," Change.org; Ralf Fücks et al., "Offener Brief," *Zeit*, 5 / 4 / 2022. Also see Alexander Neubacher, "'Nie wieder Krieg' kontra 'Nie wieder Auschwitz': Was lehrt uns die Geschichte?" *Spiegel*, 5 / 4 / 22.

8. DB-P / SB, 19. Sitz., 20. Wahlperiode (2 / 27 / 2022), 1377.

ARCHIVAL SOURCES AND INTERVIEWS

ARCHIVAL SOURCES

Political Archives

Bundesarchiv (Dienststelle Berlin)
Parlamentsarchiv des Deutschen Bundestags (Berlin)
Politisches Archiv des Auswärtigen Amtes (Berlin)
Presse- und Informationsamt der Bundesregierung (Berlin)

Party Archives

Archiv der sozialen Demokratie der Friedrich-Ebert-Stiftung (Bonn)
Archiv des Liberalismus der Friedrich-Naumann-Stiftung (Gummersbach)
Archiv für Christlich-Demokratische Politik (Sankt Augustin)
Archiv Grünes Gedächtnis (Berlin)

Media Archives

Deutsches Rundfunkarchiv (Potsdam)
Historisches Archiv des Bayerischen Rundfunks (Munich)
Historisches Archiv des Norddeutschen Rundfunks (Hamburg)
Historisches Archiv des Südwestrundfunks (Baden-Baden)
Historisches Archiv des Westdeutschen Rundfunks (Cologne)

INTERVIEWS AND CORRESPONDENCE

Bahr, Egon, federal minister
Barth, Ariane, journalist

Dach, Rolf, diplomat
Dingels, Hans-Eberhard, head of SPD's External Affairs Bureau
Dohnanyi, Klaus von, federal minister, state secretary
Duve, Freimut, politician, journalist
Fröhder, Christoph-Maria, television journalist
Grobe-Hagel, Karl, journalist
Gutman, Roy, journalist
Gysi, Gregor, politician
Hamm-Brücher, Hildegard, minister of state
Haubold, Erhard, journalist
Hauser, Monika, gynecologist, founder of Medica mondiale
Hellbeck, Hannspeter, diplomat
Heynowski, Walter, documentary filmmaker
Hofwiler, Roland, journalist
Hornhues, Karl-Heinz, politician
Libal, Michael, diplomat
Manoschek, Walter, political scientist
Müller, Edith, politician
Neudeck, Rupert, journalist, founder of Cap Anamur
Neumann, Volker, politician
Nolte, Ernst, historian, philosopher
Pfetten-Arnbach, Berthold Freiherr von, diplomat
Pflaum, Hannelore, journalist
Pflaum, Klaus-Dieter, journalist
Pilz, Christel, journalist
Pütter, Benjamin, social activist, assistant to Petra Kelly of the Greens
Quistorp, Eva, politician
Ranke-Heinemann, Uta, theologian
Rathfelder, Erich, journalist
Röhl, Klaus Rainer, journalist
Schanz, Dieter, politician
Schilling, Hans-Jürgen, secretary-general of the German Red Cross
Schmid, Thomas, journalist
Schmidt, Helmut, federal chancellor
Schwarz, Stefan, politician

Schwarz-Schilling, Christian, federal minister, High Representative for
 Bosnia and Herzegovina
Semler, Christian, journalist
Siemes, Hans-Dieter, diplomat
Sontheimer, Michael, journalist
Steger, Hans Alfred, diplomat
Stiglmayer, Alexandra, journalist
Studnitz, Ernst-Jörg von, diplomat
Thumann, Michael, journalist
Warnecke, Angela, physician
Wechmar, Rüdiger von, diplomat
Welser, Maria von, television journalist
Widmann, Carlos, journalist
Wolf-Borchert, Frieder, assistant to Petra Kelly

ACKNOWLEDGMENTS

German responses to foreign genocide first piqued my curiosity in the summer of 1992. I was living at the time in Germany, where I heard shocking reports that Serbs had set up "concentration camps" in Bosnia. I vividly remember television images of emaciated men with shaved heads standing behind barbed wire. The images resonated, for obvious reasons, and I distinctly recall thinking that this could not be true, that there could not be *concentration camps* in Europe—in 1992! I also recall a great deal of skepticism in Germany, where policy makers and other public figures struggled to formulate a "proper" response.

There were other inspirations besides the horrific news reports of the early 1990s. During a brief hiatus from academe in 2001–2002, I worked at the Human Rights Office of the City of Nuremberg, organizing international conferences and hosting German-born Jews who had fled their country of birth in the 1930s. Since arriving at Wayne State University in 2003, I have regularly taught a lecture course titled World History since 1945, which sparked my interest in connections between Germany and other parts of the globe. Many academics emphasize how their own research informs their teaching. In my case, the opposite has also been true. There were two other important stimuli: Samantha Power's investigation of American responses to genocide, *"A Problem from Hell": America and the Age of Genocide,* and Paul Berman's *Power and the Idealists,* which traces the political evolution of a small group of

European student "radicals" from the late 1960s to the late 1990s, when they became ardent "humanitarian interventionists." I thank Daniel Mufson for introducing me to Berman's book. Little did he know how that recommendation would shape my life over the next decade and a half.

I have incurred a number of other debts while working on this book, and it is with great pleasure that I acknowledge them. *Never Again* could not have been written without support from numerous individuals and institutions in the United States, Germany, and Britain. This includes the Freiburg Institute for Advanced Studies (FRIAS), where I had an extended stay as a Marie Curie Senior Fellow. The Leverhulme Trust funded an equally generous visiting professorship at Nottingham Trent University in the UK, where Bill Niven welcomed me with warm hospitality. Several years earlier, Martin Sabrow and Stefan-Ludwig Hofmann were gracious hosts at the Center for Contemporary Studies in Potsdam, where I was a Leibniz Fellow. Because of my previous stint as a Chancellor Fellow in the mid-1990s, the Alexander von Humboldt Foundation in Bonn funded two return trips to Germany to conduct new research. Last but not least, Wayne State University awarded me a Board of Governors Distinguished Faculty Fellowship, a Career Development Chair, and a Humanities Center Research Fellowship. The Department of History kindly provided funding for conference travel and the licensing of images for this book. I am also grateful to my doctoral student, Katie Chaka Parks, who provided invaluable support as a research assistant during the final stage of this book.

Dozens of German politicians, diplomats, journalists, filmmakers, and human rights activists generously shared their knowledge with me in interviews and written exchanges: Egon Bahr, Ariane Barth, Rolf Dach, Hans-Eberhard Dingels, Klaus von Dohnanyi, Freimut Duve, Christoph-Maria Fröhder, Gregor Gysi, Karl Grobe-Hagel, Hildegard Hamm-Brücher, Erhard Haubold, Monika Hauser, Hannspeter Hellbeck, Walter Heynowski, Roland Hofwiler, Karl-Heinz Hornhues, Michael Libal, Walter Manoschek, Edith Müller, Rupert Neudeck, Volker Neumann, Ernst Nolte, Berthold Freiherr von Pfetten-Arnbach, Hannelore and Klaus-Dieter Pflaum, Christel Pilz, Benjamin Pütter, Eva Quistorp, Uta Ranke-Heinemann, Erich Rathfelder, Klaus Rainer Röhl, Dieter Schanz, Hans-Jürgen Schilling, Thomas Schmid, Helmut Schmidt, Stefan

Schwarz, Christian Schwarz-Schilling, Christian Semler, Hans-Dieter Siemes, Michael Sontheimer, Hans Alfred Steger, Alexandra Stiglmayer, Ernst-Jörg von Studnitz, Michael Thumann, Angela Warnecke, Rüdiger von Wechmar, Maria von Welser, Carlos Widmann, and Frieder Wolf-Borchert. Some have since become friends and acquaintances; others, I am sad to write, did not live to see publication of this book.

I conducted research in more than a dozen archives and would like to thank those persons who were especially helpful: Christoph Becker-Schaum (Archiv Grünes Gedächtnis), Jana Behrendt (Historisches Archiv Baden-Baden), Johannes Freiherr von Boeselager (Politisches Archiv des Auswärtigen Amts), Klaus Frese (Presse- und Informations-amt der Bundesregierung), Mary Ellen Jensen (Alamy), Bettina Just (Dokumentationszentrum und Museum über die Migration in Deutsch-land), as well as Bernd Brettschneider and Christoph Rohde (Nord-deutscher Rundfunk). Christine Marie Czaja kindly granted me access to the papers of her father, Herbert Czaja, housed in the Archiv für Christlich-Demokratische Politik.

Colleagues and friends across Europe and North America have given me the opportunity to present my findings. My thanks to Celia Applegate, David Blackbourn, Frank Bösch, Mary Fulbrook, Thomas Großbölting, Konrad Jarausch, Thomas Kühne, Charles Maier, Thomas Mergel, Paul Moore, Deb Neill, Pam Potter, James Retallack, Marc Silberman, Helmut W. Smith, and Chris Young. A word of thanks as well to other friends, family members, and colleagues who have served as a sounding board and source of good cheer for many years: Mark Baker, John Bukowczyk, Lisa Della Pietra, Lelove Felter, Will Gray, Jaclyn Green-berg, Donna Harsch, Victoria Johnson, Eric Kurlander, Katie Lemire, Ulrich Mählert, Thomas Maulucci, Patrice Poutrus, John Powell, Bob Sansky, Norbert Schürgers, Aephraim Steinberg, Yvonne and Troy Stevens, Anna Stavrakopoulou, Jutta Taschka, and Alison Wittenberg. I regret that my mother, Lois Sansky, did not live to see the publication of this book.

Don Fehr of the Trident Media Group helped me craft my book pro-posal, and I have him to thank for putting me in contact with Kathleen McDermott at Harvard University Press. Kathleen has been everything I always wished for in an editor: curious, conscientious, and compassionate.

I am also grateful for the helpful assistance of her dedicated and responsive colleagues Kate Brick, Lisa Roberts, Stephanie Vyce, and Aaron Wistar. Julie Ericksen Hagen painstakingly copyedited the final manuscript and taught me more than I ever wanted to know about some of my more egregious verbal tics. John Donohue of Westchester Publishing Services deserves my heartfelt thanks as well for his patience and meticulous attention to detail during the final production process.

My wife, Sylvia Taschka—historian, novelist, and poet extraordinaire—has accompanied me through every stage of this book, from its inception to the final inspection of the proofs. I could not have written it without her patience, love, and unwavering support. Our daughter Hannah arrived with the proofs of my last book but is now old enough to have read and provided invaluable feedback on various iterations of this one. Hannah has a sense for language and nuance beyond her years—and my own. Rebekka, our younger daughter, has lived her entire life with *Never Again,* occasionally to her chagrin. A gifted singer and songwriter, her music has brightened my countless days grappling with a profoundly somber topic. This book is dedicated with love, affection, and gratitude to these three talented women in my life.

INDEX